The Life-Course of Serious and Violent Youth Grown Up

The Life-Course of Serious and Violent Youth Grown Up addresses significant gaps in the literature on youth involved in chronic, serious, and violent offending. Through longitudinal research and a long follow-up into adulthood, it challenges common perceptions about offending outcomes.

Using theoretically grounded, methodologically sophisticated and empirically driven research, this book culminates 20 years of data emerging from the Incarcerated Serious and Violent Young Offender Study (ISVYOS). Initiated in 1998 to understand the origins of serious and violent youth offending, it follows 1,719 formerly incarcerated youth through adulthood and offers a contemporary perspective to questions about chronic offending in adolescence and social and offending outcomes in adulthood. The authors provide a theoretically framed examination of new findings from the ISVYOS regarding participants' justice system involvement, from onset to persistence to desistance. Most participants experienced continued involvement in the justice system in adulthood. However, contrary to past literature, ISVYOS findings challenge static descriptions of chronic offending and notions of the youth "super predator." ISVYOS findings also challenge assertions that experiences and risk factors in childhood and adolescence are not informative of adult justice system involvement. Together, the findings call for a more humanistic approach that recognizes that the complex lives of individuals formerly incarcerated in adolescence implies that desistance does not happen by default.

This book will be of great interest to scholars, researchers, and students of forensic psychology, developmental and life-course criminology, youth justice, and violent crime.

Evan C. McCuish is an assistant professor at Simon Fraser University and is the Principal Investigator of the Incarcerated Serious and Violent Young Offender Study. He is the recipient of the Simon Fraser University Dean's Convocation Medal for Academic Excellence, the American Psychology-Law Society Outstanding Dissertation Award, and the American Society of Criminology Division of Developmental and Life-Course Criminology Early Career Award. His research interests include criminal careers, desistance, developmental criminology, foster care, gang involvement, psychopathy, sexual offending, and violence.

Patrick Lussier is a professor of criminology at the School of Social Work and Criminology at Université Laval, Canada. In 2005, Professor Lussier received the Academic Gold Medal from the Governor General of Canada for the excellence of his PhD dissertation. Since 2019, he has been the editor of the *Canadian Journal of Criminology and Criminal Justice*. His field of expertise is at the intersection of criminology and criminal justice and includes, among other things, the etiology of criminal conduct, sexual offending, risk assessment and management, and quantitative research methods.

Raymond Corrado is a professor in the School of Criminology at Simon Fraser University. He has published over 100 articles and book chapters on a variety of policy issues, including juvenile justice, violent young offenders, mental health, adolescent psychopathy, victimization, child/adolescent case management strategies, and terrorism.

Routledge Studies in Criminal Behaviour

The Psychology of Crime, Policing and Courts
Edited by Andreas Kapardis and David P. Farrington

The Sexual Murderer
Offender behaviour and implications for practice
Eric Beauregard and Melissa Martineau

Psychological Violence in the Workplace
New perspectives and shifting frameworks
Emily Schindeler, Janet Ransley, and Danielle Reynald

Domestic Homicide
Patterns and Dynamics
Marieke Liem and Frans Koenraadt

Intergenerational Continuity of Criminal and Antisocial Behaviour
An International Overview of Studies
Edited by Veroni I. Eichelsheim and Steve G. A. van de Weijer

Evidence-Based Offender Profiling
Edited by Bryanna H. Fox, David P. Farrington, Andreas Kapardis, and Olivia C. Hambly

Empathy versus Offending, Aggression and Bullying
Advancing Knowledge using the Basic Empathy Scale
Darrick Jolliffe and David P. Farrington

The Life-Course of Serious and Violent Youth Grown Up
A Twenty-Year Longitudinal Study
Evan C. McCuish, Patrick Lussier, and Raymond Corrado

For more information about this series, please visit: https://www.routledge.com/Routledge-Studies-in-Criminal-Behaviour/book-series/RSCB

"This book describes an outstandingly important longitudinal study of a large sample of incarcerated Canadian boys and girls. It is a brilliant contribution to developmental and life-course criminology, advancing knowledge especially about criminal career features, offending trajectories, the importance of psychopathy, and theories of desistance. It includes interesting case histories and draws policy implications. It should be read by all criminologists, psychologists, and social scientists who are interested in the development of criminal careers."

David P. Farrington, Emeritus Professor of Psychological Criminology Cambridge University

"This remarkable book tells the story of the spell-binding story of 1700 offenders followed from adolescence to mature adulthood in Canada's Incarcerated Serious and Violent Young Offender Study. The science is terrific, and it's careful. There are rich quantitative data and qualitative data. But unlike most criminology writing, the book doesn't hide behind a fastidious over-focus on measurement, methodology, and theory. Instead, the book grapples up close and personal with the reality of chronic, serious, and violent offenders. It deals with factors typically omitted, such as foster care, drug addiction, gang membership, and custodial sentences. This book gets in there and gets its hands dirty. The result is eye-popping new information about where offenders come from and where they go when they grow older, and why. The book ends with a plea for criminology to look more at crime from the perspective of justice system professionals tasked with controlling it. I can't recommend it too strongly, for students, researchers, and justice system professionals."

Terrie E Moffitt, Nannerl O. Keohane University Professor, Duke University, Professor of Social Behaviour and Development, Social, Genetic and Developmental Psychiatry Centre, and Associate Director, Dunedin Multidisciplinary Health and Development Study

The Life-Course of Serious and Violent Youth Grown Up

A Twenty-Year Longitudinal Study

Evan C. McCuish, Patrick Lussier, and Raymond Corrado

Routledge
Taylor & Francis Group
LONDON AND NEW YORK

First published 2022
by Routledge
2 Park Square, Milton Park, Abingdon, Oxon OX14 4RN

and by Routledge
605 Third Avenue, New York, NY 10158

Routledge is an imprint of the Taylor & Francis Group, an informa business

British Library Cataloguing-in-Publication Data
A catalogue record for this book is available from the British Library

Library of Congress Cataloging-in-Publication Data
A catalog record has been requested for this book

ISBN: 978-0-367-28099-4 (hbk)
ISBN: 978-1-032-06081-1 (pbk)
ISBN: 978-0-429-29965-0 (ebk)

Typeset in Times New Roman
by MPS Limited, Dehradun

This book is dedicated to participants from the ISVYOS who took their time to share their stories with us.

Contents

Foreword

Why do people commit crime? Why do some stop? Why do some continue? And most importantly, how do we carry out a study to answer these questions. A "how-to" is in your hands right now.

The Life-Course of Serious and Violent Youth Grown Up by McCuish, Lussier, and Corrado is a tour-de-force for the field of developmental and life-course criminology. It details in painstaking but necessary fashion a 20-year longitudinal study of a cohort of incarcerated boys and girls in Canada. As someone who was involved in a similar study in the United States, the Pathways to Desistance Study, I have a deep appreciation for the blood, sweat, and tears that are carried out when conducting such a study. But we as life course criminologists owe these authors – and more importantly – their study subjects – much gratitude because there is much to learn from this work.

Because the sample is justice-involved, knowledge about their criminal careers, life background, and psychosocial function is critical for developing an understanding as to what factors may promote desistance and what factors may discourage it. Studying the issue of desistance is best done with an offender-based sample because they are, after all, the policy-relevant group. There are some success stories with some of the sample members, and then some not-so-good stories, thereby showcasing the heterogeneity that lies within the offender sample. The key for us researchers is to take the lessons learned about the successful outcomes of these youth and build intervention (and prevention) strategies to encourage the desistance process. After all, the clock to the onset of crime starts at birth and that is where we need to start looking at the risk and protective factors that may help to shape a pathway to crime or a pathway away from crime.

Aside from the important theoretical, empirical, and policy findings contained in McCuish et al., I also am thankful for their taking the time to describe the process of carrying out such a research study. Every single person contemplating such a study needs to think carefully about what is involved in such an effort. Reading this book and the details of the study will save you from a few bouts of head-banging – not the music version but instead the wall version. All kidding aside, this was a very important addition to this book.

In short, every now and then, a book comes along that is a culmination of an undertaking of many years of work by many different people, from the academics, to the students, to the staff, and to the study subjects. Do not take this one for granted. This book, and the study it was built upon, is a treasure.

Alex R. Piquero
Chair and Professor of
Sociology and Arts & Sciences Distinguished Scholar,
University of Miami & Professor of Criminology,
Monash University.

Preface

At age 25, John, who is one of the members of our Incarcerated Serious and Violent Young Offender Study (ISVYOS),[1] saw a man sitting at a bench outside a park. According to John, the man was smiling and looked "too happy" and so John stabbed the man in the leg and ran away. There was no other interaction between John and the victim. John was angry about a negative incident with a friend and did not appreciate the victim's attitude that contrasted with his own. He showed no remorse for his offense. He claimed that the victim deserved it and was "a fucking bitch" for not fighting back. He received a five-year sentence for this offense. It was one of many associated with John's high-rate and persistent pattern of offending through adulthood. To some, this represents a senseless, random, unprovoked attack against a stranger. This book takes the perspective that examining the development of individuals over time can help highlight risk factors and life events that may be useful for making sense of such offenses and for thinking more clearly about prevention.

Ten years prior to this offense, we interviewed John while he was incarcerated at the Burnaby Youth Custody Centre (BYCC). John reported that he did not know his father and no longer wished to have a relationship with his mother and younger brother, who was also involved in the youth justice system. John reported that his mother had a drinking problem and that she used alcohol while pregnant. John was diagnosed with fetal alcohol spectrum disorder (FASD). John denied experiencing physical abuse, but information from his case file indicated that his mother's intimate partners had abused him, his mother, and his brother. Youth justice practitioners reported that John had severe unresolved trauma from the abuse he experienced and witnessed. He was engaging in criminal behavior before age 12, which meant that he was offending before Canada's justice system could hold him criminally responsible and formally intervene. At school, he bullied students, disrupted classes, and hit teachers. Outside of school, he reported involvement in instrumental forms of aggression, such as beating someone up who did nothing to him and assaulting others to get what he wanted. In effect, while his stabbing offense at age 25 appeared to be a random attack, this type of behavior was not an anomaly for John. The continuity of antisocial and criminal behavior across developmental stages is a key theme of this book.

Partly because of his repeatedly aggressive behaviors, John was moved from his mother's home and into the care of the Ministry of Children and Family Development (MCFD). In his interview, John reported living in more than 30 different foster care facilities. John was unsure where he was going to live upon release from custody as his index offense involved uttering threats towards a staff member at the Group Home he lived at prior to incarceration. John reported his involvement in a wide range of crimes, including violating court orders, possessing and selling drugs, stealing cars, robberies, and assaults, including assaults with the use of a weapon. He reported that he typically offended because he was "bored", "just felt like it", "was using drugs", and "to see what it was like". During adolescence (ages 12–17) he spent just under 1,000 days in custody and incurred 26 convictions, nine of which were for violent offenses. John's story is not unique to our sample. The youth who are the focus of this book perpetrated a wide range of antisocial and criminal behaviors that escalated in severity during adolescence.

John's offenses were related to his social environment, which included little monitoring from caregivers and few structured activities. He dropped out of school around age 13 and spent free time using drugs with youth that he met while in foster care. John indicated in his interview that he started drinking before age 10 and first used ecstasy at age 13. He reported that not a single thing about his adolescence made him happy. He described himself as unattractive and poor. He believed that others viewed him this way as well. His mental health profile assessed via the Massachusetts Youth Screening Instrument-2 revealed clinical concerns about his anger and irritability. He displayed these traits during his interview by communicating that he resented people who did not fight and called them "goofs".[2] He scored 25/40 on the Psychopathy Checklist: Youth Version, which was only slightly above average for our sample (but about 10 points higher compared to incarcerated youth from other studies; e.g., Cauffman et al., 2009). Practitioners noted that John had serious problems with family relationships, lacked parental supervision, had precarious living arrangements, and his antisocial attitudes and resistance to justice system intervention were major factors in his continued involvement in crime. He was noted to have poor problem-solving skills, engaged in denial, had a learning disability, FASD, anger control problems, poor social skills and self-esteem, experienced neglect and physical abuse, and associated with a negative peer group.

We also asked John about his experiences in custody. During a four-month stay at BYCC, John reported five occasions in which he had instigated fights with other residents. His file information showed a slightly different story. He was the subject of 19 incident reports recorded by custody staff. These incidents related to physically fighting with other residents and being verbally abusive towards staff. Staff mentioned one incident in which John made sexually inappropriate remarks and exposed his genitals to staff and residents.

These 19 reports were not unusual for the sample. Some participants were the subject of over 100 such reports in adolescence. John reported that while in custody he frequently felt depressed, anxious, and had trouble concentrating. He noted that family did not visit, were not helpful, and that he could not count on them. He felt the same way about residents and staff. He did not find it difficult to be away from his family but found it extremely difficult to get along with other residents. He refused to participate in most programs in custody except for cooking. He attended school while in custody, but did not enjoy it, did not find it helpful, and routinely walked out of class.

John's story did not improve in adulthood. Risk/needs factors identified in adolescence remained unaddressed. His family relationships, living situation, relationships with intimate partners, and behavioral and emotional stability represented major barriers to desistance from crime. Clinicians were concerned that John's near-daily use of crystal methamphetamine had placed him in a drug-induced psychosis. During the trial for the abovementioned stabbing, he was diagnosed with antisocial personality disorder. Between ages 18 and 26 (his age at the time of this writing), he incurred 9 convictions and spent 1,397 days in custody. John was sentenced to a federal penitentiary for the stabbing and is not eligible for release until he turns 30.

This is an extreme case when considering the typical youth involved in the justice system. However, John's background was typical for this sample; an individual with a negative family environment was placed in foster care, their substance use escalated especially after meeting older antisocial peers, and through these new peer associations they became involved in the youth justice system. Not all stories with the same beginnings have the same endings. Some participants' adulthoods represented a continuity of their experiences in adolescence. Some found adulthood and associated independence as a means of respite from a negative social environment. We examine this stability and change for the ISVYOS sample with attention to the role of the youth justice system in influencing why some experience continuity and others change.

Youth justice systems throughout history have been presented with competing philosophies on how to respond to youth such as John (e.g., deterrence/punishment versus rehabilitation/treatment). The ISVYOS was implemented to address ideological thinking, misconceptions, and short-term views that are often common denominators in the enactment of youth justice policies. In the midst of these policy shifts and debates, extraordinary expectations are placed on practitioners (e.g., counselors, social workers, psychologists, probation officers) working with multi-needs youth caught in this system. They work in less-than-ideal conditions. Programs are underfunded or not tailored to the diverse needs of clients. Practitioners working with youth in custody have access to their client for only a short time-period. This access takes place in an environment where their client is surrounded by other residents presenting with similar difficulties and who resent authority, justice system professionals, and the justice system at large. In effect, practitioners are given maybe a few months to make a difference with respect to risk factors that often have been influencing a youth's criminal behavior for several years. For youth in custody, at least based on our sample, chances are that they will repeatedly re-enter the youth justice system, which may paint a pessimistic perspective regarding the efficacy of treatment efforts and the young person's transition to adulthood. However, practitioners do not have the benefit of knowing what will happen to these kids when they become eligible for the adult justice system. What happens to the 16-year-old who has conduct disorder, an addiction to crystal methamphetamine, a traumatic family situation, unstable living conditions, and a negative peer group? This book aims to provide some insight into this question by describing the childhood, adolescence, and adulthood of such persons. This book therefore focuses on answering the question of "*Who is the serious and violent youth grown up?*".

Criminological theory traditionally was not developed having in mind the complexity of the risk/needs profiles of youth like John who are involved in serious and violent offending. Theories were often focused on a single factor or interrelated set of factors designed to understand youth delinquency (Akers, 1979; Agnew, 1992; Gottfredson & Hirschi, 1990; Hirschi, 1969; Sykes & Matza, 1957). When we juxtapose these theories against John's background, it seems that theories that rely on a single risk factor or collection of similar risk factors (e.g., labeling, low self-control, social bonds, social learning, strain) are not sufficient for fully understanding John's initial and continued offending. With some exceptions (e.g., Mulvey et al., 2004), criminology has overlooked individuals in the deep-end of the youth justice system. The consequence is a lack of understanding of the individuals involved in the most frequent rate of offending and most severe types of offending. This book was written to bring attention to the needs of these youth, their patterns of justice system involvement in adulthood, and the association between the two.

Impetus for the book

There is a long tradition of research on the origins and development of offending over the life-course. This tradition was initiated by the pioneering work of American scholars Sheldon and Eleanor Glueck from Harvard Law School. Many scholars followed the Gluecks' path by using longitudinal data to identify and describe risk and protective factors associated with crime and delinquency over the life-course. This type of research is referred to as developmental and life-course (DLC) criminology. The Gluecks' work was valuable because, although not fully recognized at the time, it marked a shift from the view that delinquency was the result of a single factor. The Gluecks' work eventually influenced the emergence of the risk factor approach to the study of juvenile delinquency (e.g., West & Farrington, 1973) and the examination of different risk factors associated with different hypothesized patterns of offending (e.g., Moffitt, 1993). However, the Gluecks' sample was composed of *wayward youth*. It is unclear how these youth compare to contemporary youth involved in chronic, serious, and violent offending and who experience incarceration. Nevertheless, the Gluecks' work cleared a path to the longitudinal examination of delinquency. Doing so influenced a generation of scholars.

Scholars that followed the Gluecks were attuned to criminology's past research design flaws, which included inattention to both comparison groups and generalizability. Accordingly, initial DLC research focused on community populations. The emphasis on generalizability brought legitimacy to the field and answered important questions about antisocial and criminal behavior more broadly. Youth involved in more serious and chronic offending were largely absent from early survey studies conducted in schools and therefore findings about the causes and correlates of youth antisocial and criminal behavior were skewed towards individuals not involved in the justice system (Cernkovich et al., 1985). Rather than assume that these important insights can be directly adopted by practitioners and policymakers responding to serious and violent offending, the ISVYOS empirically examines the correlates of the longitudinal development of offending for formerly incarcerated youth. Are findings from prior community-based studies (West & Farrington, 1973) and studies of wayward youth (e.g., Glueck & Glueck, 1950) applicable to the challenges faced by incarcerated youth born in the 1980s and 1990s? Such challenges included rises in the availability of particularly harmful drugs (e.g., crack cocaine, crystal methamphetamine), gang involvement, and economic changes impacting the funding of social welfare services.

Some DLC researchers, including Professors Stephen Cernkovich, Peggy Giordano, John Laub, Marc Le Blanc, Rolf Loeber, Alex Piquero, Ed Mulvey, and Robert Sampson, understood the important policy implications of studying at-risk samples of young persons involved in chronic and serious offending. We wrote this book to add to the work of these and other scholars by highlighting the utility of a DLC approach to youth justice system policy. Rather than assume that these young persons are destined to offend at a high rate in adulthood (DiIulio, 1995), this book uses theoretically-grounded research from the ISVYOS, a 20-year longitudinal study. The ISVYOS was initiated in 1998 to address a large gap between the public and policymakers' concerns regarding youth involved in serious and violent offenses and the lack of empirical research within criminology that focused on this group. Thus, although there was growing awareness of such persons and a desire to develop policies and practices for responding to them (or better yet, providing interventions and humanistic services to prevent such outcomes in the first place), there was also a lack of data to provide empirical evidence to justify policy shifts or to push back against ideological thinking. Between 1998 and 2011 the ISVYOS recruited 1,719 youth incarcerated in various custody facilities throughout the province of British Columbia (BC), Canada. Some of the oldest participants are now in their forties. The ISVYOS provides a contemporary comparison point to the Gluecks' research at the beginning of the 20th century and then extended by Laub and Sampson (2003) several decades later.

The ISVYOS sample is also likely different (i.e., more severe in risk factor profiles and offending patterns) compared to their contemporaries in the United

States. During the recruitment period (1998–2011), adolescents in the province of BC were incarcerated at a rate ranging between approximately 40 to 80 per 100,000 (Statistics Canada, 2020a). To put this into context, researchers would need to sample approximately 1,500 youth in the community to find just one youth who experienced incarceration. During a similar period, adolescents in the United States were incarcerated at a rate ranging between 196 and 355 per 100,000 (OJJDP, 2019). Directly south of the BC border, in Washington State the rate of adolescent incarceration ranged from approximately 150 and 300 per 100,000 (ACLU, 2020). These differences are underestimated because Canada does not incarcerate its adolescents in adult facilities, whereas in the United States, approximately 10% of incarcerated youth are incarcerated with adults (Sawyer, 2019). The adolescents in the United States whose offenses are so serious that they are detained with adults are adolescents in Canada who would remain in youth detention facilities. Thus, compared to the United States, youth who are incarcerated in Canada are likely a narrower group of individuals (i.e., less likely to include persons involved in relatively trivial offenses). We believe that these data help address gaps in the scientific literature regarding the adult outcomes of formerly incarcerated youth, including risk/needs factors in adolescence contributing to adult offending and social outcomes.

Organization of chapters

This book is divided into three sections. Section One covers Chapters 1–3. These chapters include a description of theoretical and policy developments and debates that were instrumental in guiding the focus of the ISVYOS on youth involved in chronic, serious, and violent offending. Chapter 1 describes four pillars of DLC criminology: (1) criminal career research, (2) developmental criminology, (3) propensity theories, and (4) life-course criminology. The principles of these four pillars dictated the research questions answered in this book. Chapter 2 focuses on how criminology has defined, measured, and explained chronic offending. It also describes research design qualities needed to make reliable and valid conclusions about chronic offending and offending trajectories. Chapter 2 looks at the validity of three major questions addressed in this book: (1) is chronic offending an empirical reality; (2) what does this pattern of offending look like; and (3) are childhood and adolescence risk/needs factors informative of this type of offending trajectory? Chapter 3 describes the origins of the ISVYOS, including the youth justice context at the time it was initiated, and why it is suitable for addressing the types of questions and research design needs outlined in prior chapters.

Section Two includes five chapters that use principles from DLC criminology's four pillars to address fundamental questions about crime over the life-course. Chapter 4 uses a criminal career lens to answer questions about the prevalence, frequency, severity, and duration of justice system involvement for the ISVYOS sample. Chapter 5 models conviction trajectories to study the full longitudinal sequence of participants' justice system involvement. Even among this sample of individuals with relatively similar beginnings (i.e., all were incarcerated in adolescence), do participants experience divergent outcomes in adulthood? Chapters 4 and 5 help *describe* the nature of justice system involvement for the sample. Chapters 6–8 use developmental, propensity, and life-course theories to help *understand* the onset, persistence, and desistance stages of a person's trajectory.

Chapter 6 recognizes the developmental criminology assertion about criminal behavior as just one aspect of the broader domain of antisocial behavior by examining participants' self-reported involvement in antisocial behavior across multiple dimensions (e.g., aggression, substance use) and contexts (e.g., at school, at home). For incarcerated youth, does antisocial behavior always begin in childhood? Is this behavior always frequent and diversified or is there heterogeneity in antisocial behavior patterns even among this relatively homogenous sample? This chapter also looks at whether participants' childhood and adolescence behavioral patterns were informative of chronic and persistent offending through adulthood.

Chapter 7 examines the propensity theory assertion that stable characteristics in childhood/adolescence influence the stability of offending over the life-course. Leading propensity theorists showed that there were limitations of strictly sociological theories of crime (e.g., Gottfredson & Hirschi, 1990; Nagin & Paternoster, 2000). However, such theories tended to look at broad constructs like low self-control that are ubiquitous for individuals in the justice system and therefore are not suited to explaining differences in offending *among* such persons. This chapter looks at whether features of psychopathy assessed in adolescence are informative of persistent justice system involvement through adulthood.

Chapter 8 addresses questions from life-course theories about desistance from offending. In contrast to propensity theories, life-course criminology stressed that not all cards are played in childhood and adolescence. Instead, adulthood life events, transitions, and turning points can impact a person's justice system involvement. Chapter 8 examines whether ISVYOS participants found jobs, positive relationships with intimate partners, and stable living situations in adulthood. It then examines whether these adult sources of informal social control influence desistance from crime. Chapter 8 also examines whether certain characteristics in adolescence act as barriers to benefiting from these different sources of informal social control. This chapter also examines whether change in these adult outcomes helped produce change in adult justice system involvement.

Section Three focuses on policy and research design implications. Chapter 9 examines differences in justice system trajectories between two cohorts of participants from the ISVYOS that were under the purview of different pieces of youth justice legislation that adhered to different principles about the way to respond to youth involved in crime. Did Canada's transition to a more rehabilitation-oriented youth justice system have implications for adult justice system involvement? Chapter 10 describes operational lessons from the

ISVYOS and our experiences collecting data on this hard-to-reach, and sometimes hard-to-interview sample. This chapter details the experience of interviewing incarcerated youth, how to build rapport, manage participant misbehavior, and respond to deceitfulness during the interview. Chapter 11 concludes the book by summarizing the major points from each chapter and what these points mean for helping youth in custody desist from offending.

Notes

1 The description of case studies presented in this book followed the recommendations of the American Psychological Association (2010) by altering identifying details, including the use of pseudonyms, to maintain confidentiality. The alterations do not impact the interpretation of the risk/needs factors of cases presented.

2 In prison culture, the term "goof" initially was used to refer to a person who sexually offended against a child. It can be used more broadly as a means to provoke a fight.

Acknowledgments

The three authors are only part of the large research team that was required to implement the study, collect data, and code and enter these data. Since 1998, close to 100 undergraduate and graduate students worked on this project. The data provided in this book would not be possible without this team. Certain of these people played an especially large role, including Irwin Cohen, Stephanie Dawson, Karine Descormiers, Lauren Freedman, Sarah Kuehn, Amanda McCormick, Alan Markwart, Zina Lee, Candice Odgers, Adrienne Peters, Amy Prevost, and Gina Vincent. A special thanks to Kelsey Gushue, Taline Blakley, Hana Ryu, and Marjan Heirati for their editorial assistance.

We would also not have a team to begin with if not for the support received from various practitioners from the Ministry of Children and Family Development. We are especially indebted to Mark Caros, Andrew Cronkhite, Chris Devlin, Nerina Holderness, Jeremy Leveque, Emily Lindh, Anita McDonnell, Kim McKinney, Marty Mueller, Denise Townsend, and the numerous staff throughout custody centers in British Columbia that facilitated our access to participants.

The data collected in this book would not have been possible without the assistance of funding from the Social Sciences and Humanities Research Council of Canada.

We are grateful to Charlotte Endersby, Arunima Aditya, and Lydia de Cruz for believing in our project and helping us publish with Routledge.

Evan McCuish

I would like to thank my wife for her support, feedback, and helpful ear during the process of writing this book. I would also like to say thank you to the Staff at the JJ Bean in Suter Brook for providing me with the coffee that made this book possible.

Patrick Lussier

I cannot say enough about the support from my partner and two children who provided enough support, understanding, joy, and comfort, but also at times, the necessary distractions to go through a long-term project such as this one with a fresh and positive mindset.

Raymond Corrado

I have been inspired at this later point in my career by my wife, Patricia Massitti, who has been so courageous in fighting through her fundamental challenge while encouraging me to continue being a part of such a wonderful team of graduate researchers, colleagues, and dear friends.

Acronyms

AL	Adolescence-Limited Offending
ALC	Adolescence-Limited Criminology
BC	British Columbia
BCF	Blumstein, Cohen, and Farrington
BIC	Bayesian Information Criterion
CORNET	Corrections Network
CPO	Chronic and Persistent Offending
CSDD	Cambridge Study in Delinquent Development
CYA Study	California Youth Authority Study
DLC	Developmental and Life-Course
EOFD	Early Onset-Fast Desistance
EOSD	Early Onset-Slow Desistance
GH	Gottfredson and Hirschi
ISVYOS	Incarcerated Serious and Violent Young Offender Study
LCA	Latent Class Analysis
LCP	Life-Course Persistent Offending
MCFD	Ministry of Children and Family Development
PCL:YV	Psychopathy Checklist: Youth Version
PCL-R	Psychopathy Checklist - Revised
PO	Probation Officer
PYS	Pittsburgh Youth Study
RA	Research Assistant
RNR Model	Risk, Need, Responsivity Model
SL	Sampson and Laub
SPGM	Semi-Parametric Group-Based Modeling
SRD	Self-Reported Delinquency
SRO	Self-Reported Offending
SRP	Slow Rising Persistent
UJD Study	Unraveling Juvenile Delinquency Study
YCJA	Youth Criminal Justice Act
YOA	Young Offenders Act

Section I

Context

This section describes the theoretical, methodological, empirical, and policy backdrop that helped frame the empirical chapters in this book. Chapter 1 describes major paradigms in the history of criminology, including the developmental life-course paradigm that Cullen (2011) described as the heart of contemporary criminology. Chapter 2 describes perspectives on the measurement and explanation of chronic offending. A major focus of this book is on debates about the existence of a pattern of chronic and persistent offending and whether this type of offending pattern can be understood based on characteristics and experiences in childhood/adolescence. Chapter 3 describes the origins of the ISVYOS and the ways in which the data from this study are suitable for addressing core questions raised in Chapters 1 and 2. In addition to providing the backdrop for the empirical analyses in this book, this section illustrates that, despite a century of research on youth offending, there is still much to be learned about those youth who are involved in chronic, serious, and violent offenses.

1 Historical contexts and perspectives on offending over the life-course

Introduction

In the 1990s, against the backdrop of a significant decline in crime rates in Canada and the United States (Blumstein et al., 2006; Ouimet, 2002), paradoxically, there were growing concerns about youth crime. Some referred to youth involved in serious and violent offenses as dangerous "superpredators" (DiIulio, 1995) and "fatherless, Godless, and jobless" (Bennett et al., 1996, 27). Despite the crime drop, DiIulio (1995) asserted that over the next decade there would be hundreds of thousands of additional "superpredators" in the United States. These assertions and depictions were harmful as well as inaccurate given contemporary trends in youth crime[1] (e.g., Howell, 2009; Payne & Piquero, 2020). However, such claims garnered substantial media attention and elicited calls for a transition to more punitive, deterrence-based models of youth justice (see Corrado et al., 2006).

Amidst what some described as a moral panic over youth violence, policymakers overreacted with legislative changes that impacted the youth justice system (Howell & Lipsey, 2004). This led to reforms in Canada by a newly elected government that espoused a tough-on-crime philosophy. By the late 1990s, Canada was incarcerating its youth population at a rate higher than most Western industrialized nations, including the United States. At that time, there was a clear lack of research examining youth in the justice system, especially from a developmental and life-course (DLC) criminology viewpoint. This implied that although there was a growing awareness of youth involved in serious and violent offenses, and a desire to develop policies and practices for responding to this group (or better yet, preventing youth from heading down this path), there was also a lack of data suitable for addressing important theory and policy questions regarding these youth.

Data presented in this book are from the Incarcerated Serious and Violent Young Offender Study (ISVYOS) in British Columbia (BC), Canada. The ISVYOS began in 1998 as an exploratory study intended to address the lack of research regarding youth involved in chronic, serious, and violent offending. A wide range of risk/needs factors were measured relating to individual, familial, and school domains. The measurement of these factors was driven by sociologically oriented theories of deviancy (e.g., strain, labeling, social control) and by the risk factor prevention paradigm rooted in early longitudinal studies such as West and Farrington's (1973) Cambridge Study in Delinquent Development (CSDD) and then later formalized by models such as Catalano and Hawkins' (1996) social development model. Accordingly, while gaps in the knowledge base regarding chronic, serious, and violent offending existed, the ISVYOS' approach to addressing these gaps was not based on the introduction of a new framework for studying this phenomenon. The exploratory focus on risk factors was also part of the rejuvenation of forensic psychology and correctional treatment and intervention (Andrews et al., 1990), which highlighted gaps in sociologically oriented theories of offending. By 2011, the ISVYOS transitioned towards a research design that facilitated the description and explanation of adulthood offending patterns as outlined by DLC criminology.

There are many ways to reflect on scientific developments in criminology (see Farrington, 2003; Piquero et al., 2003). Different perspectives have been proposed to describe (1) macro-level explanations of crime rates across time and place, (2) explanations of crime events, and (3) micro-level explanations of criminal behavior across individuals. Given that the ISVYOS data pertain to individuals, our review of the history of major paradigms in criminological research focused only on micro-level explanations. We believe that the past 100 years of research on criminal behavior at the individual level[2] can be divided into three major paradigms.

The first paradigm is characterized by a medical/psychiatric viewpoint that we refer to as the psychiatrization of offending paradigm.[3] The Unraveling Juvenile Delinquency (UJD) Study initiated by Sheldon and Eleanor Glueck represents the major research contribution now attributed to this paradigm. The Gluecks' research was more sophisticated compared to other studies of this era. They created control groups, included various measures and instruments to capture multiple risk factor domains hypothesized to influence offending, and examined the influence of these factors from a longitudinal perspective. However, the Gluecks' multifactor research was criticized based on an ideological divide between sociologists and psychiatrists (Laub & Sampson, 1991). This criticism shifted research from an emphasis on sometimes vague and subjective descriptions of mental disorders to the sociological construction of crime. This second paradigm was referred to by Cullen (2011) as the adolescence-limited criminology (ALC) paradigm because of its almost exclusive focus on youth delinquency. During this paradigm, Kornhauser (1978) and others (e.g., Schuessler & Cressey, 1950; Tennenbaum, 1977; Waldo & Dinitz, 1967) were largely successful in discrediting the Gluecks' work and other research that linked personality to antisocial and criminal behavior (Posick & Rocque, 2018). The predominant focus of the ALC paradigm was on the understanding of youth delinquency through the lens of sociological theories. The emergence of longitudinal studies testing these sociological theoretical perspectives highlighted the importance of looking past adolescence. This gave way to the DLC paradigm, which we see as providing a balance between the first two paradigms that at times seemed to represent ideological attempts to swing the research pendulum towards a specific academic discipline.

This chapter reviews key principles and debates within and between each paradigm. Collectively, these paradigms contributed to a century of research on behavior in adolescence and helped inform the types of questions addressed in this book. Understanding the shifts that occurred between different paradigms in many ways explains, despite a century of research, gaps in the knowledge base concerning incarcerated youth and their patterns of offending through adulthood. The ALC paradigm was especially influential in the purposeful neglect of research on such individuals. Theories and research design traditions passed down from the ALC paradigm directed DLC research interests away from individuals whom justice system practitioners were responding to as part of service delivery. The ISVYOS data are suitable for extending DLC research interests and questions to youth who experience incarceration as a result of serious and violent offending.

The psychiatrization of criminal behavior paradigm

In the mid-19th century, some studying crime believed that physical and psychological characteristics were proximal indicators of the genetic underpinnings of crime (e.g., Ellis, 1890; Fink, 1938). This research era was dominated by physicians focusing on body-type, IQ, and personality as correlates of criminal behavior. Individuals involved in crime, especially those who recidivated or offended violently, were labeled as "feeble-minded" or "defective". Findings were often based on case studies or highly specific samples of persons referred by courts to psychiatrists because of the perceived uniqueness of the person or offense. Research of the time relied on crude measures, subjective opinions, and tests insensitive to the cultural, educational, and language capabilities of persons involved in this research (Rafter, 1997).

This focus on micro-level explanations of crime emerged from macro-level changes in social structure. In response to the demand for increased testing of fitness to serve in the military during World War II, the United States experienced a ten-fold increase in the number of employed psychiatrists (Jenkins, 1998). Following the war, there was a surplus of psychiatrists given that their services were no longer needed for fitness assessments. This was addressed by employing such individuals for the purpose of assessing persons involved in serious and violent offenses (Jenkins, 1998). Given their training, it is not surprising that their assessments were used to make broad statements about psychopathology and the origins of criminal and antisocial behavior. This approach was especially salient in the assessment of persons involved in sexual offenses (Tappan, 1955) and led to policies that were predicated upon the psychiatric perspective that certain persons represented a long-term and unchangeable danger to the public (Sutherland, 1949). Evaluating a person's "dangerousness" became a hallmark of the justice system. Medical personnel played a central role in diagnosing mental disorders, yet gave little attention to the reliability and validity of formal measures. In most cases, there was no development of measurement tools at all, relying instead on unstructured clinical judgment and impressions (Lussier et al., 2020a).

Key hypotheses associated with the psychiatric perspective were debunked by more rigorous analyses (e.g., Goring, 1913). The Gluecks' research marked the growth of a rehabilitation ideology that departed from biologically driven views (see also Aichorn, 1935; Friedlander, 1945). This work called for the individualization of justice given that persons may react differently to the same justice system response. Some forms of intervention might be more appropriate than others (e.g., Glueck, 1958).[4] These views supported the investigation of psychological, familial, and social factors that contributed to delinquency but that also could be modified through intervention.

The Gluecks (1950) were among the first to document, describe, and compare youth delinquency in the general population and were largely responsible for the introduction of longitudinal research on how delinquency develops over time. Contrary to the highly specific samples found in most studies associated with this paradigm, the Gluecks collected information from the Boston area on 500 adjudicated boys and 500 boys from public school who had no criminal record. They collected detailed official, self-report, and parent and teacher reports for both groups. They also followed participants into their late 20s. The inclusion of a comparison sample and a longitudinal framework highlighted their efforts to establish scientific facts with methodological rigor unequal before in criminology. The Gluecks' research is now well-known for highlighting the continuity of offending over time.

Some researchers valued the study of individual-level factors (i.e., risk factors internal to the specific person) associated with offending variability. These researchers, whom we will refer to as psychocriminologists, looked for ways to expand the Gluecks' research to better understand the ways to increase rehabilitation prospects. This aligned with individualization principles in justice system sentencing decisions (Coffee, 1975). Understanding individual differences that contributed to a person's involvement in crime and delinquency, not just in terms of psychological functioning but also in terms of social context and familial background, was paramount to the rehabilitative approach. This group (e.g., Jesness, 1988; Quay, 1964; Yochelson & Samenow, 1976) became known for their research studying the personality-crime association, recognizing heterogeneity among youth involved in criminal behavior, developing assessment tools, and identifying key clinical indicators for treatment purposes. These researchers argued that individual differences captured someone's propensity to act in an antisocial and criminal manner. Ultimately, the emergence of psychocriminology and the use of individual-level factors associated with offending and, more importantly, treatment needs, was not interpreted by all as a sign of scientific advancement.

Sociocriminologists, although interested in explanations of offending at the individual-level, typically rejected arguments that risk factors internal to the individual (i.e., individual-level risk factors) were important. Sociocriminologists valued the study of social class structure, economic deprivation, and sociocultural explanations of deviance and crime. Dr. Edwin Sutherland strongly opposed the notion of psychopathy and other indicators of psychopathology. This opposition was justified because psychologists and psychiatrists of the time provided vague descriptions of these disorders but nevertheless used such disorders to create impactful laws (Sutherland, 1949). Sutherland's writings were not a response to the risk factor model of the late 20th century but rather a response to comments by Earnest Hooton (1939) and others who argued for a eugenics movement (Cullen, 2011). Sociologists and legal scholars were concerned that the psychiatric/medial approach was atheoretical and lacked a formal tradition of research design, measurement, and analysis (e.g., Sutherland, 1937). While this was an accurate characterization of the psychiatric/medical approach, it was not true of the Gluecks' research. Arguably, the Gluecks' work was an empirically driven albeit atheoretical research program focused on meticulously[5] collecting and analyzing information from large samples of youth involved in crime but also samples from the general population. Their exploratory search for risk factors aimed to establish some baseline empirical knowledge about the causes of juvenile delinquency. Nevertheless, sociologists misrepresented the Gluecks' work based on the perception that it represented an extension of the ideological thinking of the eugenics movement (also see Laub & Sampson, 1991). The clash between individual-focused and sociological-oriented explanations of antisocial and criminal behavior was only beginning.

Sociologists argued that explanations of delinquency based on individual-level risk factors had no place in criminological scholarship and that focus should be exclusively on a youth's social environment (Kornhauser, 1978; Schuessler & Cressey, 1950; Sutherland, 1947; Tennenbaum, 1977; Waldo & Dinitz, 1967). It is important to contextualize the literature at the time of this critique. Personality research was characterized by major research design flaws and fuzzy, undefined constructs, but yet had a major influence on justice system policy (Sutherland, 1949). Criticism of psychological perspectives on offending were warranted, but criticisms often waded into ideological territory-marking rather than legitimate research criticisms (Laub & Sampson, 1991). For example, Sutherland asserted that the Gluecks' research on youth involved in delinquent behavior and their outcomes in adulthood did not make a substantial contribution to explanations of criminal behavior. Sutherland was considered successful in his attack on the Gluecks' research (Posick & Rocque, 2018), which opened the door for a new generation of sociocriminologists, including his own students, to help explain offending. This new generation refocused criminological research on the period of adolescence and brought forward new theories, research design philosophies, and analytic strategies that helped establish the ALC paradigm (Cullen, 2011).

The adolescence-limited criminology paradigm

The ALC paradigm focused the investigation of delinquency away from the individual and closer to their environment. This paradigm stressed the importance of socioeconomic disadvantage, peers/delinquent subcultures, and informal social control/social bonds. The message of the ALC paradigm was clear: it is not the person, but the social system that the person functions in, that needs to change. The ALC paradigm recognized that crime peaked during adolescence and therefore sociological theories focused on understanding adolescent delinquency. It was believed that this approach allowed for broader theoretical generalizations than what was afforded by earlier research on specialized samples of justice-involved persons (Cullen, 2011). Although Sutherland's research mostly concerned adults involved in crime-as-profession (e.g., Sutherland, 1937), his arguments against psychiatrists' views on offending laid the foundation for the ALC paradigm. Research needed to move away from assumptions that marginalized people were predisposed to offending due to an inherent psychological or medical condition.

Sociologists and criminologists trained in sociology, some of them by Sutherland, pushed back against assertions from the early 20th century that a psychological disorder or personality trait was responsible for crime. Sociocriminologists viewed crime as a product of rational thinking, even if such rationality was bound by contextual and situational factors (e.g., time and opportunity to offend, information available at the time of the offense, the influence of peers on behavior). This approach recognized that for some individuals, to make it good, was to make money, make money fast, have some power and influence, and to be prepared to defend what they possessed illegally (e.g., Sykes & Matza, 1957). Such persons were described as innovators who adapted in their own ways to society's rules and laws (e.g., alcohol prohibition). They learned through socializing with other persons involved in similar behavior regarding how to "make it" without relying on conventional and legitimate means (Akers et al., 1979; Sutherland, 1947).

Sutherland's differential association theory was one of the ALC paradigm's dominant theoretical perspectives. It was also used to double-down on Emile Durkheim' insistence that ideas from other disciplines were unwelcome (Posick & Rocque, 2018). Sutherland's (1947) first principle of differential association theory explicitly rejected biological explanations of criminal behavior that underscored perspectives from the Gluecks and others that adopted a psychological perspective. To leave no ambiguity, Sutherland suggested that sociology become solely responsible for criminological research (Laub, 2006). Sutherland's stature helped this suggestion have a lasting impact on the direction of criminological scholarship (Laub & Sampson, 1991), at least in the United States.[6] Although Sutherland's concerns about individual-level risk factors were warranted, it may have led to an over-correction by criminological research. The ideological pendulum swung to the opposite side.[7] On a positive note, there was an increased impetus to avoid the pitfalls of early research by physicians and psychiatrists. This ushered in a new wave of researchers who used survey-based instruments, administered mostly to high school students, to test theories about delinquent behavior.

In contrast to the atheoretical nature of the Gluecks' work, the ALC paradigm was a time for theory-testing. Influenced by Sutherland's adoption of an analytic induction approach, a plethora of sociologically oriented theories emerged. These included social learning theory (Akers et al., 1979), social bond theory (Hirschi, 1969), and techniques of neutralization (Sykes & Matza, 1957). Although the ALC paradigm was driven by Sutherland's (1947) emphasis on theory-building, it only viewed theory as valuable if it was oriented in sociology. Theory-building was the vessel that allowed sociological positivism to persist through the 1980s (Laub & Sampson, 1991). Sociologically oriented theories were constructed with two major principles in mind. First, such theories were general theories aimed at explaining youth delinquency. Explanations of broad-based antisocial behaviors required making assumptions that the causes of teenage drinking and the causes of sexual homicide were the same. In most cases, such theories did not reference more serious forms of offending. Second, parsimony was a major emphasis of theory construction. As a departure from the risk factor paradigm initiated by the Gluecks, theories from the ALC paradigm emphasized a single factor or set of interrelated factors as fully responsible for the development of youth delinquency. These monocausal general explanations of crime rejected theoretical integration on the basis that theories have contradictory principles that make them incompatible (Hirschi, 1979). Any multifactor theoretical perspective implies that all risk factors in the model have an imperfect association with criminal behavior. Multifactor theoretical perspectives were categorically rejected based on adherence to the analytic induction perspective that if the correlation between a risk factor and offending does not equal 1.00, then that risk factor cannot be a cause of crime and the theory is falsified (Hirschi & Selvin, 1970).

In the wake of multiple new theories, it was assumed that through empirical testing, one would eventually be declared the winner (Hirschi, 1979). This did not occur (Bernard & Snipes, 1996). The monocausal nature of theories from the ALC paradigm meant that testing a single theory did not allow for examinations of whether sociological constructs like strain, family poverty and dysfunction, poor supervision, neighborhood violence, and delinquent subcultures were tapping into distinct phenomena. If these constructs were all interrelated, then if one was associated with criminal behavior, others were also likely to be associated with criminal behavior. For example, Short (1960) pointed out that the ambiguity of principles of differential association theory allowed for a variety of interpretations regarding how to empirically examine the status of the theory (for further critiques see Kornhauser, 1978; Matsueda, 1988). Thus, instead of falsification, the same theories remained but were tested in different ways. For several decades, theoretical explanations from the ALC paradigm were fragmented, disjointed, and relatively simplistic at best (Farrington, 2003), unfalsifiable at worst (Bernard, 1990).

Nevertheless, the ALC paradigm was a positive step away from mostly pseudo-scientific explanations of crime that pervaded the late 19th and early 20th centuries. The ALC paradigm brought important sociological constructs back into the equation and highlighted the value of theory to help explain, and not just predict, criminal behavior (for a discussion, see Wikstrom, 2006). Ultimately though, this paradigm was too narrowly focused on sociological perspectives, developed unfalsifiable theories that were subject to endless empirical tests, and left few puzzles that could be solved without looking outside this paradigm (Cullen, 2011). The paradigm's position on excluding individual-level factors in the explanation of crime at the individual-level represented a severe overcorrection and pigeonholed the breadth of research questions for the ALC paradigm to address. Another issue was that the paradigm's almost exclusive focus on delinquency among high school students meant that research from this paradigm had little to offer during conversations about the rapidly increasing U.S. prison population in the 1980s and the associated punitive stance of this era (Blumstein & Beck, 1999; Tonry, 1999).

This opened the door for the emergence of a new generation of research. The general theory of crime emphasizing low self-control (Gottfredson & Hirschi, 1990) and strain theory (Agnew, 1992) were direct responses to the rejection of individual-level factors during the ALC paradigm (Hirschi & Hindelang, 1977). In fact, these two theories borrowed concepts that were germane to psychology (e.g., theories of self-regulation and coping with anxiety). Although both theories espoused monocausal explanations of offending rather than integrated perspectives, they highlighted the fruitfulness of considering constructs from different disciplines. These theories helped the field of criminology transition to the DLC criminology paradigm that espoused concepts from both sociology and psychology, including the integration of concepts from both disciplines and over the life-course. Paradoxically, this contrasted with Gottfredson and Hirschi's (1990) emphasis on monocausal explanations and the rejection of the importance of longitudinal research.

The developmental and life-course criminology paradigm

Theories from the DLC paradigm built upon theories from the ALC paradigm by paying attention to how offending unfolded over the life-course. For example, Sampson and Laub's (1993) age-graded theory of informal social control in some ways extended Hirschi's (1969) social bond theory to consider social bonds in adulthood. The focus on longitudinal research revitalized the Gluecks' research traditions. Doing so revealed several findings that could not be explained by theories from the ALC paradigm (Farrington, 2019). As well, contrary to the ALC paradigm, the DLC paradigm pays attention not only to the emergence of antisocial behavior among high school students but also to what youth involved in serious and violent offenses have to say about their involvement in offending (e.g., Cullen, 2011). This shift opened the door for the ISVYOS to contribute to a number of criminological puzzles regarding individuals involved in a frequent and serious pattern of offending.

We see four pillars to the DLC paradigm: the criminal career perspective, developmental criminology, propensity theories, and life-course criminology (also see Farrington, 2003). The criminal career perspective emerged first and provided a set of research questions for the other three pillars to address. Although these latter three pillars include research on the entire criminal career, developmental criminology tends to focus on the onset of offending, propensity theories on the persistence of offending, and life-course criminology on desistance from offending. These pillars also do not each represent one specific theory. Rather, they provide an overarching philosophy framing how researchers think about the development of criminal behavior. We begin with a description of the criminal career research pillar as the atheoretical initiator of the DLC paradigm.

Criminal career research

The criminal career perspective provides a framework for examining an individual's longitudinal sequence of offending. As opposed to offering hypotheses about such sequences, the criminal career framework describes concepts and parameters of offending that other theories should explain. Criminological theory was expected to become more sophisticated as the field established its own research methods (Goff & Geiss, 2008). That criminological theory matured after the criminal career perspective established a framework for data collection was not a coincidence. For parsimony, we start in the 1970s[8] with the Philadelphia Birth Cohort study. Wolfgang et al. (1972) examined nearly 10,000 boys born in Philadelphia in 1945. One of their major discoveries was the identification of a small percentage of individuals (6% of the sample; 18% of all participants involved in crime) that were responsible for most (52%) of all delinquent behavior in the cohort and the vast majority of serious offenses such as murder (71% of all such offenses), robbery (82% of all such offenses), and rape (73% of all such offenses). The identification of what are often referred to as "chronic offenders" paved the way for criminal career research that looked beyond whether antisocial or criminal behavior was present or absent. Instead, criminal career research introduced to the field a variety of offending parameters, including age of onset of offending, chronic offending, the severity or versatility of criminal behavior, offense specialization, duration of offending, and desistance or the age at which a person stops offending (e.g., Blumstein et al., 1982; Tracy & Kempf-Leonard, 1996). These parameters required attention to different stages of the life-course, which meant that longitudinal research was necessary. This opinion was not shared by all.

For nearly a decade, Michael Gottfredson and Travis Hirschi (1987, 1988; also see Hirschi & Gottfredson, 1983) debated Al Blumstein, Jacqueline Cohen, and David Farrington (see Blumstein et al., 1988a, 1988b) about the merits of criminal career research. This debate covered many different points of contention (see Table 1.1 for a summary). Gottfredson and Hirschi (GH) argued that there was no such thing as career criminals (i.e., persons that made a living via the perpetration of crime). Blumstein, Cohen, and Farrington (BCF) explained the GH's characterization of criminal career research as being concerned with career criminals was inaccurate. GH argued that individuals were characterized by an antisocial propensity to offend, that this propensity was stable over the life-course, and this produced stable between-person differences in offending. Accordingly, longitudinal research was unnecessary. BCF argued that offending was dynamic; longitudinal research was necessary to capture change in offending and resolve questions of causal order. GH argued that age of onset of offending had no impact on a person's likelihood of later offending. BCF argued that parameters like age of onset of offending helped measure important differences among persons involved in crime. GH argued that what predicts crime at one point in the life-course also predicts crime at any other point in the life-course. BCF argued that risk factors for crime varied depending on a person's developmental stage.

Perhaps the biggest disagreement concerned the nature of the age-crime curve. Both groups agreed that, at the aggregate level, crime peaks in late adolescence and sharply decreases thereafter. GH asserted that the age-crime curve was invariant across persons involved in crime. Any differences in frequency of offending over the life-course was a matter of differences in opportunity; persons involved in crime may differ in degree, but not in kind. BCF argued that the decline in the age-crime curve was because some persons stopped participating in crime altogether and a small portion of potentially qualitatively distinct persons persisted in their involvement in crime at a level resembling their offending in adolescence. Thus, this debate was a matter of whether the peak in offending in adolescence was the result of individuals increasing their frequency of offending during this period (GH) or the result of a higher proportion of all youth participating in criminal behavior (BCF).

Table 1.1 The criminal career debate

	Propensity approach (Gottfredson and Hirschi)	*Criminal career approach (Blumstein, Cohen, & Farrington)*
Point of Contention		
Career criminals	Persons that make enough money via crime to make this their sole means of income do not exist.	Not necessary to weigh in on this position because criminal career research is not about "career criminals".
Longitudinal research	Criminal propensity fully explains differences between those involved or not involved in crime and its stability implies that longitudinal research was unnecessary.	Longitudinal research is necessary for resolving questions about causal order.
Differences among individuals involved in crime	Individuals involved in crime are characterized by the same trait. Differences in offending only vary due to differences in opportunities for crime.	There is heterogeneity in risk factor profiles among persons involved in crime and this heterogeneity helps explain differences in offending over the life-course.
Age-graded risk factors	Stable risk factor or set of risk factors identified by childhood; no such thing as age-graded risk factors.	Risk factors are age-graded; what matters for offending will vary across age.
The age-crime curve	All individuals involved in crime follow the age-crime curve; variation around this curve is the result of differences in opportunity.	There are different trajectories of offending over the life-course with different ages of onset, slopes, peaks, and endpoints.
Peak in the age-crime curve	The peak in the age crime curve is a result of the opportunity in adolescence to offend more frequently.	The peak in the age crime curve is a result of an increase in the proportion of youth who participate in criminal behavior.
Participation versus frequency	Necessary to distinguish participation from non-participation but not necessary to distinguish variability in the frequency of offending.	Factors that impact participation in crime may not be the same as the factors that impact differences in frequency of offending; variability in both parameters.

Empirical studies tended to support BCF's perspective (e.g., Nagin et al., 1995; for reviews, see Le Blanc & Loeber, 1998; Piquero et al., 2003). This support helped influence the initiation of dozens of longitudinal studies (see Piquero, 2008). Farrington (2003) summarized findings from these studies in his description of ten widely accepted conclusions about the nature of criminal careers (see Table 1.2). At the end of this book, we reflect on how

Table 1.2 Farrington's widely accepted conclusions about the development of offending

		Criminal career parameters					
	Nature of the conclusion	*Prevalence*	*Onset*	*Persistence*	*Frequency*	*Diversity*	*Other*
#1	Offending peaks in late adolescence.	X					
#2	Onset of offending is most common between ages 8 and 14 and termination from offending is most common during the 20s.		X				
#3	Onset of offending and continuity/frequency of offending are negatively correlated.		X				
#4	There is some continuity between antisocial behavior across different developmental stages.			X			
#5	Most of all crime is perpetrated by a minority of all persons.				X		
#6	Persistent offending is characterized by involvement in a wide range of crimes as opposed to specializing in a particular crime-type.			X			
#7	Specific types of crimes tend to be a manifestation of a general antisocial tendency as opposed to a proclivity for engaging in a certain crime-type.					X	
#8	Co-offending is more likely during adolescence than adulthood.						X
#9	Motivations for crime in adolescence tend to be both reactive (e.g., anger, negative emotional states) and instrumental (e.g., for profit or fun) whereas crimes in adulthood tend to be driven by the latter motive only.						X
#10	Different types of crime tend to be first committed at different ages.		X				

Note: Cells marked with an "X" denote the criminal career parameter to which the conclusion applies.

findings from our empirical chapters align with these conclusions. These conclusions highlighted three fundamental aspects of offending: (1) it tends to be patterned, (2) it is dynamic, and (3) age and aging matter. While these conclusions were important, the atheoretical nature of the criminal career perspective implied that it was not suited to answering questions about these different aspects of offending (Wikstrom, 2006). Thus, the criminal career perspective gave way to theory.

Theoretical perspectives on crime over the life-course

In Table 1.3 we defined some core ways of thinking about the unfolding of crime over the life-course. DLC theories, while all interested in explaining offending over the life- course, can be distinguished according to their endorsement of the following principles: (1) a single construct or set of interrelated risk factors is responsible for all criminal behavior (i.e., monocausality), (2) there are distinct trajectories of criminal behavior over the life-course, (3) at least one of these trajectories is characterized by a high rate of offending that persists across adolescence and adulthood, (4) longitudinal research is necessary to address the causes of crime and desistance over the life-course, (5) criminal behavior is explained by an antisocial propensity that remains stable over the life-course, (6) human agency plays a role in desistance from criminal behavior, regardless of a person's background or risk factors, (7) risk and protective factors are age-graded (i.e., factors important for explaining offending vary according to a person's age), and (8) the factors explaining the onset and continuity of criminal behavior are different from the factors that explain desistance (i.e., asymmetrical causation).

The remaining three pillars of the DLC paradigm offer different perspectives on the unfolding of crime over the life-course. Table 1.4 looks at how developmental, propensity, and life-course theories vary in their endorsement of these different principles. Developmental criminology theories emphasize the onset of offending early in the life-course; propensity theories emphasize the examination of offending persistence between adolescence and adulthood; life-course theories emphasize desistance during the later stages of adulthood. Accordingly, we discuss these perspectives linearly; that is, from onset to desistance. The book's empirical chapters are also organized in this manner.

Developmental criminology

Contrary to criminology programs of the 1960s and 1970s in the United States, which were typically housed within sociology departments, Université de Montréal (Canada) established criminology as a specific discipline, albeit one heavily influenced by sociology. Marc Le Blanc, a graduate student of this program who became a faculty member, was influenced by developmental psychology (Fréchette & Le Blanc, 1989). Le Blanc became a key figure for the

Table 1.3 Key theoretical principles underscoring perspectives on crime over the life-course

Principle	*Description/Meaning*
Longitudinal Research Design	Longitudinal research, sometimes referred to as panel data, requires the collection of data, often the same measures, on the same person, at multiple points in the life-course. Contrasts with cross-sectional data, which refers to the administration of surveys or interviews to individuals at a single point in the life-course.
Distinct Offending Patterns	Involves the assertion that, among the population of individuals involved in crime, it is more accurate to suggest that the variability in the onset, volume, and persistence of offending over time is such that it is more appropriate to categorize persons into different groups. This is not to say that there are naturally occurring, taxonomic "groups" of persons involved in crime, only that there is simply too much heterogeneity in offending to rely on a single trajectory pattern to accurately describe offending patterns for all persons.
Life-Course Persistent Offending	Describes the intersection of two main criminal career parameters: frequency and persistence. The former describes a person's volume of offending and the latter describes offending that continues across multiple developmental stages. Disagreement exists with respect to whether life-course persistent offending requires that an individual continue to offend at a high rate essentially from the start of childhood until death or whether this type of pattern describes involvement in a high rate of offending early in the life-course that continues through later stages of adulthood.
Monocausality	Regardless of whether all offending is best described by a single pattern or multiple patterns, only a single factor or set of factors is needed to explain all offending at any point in the life- course.
Asymmetrical Causation	Risk or protective factors that help explain the development of one criminal career parameter (e.g., onset) may not be useful for helping to explain other parameters (e.g., persistence, versatility, desistance).
Age-Graded Risk Factors	The risk factors important to offending at one developmental stage may not be applicable at a different developmental stage. This principle is not inconsistent with monocausality. For example, a single type of risk factor may take on different forms at different ages and therefore a monocausal theory may still describe different risk factors.
Antisocial Propensity	Describes a single factor or construct that emerges early in the life-course, demonstrates relative stability,† and relates to offending. Antisocial propensity does not go away, but external factors (e.g., aging) can impact how it is expressed.
Human Agency	Describes a person's ability to regulate behavior, form plans, put plans into action, and reflect on such plans. Human agency allows individuals in otherwise high-risk situations for criminal behavior to abstain from such behavior.

† Relative stability means that individuals do not change. Or, an individual may experience a certain level of change, but this level of change is typical for all persons and therefore the individual's level of antisocial propensity does not actually change relative to their peers' level of antisocial propensity.

Table 1.4 Theoretical principles and their applicability to perspectives on crime over the life-course

	Theoretical Perspectives		
	Dual taxonomy (developmental criminology[††]*)*	*General theory of crime (propensity theory)*	*Age-graded theory of informal social control (life-course criminology*[†]*)*
Theory Principles			
Longitudinal Research Design	Cross-sectional research will not allow for distinctions between adolescence-limited and life-course persistent offending. Longitudinal research into adulthood is needed to differentiate the latter from the former.	Longitudinal research is unnecessary given the underlying propensity for criminal behavior that results in stable between-person differences.	Criminal behavior is dynamic and thus must be measured over time. Similarly, longitudinal research is needed to capture life events that alter a person's criminal trajectory.
Distinct Offending Patterns	Two offending patterns over the life-course (adolescence-limited and life-course persistent) that vary in terms of both *degree* and *shape.*	All individuals' offending patterns follow the age-crime curve. Crime declines steadily with age across all individuals involved in crime.	Tends to assert that trajectories vary in *degree* rather than *shape.*
Life-Course Persistent Offending	A small proportion of all individuals account for the majority of all crime; signs of antisocial behavior begin as early as five years old. Such behavior persists at a high rate across the life-course.	Differences in frequency of offending amount to differences in opportunity; no such thing as life-course persistent offending.	A high rate of offending in adolescence does not help identify persons involved in a high rate of offending in adulthood; a trajectory characterized by life-course persistent offending does not exist.
Monocausality	Different patterns of offending must be explained using different sets of risk factors.	A single construct (low self-control) explains all crime, all the time.	General offending persistence and desistance is the result of informal social control. Sources of informal social control function similarly across all persons.
Asymmetrical Causation	Asymmetrical causation does not exist. The life-course persistent trajectory shows no pattern of desistance and the maturity gap explains why individuals	Low self-control is responsible for onset and continuity of criminal behavior, but the effects	Factors responsible for onset and continuity of offending are also responsible for desistance from offending (i.e., persistence and desistance are two sides of the same coin).

(*Continued*)

Table 1.4 (Continued)

	Theoretical Perspectives		
	Dual taxonomy (developmental criminology††)	*General theory of crime (propensity theory)*	*Age-graded theory of informal social control (life-course criminology†)*
	associated with the adolescence-limited trajectory offend in adolescence and desist in adulthood.	of aging are responsible for desistance.	
Age-Graded Risk Factors	The adolescence-limited trajectory is characterized by risk factors specific to this developmental stage (e.g., learning from delinquent peers, attempting to bridge the maturity gap).	Low self-control emerges in childhood and is solely responsible for criminal behavior. There is no need to measure different risk factors at different ages.	Although adhering to monocausal explanations, the type of informal social control relevant for offending persistence/desistance is age-graded.
Antisocial Propensity	Individuals characterized by a life-course persistent pattern of offending have a stable antisocial/criminal propensity that resembles the general theory of crime.	Low self-control characterized by relative stability (i.e., possibility of within-individual change but such change does not result in between-person differences).	There is no propensity for criminal behavior. The life-course is characterized by instability, random events, human agency, and macro-level factors that can influence individual-level behavior.
Human Agency	Human agency may be useful for understanding why those associated with an adolescence-limited trajectory desist from crime, but individuals associated with a life-course persistent offending trajectory will experience cumulative disadvantage/selection effects that inhibit their ability to alter their criminal trajectory.	Human agency is irrelevant because those with low self-control will lack discipline, determination, and future orientation.	Human agency helps explain why youth involved in a high rate of offending do not necessarily become adults involved in a high rate of offending, even in the presence of risk factors in adolescence.

† Sometimes referred to as dynamic theories or state dependence theories.
†† Sometimes referred to as typological theories.
Note: Cells with gray shading denote that the principle listed is endorsed by the theoretical perspective in question.

development of an integrated criminology that recognized the importance of longitudinal research framed by the developmental perspective (Lerner & Kauffman, 1985). His team implemented a two-sample longitudinal research study composed of a sample of high schoolers and a sample of adjudicated youth (Le Blanc & Fréchette, 1989). This study did not get the attention it deserved at the time, in part because the project's findings were typically published in French (Morizot & Kazemian, 2014). This study, along with research from the Pittsburgh Youth Study (PYS; Loeber et al., 2008), helped Le Blanc and Rolf Loeber formalize tenets of developmental criminology. The developmental psychology roots of this pillar of DLC criminology influenced a transition from the ALC paradigm's focus on youth delinquency to an interest in the childhood origins of antisocial behavior and its continuity over developmental stages (Le Blanc & Fréchette, 1989; Le Blanc & Loeber, 1998; Loeber & Le Blanc, 1990). Unlike theories from the ALC paradigm, developmentalists were interested in moving beyond between-group questions about which individuals did or did not have low self-control, strain, social bonds, or delinquent peers. This interest manifested in four ways.

First, developmentalists recognized the importance of placing theoretical constructs and mechanisms in the context of neurological, cognitive, emotional, and social development. Drinking alcohol at age 10, 17, and 25 years old is the same behavior, but carries a different meaning from human development, legal, and sociocultural perspectives. Recognizing the importance of developmental stages and developmental milestones is pivotal for the formalization of a prevention-oriented theory of antisocial and criminal behavior. Not recognizing these differences can lead the justice system to impose adult-like sentences on youth who have perpetrated serious offenses, even though such offenses may not be reflective of a stable propensity to act in a criminal manner but instead represent a small, transitory period of this person's life. Disproportionately punitive justice system responses may only further entrench the young person in criminal behavior.

Second, developmental criminologists were interested in within-individual change; that is, the extent to which someone's self-control, strain, social bonds, and/or associations with delinquent peers change over time. Although Sampson and Laub (2005b) presented developmental criminology as a deterministic perspective, others described developmental criminology as open to the idea of change over the life-course (Thornberry, 1994). The developmental approach believes that the dynamic aspect of human development is predictable to some extent. It rejects the suggestion that human development and adult outcomes are simply the result of random variations. Developmental criminology does not believe that prediction is perfect, but uses the link between the past and future to help understand ways of providing humanistic interventions.

Third, unlike ALC theories, developmentalists were cognizant that youth are not strictly passive receptacles of environmental influences. Youth are partly responsible for their own development (Moffitt, 1993). It is not just that youth are influenced by their family and peer environments (e.g., learning and acquiring skills, competence). Youth have some agency in defining their social circle, identity, preferences, and activities, which can influence their trajectory in adolescence and adulthood. Late adolescence and adulthood provide opportunities for the establishment of independence from a person's social environment (e.g., moving out of the family home, financial independence, university), which allows individuals to have greater decision-making power in how they shape their environment.

A fourth principle that sets developmental criminology apart from other theoretical perspectives is an emphasis on explaining offending across different life stages and distinguishing different trajectories of offending that have unique causal origins (Lahey & Waldman, 2005). This principle addressed Bernard and Snipes' (1996) concern that crime covers a wide range of different behaviors that have diverse causes and cannot be explained by a single general theory of crime. While other DLC theories also examine offending over the life-course, for many of these theories, explanations for offending are the same across all stages of the life-course. Taken together, these four principles paved the way for the incorporation of individual-level factors into multicausal theories.

The dual taxonomy as a developmental theory

Moffitt's (1993) dual taxonomy is one of the most influential criminological theories of the last several decades (Cohn & Farrington, 2008). The dual taxonomy provides a theoretical explanation for the criminal career research perspective that an increase in the number of individuals perpetrating crime in adolescence is responsible for the peak in the age-crime curve and the drop in the age-crime curve is a result of these same individuals terminating their involvement in offending in adulthood. The dual taxonomy disaggregates the age-crime curve into adolescence-limited (AL) and life-course persistent (LCP) offending trajectories. The AL trajectory characterizes approximately 90% of all individuals who offend. A fundamental distinction between these two trajectories relates to the age at which offending begins. The focus on the onset of offending as a means of understanding future offending is one of several principles that makes the dual taxonomy distinct from propensity and life-course theories.

The dual taxonomy is sometimes referred to as a typological theory (Blokland et al., 2005) because it offers different explanations of offending for the two trajectories, which makes it unique from life-course and propensity theories. The dual taxonomy uses principles from life-course theories to explain AL offending and principles from propensity theories to explain LCP offending. For the AL trajectory, criminal behavior emerges in mid-adolescence through social learning mechanisms and an individual's desire to bridge the maturity gap (Moffitt, 1993). Individuals associated with AL offending seek certain status symbols and the autonomy associated with adulthood but lack the legitimate means to achieve them. These individuals observe the rewards experienced by LCP offending and mimic this behavior. AL offending involves less serious offenses that discontinue in early adulthood due to new opportunities afforded by this developmental stage that allow individuals to achieve their goals through conventional means. Abstention from crime continues in adulthood because of a person's desire to avoid jeopardizing newfound prosocial adult roles. For some associated with an AL trajectory, crime may continue in adulthood because they experience snares (e.g., joining a gang, substance use, poor educational attainment; McGee et al., 2015; Petkovsek et al., 2016) that act as a barrier to prosocial adult roles that facilitate desistance.

LCP offending is hypothesized to result from a combination of having a neuropsychological deficit and experiencing family adversity. This combination forms a person's propensity for continued offending. The interaction of individual and family risk domains leads antisocial behavior that emerges in early childhood and continues over the life-course via one of two mechanisms. One mechanism is contemporary continuity, which describes how the interaction between childhood traits and childhood environment directly influence continued offending over the life-course. The other mechanism is cumulative continuity, which describes how the interaction between childhood traits and a negative environment interact to increase the likelihood of accumulating additional risk factors that independently influence continued criminal behavior. For example, the temperament of certain children may negatively influence how parents respond to their children, and exposure to harsh parenting practices can lead to poor school performance, disruptive behavior, alienation from prosocial peers, and an increased likelihood of dropping out of school, all of which directly influence offending as well. Regardless of whether contemporary or cumulative continuity mechanisms influence LCP offending, individuals associated with this trajectory experience a more challenging transition into adulthood because their opportunities for key turning points are limited (e.g., difficulty finding employment, less likely to attract a prosocial marital partner who promotes resistance). For individuals following a LCP offending trajectory, even when informal social controls are present, they are less likely to influence desistance (e.g., marrying a partner who encourages their antisocial behavior; Moffitt et al., 2002).

To sum up the principles of the dual taxonomy, unlike ALC theories and several propensity and life-course theories, the dual taxonomy is not a monocausal theory (Blokland et al., 2005). Instead, it relies on qualitatively different types of risk factors to explain different patterns of offending that vary in degree and kind. Moffitt (1993) asserted that the LCP pattern of offending required a unique explanation from other patterns of offending, including the predominant AL taxon. Longitudinal research that follows individuals well into adulthood is required to address this assertion. Moffitt considers individuals associated with the LCP trajectory to have a stable antisocial propensity that manifests in childhood. This propensity implies that, for this small group of individuals, human agency will be insufficient for altering their course of offending. The accumulation of disadvantage early in the life-course can have cascading effects on opportunities to experience or benefit from adult roles and other positive life events that help explain why individuals associated with the AL trajectory stop offending. The dual taxonomy is an age-graded theory because it relies on different risk factors to explain offending with an onset in early childhood (i.e., neuropsychological deficits) versus offending with an onset in middle adolescence (i.e., differential association). This theory does not comport with asymmetrical causation because LCP offending is not associated with desistance from crime, and for AL offending, the maturity gap explains initial involvement in crime as well as why desistance occurs.

With respect to empirical evidence for the dual taxonomy, studies typically supported the notion that there are different patterns of criminal behavior over the life-course. However, such studies also showed that Moffitt's two trajectories insufficiently accounted for the heterogeneity of offending (Jennings & Reingle, 2012; Piquero, 2008). Additionally, other studies indicated that the highest-rate trajectories identified were not characterized by offending that was stable between adolescence and later adulthood (Laub & Sampson, 2003; Nagin et al., 1995; Piquero, 2008; c.f., Blokland et al., 2005). Others found that offending in the AL trajectory was not restricted to the period of adolescence (Moffitt et al., 2002). This is at least in part due to the impact of snares (McGee et al., 2015) and sociocultural changes that occur during a recently defined life-stage in-between adolescence and adulthood, referred to as emerging adulthood (Arnett, 2000). This period may create a context conducive to the persistence of certain forms of offending. Perhaps most importantly, it has been difficult to identify risk factors that differentiate AL and LCP offending trajectories (Blokland et al., 2005; Day et al., 2012; Fergusson et al., 2000; Landsheer & van Dijkum, 2005; van der Geest et al., 2009; van Domburgh et al., 2009; Ward et al., 2010). This is partly because studies lacked sufficient base rates of chronic offending and partly because of the failure to measure the propensity for LCP offending in a manner that aligned with Moffitt's description (for similar arguments, see Robins, 2005; van der Geest et al., 2009).

Propensity theories

Propensity theories, sometimes described as population heterogeneity theories (Nagin & Paternoster, 2000), focus on hypothesized time-stable between-person differences in propensity for antisocial and criminal behavior. Different propensity theories share many of the same principles; where they differ is with respect to which individual-level construct is asserted to capture propensity (e.g., IQ, low self-control, psychopathy; see DeLisi, 2016; Nagin & Paternoster, 2000; Wilson & Herrnstein, 1985). These constructs vary within the population and are asserted to be characterized by relative stability. Relative stability implies that the construct either (a) remains stable within the individual over the life-course or (b) shows slight within-individual variations over time, but such change is not more than expected for the population that they were drawn from and thus does not result in rank-order differences between persons (Na & Paternoster, 2012; Nagin & Paternoster, 2000). Stable between-person differences in criminal propensity correspond with stable between-person differences in offending. Accordingly, unlike principles of the criminal career framework, pure propensity theories suggest that the correlation between past and future offending is spurious. A person's time-stable propensity for crime fully accounts for this relationship (Nagin & Paternoster, 1991). We use the term "pure" propensity theories because some propensity theories assert that both propensity and situational characteristics are important in the unfolding of criminal behavior (Nagin & Paternoster, 1993; Wikström & Treiber, 2009). Propensity theories tend to be monocausal explanations of crime (Nagin & Paternoster, 2000), but they are not restricted to such explanations (e.g., Lahey & Waldman, 2003, 2005; Wilson & Herrnstein, 1985).

General theory of crime as a propensity theory

Including Gottfredson and Hirschi's (1990) general theory of crime under the umbrella of DLC theories may seem surprising given that these authors were directly opposed to the criminal career framework. However, the general theory of crime fits within the overarching purpose of the DLC paradigm, which is to provide a framework for research on offending over the life-course, even if the theory suggests that longitudinal research is not necessary to study offending over the life-course. In effect, by suggesting that crime need not be studied through longitudinal research, the general theory of crime offers an important and parsimonious perspective on crime over the life-course.

While often pitted against life-course theories, Paternoster and Brame (1997) illustrated several similarities between the general theory of crime and life-course theory. For example, both offer monocausal explanations of offending. The general theory of crime suggests that low self-control sufficiently explains all offending at all stages of the life-course. Low self-control is represented by a constellation of personality features, including impulsivity, desire for instant gratification, failure to be forward-thinking, and preference for physical rather than verbal behaviors. Low self-control emerges because of the failure of parents to appropriately monitor the child, recognize misbehavior, and respond to this misbehavior with parenting strategies that help correct the behavior without relying on coercion (Gottfredson & Hirschi, 1990). According to the general theory of crime, once low self-control emerges, it remains stable over the life-course. The general theory of crime is consistent with the principle of asymmetrical causation because the theory suggests that deficits in self-control cause crime, but that desistance results from "inexorable aging" that results in burnout and reduces opportunities for criminal behavior (Gottfredson & Hirschi 1990, p. 141). This uniformed effect of aging means that all persons involved in crime are characterized by the same age-crime curve. Variation around this curve is a matter of differences in exposure to opportunities for criminal behavior.

In sum, the general theory of crime stands out for its parsimony. It is a monocausal theory that suggests that qualitatively distinct patterns of offending do not exist. This, therefore, implies that there is no LCP offending pattern. Longitudinal research is viewed as inefficient and unnecessary because criminal behavior is the result of a general antisocial propensity (i.e., low self-control) that remains stable beyond childhood and produces stable between-person differences in offending. Any relationship between human agency and desistance is fully accounted for by low self-control; those with low self-control will also have the lowest levels of human agency. The general theory of crime is not an age-graded theory because low self-control is asserted to explain criminal behavior at all ages. Other risk factors that correlate with criminal behavior, including those that emerge later in the life-course, are asserted to be a product of low self-control and therefore their association with offending is spurious. The theory aligns with the asymmetrical causation principle because low self-control causes offending, but aging explains declines in offending.

In terms of its empirical status, the general theory of crime's proposition that low self-control sufficiently explains all crime, all the time is inaccurate. A meta-analysis of studies examining this relationship showed that low self-control is important, but not sufficient, for explaining criminal behavior (Pratt & Cullen, 2000). Social learning constructs were identified as more important than low self-control when it came to explaining the age-crime curve (Sweeten et al., 2013). Pratt and Cullen (2000) noted that the relationship between low self-control and offending was weaker when longitudinal studies accounted for the temporal order between the two. This finding likely resulted because low self-control lacks the within-individual and between-person stability (e.g., Barnes et al., 2017; Hay & Forrest, 2006; Na & Paternoster, 2012) hypothesized by Gottfredson and Hirschi (1990). In effect, if there is such a thing as antisocial propensity, it is not captured by low self-control. Finally, with respect to assertions about the invariance of the age-crime curve, most studies of longer-term patterns of offending identified at least one trajectory characterized by offending that started in adolescence and ended in early adulthood and at least one trajectory characterized by a high rate of offending between adolescence and adulthood (Jennings & Reingle, 2012; Piquero, 2008). In other words, these studies provided evidence against the invariance of the age-crime curve (Nagin et al., 1995).[9]

Despite the lack of empirical support for several of its principles, Gottfredson and Hirschi's (1990) theory served as a more contemporary, clearer, and productive version of the Michael-Adler (1933) Report.[10] Like the Michael-Adler Report, their book was critical of existing criminological theory and research, especially sociological positivism, for ignoring individual-level risk factors. Gottfredson and Hirschi (1990) started with an extremely parsimonious viewpoint on the development of crime over the life-course, which challenged criminologists to refine, test, and clarify their own theoretical positions. Gottfredson and Hirschi essentially forced criminologists to step back and provide evidence that greater theoretical complexity was necessary for the explanation of criminal behavior. This included requiring criminologists to address (a) whether certain persons had an underlying propensity for criminal behavior that rendered longitudinal research unnecessary, (b) whether low self-control sufficiently explained all crime, (c) whether correlations between other risk factors and crime were fully accounted for by low self-control, (d) whether the decline in the age-crime curve was a result of all persons involved in crime slowing down in their level of offending, and (e) whether a person's decline in frequency of due to offending was simply inopportunity brought about by the effects of aging. This last point was given particular consideration by life-course criminologists.

Life-course criminology

Life-course theories are rooted in sociology (Elder, 1994) and describe how social roles and local life circumstances, which are tied to age, human agency, and historical context, influence the dynamic nature of human development (Elder, 1998). Life-course theories are unique from propensity theories because they assert that the relationship between past and future offending is due to a state dependence process, whereby prior offending negatively alters a person's life circumstances. For example, incarceration may result in a person losing their job, which may weaken their sources of informal social control, which in turn increases their likelihood of future offending. Similar to the general theory of crime and theories from the ALC paradigm, life-course theories often consider a single causal factor to explain offending and do not provide different explanations for different patterns of offending (Blokland et al., 2005). Unlike ALC theories, life-course theories of crime have been especially focused on adulthood. Laub (2006) clarified five major principles of life-course criminology. First, the absence of social ties, especially to family and school, is most important for explaining the development of offending. Second, there is much continuity in antisocial and criminal behavior from childhood through adulthood.[11] Third, social ties in adulthood result in change over the life-course. The acquisition of social ties is not accounted for by childhood propensity (e.g., temperament in childhood does not account for which individuals acquire social ties later on). Fourth, a main reason for change over the life-course is human agency, which refers to the ability of individuals to actively change their offending trajectory. Fifth, the goals of prevention and rehabilitation should be given equal weight by the justice system.

Laub (2006) clarified that although sociological explanations of crime were important, Sutherland's sociological positivism hindered the evolution of criminological research. Unlike Sutherland's emphasis on abstraction of analysis, Laub (2006) argued that a paradigm should be based on facts and open to exploration by a range of disciplines, including disciplines like psychology and biology that focused on individual-level factors rather than a person's social environment. Life-course criminology's openness to different academic disciplines was influenced by reanalyzing and updating the Gluecks' UJD Study (see Laub & Sampson, 1993, 2003; Sampson & Laub, 1997). Although open to the potential importance of individual-level factors, Laub (2006) asserted that the "strongest and most consistent effects on both official and unofficial delinquency flow from the social processes of family, school, and peers" (p. 242).

Whereas Elder's (1994, 1998) initial sociologically based life-course theory was influenced by developmental principles (also see McAdams, 1993), Laub's (2006) version of life-course theory paid less attention to developmental criminology. In fact, despite suggesting an openness to different disciplines, none of the five principles of life-course criminology reference individual-level factors, except to suggest that childhood and adolescence personality factors did not interfere with social ties in adulthood. However, unlike Sutherland's sociological positivism, Laub's (2006) lack of emphasis on individual-level factors was rooted in empirical research. Laub and Sampson's (1988) re-examination of the Gluecks' data, which were collected specifically for the purpose of testing multicausal perspectives on crime, led to their empirically driven rejection of the importance of childhood and adolescence risk factors for offending in adulthood (also see Laub & Sampson, 2003; Sampson & Laub, 2005a). A closer look at these statements is important given that their age-graded theory of informal social control is the major theoretical perspective to come from life-course criminology (also see Warr, 1998).

The age-graded theory of informal social control as a life-course theory

The age-graded theory is focused on explaining desistance rather than onset and/or continuity. This is partly because it does not view childhood and adolescence risk factors as informative of offending beyond these developmental stages. Thus, this theory focused on how different sources of informal social control, referred to as turning points, alter a person's offending trajectory in ways that promote desistance (Laub & Sampson, 2001). Desistance is not an abrupt event but a process of slowing down in the frequency of offending over time. This process is gradual because it takes time to acquire, value, and maintain sources of informal social control (Nguyen & Loughran, 2018). Informal social control is acquired via a sociogenic process whereby social structure induces turning points that influence desistance. Individuals do not necessarily actively pursue employment, marriage, or parenthood

(Sampson & Laub, 2005a). The social structure that a person is embedded within can also funnel them into adult roles (Laub & Sampson, 1993). The effect of informal social controls on desistance is a collateral consequence of fulfilling the responsibilities associated with newfound adult roles. The maintenance of a person's adult role is a reciprocal process. After entering a new role, individuals will alter their identity to conform to role expectations. Doing so crystalizes the individual's position in that role and reinforces desistance (Laub & Sampson, 2003).

The timing of informal social controls matters because the capacity to experience, benefit from, and value adult roles is age-graded. For example, employment during later stages of adulthood has a more pronounced impact on desistance than employment that occurs earlier in adulthood (Uggen, 2000). The quality of informal social control also matters. Individuals must have the desire to alter their behavior to avoid jeopardizing their new social roles and associated identity built from that role. A marriage must have a strong emotional attachment, a person must enjoy their profession, and parenthood must be defined by a desire to nurture one's child and see them succeed (Laub & Sampson, 2001; Nguyen & Loughran, 2018). Although the timing of desistance can be impacted by formal sanctions that disrupt experiences of informal social control (Sampson & Laub, 2016), all persons involved in crime will eventually desist, and this is in part because turning points in the life-course can be structurally induced (Laub & Sampson, 2003). Macro-level social factors funnel individuals into different roles even if the individual did not actively pursue this role or did not pursue this role specifically to avoid criminal behavior.

In sum, the age-graded theory of informal social control is a monocausal theory (Blokland et al., 2005) that rejects Moffitt's dual taxonomy because of the typological nature of Moffitt's theory and because of the belief that LCP offending is not an empirical reality (Laub & Sampson, 2003). Sampson and Laub (2005a, 2005b) view the age-crime curve as invariant, meaning that offending patterns differ in degree, not kind. Therefore, distinct explanations for different offending patterns are not required. Differences in the degree of offending reflect differences in the timing of key turning points. Unlike Gottfredson and Hirschi's (1990) perspective, life-course theory prioritizes the use of longitudinal research to capture turning points and changes in offending. The age-graded theory explains that risk factors in adolescence do not preclude the capacity to change in adulthood because human agency allows individuals to change through motivation. Turning points are age-graded, meaning that informal social controls such as employment, marriage, military service, and parenthood differentially relate to desistance depending on a person's age. Age indicates a person's level of maturity and capacity to benefit from turning points. Proponents of this theory reject the criminal career principle of asymmetrical causation; the absence of informal social controls explains offending and the presence of informal social control explains desistance.

Sampson and Laub's re-examination of the Gluecks' (1950) UJD Study initially reported that (1) youth involved in a high rate of offending continued this pattern in adulthood and (2) that this pattern of offending was explained by a range of different risk factors (Laub & Sampson, 1993). However, Sampson and Laub (2005b) later reported that evidence for both findings dissipated with a longer follow-up period. This led Laub and Sampson (2003) to argue that it was necessary to measure informal social controls in adulthood to understand desistance. Through qualitative interviews with a subsample of men from the UJD Study, Laub and Sampson (2003) identified employment, marriage, parenthood, and military service as key turning points in the life-course. They reported that because of human agency and macro-level processes, even the highest-risk youth desisted from criminal behavior. This perspective was diametrically opposed to Moffitt's (1993) theory on life-course persistent offending and is why life-course theories are sometimes referred to as a middle-ground between propensity and developmental theories (Paternoster & Brame, 1997). Other tests of life-course theoretical assertions showed that informal social controls offered a modest explanation of desistance (e.g., Blokland et al., 2005). Some scholars suggested that informal social controls were a *result* of desistance (e.g., Skardhamar & Savolainen, 2014).

Summary

We described three major paradigms in the last 100 years of research on criminal behavior at the level of the individual. The psychiatrization of offending paradigm included groundbreaking work by the Gluecks regarding the use of longitudinal research methods with control groups and the establishment of temporal order to study the relationship between past and future offending. This paradigm also included research that was ideological, poorly conceived, and of limited scientific value. This research and the Gluecks' research tended to be lumped together by sociocriminologists who sought to make sociology the sole field responsible for the study of criminal behavior. Sutherland's work and the work of his students brought forward the ALC paradigm and its emphasis on theory-building and theory-testing to understand youth delinquency. Although the ALC paradigm was interested in research on criminal behavior at the level of the individual, it rejected the importance of individual-level risk factors and integrated theoretical perspectives. Instead, the causes of criminal behavior were thought to arise from a person's social environment. While these were presented as theories of crime, the reliance on studies of high school and college samples meant that most research was focused on explanations of minor forms of antisocial behavior. Two theories that emerged towards the end of the ALC paradigm, the general theory of crime (Gottfredson & Hirschi, 1990) and strain theory (Agnew, 1992), opened the door for a focus on individual-level risk factors for offending.

The DLC paradigm offered a framework for studying offending over the life-course. One of its four major pillars, the criminal career perspective, identified different offending parameters to measure, such as onset, persistence and desistance. The other three pillars, represented by developmental criminology, propensity theories, and life-course criminology, provided sometimes contradictory explanations of these different parameters. Part of the reason for this contradiction relates to the tendency for each perspective to prioritize the explanation of a particular aspect of offending. Developmentalists emphasized age of onset of offending, propensity theorists emphasized continuity of offending, and life-course theorists emphasized desistance from offending. In some ways, the disagreement observed here resembles the parable of the blind men and the elephant. Each perspective is looking at a different aspect of the criminal career, and each perspective can provide valuable insight into that aspect. These past theoretical debates provided the backcloth for the ISVYOS and its investigation of the roles of propensity, interacting forces of various risk factors, and the role of informal social control in offending over the life-course.

Chapters 4–8 examine what can be learned about youth involved in serious and violent offending when looking at their justice system involvement through the lens of the four pillars of DLC criminology. Given Laub and Sampson's (2003) assertions about the lack of stability in offending between adolescence and adulthood and the relative unimportance of risk factors in childhood/adolescence to understanding adult offending, we take some time in Chapter 2 to revisit approaches to defining, measuring, and explaining chronic offending. The complexity of the backgrounds of youth like John (see Preface) and others involved in serious and violent offenses illustrates why a more comprehensive approach is needed. Setting aside territory-motivated depictions of different theoretical perspectives can help provide a fuller understanding of offending.

Notes

1 When we collected data at BYCC, there were approximately 100 residents. As of 2020-11-05, there were seven residents.

2 By this, we mean explanations of offending by persons as opposed to institutions, groups, or aggregate-level data (e.g., crime rates). This is also not the same as individual-level risk factors, which identify specific characteristics internal to the individual (e.g., low self-control) important to offending as opposed to risk factors describing the person's social environment (e.g., peer delinquency).

3 Psychiatrization refers to the tendency to infer that criminal behavior must be inherently the result of psychopathology (Kecmanovic, 1983).

4 Glueck (1958) referred to the individualization of sentencing in these words: "in the case of any specific offender (it) means, first, to differentiate him from other offenders in personality, character, sociocultural background, the motivations of his crime and his particular potentialities for reform or recidivism; and, secondly, to determine which, among a range of punitive, corrective psychiatric and social measures, is best adapted to solve the special set of problems by that offenders in

such a way as materially to reduce the probability of his committing crimes in the future" (461).

5 To be sure, it was meticulous at the time, but was hardly meticulous compared to later advancements in the understanding of measurement and construct validity germane to forensic psychology (Cronbach & Meehl, 1955).

6 In Canada, Denis Szabo founded the School of Criminology at Université de Montréal in 1960 based on his perspective that sociology was only part of the necessarily interdisciplinary approach to understanding criminal behavior (Szabo et al., 1968). Sociocriminology and psychocriminology were part of an overarching perspective rather than two competing perspectives. This tradition transcended throughout Canada (Fenchel & Winterdyk, 2019). However, given the number of criminology and criminal justice programs in the United States combined with the tendency for the most prestigious journals to be hosted by U.S.-based organizations, societies, and publication companies, this work was overshadowed, at least at the time, by the sociocriminology/psychocriminology debate.

7 Another reason for sociology's territorial defence of criminology related to conclusions from the Michael-Adler (1933) report that the study of crime should be conducted by persons with no history of criminological training. From this point on, "criminology became captive to the discipline of sociology" (Goff & Geiss, 2008, 361).

8 Principles of the criminal career perspective emerged over 50 years earlier with the Gluecks' (1930, 1945) examination of the relationship between age of onset and persistence, the stability of criminal behavior, and the relationship between aging and desistance.

9 That said, others debated whether semi-parametric group-based modeling was an appropriate analytic strategy for making claims about the presence of distinct groups given the possibility that the analysis forces groups where none exist (Sampson & Laub, 2005a, 2005b; Skardhamar, 2010).

10 Jerome Michael and Mortimer Adler were contracted by the Bureau of Social Hygiene of New York City to evaluate the state of criminology. Their report indicated that criminology was held back by the incompetence of sociologists and psychologists who studied crime. According to the report, there was not only a lack of useful data but also a lot of unsubstantiated claims based on such data. A major recommendation of the report included the establishment of a federal institute for examining the causes of crime. This institute was to include a wide range of professionals including statisticians, engineers, economists, and physicists. Notably, they also recommended including one criminologist, provided that this person lacked any formal training and research in the field. That said, there were several critical responses to the report from both criminologists and non-criminologists that targeted the validity of most of Michael and Adler's (1933) assertions (Goff & Geiss, 2008).

11 Despite this assertion, Sampson and Laub (2003) described how there was a lack of evidence that high rates of adolescent offending were informative of high rates of later adult offending.

2 The search for chronic offending

Introduction

Wolfgang and colleagues' (1972) analyses of the Philadelphia Birth Cohort found that a small group of persons were responsible for the majority of all crime. This phenomenon was termed chronic offending and captured the attention of scholars, policymakers, crime analysts, law enforcement, and justice system practitioners. The four pillars of DLC criminology (see Chapter 1) provided different perspectives on chronic offending and its relevance for policy. Some criminal career research investigated the utility of selective incapacitation as a means of curbing future offending (i.e., instituting lengthy sentences to individuals believed to be involved in chronic offending to prevent future offending; Greenwood & Abrahamse, 1982). Certain propensity theorists viewed chronic offending as a myth and, therefore, neutralization policies like selective incapacitation were ineffective (Gottfredson & Hirschi, 1986). Life-course researchers agreed that neutralization techniques for chronic offending were not the solution. The randomness of life events, the impact of a person's social structure on funneling them into adult roles, and human agency implied a substantial capacity for change. Neutralization policies might result in state dependent effects (e.g., incarceration reduces access to informal social control) that have the collateral consequence of increasing the likelihood of continued offending (Sampson & Laub, 1993). Developmentalists viewed chronic offending as evidence of the need for early, proactive, empirically-driven intervention strategies (e.g., social assistance, psychoeducation; Farrington & Welsh, 2008). In sum, the different DLC pillars' perspectives on chronic offending were fairly predictable based on their respective theoretical principles (see Table 1.4 of Chapter 1).

Research on chronic offending became a lightning rod in academic circles and an important focus of criminological scholarship from the 1980s onward. The notion that a small group of individuals were responsible for the majority of all crime raised several questions. Are persons involved in a pattern of chronic offending a group with theoretical relevance or simply a statistical artifact (e.g., all offending distributions will identify a small group of individuals at the tail-end; Blumstein & Moitra, 1980)? Can persons associated with chronic offending be meaningfully distinguished from persons associated with non-chronic patterns of offending? A challenge in interpreting this work is that researchers often mean different things when discussing chronic offending (Jolliffe et al., 2017; Whitten et al., 2017, 2019). We refer to chronic offending as the point at which a person's volume of offending (i.e., frequency) meets a certain threshold so as to justify such a label (e.g., Wolfgang et al., 1972). How this threshold is defined varies across measurement strategies, but what many strategies have in common is that they measure chronic offending in static terms; once someone reaches the threshold for chronic offending, their status does not change.

Somewhat more recently, especially following Moffitt's (1993) dual taxonomy and the availability of semi-parametric group-based modeling (SPGM) in different statistical software packages, other researchers have used the term chronic offending to describe a high-rate (i.e., high volume) and persistent (e.g., extends across multiple age-stages) pattern of offending. For clarity and to avoid confusion with Wolfgang et al.'s (1972) initial, static definition of chronic offending, which relies solely on measuring a person's frequency of offending, we refer to high-rate and persistent offending as chronic and persistent offending (CPO).

Measuring chronic offending: Wolfgang's approach

Interest in chronic offending was popularized by Marvin Wolfgang and colleagues' (1972) research on 10,000 youth from the Philadelphia Birth Cohort study. This cohort included boys born in 1945 who were followed until at least age 18, some of whom were followed until age 30 (Wolfgang, 1983). A key discovery from these data was the identification of a small percentage of the cohort (6% of the full sample and 18% of all delinquents) who were responsible for the majority (52%) of all arrests in adolescence for the cohort (Kempf-Leonard et al. 2001; Wolfgang et al., 1972). Those that met the threshold for chronic offending had a minimum of five arrests. Their measure of chronic offending can be interpreted from two perspectives: (1) chronic offending is the minimum percentage of the sample required to account for 50% of all offenses perpetrated by the sample during adolescence or (2) individuals with at least five arrests exemplify chronic offending.

Wolfgang et al.'s (1972) research set in motion the use of longitudinal studies to identify chronic offending and associated risk factors. This included studies of community-based samples in England (e.g., the CSDD), the United States (e.g., the Denver Youth Survey, the Rochester Youth Development Study, the PYS), New Zealand (the Dunedin Multidisciplinary Health Study), and Canada (the Montreal Two-Sample Longitudinal Study on Delinquency). Like the Philadelphia Birth Cohort, these studies observed that a small proportion of their sample were disproportionately responsible for criminal behavior.

Wolfgang et al.'s findings highlighted that there was heterogeneity *among* individuals involved in crime and not just heterogeneity between individuals who were arrested and those who were not. However, their criteria for chronic offending, and the criteria identified in other community-based studies, was not practical for policy purposes. Five arrests helped discern between less and more serious patterns of offending in community studies, but five arrests among populations of persons in contact with police was far too inclusive (Chaiken & Chaiken, 1982). Extending Wolfgang et al.'s definition to justice-involved samples resulted in a lack of specificity in the measurement of chronic offending.

To address critiques about the arbitrariness of Wolfgang et al.'s (1972) measurement approach, Piquero et al. (2007) presented a formula for calculating the probability of reoffending. These probabilities could be inspected, collectively, to interpret the point at which offending frequency met the threshold for chronic offending. This involved looking at all persons with k adjudications and examining the probability that these individuals experienced k_{+1} adjudications. This procedure identifies the point at which (a) the probability of reoffending at offense k is low compared to offense k_{-1}, but (b) the probability of a "next offense" (i.e., k_{+1},k_{+2},k_{+3}, etc.) remains high and stable for the sample with k adjudications. To illustrate, if a hypothetical sample of persons with five offenses had a 0.40 probability of committing a sixth offense (i.e., perpetrating a sixth offense was unlikely), but the subsample of persons with six offenses had probabilities of 0.92, 0.90, and 0.89, for committing a seventh, eighth, and ninth offense, respectively, then all persons with at least six offenses would be identified by a pattern of chronic offending. Essentially, these probabilities show that a sizeable proportion of this hypothetical sample with five offenses do not make it to a sixth offense, but among those that do, it is likely that more offenses are to follow.

The quest for less subjective measures of chronic offending, combined with the plethora of longitudinal studies that emerged following the Philadelphia Birth Cohort, led to researchers' interest in whether chronic offending was also stable across developmental periods. Will individuals defined by chronic offending at one age-stage also be defined by chronic offending at another age-stage? One of the more parsimonious approaches to examining stability in chronic offending used a cross-tabulation method (Le Blanc & Kaspy, 1998) to compute whether chronic offending was present at two different age intervals. The introduction of a time component helped identify the dynamic nature of chronic offending that was masked by static measures that only looked at chronic offending over a single period of time (for a demonstration, see Deslauriers-Varin & Beauregard, 2014). Le Blanc and Kaspy's (1998) cross-tabulation method focused on the total volume of offending across just two different windows of measurement, making its investigation of the potentially dynamic nature of offending limited. This means that analyses must either investigate two measurement points that are not meaningfully distant from one another (e.g., chronic offending at age 16 and chronic offending at age 17) or two measurement points that are so distant from one another (e.g., chronic offending between ages 12–17 and chronic offending between ages 18–23) that bigger questions are raised about what happens *within* these two aggregated periods. Looking into the black box of what happened within these different aggregate periods required new theories, definitions, and measurement strategies that simultaneously accounted for two key components of offending: volume and persistence.

From Wolfgang's chronic offending to Moffitt's life-course persistent offending

Static indicators of chronic offending were identified almost by accident. Wolfgang et al. did not conceive of a theoretical version of what chronic offending is, how it develops, and its relationship with other criminal career parameters. This initial definition and measurement approach found a way to reduce a dimensional parameter of the criminal career (i.e., frequency) as either present (chronic) or absent (non-chronic) according to some threshold. Moffitt (1993) referred to LCP offending in ways that required researchers to think about chronic offending as the intersection of volume and persistence. LCP offending is therefore one example of a CPO trajectory. We do not say that LCP offending *is* CPO, because LCP offending requires data over the *entire* life-course. A CPO trajectory describes persistence across age, but not necessarily across the entire life-course.

According to Moffitt (1993), CPO was just one symptom of something bigger; a syndrome that manifests itself in various ways and in multiple contexts. Gottfredson and Hirschi (1990) raised similar ideas by suggesting that offending and involvement in *analogous behaviors* go hand-in-hand. Moving on from static concepts of chronic offending was appealing because Moffitt's LCP concept provided a life-course view of a phenomenon of extreme social importance. Wolfgang's description of chronic offending was only measured during adolescence. Moffitt's description of LCP offending required researchers to make better use of their longitudinal data. Moffitt also provided a set of hypotheses that gave researchers a clear path for testing theoretical assertions about *why* CPO developed and not just whether it developed or how prevalent it was.

From a policy standpoint, Moffitt's description of LCP offending was more useful than static notions of chronic offending. For one, Blumstein and Moitra (1980) pointed out that because crime distributions are positively skewed, virtually any study will find evidence of a group of persons towards the tail-end of this distribution who can be characterized by a pattern of chronic offending. Therefore, it was necessary to develop conceptualizations of chronic offending that would not be disregarded as a statistical artifact. Moffitt (1993) described LCP offending as also characterized by more serious offending and a very early onset of offending, meaning that researchers were looking for more than just the tail-end of a distribution. Chronic offending required a wait-and-see approach. Individuals could not be defined by a pattern of chronic offending until they reached some pre-defined threshold. Nothing was mentioned about precursors or warning signs for chronic offending. Moffitt's theoretical perspective was more suited to proactive, humanistic interventions early in the life-course and provided different theory-informed and policy-driven avenues for the investigation of CPO.

To measure volume and persistence simultaneously, researchers needed an analytic strategy capable of measuring offending trajectories.[1] SPGM (Nagin & Land, 1993) is the most common analytic strategy used to measure CPO (see Piquero, 2008). SPGM assumes that representing an entire population by an "average" trajectory (e.g., the aggregate age-crime curve) poorly accounts for the heterogeneity of individual offending patterns. However, it also acknowledges the inordinate number of parameters needed to measure trajectories for each person in a sample. To find a balance, SPGM uses a grouping method to identify the number of aggregate trajectories that fits a sample best. Using the maximum probability of correct assignment rule, individuals are assigned to the trajectory identified by SPGM that best resembles their own trajectory pattern. One assumption made by SPGM, which does not always hold true (Skardhamar, 2010), is that there is heterogeneity in offending patterns when comparing individuals assigned to different offending trajectories but homogeneity when comparing individuals within the same trajectory.

Importantly, trajectories identified using SPGM represent a statistical approximation of the reality of offending as an unknown continuous distribution. Therefore, it is important that researchers not present a given trajectory as if it is a naturally occurring taxon within the population of interest (Skardhamar, 2010). Users cannot describe a theoretical pattern of CPO (e.g., LCP offending) and tell SPGM to look for such a pattern. SPGM tells the user what offending trajectories look like in the sample based on the specified model criteria and it is left to the researcher to decide if any pattern resembles CPO. The lack of standardized criteria to interpret when a particular trajectory represents CPO makes comparisons across studies difficult (see Chapter 5). What might be defined as a CPO trajectory in a community sample may more closely resemble the lowest rate trajectory in a sample of persons involved with the justice system. For example, examining conviction trajectories between ages 10–31 for members of the CSDD, Nagin et al. (1995) defined their "high-level chronic" trajectory as their CPO trajectory. Individuals in this trajectory averaged less than 0.5 convictions at each year of age between ages 20–31. In contrast, examining conviction trajectories between ages 12–32 among a sample of adjudicated youth from the Harreveld Study in the Netherlands, van der Geest et al. (2009) found that their CPO trajectory never averaged fewer than two convictions per year between ages 14–32. In effect, researchers have paid attention to the shape of CPO trajectories, but much less attention to the scale of the y-axis, meaning that the volume of offending varied greatly between CPO trajectories from different studies. Accordingly, *markedly different trajectories have been used to indicate CPO.*

On the other hand, some researchers were less concerned with comparisons across studies and more concerned with the value of Moffitt's hypotheses. Research on CPO is far from perfect, but gaps are understandable given the complexity of the phenomenon under study and the fact that addressing these gaps literally requires time (i.e., a longer follow-up period). Others saw things differently and rejected the idea that CPO could be understood from risk factors in childhood/adolescence and even the idea of CPO as an empirical reality.

Confronting Sampson and Laub's critique of Moffitt and developmental criminology

Sampson and Laub (SL) published a body of work critical of developmental criminology, especially Moffitt's dual taxonomy. Their expansion of the Gluecks' UJD Study represented the first longitudinal study of system-involved youth who were followed into late adulthood. Their findings were published in a widely cited book (Laub & Sampson, 2003) and in the field's flagship journal, *Criminology* (e.g., Sampson & Laub, 2003). SL suggested that Moffitt's notion of LCP offending was not an empirical reality because participants from the UJD Study who had the highest rate of offending in adolescence were not also the participants who had the highest rate of offending in adulthood. They presented these findings as evidence that developmental criminology overemphasized the stability of offending over the life-course. They also asserted that "we cannot predict long-term trajectories of offending … the childhood (developmental) paradigm cannot provide the answer" (Sampson & Laub, 2005b, p. 75). SL (2003) concluded that developmental criminology had relatively limited utility and were confident that other research would produce similar findings:

> Where our data are strong, and perhaps unsurpassed, are in setting up the possibility to examine long-term trajectories of crime and the existence of life-course-persistent offender groups. It would be hard to find an analytic script that would be more conducive to finding troubled men than the one laid out in the behavioral story of the delinquent group in the Gluecks' *Unraveling Juvenile Delinquency* … and yet we have failed to find convincing evidence that a life-course-persistent group can be prospectively or even retrospectively identified based on theoretical risk factors at the individual level. (emphasis in the original, p. 588)

We argue that SL's data and analyses were poorly suited for making conclusions about Moffitt's dual taxonomy, CPO trajectories, and risk/need factors in childhood/adolescence hypothesized to be important to CPO trajectories. Our perspective, and part of the impetus for this book, is that testing developmental criminology principles is more complex than implied by this research and that the failure to recognize this complexity is partly because of inattention to the role the justice system plays in impacting offending over the life-course. The consequence of SL's failure to recognize this complexity and associated research design requirements was the rejection of an important perspective (Lussier et al., 2020b).

Debunking Sampson and Laub's claims about CPO trajectories

SL's conclusions regarding Moffitt's theory were based on major research design flaws (see Table 2.1 for a summary). We highlight four minimum research design criteria for describing and explaining CPO trajectories: (1) the inclusion of individuals at-risk of CPO, (2) the measurement of behaviors that are considered by the justice system to be criminal, regardless of age-stage, (3) measurement of exposure time, and (4) the specification of appropriate risk factors for the prediction of CPO. We believe that these flaws were overlooked or disregarded by SL to challenge developmental criminology while promoting life-course criminology. We do not share this forced dichotomy of life-course *or* developmental criminology. Developmental and life-course criminology offer useful approaches to solving different questions.[2]

The *first research design flaw* that justifies tempering SL's critique of Moffitt's theory relates to their presentation of their sample as well-suited for studying CPO. SL (1993) critiqued DLC research on the basis that:

> Prior data bases often do not include sufficient samples of serious or persistent criminal offending … many studies of juvenile delinquency are characterized by an analysis of truancy, running away, and other relatively minor offenses, and by samples where State sanctions are infrequent… Focusing on minor deviance therefore precludes the study of how the mechanisms of official delinquency control may alter later adult development. (p. 23)

We agree with this statement. However, SL wrongly presented the UJD Study as a sample that was substantially different from prior studies of delinquency that characterized the ALC paradigm. The Glueck boys were wayward youth involved in minor offenses. Looking back at the early days of the Industrial School for Boys in Shirley Massachusetts, one of two training schools used for participant recruitment, more than a quarter of residents were admitted for being stubborn, idle and disorderly, stealing fruit, and drinking (Masis, 2009). This is hardly what Moffitt (1993) had in mind when describing LCP offending. These are the types of behaviors that

Table 2.1 Issues with Sampson and Laub's conclusions about developmental criminology

Developmental principle	*SL's conclusion*	*UJD Study data issue*	*Implication*
LCP offending found disproportionately in adjudicated samples (Loeber & Farrington, 1998).	If LCP offending cannot be identified in the high-risk UJD Study, it cannot be identified anywhere else.	The highest-rate offending trajectory more closely resembled low-rate trajectories in contemporary studies of adjudicated youth.	The UJD Study was not comprised of the types of persons Moffitt hypothesized as being associated with LCP offending.
LCP offending defined by high-rate, serious, and persistent offending (Moffitt, 1993).	Youth in the UJD Study showing the highest rate of offending did not show persistence in this behavior in adulthood; lack of offending continuity. If not in this sample, where else?	Serious offenses rare; status offenses and public order offenses more typical of the sample. Many behaviors no longer criminal under contemporary justice systems.	Criminal behavior in adolescence not considered criminal if repeated in adulthood.
Individuals involved in serious offenses disproportionately associated with LCP offending (Moffitt, 1993).	Same as above.	Failed to account for exposure time at all, or at best only through age 32.	Individuals involved in high-rate and serious offending most likely to experience restrictions in exposure time due to incarceration and early mortality. Underestimated the prevalence of persistence.
Early childhood risk factors associated with LCP offending (Moffitt, 1993).	Early childhood risk factors not related to LCP offending.	Mismeasurement of risk factors; inclusion of risk factors irrelevant to LCP offending; exclusion of risk factors relevant to LCP offending.	Inappropriate test of Moffitt's perspective. Whether risk factors in childhood/adolescence were informative of adult offending requires further research.

Notes: SL = Sampson and Laub. UJD Study = Unraveling Juvenile Delinquency Study. LCP = life-course persistent.

Moffitt hypothesized would be perpetrated by individuals associated with an AL trajectory who were trying to mimic the behavior of those associated with LCP offending. Further, SL (1993) noted that "the use and sale of drugs like cocaine and heroin were not prevalent in this study" (p. 3). Similarly, violent offending was rare for UJD participants (never eclipsing an average of 0.07 offenses per year for the sample; see Laub & Sampson, 2003).

It is not just that the Glueck boys' offending and contact with the justice system was non-serious; it was also infrequent. Regardless of whether offending trajectories were measured through age 32 or through age 70, the highest-rate trajectory peaked at just 2.5 arrests per year. Individuals assigned to the highest-rate trajectory rarely exceeded *an average of 1.5 arrests* at a given year of age. How does this compare to more contemporary research on adjudicated youth? In the Harreveld Youth Study in the Netherlands, even though the study relied on the narrower category of convictions compared to the measurement of arrests in the UJD Study, the highest-rate trajectory peaked at approximately five convictions and averaged approximately 3.5 convictions at each year of age (van der Geest et al., 2009). In the California Youth Authority (CYA) Study, Piquero et al. (2001) found that individuals in their highest-rate trajectory averaged approximately 6.5 arrests per year between ages 18–33. In effect, the highest-rate group found in contemporary samples of adjudicated young persons had a rate of offending 3–4 times higher than in the UJD Study. Based on data from the Criminal Careers and Life Course Study, also from the Netherlands, individuals associated with the highest-rate trajectory averaged approximately three convictions per year up to age 72 (Blokland et al., 2005).

How does the UJD Study compare to community-based studies? When the CSDD examined trajectories among children from higher-risk neighborhoods in South London, despite looking at convictions rather than arrests, participants assigned to the "high-level chronic" trajectory peaked at 1.65 convictions in the combined years of ages 18–19 (Nagin et al., 1995). Similar findings were observed in a study of youth sampled from New Zealand communities (Ferguson et al., 2000). In sum, the rate of offending in the UJD Study was more similar to rates of offending found in community populates than to studies of adjudicated youth from more contemporary samples. Therefore SL failed to address their own assertion regarding the need for datasets with a sufficient subsample of participants involved in serious of persistent offending.

The second research design flaw that justifies tempering SL's critique of Moffitt's theory relates to the measurement of criminal behavior. As indicated in the quote above, SL (1993, p. 23) believed that studies of CPO needed to prioritize the examination of serious offending rather than minor deviance. Yet, minor deviance comprised the bulk of crimes perpetrated by members of the UJD Study. Specifically, offenses classified as "other" were the most common crime type for the sample (Figure 7 from Sampson and Laub [2003]). These 'other' offenses included status offenses (i.e., behaviors considered to be crimes in adolescence but not in adulthood) and public order offenses (e.g., gambling, vagrancy, speeding, conspiracy, lewdness, desertion, failure to pay child support, hunting near a dwelling). Our point here is that the most common types of behaviors perpetrated by participants in the UJD Study would not be considered criminal offenses in most contemporary justice systems. Alcohol and drug offenses were twice as common as violent offenses for the UJD Study sample (Sampson & Laub, 2003), which is also problematic given that alcohol and some drug offenses are unlikely to be prosecuted in contemporary justice systems.

The biggest concern about the inclusion of nuisance-based offenses is that measuring status offenses favors the identification of discontinuity in offending between adolescence and adulthood. This is because continued involvement in status offenses in adulthood will not actually be treated as punishable behaviors. For UJD Study participants, behaviors that resulted in their involvement in the youth justice system, if continued into adulthood, would not result in their involvement in the adult justice system. Status offenses are an epiphenomenon of adolescence (e.g., Le Blanc, 2008) and therefore unhelpful for distinguishing who does or does not enter the youth justice system. In fact, decisions to arrest or prosecute youth on the basis of status offenses has more to do with socioeconomic status, race, and gender than the actual behavior (Bell, 2014).

We are not criticizing research on different types of antisocial behavior. It is important to learn about all forms of antisocial, delinquent, and criminal behavior (Loeber & Le Blanc, 1990). Our issue is with SL (1993) acknowledging the importance of focusing on more serious criminal behavior when studying CPO yet failing to do so in their own work. This did not stop them from making strong, sweeping conclusions about the value of developmental criminology.

The third research design flaw that justifies tempering SL's critique of Moffitt's theory relates to the issue of failing to appropriately account for exposure time. Researchers studying offending trajectories over the life-course recognized that even if individuals were followed for an identical length of time, how this time was experienced varied, and this had implications for opportunities for continued offending. Incarceration is one factor that restricts a person's opportunity for continued offending. Using data from the CYA Study, Piquero et al. (2001) illustrated that the prevalence of desistance was 20% lower once accounting for time incarcerated (i.e., offending continuity was underestimated). Similar observations were made when looking at the UJD Study (Eggleston et al., 2004). Despite this, SL's (2003) analysis of offending trajectories from the UJD Study either only examined exposure time up until age 32 (i.e., only half the study period) or did not control for exposure time at all (see original argument by Robins, 2005). Blokland et al. (2005) speculated that individuals involved in the highest rate of offending in SL's data were only involved in relatively minor crimes/nuisance behaviors that escaped more punitive responses from the justice system. Incarceration is particularly likely to constrain the behavior of individuals involved in the most serious offenses and those who have lengthy criminal histories, as both are used as aggravating circumstances in sentencing decisions (e.g., Clancy et al. 1981). This makes it difficult to identify CPO trajectories (Bushway, 2013). At some point, an individual associated with a CPO trajectory will receive a lengthy custody sentence that limits their ability to participate in crime for several years.

The failure to account for time incarcerated may, on top of the low base-rate problem, help explain the limited predictive validity of the risk factors included in SL's analyses. Persons with a history of frequent offending who receive lengthy sentences are, theoretically, also more at-risk of future offending. Yet, when time incarcerated is not accounted for, such individuals are assigned to lower-rate trajectories (McCuish, 2020). These lower-rate trajectories should be comprised of lower-risk persons (e.g., risk factors are less prevalent and less severe). The inclusion of both high-risk and low-risk persons in the same low-rate offending trajectory increases the likelihood of rejecting the importance of risk factors hypothesized to be important to CPO, as well as protective factors hypothesized to be important to desistance.

Mortality is another factor to account for when measuring exposure time. Analyses of the UJD Study data showed that "when those who are dead are assumed to have desisted, the high-rate chronic population is under-estimated" (Eggleston et al., 2004, 21). However, SL (2003, 578) viewed this as evidence against both the possibility of a LCP offending trajectory and the policy value of Moffitt's theoretical perspective.[3]

> It remains true that high-rate offenders die earlier, but then again developmental theories make claims about offending over the full life course and the ability of individual differences and childhood factors to predict long-term patterns of offending. **If high-rate offenders tend to die early, say before age 30, then the idea of life-course-persistent offending loses much of its appeal. Early mortality among higher rate offenders takes away from the policy implications of Moffitt's LCP offenders.** (emphasis our own)

That individuals following an LCP-path suddenly 'desist' because they are deceased is an odd way of claiming that LCP offending has limited policy appeal. Such individuals were literally characterized by offending over their entire life-course. In our study, of the 1,719 members of the ISVYOS, more than 100 are deceased. These young persons passed away due to gang or family violence, substance use, suicide, and drinking and driving. If Moffitt's notion of LCP offending helps identify individuals who are along this track, and only depart from this track because of early mortality, we think that such information carries incredibly important humanistic policy implications, including the need to develop intervention strategies to help avoid the harm that befalls the individual and their family and friends. Preventing future victimization and trauma/strain to the individual and their family should be as important to policy as preventing crime perpetrated by these individuals. Unfortunately, SL could not see that early mortality highlighted the importance of acknowledging the victimization-offending overlap, early detection and intervention, and not just faith-in-the-making.

The *fourth research design flaw* that justifies tempering SL's critique of Moffitt's theory relates to the risk factors they considered relevant to the prediction of CPO. SL (2003, 586) put out a challenge to anyone questioning their findings:

> For our results to be invalid, the critic must point to an isolated risk factor that is uncorrelated with the more than dozen indicators we summarized. Recall that our strategy was based on the constellation of multiple risk factors within the same boy.

SL's assertion assumes that the only way to invalidate their results is to identify a particular risk factor neglected by their analyses. Although we believe that SL overlooked features of psychopathy as a key risk factor for CPO (see Chapter 7), other reasons that justify a closer look at their findings include (1) low base rates of CPO, (2) the reliability of the risk factors they examined, (3) poorly justified measurement decisions, and (4) the inclusion of irrelevant risk factors.

With respect to the low base rate issue, sufficient base rates are needed to facilitate conducting the appropriate statistical analyses (Copas & Tarling, 1986; MacLennan, 1988). Those characterized as "high rate" comprised just 2–3% of the UJD study sample. When examined through age 32, only 11 participants were in the highest rate trajectory (Laub et al., 1998). SL's (2003) comparisons between trajectories sometimes included as few as five individuals in their highest rate trajectory (see Blokland et al., 2005 for original argument). This low base rate problem and associated issues with statistical power in predicting problem behavior may have contributed to SL's failure to identify risk factors in childhood/adolescence that differentiated individuals in this trajectory from other trajectory groups.

With respect to the reliability of risk factors measured, the types of individual-level risk factors examined by SL were emblematic of the issues Sutherland (1949) identified with measures used during the psychiatrization of offending paradigm. When Donald West was planning the CSDD, he avoided using the Gluecks' research instruments because of concerns about their reliability (Farrington, 2020). For example, SL used low IQ as an indicator of childhood risk and then concluded that the failure of low IQ to predict their CPO trajectory was evidence against developmental criminology. However, Glueck and Glueck (1950) mentioned that there were large discrepancies between their IQ test scores and the IQ scores found within the files of members of their sample and therefore this measure may have been unreliable. Further, it was unclear how personality traits were measured in the UJD Study, other than the fact that "detailed psychiatric assessments" were used (Sampson & Laub, 2003, 571). The degree of detail in these assessments, whether the same assessment was used for each participant, whether interrater reliability was ever conducted, and a range of other requirements for establishing construct validity (Cronbach & Meehl, 1955) were not performed or at least not reported. Reviews of the process of measuring risk during the Gluecks' era revealed issues with clinical biases (e.g., reliance on Rorschach tests, subjective, uninformed opinions of persons involved in crime that were based on myths and misperceptions of what constitutes risk for offending; Lussier et al., 2020). Forensic psychologists considered this type of unstructured clinical judgement to lack reliability. Recognition of this resulted in a revolution in risk assessment (Hart et al., 2016). Impetus on psychometric properties of measures of risk factors at the time of the UJD Study was not what it is today (Forth et al., 2003; Lahey & Waldman, 2003; Mathesius et al., 2017).

With respect to poorly justified measurement decisions, SL (2003) dichotomized their indicators of personality traits and failed to provide a justification for thresholds used. Contemporary measurement of key personality variables emphasizes "little compelling evidence that the categorical model of personality disorder should be retained" (Trull & Durrett, 2005, 372). SL also dichotomized temper tantrums as present or absent. Temper tantrums are among the most common behavioral problems among children (Potegal & Davidson, 2003) and, therefore, may be too broad to distinguish individuals associated with a CPO trajectory from individuals associated with non-CPO trajectories. The prediction of CPO must examine risk factors that are theoretically relevant, sensitive (i.e., typical to CPO), and specific (i.e., atypical of non-CPO patterns; see McCuish et al., 2018a).

With respect to the inclusion of irrelevant risk factors, criminology, in general, has a history of trying to predict CPO using risk factors that may be important for distinguishing between offending and non-offending, but are too common among persons involved in crime to help distinguish which individuals are at risk of CPO (McCuish et al., 2014; van der Geest et al., 2009). Looking specifically at SL's (2003) analyses, across the six trajectories they identified, dichotomous measures like "extroversion" and "adventurous" were found in approximately 50% or more of persons within each trajectory. These are too ubiquitous to help explain LCP offending/CPO. As noted by Robins (2005), SL's approach of aggregating a range of risk factors was inappropriate because included in their risk factor scale were risk factors not hypothesized to be specific to CPO or Moffitt's hypothesized LCP offending trajectory (e.g., IQ, low maternal supervision, poverty).[4] Including irrelevant risk factors and then proclaiming that risk factors in childhood/adolescence are not useful for understanding adult offending is a disingenuous test of Moffitt's theory. Nevertheless, SL (2003, 588) concluded:

> We can say with some confidence that adult trajectories of offending among former delinquents cannot be reduced to the past… Differences in adult criminal trajectories cannot be predicted from childhood, contra the National Summits of the policy world and apparently much yearning among criminologists.

Several of the empirical chapters in this book support a different conclusion, one that recognizes the importance of experiences in childhood and adolescence.

Summary

There is a small group of individuals responsible for a disproportionate number of crimes. However, the label and measurement of this chronic offending phenomenon remain debated. Such debates are a normal part of the social sciences when confronted with complex and multidimensional phenomenon (Posick & Rocque, 2018). Developmental criminologists agree that there is a small group of children that are worth thinking about for the purpose of developmental prevention through care, service, and intervention (e.g., Farrington & Loeber, 2001). Others feel that the life of individuals on a path of crime might be best left alone (Laub & Sampson, 2003). SL's critique of developmental criminology was made over a decade ago. We might be a day late, but we do not believe that we are a dollar short in our assessment of the veracity of SL's critique.

SL are right to be concerned about the use risk factors in childhood/adolescence to make strong conclusions about a young person's fate in adulthood given how such labels could perpetuate self-fulfilling prophecies, neglect by parents and teachers, or unfair targeting by justice systems (Bernburg et al., 2006). SL's critique seems based on misconceptions about the principles of developmental criminology (e.g., protection and education of marginalized children as opposed to control and deterrence). Nordic criminology and criminology in Western/Northern Europe and Canada for decades emphasized that the purpose of intervention was to help create equity through social services. We are not talking about using incarceration for deterrence and selective incapacitation. The history of mass incarceration in the United States (Blumstein & Beck, 1999) might have led SL to be apprehensive of policies with long-term prediction in mind. However, developmental criminology and the examination of CPO are not just about long-term prediction of offending. Rather, it is about understanding that exposure to early risk factors carries potential long-term consequences but that these risk factors can be intervened on through appropriate social services and psychoeducational interventions.

SL (2003) commented that "if high-rate offenders tend to die early, say before age 30, then the idea of life-course-persistent offending loses much of its appeal" (p. 578). It is unfortunate that SL do not see the policy-value in trying to, for example, provide services that can help young persons from dying. Developmental criminology can be used to help guide the prevention of CPO and thus decrease the likelihood of early mortality. These are children and youth who are often born into remarkably disadvantaged/oppressive situations (see the description of John's background in the Preface). SL's stance on desistance by default and aging out of crime due to the randomness of life events reflects a laissez-faire attitude that may have disastrous consequences with the potential of perpetuating inequality, including inequality in victimization and early mortality.

For individuals in extremely difficult circumstances on a potential path to CPO, the assumption that they will have similar levels of human agency so as to simply pull themselves up by their bootstraps is out of touch with empirical findings showing how individual-level factors and social/historical situations and contexts impact between-group differences and within-individual change in agency. For example, experiencing discrimination influences poorer sleep quality (Yip et al., 2020) which in turn produces lower levels of self-control (Meldrum et al., 2015), which has implications for human agency. It is also out of touch with the life circumstances of participants from the ISVYOS. This is not to say that such participants have lower levels of agency compared to others, only that they face an uphill battle given the disadvantages and oppressive circumstances they are in. It is quite possible that without intervention, even more individuals in the ISVYOS sample would be deceased or continuing a pattern of CPO. Intervention does not mean incarceration only, and when incarceration is used, it can be used for treatment and rehabilitation rather than deterrence and punishment (Corrado et al., 2010). Researchers have established the importance of using custody to focus on humanistic, person-centered intervention strategies, including trauma-informed practices (Viljoen et al., 2019), that help individuals avoid offending but also improve other domains of functioning (e.g., interpersonal relationships, school, work, civic responsibility).

Notes

1 A trajectory refers to a measure of the frequency that a given outcome occurs within a given measurement window. Typically, an offending trajectory measures the number of offenses (e.g., arrests, convictions, self-reported crimes) at each year of age.

2 Ironically, the life-course approach espoused by SL was based on Dr. Glen Elder's (1998) theoretical work that embraced the developmental perspective.

3 Although SL accounted for mortality, doing so revealed that most of their participants were not included in follow-up analyses. Eggleston et al.'s (2004) analysis of the UJD Study noted that "if there are different members included in a trajectory group given different lengths of follow-up, for instance, this fact could potentially change the results of subsequent tests that are based on the characteristics of people in the identified trajectory groups" (24). In effect, because many individuals in the UJD Study sample were deceased, (a) the

modeling of trajectories may have carried certain biases impacting the reliability of the prediction of trajectories via characteristics in adolescence and (b) as time went on, fewer and fewer individuals were included in the estimation of the tail-end of trajectories. These individuals were not excluded from analyses altogether; they were assigned to a particular trajectory, but they were not used to help calculate the rate of offending within that trajectory following their death. This creates issues with, among other things, low base rates of persons with a pattern of CPO.

4 Inclusion of less important risk factors in the same scale is problematic because the scale gives equal weight to all items (Robins, 2005).

3 The Incarcerated Serious and Violent Young Offender Study

Introduction

Chapter 2 established a minimum of four research design needs for studying CPO trajectories: (1) a sufficient sample of individuals involved in serious and violent offenses, (2) the measurement of behaviors that are considered by the justice system to be criminal, regardless of age-stage, (3) the measurement of exposure time, and (4) the reliable measurement of risk factors theoretically relevant to the development of CPO. This chapter identifies how the ISVYOS meets these needs. First, we situate the ISVYOS within the broader research and policy context that motivated its initiation in 1998.

Before the late 1960s, Canada's incarceration rate was higher than most Western industrialized nations, including the United States (Hogarth, 1967). This period coincided with the development of university programs across Canada focused on criminology, sentencing, and the justice system. It also marked a period characterized by penal reform that stressed that the historical overreliance on incarceration was a social issue. These reforms formally recognized the role and importance of probation officers and the use of presentence reports to assist judicial decision-making. They also favored the increased use of community-based sentences as an alternative to incarcerating adults (e.g., Dombek & Chitra, 1980; Hogarth, 1971). Paradoxically, reforms in Canada's youth justice system moved away from the *parens patriae* philosophy (e.g., children in need of protection) emphasizing the rehabilitative needs of the child (Trépanier, 1999a) and towards an emphasis on due process and the use of punitive sentences. In effect, there was a switch from a focus on the child to a focus on the offense (Leschied & Gendreau, 1986).

This youth justice reform included the adoption of the 1984 Young Offenders Act (YOA). Under the YOA, through the 1990s, Canada incarcerated approximately 700 youth per 100,000 in the population (Bell, 2014) compared to approximately 350 youth per 100,000 in the population in the United States (Smith, 1998). There were therefore important questions for researchers to address about youth incarceration in Canada. Was the judicial system more likely to incarcerate youth involved in relatively trivial offenses or was serious and violent youth offending on the rise (Corrado & Markwart, 1994; Doob, 1992)? There was at least some evidence that both explanations were true (Corrado et al., 2000). At the time, however, criminological scholarship in Canada focused almost entirely on sociolegal perspectives and, with some exceptions (e.g., LeBlanc & Fréchette, 1989), neglected the study of the young persons in this system.

Concurrent to the rise in Canada's youth incarceration rate was the growing theoretical and policy interest related to major cohort studies identifying a small percentage of youth who accounted for the majority of all offending. This small group caused major political controversies concerning whether the appropriate legal/policy response was to transition towards punitive and deterrence-based models of youth justice (Loeber & Farrington, 1998). However, criminologists' understanding of this group was relatively limited because community-based longitudinal studies included few youth with histories of incarceration. It is therefore unsurprising that debates about the most appropriate response to such youth played out across political lines and the social sciences had a relatively minor role in shaping this response. Media portrayed youth crime as an epidemic (for a discussion, Corrado & Markwart, 1994) and this portrayal was used to justify a more punitive, deterrence-based model of youth justice to protect the public (e.g., Howell et al., 1995).[1] When some made claims about child "superpredators" (DiIulio, 1995) there was little research on youth in the justice system that could be used to counter such claims.

Who is the youth repeatedly involved with the justice system? What is the impact of the justice system on these young persons? The DLC paradigm at least provided a framework for studying such individuals. This growing interest, combined with new theoretical perspectives from the DLC paradigm but a lack of data to appropriately address major policy and theoretical questions, served as the catalyst for the ISVYOS.

Developing and implementing the ISVYOS

Custody centers are not easy for researchers to access (Fox et al., 2011). This is especially true of youth custody centers where there is the added need to protect persons who are too young to consent to participate in research. Throughout the 1980s, Professor Raymond Corrado was the project director for the province of British Columbia (BC) on a Canadian study of youth justice policy in six provinces. The purpose of this study was to determine the philosophical direction of the new (at the time) federal legislation, the YOA. While the intention was to move towards a system where youth were held more accountable (e.g., longer custody sentences; Caputo, 1987), this law/policy change was not supported by many youth justice system professionals in BC. The goal was to reserve the use of custody for only those youth involved in serious or violent offenses. Another goal, brought about by the YOA, was the abolishment of status offenses. Thus,

ISVYOS participants were never incarcerated for behaviors like truancy, alcohol use, or incorrigibility (i.e., addresses the first and second research design needs for studying CPO identified in Chapter 2).

An oversight committee was formed to review the approach to youth justice in BC. Gordon Hogg, the Director of BC's largest custody facility, the Willingdon Youth Detention Centre in the Greater Vancouver region, and his colleague, Alan Markwart, a former youth probation officer and youth justice policy specialist, nominated Raymond Corrado for this committee. The committee produced an unpublished report that illustrated a gap between what practitioners believed would work (i.e., rehabilitation) and what Federal policymakers and some members of the public wanted to see as the official response to youth crime (i.e., punishment). The report showed that youth in custody had an array of unmet service needs due to major trauma and associated negative outcomes, including foster care placement, self-medicating with drugs and alcohol, survival-directed behaviors (e.g., break & enters, drug trafficking, sex work), early/continuous school problems and dropouts, and unstable/unhealthy housing conditions (also see Teplin et al., 2003). Given short-term custody sentences, coordination was needed between custody facilities and community-based government ministries and non-profit organizations that could help ensure that programming in custody continued in the community. In practice, it was challenging to coordinate systematic case planning and service delivery, particularly to multi-problem and geographically mobile youth in the community (Bala et al., 2009).

In response to the committee's findings, the Ministry of Children and Family Development (MCFD) was established as the ministry responsible for all youth in conflict with the law in BC.[2] Mr. Hogg was appointed as minister of MCFD and Mr. Markwart as assistant deputy minister responsible for all services for incarcerated youth. Both were aware of the absence of research on this population, especially in Canada. This was not surprising given that Canadian criminology at the time was more heavily represented by scholars concerned with critical theory and the sociolegal response to crime. In light of this, Mr. Hogg and Mr. Markwart encouraged and assisted Raymond Corrado in initiating the ISVYOS. MCFD allowed the study to approach all youth in all custody facilities in the province to participate. Although research goals varied over time (discussed below), from 1998 through 2011, research assistants (RAs) from the ISVYOS entered custody facilities throughout the province of BC to interview youth. In all, the ISVYOS required a partnership between academics, youth justice professionals, and government representatives that has persisted for over two decades.

Maintaining data collection for over 20 years

Unlike major longitudinal studies in the United States that receive millions of dollars at a time to focus on long-term data collection, grant strategies in Canada are not well-suited for the support of longitudinal studies, especially those that span multiple decades. Federal granting agencies fund criminological research only for short-term periods. This funding strategy influenced the ISVYOS, including how the project collected data. The ISVYOS relied on securing many short-term grants and thus was initially designed with short-term goals in mind. Data collection began in 1998 and remains ongoing. Collecting data through 2021 was not part of the initial plan. However, motivated especially by theories from the DLC paradigm, it became clear that longitudinal research was necessary to appropriately understand youth in custody and their experiences. Thus, the ISVYOS pieced together different short-term aims, representing three major phases of the study thus far, to create a longitudinal project. This longitudinal component assisted with the exploration of research areas relevant to the DLC paradigm. Table 3.1 summarizes how the different phases of the study comport with these research areas and the longitudinal sequence of the study is described in Figure 3.1.

Phase one: Profiles of incarcerated boys and girls

The first phase of data collection ran between 1998–2002 and involved interviews with boys and girls in various custody centers throughout Metro Vancouver, the Fraser Valley, Vancouver Island, and the Okanagan. This region of BC is approximately half the size of Texas in terms of square miles. Participants recruited during this phase are referred to as Cohort I. The purpose of this first phase was to provide a cross-sectional snapshot of the risk/needs profiles of incarcerated youth. The first step in the data collection process involved recruiting youth to participate in a structured interview, referred to as the intake interview. This was a survey-based instrument covering a range of different risk factors and constructs that were specified by criminological theories to be important to criminal behavior, including substance use, victimization experiences, self-identity, family problems, and attitudes towards the justice system. In line with developmental criminology interests (e.g., LeBlanc & Loeber, 1998), attention was given to the age of onset of different behaviors and risk factors. Other themes included investigating whether sentencing practices in BC were such that judges were incarcerating girls, not because of the severity of their offense, but to remove them from a dangerous social environment (Corrado et al., 2000). This concern with protectionist sentencing practices suggested that girls might be unfairly punished by the justice system given that judges were not relying on traditional bases for sentencing decisions.

Participants who completed the intake interview were eligible to participate in a semi-structured interview used as part of the procedures for scoring the Psychopathy Checklist: Youth Version (PCL:YV; Forth et al., 2003). Participants with a complete PCL:YV rating were followed for approximately one year to identify whether they were reconvicted of a new offense (see Vincent et al., 2008).

Table 3.1 Data collection phases, associated key interviews, and applications to criminological perspectives

	Criminal career research	*Developmental criminology*	*Propensity theories*	*Life-course criminology*
Phase I: Risk Factors				
Intake Interview	• Self-reported offending linked to different criminal career parameters.	• Association between age of onset and key risk factors. • Measurement of criminal versatility. • Links between onset of criminal behavior and frequency of criminal behavior. • Risk factors used to predict continuity/ frequency of offending over age-stages.	• Different measures of self-control can be used to capture Gottfredson and Hirschi's notion of criminal propensity.	• Risk factors measured in the intake interview used to predict likelihood of experiencing positive turning points in adulthood (i.e., investigation of selection effects).
PCL:YV	NA	• Used to predict continuity/ frequency of offending over age-stages.	• Suitable for measuring criminal propensity.	• Used to predict likelihood of experiencing positive turning points in adulthood (i.e., selection effects).
Phase II: Expanding What We Know				
Intake Interview	• Self-reported offending linked to different criminal career parameters.	• Association between age of onset and key risk factors. • Measurement of criminal versatility. • Links between onset of criminal behavior and frequency of criminal behavior. • Risk factors used to predict continuity/frequency of offending over age-stages.	• Different measures of self-control used to capture Gottfredson and Hirschi's notion of propensity.	• Risk factors measured in the intake interview used to predict likelihood of experiencing positive turning points in adulthood (i.e., selection effects).

(*Continued*)

Table 3.1 (Continued)

	Criminal career research	*Developmental criminology*	*Propensity theories*	*Life-course criminology*
PCL:YV/ CAPP-IRS	NA	• Used to predict continuity/ frequency of offending over age-stages.	• Suitable for directly measuring criminal propensity.	• Used to predict likelihood of experiencing positive turning points in adulthood (i.e., selection effects).
MACI	NA	• Used to predict continuity/ frequency of offending over age-stages.	• Suitable for directly measuring criminal propensity.	• Used to predict likelihood of experiencing positive turning points in adulthood (i.e., selection effects).
Exit Interview	NA	Identify custody-based interventions informative of desistance.	• Suitable for examining outcomes of a criminal propensity (e.g., low self-control and its relationship to a person's responses to their custody environment).	• Used to explore the role of prison as a turning point associated with desistance.
Phase III: Adult Outcomes				
Criminal History Data	• Measures different parameters of the criminal career.	• Used to examine the relationship between past and future offending, including measures of versatility, chronicity, persistence.	• Used to examine whether all individuals follow the same age-crime curve. • Used to examine the presence of persistent offending.	• Used to operationalize desistance from (official) criminal behavior.
Repeated Measures of Risk/Protective Factors	NA	• Used to examine the association between change/stability in risk factors and change/ stability in offending.	• Used as outcomes of a person's risk/needs factors in childhood/adolescence.	• Used to operationalize different turning points, including family, employment, marriage, housing, etc.

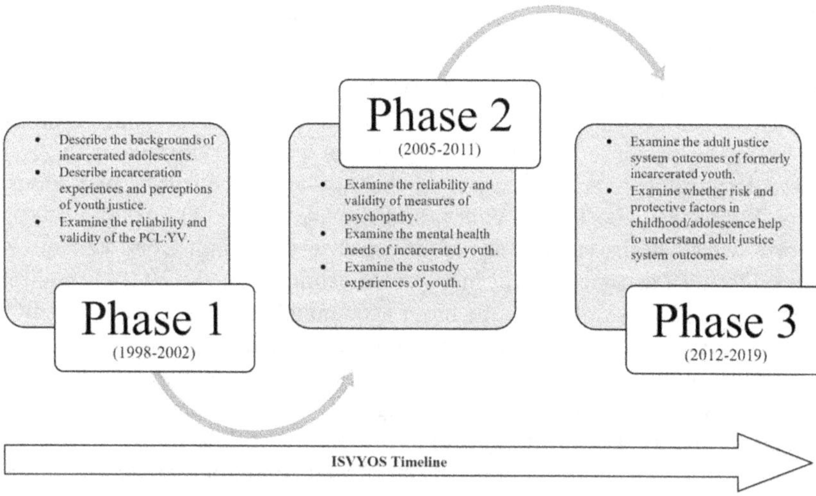

Figure 3.1 Description of the research questions examined in each major phase of the ISVYOS.

Towards the end of data collection in Phase One, the Canadian Federal government began the process of repealing the YOA because of policy concerns about the over-use of custody for minor offenses as well as the perceived lack of sufficiently punitive responses to serious and violent youth offending, which received major media attention. For example, in BC in 1992, teenager Jesse Cadman was fatally stabbed following an unprovoked attack by a group of teenagers. The group included one individual who was on bail and under the supervision of his father while he awaited trial for another violent crime (Tamminga, 2012). This case and others left the general public with the impression that Canada was failing to protect its citizens from serious and violent youth who were aware that they would not receive punitive sanctions (Corrado et al., 2015). Victim advocates and citizen committees called for lengthier sentences (Zytaruk, 2018). Police groups claimed that "[anti-punishment policies] made a mess of things. Now it is our turn, the punishment people. Punishment works" (see Corrado & Marquart, 1994, 345). In response, the *Youth Criminal Justice Act* (YCJA, 2002) was enacted in 2003. Two of the main goals of the YCJA included the reduction in the use of custody for young persons more generally but also the increased use of custody and lengthier custody sentences for those involved in serious and violent offenses.[3] The enactment of this new legislation allowed for a comparison of profiles of youth in custody during the YOA and YCJA (see Chapter 9) and also resulted in new questions for the ISVYOS to address.

Phase two: Expanding what we know about serious and violent youth

The ISVYOS began the second phase of data collection, which ran between 2005–2011 during the YCJA. Participants recruited during this phase are referred to as Cohort II. As part of the YCJA's initiative to reduce the use of custody, at the time of data collection, there were only three youth custody centers in the province. Cohort II participants were recruited from the two largest custody centers. The largest of the two was in Burnaby and served Metro Vancouver, the Fraser Valley, and the Okanagan. The second was in Victoria, which is the capital city of BC, and served youth from Vancouver Island. During this time, several high-profile examples of the YCJA's goal of holding serious and violent youth more accountable were witnessed. In BC, Michael Levy was paralyzed after being attacked outside of a high school dance by a group of youth who assaulted him with various weapons. One of the accused was observed laughing following his sentencing hearing. The BC Attorney General called for that youth to be brought back to court for a review of his sentence. Instead of receiving their original conditional sentence he was sentenced to custody. A second youth in the attack was sentenced as an adult and received a 10-year custody sentence (CBC News, 2007). Whereas the YOA was more commonly associated with the use of short-term custody sentences, these new cases reflected the YCJA's interest in using adult-length sentences for youth involved in serious and violent crime (Corrado et al., 2015).

Continuing with a major theme of the first phase of data collection, the Cohort II intake interview addressed developmental criminology interests in the onset of risk factors and offending behavior (see Chapter 6). The interview was based in part on an English translation of LeBlanc et al.'s (1996) *Mesures de l'Adaptation Sociale et Personnelle pour les Adolescents Québécois* (MASPAQ). The Cohort II intake interview was expanded to include additional questions about school and family life, antisocial and criminal behavior, attitudes towards offending, crime sequences, emotions prior to offending, substance use, gang activity, mental health, and fear and safety while incarcerated. All participants from Cohort II who completed an intake interview were eligible for additional interviews and assessments. The four main instruments used (see Table 3.1) were the Millon Adolescent Clinical Inventory (MACI; Millon & Davis, 1993), the PCL:YV, the Comprehensive Assessment of Psychopathic Personality – Institutional Rating Scale (CAPP-IRS), and the Exit interview. The MACI, PCL:YV, and CAPP-IRS focused on psychopathology. The MACI included 160 items related to different mental health issues. The MACI was implemented in part to examine the convergent validity of the CAPP-IRS, which is a newer measure of features of psychopathy and was adapted by the ISVYOS for use with youth (McCuish et al., 2019a). The PCL:YV was also measured to allow comparisons with Cohort I and to assess the CAPP-IRS' convergent validity. These instruments were used to evaluate whether psychopathy was informative of CPO trajectories (e.g., Corrado et al., 2015).

The Exit interview was used to examine participants' experiences in custody, including the level of support they received from friends, family, and staff while incarcerated, the level of victimization and conflict they experienced with other residents, and participation in different programs. The Exit interview helped understand life-course criminologists' interest in whether prison is a turning point promoting desistance from crime and delinquency, a pause during which young persons could access specialized interventions with rehabilitation objectives, or a negative experience that limits these young people from experiencing social, familial, educational, and/or professional growth (e.g., Sampson & Laub, 1993). Whereas socio-criminological research has consistently focused on the negative side of incarceration (Shover, 1996; Sykes, 1958; Thomas & Foster, 1972; Zingraff, 1975), initial publications using Exit interview data showed that a positive relationship with staff members was associated with a lower incidence rate of new convictions (McCuish et al., 2018b).

Phase three: The adult justice system outcomes of serious and violent youth

The first and second phases were missing the heart of the DLC paradigm: longitudinal research, including the examination of the relationship between risk/needs factors in adolescence and adult offending. This was addressed in the third phase of data collection that began in 2011. Under this phase, the ISVYOS ended its recruitment of new participants and instead measured the adult justice system outcomes of its members. This shift coincided with the emergence and proliferation of empirical research on desistance from crime (Kazemian, 2007; Sampson & Laub, 2003). The shift was also heavily inspired by the Pathways to Desistance Study (e.g., Mulvey et al., 2004), which followed a sample of formerly incarcerated boys and girls through emerging adulthood with an extensive list of repeated measures of constructs at the core of criminological and forensic psychology theories of crime.

It was clear that relying only on youth data would overestimate homogeneity among ISVYOS participants. Virtually all participants recidivated in adolescence. Drug and alcohol use characterized more than 90% of the sample. The YCJA created a system in which youth were in custody because they had perpetrated similar offenses and had a similar record of prior offending (Bala et al., 2009). Moffitt (1993) asserted that distinguishing between AL and LCP offending required looking beyond adolescence; the ISVYOS took note of this research design requirement and thus examined members' offending patterns into adulthood. Doing so addressed important policy implications about adult justice system reinvolvement among youth with histories of serious and violent offending. Was the youth justice system effective in preventing or reducing adult justice system involvement?

Examining the adult life outcomes of youth in the justice system carries certain challenges. Being able to track down individuals over prolonged periods is a significant issue and requires enormous resources (e.g., staff, time, money, computers) as well as ethical approvals from several agencies. Moreover, participants involved in antisocial behavior are especially difficult to track (e.g., Cotter et al., 2005). The ability of the ISVYOS to safely follow-up with participants in the community was also in question because participants were, for example, the subject of police duty-to-warn notifications to the public. Some were wanted for homicide. Some were murdered. Some were known to be the targets of drive-by shootings from rival gang members. Although not ideal, accessing a computerized system was used as an alternative strategy to learn about members of the sample in adulthood.

A software program for data management and storage, referred to as the Corrections Network (CORNET), was used to collect data on the adult outcomes of ISVYOS members. CORNET includes data on all individuals involved in the BC justice system. It is not restricted to data on only youth or only adults.[4] It captures the moment an individual becomes involved in the justice system and even includes information several years after a person's last criminal offense (e.g., follow-up data from practitioners while the participant is on probation). CORNET also includes a standardized risk assessment tool that provides data on risk and protective factors and adult social outcomes (e.g., employment, marriage, housing, peer relations). This allowed the ISVYOS to examine the association between risk and protective factors measured in the first two phases of the project with offending and social outcomes measured during this third phase. Doing so helped evaluate debate about whether risk factors in childhood/adolescence were informative of adult justice system involvement and social outcomes (Laub & Sampson, 2003; Moffitt, 1993).

The coding of criminal records via CORNET is repeated yearly and is recorded in such a way so as to indicate, for each person in the sample, the number of convictions incurred at each year of age and the number of days incarcerated at each year of age. Thus, we are not looking at, for example, the number of convictions each participant incurred in 2019. We are looking at the number of convictions each participant incurred at age 12, at age 13, at age 14, and so on. CORNET also includes various risk assessment tools regularly completed for all persons involved in the justice system, even after they have been convicted and sentenced. These risk assessment tools were primarily in-house measures created by BC Corrections and included youth and adult measures of risk and protective factors from a variety of domains as well as institutional maladjustment (e.g., conflicts with staff, other residents, victimization, suicidal ideation). Assessments were completed on multiple occasions in both adolescence and adulthood. Classic turning points (e.g., marriage, employment) were captured by these risk assessment tools (see Chapter 8), which allowed the ISVYOS to evaluate (a) the extent to which turning points were present in the lives of persons formerly incarcerated in adolescence, (b) whether these turning points were informative of desistance, and (c) whether risk factors and offending patterns in adolescence reduced the likelihood of experiencing these turning points or benefiting from them in terms of their influence on desistance.

Methodology

Sample

In total, 1,719 youth were recruited to participate in the ISVYOS. This included 596 members of Cohort I, who were incarcerated under the YOA between 1998–2002, and 1,123 members of Cohort II, who were incarcerated under the YCJA between 2005–2011.

Among those in Cohort I with available data, 442 participants self-identified as male (75.0% of the sample), 149 (25.2%) participants self-identified as female, and one (0.2%) participant self-identified as transgender.[5] In line with other jurisdictions in Canada, Indigenous youth were overrepresented in the sample. Although only approximately 6% of the population of BC self-identifies as Indigenous (Statistics Canada, 2013), 23.3% of the Cohort I self-identified as such. Most participants self-identified as White (61.0% of the sample) and 15.7% of the sample self-identified as a member of a non-Indigenous ethnic minority group[6] (e.g., Black, Hispanic, East Asian, South-East Asian). Interview data were available for 586 participants (98.3% of those recruited). The average age of participants at the time of their intake interview was 16.16 (*SD* = 1.26; Range = 12–19).

Among those in Cohort II with available data, 876 self-identified as male (80.6% of the sample) and 211 (19.4%) self-identified as female. The overrepresentation of Indigenous participants continued in Cohort II. Despite the YCJA explicitly including principles for reducing the use of custody for Indigenous youth, 33.3% of Cohort II participants were Indigenous (i.e., a higher prevalence than Cohort I). Most participants were White (51.2% of the sample) and 15.6% of the sample self-identified as being part of a non-Indigenous ethnic minority group (e.g., Asiatic [2.2%], Black [3.6%], and East Indian [3.9%] were among the most common non-Indigenous ethnic minority groups). Interview data were available for 962 participants (85.5% of those recruited to participate). The average age of participants at the time of their intake interview was 16.01 (*SD* = 1.29; Range = 12–19).

Procedure

Procedures for data collection were relatively similar across Cohort I and Cohort II. MCFD is responsible for the care of all incarcerated youth in BC and consented to the ISVYOS' recruitment of youth from custody centers throughout the province. Youth were eligible to participate if they were English-speaking, capable of understanding interview questions (e.g., lower functioning youth, per official file information, were excluded), and willing to provide accurate information. Data regarding refusal rates and instances in which youth were removed from the interview schedule due to perceived persistent dishonesty were not consistently recorded.

To recruit participants (see Chapter 10 for details), RAs approached incarcerated youth while they were residing in their custody center unit. Youth were typically approached to participate in the study within their first week of arrival to the custody center. All youth approached were informed that their involvement in the study would not affect their stay at the custody center. To help ensure confidentiality, interviews were conducted in a closed-door, private room away from other residents and staff. To obtain assent, participants were read and given a copy of an information sheet explaining the purpose of the study, how information would be collected (e.g., interview and file information), and that all information would be kept confidential unless the participant made a direct threat against themselves or someone else. Participants signed a form signifying that they understood the details of the study and that they could withdraw at any time.

The ISVYOS failed to record individuals who entered custody center data collection sites but were not interviewed. We are therefore unaware of the percentage of the custody population that were included in the study. That said, official statistics regarding the gender and ethnic composition of youth in custody (e.g., Malakieh, 2017) resembled what was found for the ISVYOS. Although the goal was to recruit all individuals in custody, the ISVYOS sample is likely more reflective of individuals who received lengthier sentences or were incarcerated on multiple occasions as this gave the research team more of an opportunity to recruit and interview such youth. The Canadian system never incarcerates youth with adults, meaning that youth involved in the most serious and violent offenses were not excluded from the study.

Measures

This section focuses on measures that reappear throughout the book's empirical chapters. Measures specific to a single chapter are described in that chapter (e.g., the PCL:YV in Chapter 7). The number of participants in each cohort receiving a particular interview is shown in Figure 3.2. Not all individuals who received an intake interview completed all other instruments. Typically, this was because of a lack of funding or opportunity (e.g., participant released from custody). The data presented in this book are mainly from the intake interview and criminal history data collected from CORNET.

For the intake interview, 1,548 members of the ISVYOS had available data (90.1% of the sample). There were various reasons for missing interview data (see Figure 3.3). Some members declined to be interviewed but file information was accessed through consent from MCFD (n = 149; 8.7%). Some members' intake interviews were unavailable due to administrative issues

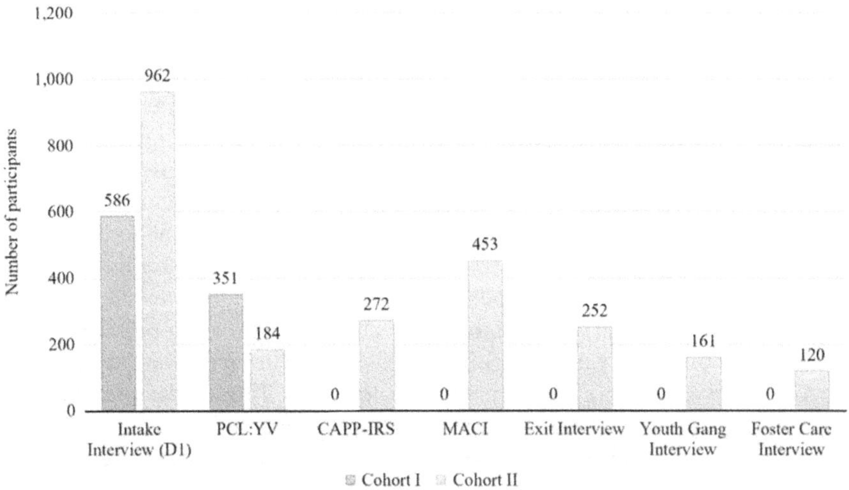

Figure 3.2 Number of participants associated with each instrument across Cohort I and Cohort II.

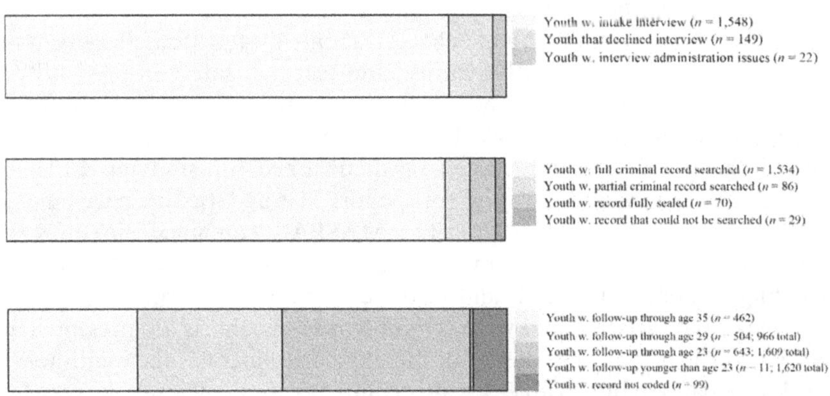

Figure 3.3 Description of 1,719 members of the ISVYOS across interview availability (top), criminal record availability (middle), and length of follow-up (bottom).

(e.g., lost interviews, unreliable data; n = 22; 1.3%). For criminal history data coded from CORNET, 1,620 members of the ISVYOS had available data (94.2% of the sample). Some members' criminal history data were unavailable due to administrative issues (e.g., they could not be searched on CORNET because the participant's name or Correctional Services number was inaccurately recorded; n = 29; 1.7%). For others, their criminal history data were missing because their CORNET file was fully sealed (n = 70; 4.1%).

There were also several reasons for missing data *among* individuals with available interview and criminal history data. Regarding the intake interview, first, some questions were unanswered because interviews were incomplete (e.g., participant refused to finish the interview or were released from custody before the interview could be finished; n = 158; 10.2% of all intake interviews). Second, sometimes participants refused to answer a specific question or reported that they did not know the answer to the question posed. Third, because of changes to the intake interview due to time, financial constraints, and changing interests of researchers, some questions were asked of some participants but not others.[7] For the second and third points, the amount of missingness was dependent on the specific variable under investigation. A codebook on the ISVYOS ResearchGate site[8] addresses the amount of missingness for different variables. In general, when questions were asked of a specific individual, data were missing for less than 10% of the sample (e.g., missing but not because the question was simply not included in the interview). Regarding criminal history data, some members' youth histories were sealed (n = 86; 5.0% of the sample). Adult criminal history data were still available for these individuals. The missing data relating to measures from the intake interview and measures of criminal history data should be kept in mind when inspecting cells within a given table.

The Intake Interview. For both cohorts, the intake interview included information regarding demographic characteristics, family structure, substance use, self-reported criminal behavior, family dysfunction, placement in foster care, mental health, self-identity, and fear and safety in prison. The focus on individual-level risk and family dysfunction aligned with Moffitt's description of neuropsychological deficits and family adversity (i.e., addressed the fourth research design need identified for studying CPO in Chapter 2). The intake interview for Cohort II was based in part on the MASPAQ (LeBlanc et al., 1996). The MASPAQ contained measures of authority conflict, covert, and overt behavior across a variety of domains, including at home, at school, and in the community. Descriptive statistics for *some* of the variables that were common to both cohorts are presented in Table 3.2. The prevalence/severity of these factors illustrates the multi-needs profiles of participants. Table 3.2 also compares these measures across female participants (n = 361) and male participants (n = 1,318). Most of these risk factors were more prevalent or more severe for female participants.

In terms of sociodemographic characteristics, the average age at the time of interview was 16.06 (SD = 1.28). Female participants were significantly younger at the time of interview compared to male participants. This may reflect Corrado et al.'s (2000) concern that the justice system tends to invoke protectionist sentencing philosophies disproportionately more so for younger girls compared to younger boys (e.g., using incarceration to protect younger girls from street entrenchment). Indigenous youth are overrepresented in Canada's justice system, and Table 3.2 shows that this was especially true for Indigenous girls, who represented a little more than 40% of all girls in the sample.

Table 3.2 Demographic characteristics, risk/need factors, and youth justice system involvement for the sample[†]

	Full sample (n = 1,719) *M (SD) / n (%)*	*Male participants (n = 1,318)* *M (SD) / n (%)*	*Female participants (n = 361)* *M (SD) / n (%)*	t/χ^2, *df*, *p*, φ/d
Demographics				
Age at Interview	16.06 (1.28)	16.16 (1.27)	15.72 (1.25)	t [1523] = 5.63, $p < .001$, $d = 0.35$
White	860 (54.8%)	681 (55.5%)	179 (52.5%)	χ^2 [2] = 43.28, $p < .001$, $\varphi = 0.17$
Indigenous	464 (29.6%)	324 (26.4%)	140 (41.1%)	
Non-Indigenous Minority	245 (15.6%)	223 (18.2%)	22 (6.5%)	
School Behavior				
Attending School	730 (47.9%)	581 (48.8%)	149 (44.6%)	χ^2 [1] = 1.86, $p = .173$, $\varphi = 0.04$
Skipping School (Before Age 12)	321 (22.9%)	247 (22.6%)	74 (24.0%)	χ^2 [1] = 0.26, $p = .609$, $\varphi = 0.01$
# of Different Schools	5.61 (5.54)	5.55 (5.53)	5.82 (5.57)	t [1424] = -0.78, $p = .438$, $d = 0.05$
Substance Use				
Substance Use Versatility[††]	4.98 (2.20)	4.74 (2.12)	5.82 (2.30)	t [495.56] = -7.65, $p < .001$, $d = 0.49$
Hard Drug Use	722 (48.0%)	489 (41.7%)	233 (70.8%)	χ^2 [1] = 87.59, $p < .001$, $\varphi = 0.24$
Family Dynamics				
Left Home (Before Age 12)	223 (16.7%)	160 (15.3%)	63 (21.8%)	χ^2 [1] = 6.92, $p = .009$, $\varphi = 0.07$
Kicked out of Home (Before Age 12)	101 (7.6%)	77 (7.4%)	24 (8.3%)	χ^2 [1] = 0.26, $p = .608$, $\varphi = 0.01$

(Continued)

Table 3.2 (Continued)

	Full sample (n = 1,719) M (SD) / n (%)	*Male participants (n = 1,318) M (SD) / n (%)*	*Female participants (n = 361) M (SD) / n (%)*	*t/χ², df, p, φ/d*
Family Dysfunction Scale††	3.04 (1.71)	2.86 (1.66)	3.70 (1.77)	t [420.77] = -7.16, p < .001, d = 0.50
Sexuality and Abuse				
Sexual Activity (Before Age 12)	132 (10.7%)	117 (12.0%)	15 (5.8%)	χ^2 [1] = 8.28, p = .004, φ = 0.08
Physical Abuse	593 (46.3%)	420 (41.3%)	173 (65.8%)	χ^2 [1] = 50.55, p < .001, φ = 0.20
Sexual Abuse	198 (17.5%)	87 (9.6%)	111 (49.3%)	χ^2 [1] = 197.58, p < .001, φ = 0.42
Self-Identity				
Positive Self-Identity	70.31 (10.16)	70.70 (10.06)	68.76 (10.44)	t [1345] = 2.81, p = .005, d = 0.19
Positive Other-Identity	64.54 (13.14)	64.55 (13.32)	64.50 (12.33)	t [1290] = 0.06, p = .955, d = 0.00
Youth Offending				
Conviction Age of Onset††	14.89 (1.76)	14.95 (1.81)	14.63 (1.43)	t [560.05] = 3.29, p = .001, d = 0.20
Convictions††	11.17 (8.66)	11.43 (9.07)	10.20 (6.62)	t [609.41] = 2.66, p = .008, d = 0.16
Days Incarcerated††	276.56 (280.06)	292.76 (293.30)	212.23 (206.50)	t [633.03] = 5.53, p < .001, d = 0.32
Any Violent Conviction	991 (61.2%)	792 (62.4%)	198 (60.7%)	χ^2 [1] = 0.31, p = .578, φ = 0.01
Sex Offending	110 (7.2%)	104 (8.4%)	7 (2.3%)	χ^2 [1] = 13.79, p < .001, φ = 0.10

† With the exception of age at intake interview, all comparisons include all persons included in the ISVYOS and not just those with an intake interview (e.g., includes persons that refused to participate).

†† Levene's test of equal variance violated.

Notes: The sum of female participants (n = 361) and male participants (n = 1,318) does not equal the total sample (n =1,719) because of missing data. The full sample does not reflect the number of members that received an intake interview (n = 1,548) nor the number of members with available criminal history data in adolescence and adulthood (n = 1,534). φ = phi effect size. d = Cohen's d effect size.

Questions about school included whether participants were attending school prior to being incarcerated, whether they skipped school (including the age they first did so), the number of times they changed schools for reasons other than grade changes (e.g., moving, expulsion), and the sum of whether they engaged in 21 different school behavioral problems (e.g., drinking, using drugs, fighting, talking back to teachers; examined in Chapter 6). Table 3.2 shows that participants regularly changed schools. Half the sample were not attending school at the time they entered custody and a quarter of the sample reported skipping school before age 12. This highlights that using school samples to capture youth involved in serious and violent offenses may be problematic because many of such youth are not actually attending school regularly.

Participants were asked about their use of nine different substances: alcohol, marijuana, hallucinogens (e.g., mushrooms, acid), ecstasy, cocaine, crack cocaine, heroin, crystal methamphetamine, and illegal use of prescription pills. Hard drug use was defined as the use of crack cocaine, heroin, or crystal methamphetamine. Simply examining substance use as present or absent would be especially uninformative given that nearly 100% of the sample reported using alcohol or marijuana. Participants averaged using about five different types of substances and half the sample reported hard drug use. Nearly 75% of girls reported hard drug use.

Questions regarding family included whether participants were ever kicked out of their home by their parents for at least 24 hours (and at what age) and whether they ever left their home by their own choice to go live somewhere else for at least 24 hours (and at what age). Girls were significantly more likely to have left their family home to live somewhere else. A series of questions were posed regarding whether a family member (and which one) had trouble with or experienced the following: alcohol abuse, drug abuse, physical abuse, sexual abuse, a criminal record, a mental health problem. These indicators were summed to create a family dysfunction scale, which girls scored significantly higher on compared to boys.

Regarding sexual development and abuse, participants were asked about whether they had engaged in sexual activity, whether they experienced physical abuse, and whether they experienced sexual abuse. Questions were also asked about the age at which sexual activity, physical abuse, and sexual abuse occurred. About half the sample reported physical abuse and 20% reported sexual abuse. Girls were significantly more likely than boys to have experienced physical and sexual abuse.

Regarding self-identity, the Good Citizen Scale (Schneider, 1990) consists of 15 items asking participants to rate themselves on a scale from 1–7 with respect to two opposing traits (e.g., Good/Bad, Dumb/Smart, Rude/Polite). Some items were reverse-coded so that higher scores always reflected the more positive identity trait. Using the same items, youth were also asked to rate how they think other people perceive them. Thus, identity includes both self-perceptions and reflections about how others see them. Girls reported a significantly less positive self-perception compared to boys.

Official Offending. Official data were coded from CORNET, which contains information pertaining to each person's movement in and out of custody as well as the exact criminal offense, date of conviction, and sentence type. CORNET only provided information about justice system involvement within the province of BC. Thus, the study did not have data on participants who became involved in the justice system of another jurisdiction.[9] However, CORNET provided data on instances in which a person was known to have emigrated outside the province. CORNET also provided data on mortality. Convictions and time incarcerated after the date of emigration outside the province or date of death were coded as missing, rather than as "zero", to avoid instances of false desistance.[10] CORNET includes both youth and adult criminal history data in the same location, which is unlike most record-keeping systems in the United States (Laub & Sampson, 2001).

The presence of offending was measured starting at age 12, which represented the minimum age of criminal responsibility in Canada. From that point on, every criminal charge (and the crime-type) that resulted in a conviction was coded at each person-period observation (i.e., frequency of convictions at age 12, at age 13, at age 14, etc.). Although the exact offense was recorded, convictions were recoded into one of seven crime types: violent, property, violation, weapon, drug, miscellaneous, and sexual.[11] For incarceration data, RAs coded the date of each admission to and release from custody. These dates were used to calculate the number of days between admission and release. Custody included days spent in sheriff's cells, remand/pre-trial centers, and centers for those sentenced to custody. Measuring time incarcerated (along with mortality and emigration) helped identify the proportion of time an individual spent in the community and thus their exposure to opportunities to offend in the community (i.e., the third research design need for studying CPO identified in Chapter 2).

Measures of justice system involvement for the period of adolescence are shown toward the bottom of Table 3.2. Chapters 4 and 5 present descriptions of justice system involvement through adulthood. Male participants averaged a significantly greater number of convictions and number of days incarcerated compared to female participants. Given these trends, it was somewhat unexpected that female participants averaged a significantly earlier age at first conviction. Once again, this may relate to Canada's court system's tendency to rely on protectionist sentencing philosophies to remove girls from a perceived unsafe environment (Corrado et al., 2000). The prevalence of having at least one violent conviction in adolescence did not vary between male and female participants. Male participants were significantly more likely to have perpetrated a sexual offense in adolescence.

As evidence of the severity of offending within this sample, for those with criminal history data available, 8.6% (n = 136) were involved in a homicide offense and 16.4% (n = 218) self-reported that they had perpetrated a homicide-related offense (including attempted murder, manslaughter, or murder). Official involvement in sexual offenses was observed for 11.8% of the sample (n = 181). In adolescence, 60% of the sample (n = 991) were convicted of a hands-on violent offense and 18.5% (n = 283) were convicted of possessing a weapon (typically a knife or firearm). The presence of serious and violent offenses separates this sample from community-based samples and even samples of adjudicated youth involved in minor and status offenses (e.g., Laub & Sampson, 2003).

Definitions of developmental stages used in the book

Traditionally, DLC research distinguished between two age-stages: adolescence and adulthood (e.g., Wolfgang et al., 1972). This book takes a slightly different approach given the recognition that society is changing in ways that impact conventional life stages (Arnett, 2000). It was important to account for the fact that research participants may not have been followed long enough to experience all these life stages. As of December 2019, the average age of participants at the time of criminal history coding was 30.57 (SD = 4.65) and ranged from ages 20 to 40. The wide range in age reflected the fact that although all participants were recruited in adolescence, for some, adolescence was as far back as 1998 or as recent as 2011. This created potential problems when examining, for example, frequency of offending for individuals with follow-up periods capturing different age-stages. Some individuals may be more frequently involved in crime than others simply by virtue of having a greater opportunity to offend. Therefore, four different age intervals were constructed to examine offending across these periods. A person's offending within a particular interval was only examined if that participant had complete data for each year of age captured in the interval (e.g., if an individual was 32 years old, they would not be included in the examination of offending outcomes between ages 12–35 or between ages 30–35).

The first interval examined was adolescence, which included ages 12–17 and spanned six years. The remaining three stages were constructed to also span six years and were labeled emerging adulthood (ages 18–23), full adulthood (ages 24–29), and mature adulthood (ages 30–35). Among the 1,620 participants whose criminal record could be searched, 28.5% were at least age 35 at the time of coding (n = 462), an additional 31.1% were at least age 29 (n = 504; 59.6% of total), 39.7% were at least age 23 (n = 643; 99.3% of total), and 0.7% were younger than 23 (n = 11). These age intervals reflect more than just identical windows of measurement. They are also associated with *potential* and *conventional* life stages and life transitions.

Individuals in the adolescence age-stage (ages 12–17) are typically in high school, living with a parent, and are employed part-time (Statistics Canada, 2015, 2018a).

Individuals in the emerging adulthood age-stage (ages 18–23) tend to have graduated from high school and are in at least the mid-point of their college education or technical/trade school (Peters, 2018). This also reflects the experience of young persons in parts of Europe (Eurostat, 2012). Employment that is at least part-time is common during this age-stage (Statistics Canada, 2018a). Individuals are likely to be single or at least non-married (Statistics Canada, 2015) and over half of individuals in this age interval live with at least one parent (Statistics Canada, 2018b). In sum, emerging adulthood in Canada and elsewhere (Eurostat, 2012; UN, 2019) is a time of opportunity where individuals are in some level of post-secondary education and have part-time employment.

Individuals in the full adulthood age-stage (ages 24–29) are expected to have completed university (Peters, 2018). The prevalence of full-time employment is about 20% higher compared to earlier age-stages (Morissette et al., 2015). Common-law partnerships are also typical (Statistics Canada, 2015), which means that compared to previous age-stages, individuals are less likely to be living with a parent (Statistics Canada, 2019a).

Individuals in the mature adulthood age-stage (ages 30–35) are more likely to become first-time parents compared to earlier age-stages, and this is true for both men (Statistics Canada, 2017) and women (Statistics Canada, 2018c). Most persons in this age-stage are married or in a common-law partnership (Statistics Canada, 2015). Employment is more likely in this stage than any other over the life-course; the percentage of persons with full-time employment is approximately 40% higher compared to adolescence, 15% higher compared to emerging adulthood, and 5% higher compared to full adulthood (Statistics Canada, 2019b). Of the different age-stages, this is when individuals are least likely to rent (Statistics Canada, 2020c) and this stage also captures the median age at which individuals in BC become first-time home buyers (Statistics Canada, 2020d).

Summary

In the 1990s, developmental criminologists were asking research questions about why some at-risk children did not become involved in serious and violent offenses in adolescence. Life-course researchers were asking questions about why some youth involved in serious and violent offenses did not demonstrate a lifelong pattern of offending. In contrast, some policymakers, some members of the public, and some researchers were asking why today's serious and violent youth was tomorrow's serious and violent adult (Corrado & Markwart, 1994). This non-DLC perspective was characterized by a tough-on-crime attitude and a belief that punishment made youth accountable for their actions. Media coverage of atypical cases of young persons involved in serious offenses fueled the public's demand for legislative changes. In other words, although DLC research increasingly recognized both continuity *and* discontinuity in offending over different stages of the life-course, public opinion and the media recognized only the continuity of offending and called for Canada's Federal government to get tougher on crime.

Some forward-thinking policymakers in BC wanted to know more about youth involved in serious and violent offending before making decisions about their response to such persons. It is in this context that the ISVYOS emerged as a research initiative to address the lack of knowledge about such youth. Thus, the purpose of the ISVYOS was to address both policy and DLC research gaps regarding incarcerated youth involved in serious and violent offenses.

Why is it valid to suggest that this was a sample comprised almost entirely of individuals involved in serious and/or violent offenses? First, legislation covering Cohorts I and II was designed to restrict the use of incarceration to youth with a history of repeated, serious, and/or violent offending. Although the YOA (Cohort I) was established to avoid using incarceration for persons involved in less serious crimes, the YCJA (Cohort II) took this initiative even further by permitting the incarceration of youth only under specific conditions.[12] Even when these conditions were met, judges were required to consider all other sentencing options (e.g., probation, community-based sentences). In effect, especially for Cohort II, it was not possible to be included in the sample if an individual (a) was not involved in a certain offense/offending pattern or (b) was identified as someone that could be better served by a community sentence.

The first phase of the IVYOS began under the YOA legislation in 1998. This phase was designed to address the lack of information, especially in Canada, about the profile of incarcerated youth. As the data accumulated, it became apparent that clinical concepts and instruments should be added to the interview protocol. Surveys and instruments that were developed for and used with general youth samples that focused on broader measures of social disadvantage could not tap into the heterogeneity of this disadvantage present at an early age for members of this sample. For example, nearly 100% of the sample used some type of illicit substance; for half the sample, questions about attachment to parents often did not apply because they had no contact with their biological parents. The second phase of the study recruited a second cohort who were placed in custody under the YCJA legislation. Recruiting participants during two different legislative frameworks allowed for an examination of the impact of a shift in the sociolegal response to youth crime (see Chapter 9). A longitudinal component was developed for the third phase of data collection to allow the ISVYOS to address questions about the continuity and discontinuity of offending and risk and protective factors over different stages of the life-course.

In Chapter 2 we identified four research design flaws that need to be addressed to make accurate conclusions about CPO: (1) a focus on youth involved in serious and violent offenses, (2) the measurement of criminal behavior rather than status offenses and public nuisance behaviors, (3) the measurement of exposure time, and (4) the reliable measurement of appropriate risk factors. Focusing on youth almost exclusively incarcerated because of their involvement in serious and violent offenses addresses the first research design need. That these youth were processed under a youth justice system that prohibited the prosecution of status offenses addressed the second research design need. The ability to measure time incarcerated, emigration, and mortality addressed the third research design need. The measurement of psychopathy, serious forms of substance use, and family dynamics aligned with theories about CPO (e.g., Moffitt, 1993), which addressed the fourth research design need. Thus, the ISVYOS was suitable for addressing some core questions of DLC research.

Notes

1 To be clear, while referring to youth crime during the YOA as an epidemic was certainly an exaggeration, at the same time, ISVYOS participants were subject to public warnings by police about their level of dangerousness and were involved in serious gang conflicts resulting in multiple homicides (Bolan, 2018).

2 MCFD acts as the guardian to youth in custody and provided consent for the ISVYOS to approach youth for participation in the study. Assent from youth was needed before starting the interview.

3 Under the YOA and YCJA, all persons between ages 12 and 17 at the time of their offense were processed through the youth justice system, regardless of the severity of their offense.

4 The use of CORNET required approval from MCFD for access to youth-based justice system data and approval from the Ministry of Public Safety and the Solicitor General was required for access to adult-based justice system data.

5 Participants were asked to self-report their 'gender' as male, female, or transgender. In hindsight, we would not have used the terms "male" and "female" given these are not reflective of gender and instead left the question open-ended.

6 The prevalence of each non-Indigenous minority group was too low to be analyzed on its own and so the "non-Indigenous minority" descriptor was used.

7 Instruments included in both Cohort I and Cohort II did not always include identical questions as the assessment protocol evolved and changed over time to address specific research grant-related objectives with more short-term objectives, to fix reliability issues with some questions, to reflect changes in the scientific literature, or simply to limit the interview duration. For example, in line with sociolegal research interests of the time, the intake interview for Cohort I included questions about perceptions of the fairness of the justice system. These questions were not included in the intake interview for Cohort II, which included more questions about mental health concerns.

8 https://www.researchgate.net/project/The-Incarcerated-Serious-and-Violent-Young-Offender-Study

9 The Province of BC is 587,031 square miles, making it twice the size of Texas. This means that individuals typically had to relocate a substantial distance before falling outside the jurisdiction of the project.

10 False desistance describes instances where individuals were identified as desisters simply because of an inopportunity to offend or to have offending behavior recorded (see McCuish, 2020).

11 Violent offenses included non-sexual hands-on offenses. Property offenses included offenses such as theft, theft of a motor vehicle, possession of stolen

property, and credit card offenses and fraud. Violation offenses included breaches of bail conditions and failure to comply with conditions of probation or other community sentences. Weapons offenses included possession and wielding of weapons without actually using such weapons against a person. Drug offenses included possession and trafficking of illegal drugs. Miscellaneous offenses included traffic-based offenses like dangerous driving, vandalism, and trespassing. Sexual offenses included sexual assault, sexual interference (relations with someone too young to consent), and possession and distribution of child pornography.

12 These conditions included (1) if they committed a violent offense, (2) if they perpetrated an offense for which an adult could receive a sentence of two years or more and they had a history of prior findings of guilt, (3) if they perpetrated an offense for which an adult could receive a sentence of two years or more and the offense included specific aggravating circumstances, or (4) if they had a history of repeated violations of court orders (see Bala et al., 2009).

Section II

Empirical answers to core DLC questions

In Chapter 1, we identified four pillars of the DLC paradigm: (1) criminal career research, (2) developmental criminology, (3) propensity theories, and (4) life-course criminology. This section focuses on the description and explanation of the justice system involvement of participants from the ISVYOS. Chapter 4 provides a description of different parameters of the criminal career across different stages of the life-course. Chapter 5 addresses questions about CPO by examining conviction trajectories across different developmental periods and risk factors in childhood/adolescence associated with CPO trajectories. Chapters 6–8 focus on the onset, persistence, and desistance criminal career parameters that have been the primary focus of developmental criminology, propensity theories, and life-course criminology, respectively. In sum, the purpose of this section is to address whether common knowledge and accepted conclusions about offending over the life-course are also true for youth who experienced incarceration as a result of involvement in serious and violent offending.

4 The justice system involvement of incarcerated youth: Old questions, new data

Introduction

Interest in criminal careers evolved from case studies from the 1930s that examined how individuals progressed to different types of offenses throughout the life-course (e.g., Shaw, 1930). This research emerged from the Chicago School and involved biographical descriptions of individuals who had a "career" in crime. Thus, this literature focused on the importance of mentorship and tutelage to the acquisition of skills facilitating the professionalization of crime perpetration (Sutherland, 1937). This sociobiographical approach (also see Chambliss, 1972; Maurer, 1940) generated interest in expanding the scope of criminal career studies to prospective longitudinal research using quantitative methods to examine individual-level patterns of offending. The Gluecks (1937) were among the first to use the term *criminal careers* to describe individual-level offending patterns in their longitudinal study of youth from the Boston, Massachusetts, area. Unlike the Chicago School's sociobiographical approach to studying the professional career aspect of offending, the Gluecks were concerned with psychosocial factors that contributed to youth offending that persisted through adulthood.[1] It was about 40 years later that more precise definitions of criminal career parameters and hypotheses about their interconnectivity were made (Blumstein & Cohen, 1979). This research essentially moved away from the strict focus on "career criminals" and instead acknowledged the heterogeneity of offending patterns. The examination of the criminal career can apply to persons involved in a single offense or hundreds of offenses and has little to do with offending as an occupation.

The criminal career framework

Blumstein et al. (1982) defined the criminal career as the longitudinal sequence of an individual's pattern of offending from first to last offense. This sequence includes four major dimensions: (1) participation, (2) frequency, (3) seriousness, and (4) length. Despite how others attempted to portray criminal career research (Gottfredson & Hirschi, 1988), this framework did not consider that individuals involved in crime were career criminals destined for CPO. Rather, the different dimensions specified by the criminal career framework reflected the notion that there was variability in crime perpetration. In retrospect, the term "criminal career" was somewhat misleading. Unlike Sutherland's work decades earlier, research on criminal careers did not refer to the idea of crime as a profession or a specialization, but simply that it had a beginning, a developmental course, and an end. The criminal career framework can help express the fact that most individuals' involvement in crime represents a small portion of their life-course. Acknowledging differences in offending patterns is also one way of identifying who does not require formal intervention and who may benefit from assistance.

The first dimension, participation, distinguishes between those who do or do not engage in criminal behavior. It denotes the proportion of a sample that has perpetrated a crime, which is often referred to as prevalence. Within samples of justice-involved persons, where the prevalence of any offending is assumed to be 100%, participation in offending can be examined across different developmental stages to distinguish which age-stages are most or least likely to be associated with offending. The age of onset of offending is another parameter of this dimension and refers to the age at first offense. Developmental criminologists argued that an earlier age of onset was informative of several other dimensions of the criminal career, especially frequency of chronic offending (Le Blanc & Fréchette, 1989).

The second dimension, frequency, refers to the volume of criminal activity (i.e., the number of offenses perpetrated). The term *lambda* is used to describe the rate of offending over some period of time. Chronic offending represents a categorical indicator of frequency or lambda and is perhaps the criminal career parameter that has received the most empirical attention. The measurement of chronic offending has undergone several iterations. As noted in Chapter 2, chronic offending refers to the point at which a person's volume of offending meets some defined threshold. That is, chronic offending refers to a static indicator of offending. This chapter defines this threshold in three ways: (1) the minimum percentage of a sample needed to account for 50% of all offenses (see Wolfgang et al., 1972), (2) probabilities of reoffending that constitute chronicity (Piquero et al.'s (2007) formula), and (3) the application of the probability formula at two age-stages to investigate different patterns of offending (Le Blanc & Kaspy, 1998).

The third dimension, severity, refers to a person's crime-mix, which is composed of the different types of crimes they have committed and the proportion of total offenses that each crime type comprises. This dimension received less attention in criminal career research, perhaps because criminal career researchers later suggested little distinction between chronic and serious offending (e.g., Farrington, 1989). Part of the inspection of offense severity involves distinguishing between offending versatility and specialization. Versatility reflects participation in a greater range of different types of offenses, whereas specialization reflects the tendency towards involvement in one specific type of offense. Developmental criminology principles suggest that versatility reflects a more serious pattern of offending whereas specialization is part of the process of desistance (Loeber & Le Blanc, 1990).

The fourth dimension, criminal career length, calculates the duration between a person's first offense (i.e., age of onset) and last offense (i.e., age of offset). The measurement of this dimension is only reliable if there is a lengthy follow-up period (Jolliffe et al., 2017; Kazemian & Farrington, 2006). This issue is referred to as right-censoring, where an individual's criminal career length is underestimated because they continued to offend after the end of the follow-up period. While criminal career researchers have been concerned with the issue of right-censoring, developmental criminologists have been concerned with the issue of left-censoring and the ability to accurately measure a person's actual onset of offending. Retrospective analyses of adult criminal careers are limited by, for example, a recall period that does not extend into adolescence. Similarly, studies that use official data will likely overestimate the age at which a person first offends given that it is unlikely that a person's first criminal offense is also the first time that they are detected, arrested, charged, and convicted.

What do we know about the criminal careers of ISVYOS participants?

Several hundred studies have examined parameters of the criminal career dimensions described above. So much so that several "widely accepted conclusions" have been made about the nature of criminal careers (Farrington, 2003). However, this research predominantly focused on children and youth from the general population who self-reported their involvement in a mix of antisocial and criminal behavior. Most of this behavior is relatively minor and circumscribed to adolescence (Basto-Pereira & Farrington, 2020). There are some exceptions, such as the CYA Study, the Harreveld Study, the Danish Longitudinal Study, and the Pathways to Desistance Study, all of which focused on criminal career parameters from adolescence until at least the early stages of adulthood for a sample of youth in the deep-end of the justice system. The ISVYOS, conducted in British Columbia, Canada, was developed to be part of this group of studies. While focusing on official involvement in crime limits some of the conclusions that can be drawn about offending more broadly (Farrington, 2003; Mosher et al., 2010),[2] knowledge of the adult justice system involvement of youth in the deep end of the justice system can help inform policymakers regarding which principles from which DLC theories help to understand justice system onset, persistence, and desistance.

The current chapter described the four dimensions of the criminal career across different stages of the life-course of ISVYOS participants. Who are the youth who are most chronic in terms of reconvictions? Are these individuals destined for a similar pattern in adulthood? Is an individual's early involvement in the justice system a warning sign that they will become a familiar face to probation officers, judges, and correctional officers for years to come?

The four criminal career dimensions were examined for four age-stages: (1) adolescence (ages 12–17; *n* = 1,620), emerging adulthood (ages 18–23; *n* = 1,609), full adulthood (ages 24–29; *n* = 966), and mature adulthood (ages 30–35; *n* = 462). Readers can refer to Chapter 3 for a description of how offending was measured and the rationale for these age-stages. Very importantly, each age-stage looked at justice system outcomes *only within that age-stage.* This was done to more closely examine the dynamic nature of offending. An individual with 30 convictions between ages 12–17 but just one conviction between ages 18–23 would not have 31 convictions during the emerging adulthood period. Instead, during emerging adulthood they would have incurred just one new conviction as the recording of convictions was not cumulative for this particular investigation of criminal careers.

Dimension 1: Prevalence of convictions

Participation indicates the proportion of individuals in the sample who were convicted or incarcerated at a given year of age or within a given age-stage. Figure 4.1 shows the annual prevalence of convictions at each age for

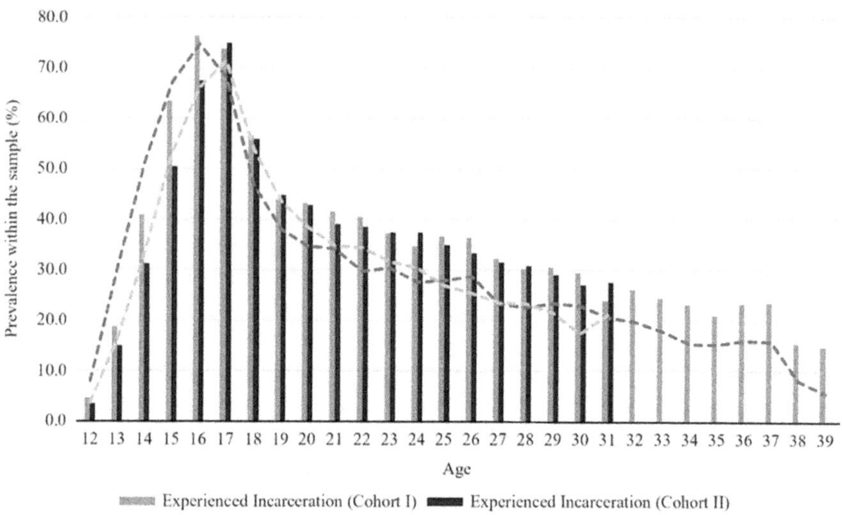

Figure 4.1 Prevalence of incurring a conviction and being incarcerated at each year of age.

Notes: For Cohort II, fewer than 10 participants were at least age 32 and so data end at age 31 for this group. For the same reason, the data end at age 39 for Cohort I.

Cohorts I and II.[3] Except for a relatively consistently higher annual prevalence of convictions during adolescence for Cohort I, both cohorts were similar in the annual prevalence of convictions at each year of age. For both cohorts, the annual prevalence of convictions peaked at the end of adolescence. For the first few years of adulthood, there was a relatively sharp decline in the prevalence of incurring at least one new conviction. This decline leveled off as individuals entered their 20s.

Regarding participation within particular age-stages,[4] the prevalence of incurring a conviction during adolescence was 96.2% for Cohort I and 93.0% for Cohort II. The prevalence of incurring a new conviction during emerging adulthood was 75.0% for Cohort I and 82.0% for Cohort II. The prevalence of incurring a new conviction during full adulthood was 58.8% for Cohort I and 60.9% for Cohort II. The prevalence of incurring a new conviction during mature adulthood was 46.1%.[5] In effect, although the prevalence of convictions declined with age, half of participants incurred a new contact with the justice system between ages 30–35.

It was possible that members of the sample were not convicted during a particular age but nevertheless experienced incarceration. Figure 4.1 includes the annual prevalence of instances in which an individual spent at least one day incarcerated. The annual prevalence of incarceration was consistently higher than the prevalence of convictions and did not conform to the classic age-crime curve in that the decline in the prevalence of incarceration following adolescence was less pronounced compared to convictions. The prevalence of experiencing incarceration during adolescence was 95.7% for Cohort I and 96.6% for Cohort II.[6] The prevalence of experiencing incarceration during emerging adulthood was 74.6% for Cohort I and 73.7% for Cohort II. The prevalence of experiencing incarceration during full adulthood was 54.0% for Cohort I and 58.4% for Cohort II. The prevalence of experiencing incarceration during mature adulthood was 42.9%. In Canada, and especially BC, incarceration is considered a last resort and used only when all other sentences (e.g., probation) are deemed inappropriate (Bell, 2014). Therefore, these results seem to suggest that although the odds of being incarcerated declined with age, a non-trivial proportion of the sample remained involved in offenses that warranted incarceration.

Of participants who did not incur a conviction in adolescence (approximately 5% of the total sample), 61.8% of this group were incarcerated in adolescence. Among participants who did not incur a conviction in emerging adulthood (approximately 20% of the total sample), 22.2% were incarcerated in emerging adulthood. Of participants who did not incur a conviction in full adulthood (approximately 40% of the total sample), 9.9% were incarcerated during this period. Finally, 9% of participants who did not incur a conviction in mature adulthood (approximately 55% of the total sample) were incarcerated during this period. The majority of individuals who were incarcerated but not convicted appeared to have been detained for offenses that they were not found guilty of or because charges were dropped. However, some participants simply did not have an opportunity to reoffend in the community during a particular age-stage because they were incarcerated for the entirety of the emerging adulthood ($n = 5$), full adulthood ($n = 7$), or mature adulthood ($n = 1$) periods. These findings also reiterated the importance of accounting for exposure time in analyses of offending.

Age at first conviction and adult reconviction

Developmental criminologists suggest that age of onset is an indicator of risk for chronic offending. There are debates as to whether this concept is best measured using self-report or official data (e.g., charges, convictions). Neither measure is perfect. The most appropriate way to measure onset is through a comparison of both self-report and official records (see Chapter 6). This chapter investigated the relationship between age of onset of official offending and incurring a conviction later in the life-course. When it comes to youth involved in particularly serious and violent crimes, does age of onset matter? The average age of onset for participants who incurred a conviction in emerging adulthood was 14.86 ($SD = 1.62$). The average age of onset of first conviction for participants who did not incur a conviction in emerging adulthood was 15.02 ($SD = 2.29$). Thus, for this sample, the age of onset of convictions did not differentiate those who were convicted in emerging adulthood (t [1443] = 1.33, $p = .185$).[7] However, a long-term association between age at first conviction in adolescence and being convicted past the period of emerging adulthood was detected.

The average age at first conviction for individuals who incurred a conviction in full adulthood was 14.62 ($SD = 1.84$). This was significantly earlier (t [827] = 3.31, $p = .001$) compared to the average age of onset of first conviction for individuals who did not incur a conviction in full adulthood ($M = 15.06$; $SD = 1.94$). The average age of onset of first conviction was 14.23 ($SD = 2.31$) for individuals who had a conviction in mature adulthood. This was significantly earlier (t [407] = 3.63, $p < .001$) compared to those who did not incur a new conviction in mature adulthood ($M = 14.94$; $SD = 1.61$).

Our findings regarding age of onset were contrary to Sampson and Laub's (2005b) assertion that the strength of the association between past and future offending would dissipate as the length of the follow-up period increased. From their perspective, the randomness of life events is supposed to take hold and dissolve the relationship between past and future offending. In contrast, developmental criminology does not see the relationship between offending at different points in the life-course as a random process impossible to understand. Crime is dynamic; both stability and change occur, and this stability and change can be understood. These findings reinforce Moffitt's (1993) perspective that differences between AL and LCP offending patterns would not emerge until later in the life-course. Moffitt held this perspective because some following an AL trajectory are ensnared in a pattern of criminal behavior that continues longer than anticipated due to, for example, the negative consequences of their criminal activity and collateral consequences of justice system involvement (e.g., delayed entry into the workforce).

Among youth involved in serious and violent crime, onset is informative of future convictions, it just takes time for differences in conviction patterns to manifest because of how pervasive offending is in earlier stages of adulthood for the sample as a whole. The nature of the ISVYOS sample is important to consider; variability in the onset of offending was limited because participants were sampled exclusively because their onset of offending began in adolescence. Cohen's *d* values were 0.23 and 0.36 for the full adulthood and mature adulthood analyses, respectively, which indicated only a small effect size (Cohen, 1988). Onset is hardly a guarantee of a prolonged pattern of justice system involvement.

Dimension 2: Frequency of convictions

The frequency dimension refers to the number of offenses a person has committed either over their lifetime or over a predefined period. The 404 ISVYOS participants who had complete data between ages 12–35 incurred 10,635 convictions. This represents an average of approximately 25 convictions per person. Sampson and Laub's (2003) examination of the arrest records of 475 individuals between ages 7–70 indicated a total of approximately 9,500 arrests (p. 565). In effect, despite 71 fewer participants, 40 fewer years of follow-up data, reliance on convictions rather than arrests, and the inclusion of girls, who average less criminal involvement than boys (see Chapter 3), individuals in the ISVYOS were responsible for more offenses than those from the UJD Study. Thus, the ISVYOS is suited for addressing limitations in past research concerning insufficient base rates of chronic offending and CPO.

More commonly, researchers are interested in the point at which the frequency of offending constitutes chronic offending. The first iteration in the measurement of chronic offending (see Chapter 2 for a review), based largely on Wolfgang et al.'s (1972) work, defined chronic offending as the smallest proportion of the sample responsible for at least 50% of all offenses. Piquero et al. (2007) developed a less subjective measure by using recidivism probabilities to define chronic offending as the point at which offending within a sample becomes rare but also likely to continue. A third approach cross-tabulates the presence of chronic offending, per reconviction probabilities, at two different aggregated age-stages (e.g., adolescence and emerging adulthood) to assess if a pattern of chronic offending was maintained (Lussier et al., 2016). Each of these three measurement strategies was performed below.

Chronic offending as the smallest proportion of a sample responsible for 50% of convictions

Wolfgang et al.'s (1972) measurement strategy resulted in identifying five arrests as the minimum volume threshold for chronic offending. They also focused solely on adolescence and did not examine whether this threshold was appropriate for defining chronic offending at other age-stages. For ISVYOS participants, 75.3% of the sample had at least five convictions in adolescence. Among those that met this threshold, convictions ranged from 5 to 50. This meant that five convictions hardly identified a homogenous group with similar levels of offending. In emerging adulthood, 46.6% of the sample had at least five convictions. In full adulthood, 35.1% had at least five convictions. In mature adulthood, 23.9% had at least five convictions. In effect, the five-conviction threshold was not useful for narrowing-down chronic offending for this sample. To find a threshold of chronic offending more appropriate for the ISVYOS, we identified the minimum percentage of the sample responsible for at least 50% of all convictions for the sample during each of the four age-stages.[8]

The percentage of ISVYOS participants needed to account for the majority of all convictions decreased across each age-stage (from 23.5% in adolescence to 9.3% in mature adulthood). Very importantly, the average number of convictions among those with a pattern of chronic offending remained relatively stable across age-stages (see Table 4.1 for a summary). Additionally, those defined by chronic offending in mature adulthood averaged 733.42 (SD = 430.97) days incarcerated during this age-stage. Those defined by chronic offending in adolescence averaged 569.03 (SD = 312.13) days incarcerated. In effect, once accounting for differences in exposure time (i.e., nearly 200 additional days incarcerated for those in mature adulthood), chronic offending in mature adulthood was associated with a rate of convictions that was nearly identical to the rate of convictions associated with chronic offending in adolescence. This contrasted with Hirschi and Gottfredson's (1983) assertion about the inexorable effect of aging on crime. To expand on this finding, the top line in the graph shown in Figure 4.2 indicates the average number of convictions at each year of age for individuals defined by chronic offending at the different age-stages of interest. While Figure 4.1 demonstrated a decline in convictions for the sample as a whole, Figure 4.2 shows that this decline is much slower for those defined by chronic offending. Moreover, when time incarcerated is accounted for, the incidence rate of convictions is quite similar when comparing chronic offending in adolescence to chronic offending in adulthood.

Chronic offending as probabilities of reconviction

Piquero et al.'s (2007) probability formula was developed to help address the subjectivity of the somewhat arbitrary 50% cut-point used above.

Table 4.1 Descriptive characteristics of chronic offending across age-stages†

	Adolescence *(n = 1,528)* M (*SD*) / *n* (%)	*Emerging adulthood)* *(n = 1,535)* M (*SD*) / *n* (%)	*Full adulthood* *(n = 880)* M (*SD*) / *n* (%)	*Mature adulthood* *(n = 410)* M (*SD*) / *n* (%)
Proportion of Sample Required to Account for >50% of all Convictions	359 (23.5%)	239 (15.6%)	109 (12.4%)	38 (9.3%)
Chronic Offending Group: Average Number of Convictions	23.82 (6.36)	23.34 (7.49)	19.73 (6.15)	17.21 (6.57)
Chronic Offending Group: Average Number of Days Incarcerated	569.03 (312.13)	885.02 (412.48)	868.07 (443.65)	733.42 (430.97)

† The average number of convictions/days incarcerated refers only to averages for those associated with chronic offending.

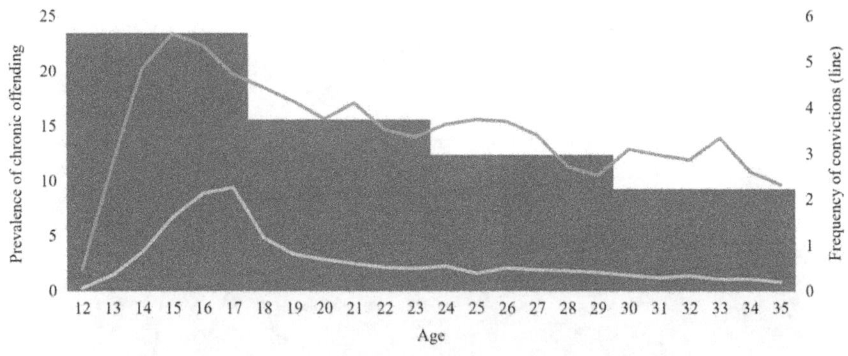

Figure 4.2 The prevalence of chronic offending was defined by the smallest percentage of the sample needed to account for at least 50% of all convictions during adolescence (ages 12–17), emerging adulthood (18 to 23), full adulthood (24–29), and mature adulthood (30–35).

Notes: The shaded area reflects the prevalence of chronic offending during each of the four age-stages examined. The top line reflects the average number of convictions for individuals included in the chronic offending group at the age-stage under examination. The bottom line reflects the average number of convictions for individuals who were not identified as showing a pattern of chronic offending.

This formula identifies the point at which having k convictions implies a high likelihood of having k_{+1}, k_{+2}, k_{+3}, k_{+x} convictions. This formula was used to identify chronic offending at each age-stage. Figure 4.3 shows the probability of a k_{th} conviction given that an individual in the sample had k_{-1} prior convictions. The point at which probabilities of reconviction demonstrate a sharp decrease followed by stability is indicative of chronicity. In other words, at which point is it rare to reach k convictions, but for those that do, they have a high probability of incurring k_{+1}, k_{+2}, k_{+x} convictions?

For adolescence, there was a probability drop between the 10th and 11th reconviction (i.e., it was rare for individuals with 11 total convictions [10th reconviction] to be convicted a 12th time [11th reconviction]); therefore, individuals with 12 convictions in adolescence were defined by a pattern of chronic offending (39.5% of the sample). For emerging adulthood, the probability drop occurred between the 13th and 14th reconviction; therefore, 15 convictions between ages 18–23 was used to define chronic offending (17.1% of the sample). For full adulthood, the probability drop occurred between the 9th and 10th reconviction; therefore, 11 convictions between ages 25–29 was used to define chronic offending (18.2% of the sample). For mature adulthood, the most substantial probability-drop was between the 11th and 12th reconviction and therefore 13 convictions defined

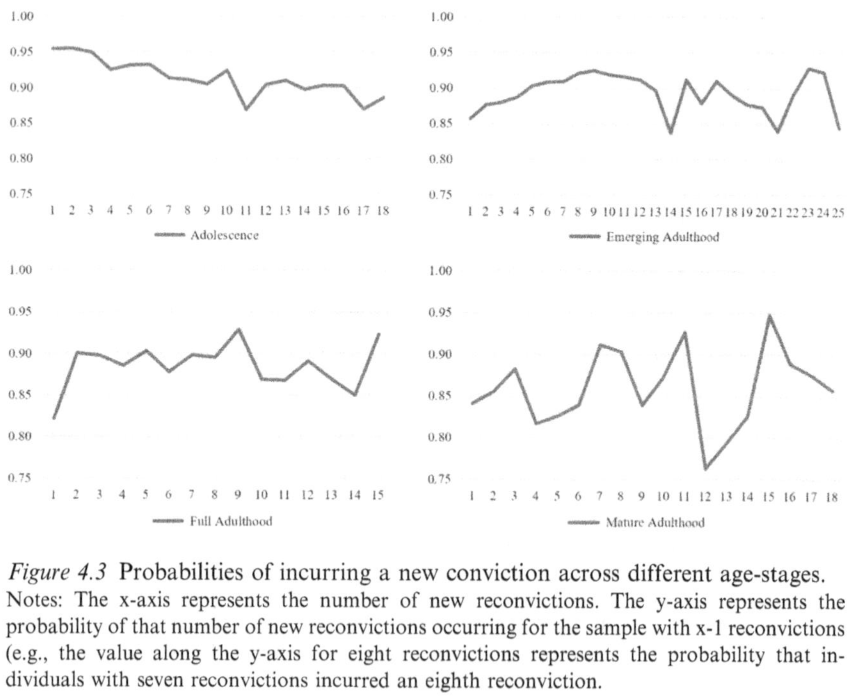

Figure 4.3 Probabilities of incurring a new conviction across different age-stages.
Notes: The x-axis represents the number of new reconvictions. The y-axis represents the probability of that number of new reconvictions occurring for the sample with x-1 reconvictions (e.g., the value along the y-axis for eight reconvictions represents the probability that individuals with seven reconvictions incurred an eighth reconviction.

chronic offending between ages 30–35 (7.1% of the sample). The higher prevalence of chronic offending in adolescence is not surprising given this was a sample defined by experiencing incarceration in adolescence.

From the perspective of practitioners, a major question concerns whether past chronic offending is informative of future chronic offending. Looking at chronic offending at one point in the life-course does not acknowledge, for example, treatment progress or other types of change. Once an individual has reached a specific volume of offending, they might be considered a "chronic offender". Is the youth "chronic offender" also the emerging adulthood "chronic offender"? Using the four measures of chronic offending based on reconviction probabilities, of those with complete data for all four age-stages (n = 404), 47.3% were never identified as having a pattern of chronic offending, 30.4% were only once identified as having a pattern of chronic offending, 15.1% were twice identified as having a pattern of chronic offending, 6.2% were thrice identified as having a pattern of chronic offending, and only 1.0% were identified as having a pattern of chronic offending for all four age-stages. In effect, chronic offending did not mean an individual would always continue this pattern of offending.

Using Wolfgang et al.'s (1972) measurement approach reduces chronic offending to a behavior that is static and fixed. We used a cross-tabulation method (Le Blanc & Kaspy, 1998) to inspect stability or change in chronic offending between each of the four age-stages (see Tables 4.2a–4.2c). For the transition from adolescence to emerging adulthood, deceleration (i.e., moving from a higher rate of convictions to a lower rate of convictions) was the most common pattern for the sample. When comparing the transition from emerging adulthood to full adulthood and full adulthood to mature adulthood, stability was most common. This included stability in terms of non-convictions/maintaining a low rate of offending as well as stability as the maintenance of chronic offending.

In Tables 4.2a–4.2c, compared to non-chronic recidivists (i.e., individuals who recidivated but did not meet the criteria for chronic offending), individuals showing a pattern of chronic offending at an earlier developmental stage were about two times more likely to show a pattern of chronic offending at the next developmental stage. In other words, these tables provided evidence of the continuity of chronic offending. To be sure, these relationships were far from perfect, which supported research on the instability of offending (Piquero, 2013; van Koppen et al., 2020). In fact, for each individual showing a pattern of chronic offending at consecutive age-stages, there was one individual who went from a pattern of chronic offending to a pattern of non-chronic offending. Of course, these cross-tabulations do not account for exposure time. It may be difficult for individuals to show a pattern of chronic offending across consecutive age-stages because recidivism sentencing premiums increase in concordance with a person's rate of offending, thus constraining their ability to continue to offend at a high rate (McCuish, 2020; Roberts, 2010).

Table 4.2a Cross-tabulation of offending statuses between adolescence and emerging adulthood (n = 1,452)

	Emerging adulthood offending status			
Adolescence offending status	*Abstainers*	*Non-recidivists*	*Recidivists*	*Chronic offending*
Abstainers	13 (15.5% / 0.9%)	19 (22.26% / 1.3%)	48 (57.1% / 3.3%)	4 (4.8% / 0.3%)
Non-recidivists	29 (45.3% / 2.0%)	9 (14.1% / 0.6%)	25 (39.1% / 1.7%)	1 (1.6% / 0.1%)
Recidivists	174 (23.8% / 12.0%)	87 (11.9% / 6.0%)	365 (49.9% / 25.1%)	105 (14.4% / 7.2%)
Chronic offending†	67 (11.7% / 4.6%)	36 (6.3% / 2.5%)	317 (55.3% / 21.8%)	153 (26.7% / 10.5%)

† Chronic offending defined using Piquero et al.'s probability formula (see Figure 4.3).
Notes: For each table, light grey area = deceleration; white area = stability; dark grey area = acceleration. Number of individuals associated with each pattern are presented in cells. The first percentage reflects the row percentage (e.g., percentage of adolescence abstainers who were also abstainers in emerging adulthood). The second percentage reflects the full sample percentage (e.g., percentage of the entire sample who were abstainers in both adolescence and emerging adulthood).

Table 4.2b Cross-tabulation of offending statuses between emerging adulthood and full adulthood (n = 876)

	Full adulthood offending status			
Emerging adulthood offending status	*Abstainers*	*Non-recidivists*	*Recidivists*	*Chronic offending*
Abstainers	126 (70.8% / 14.4%)	21 (11.8% / 2.4%)	26 (14.6% / 3.0%)	5 (2.8% / 0.6%)
Non-recidivists	56 (53.8% / 6.4%)	19 (18.3% / 2.2%)	22 (21.2% / 2.5%)	7 (6.7% / 0.8%)
Recidivists	158 (35.3% / 18.0%)	50 (11.2% / 5.7%)	165 (36.8% / 18.9%)	75 (16.7% / 8.6%)
Chronic offending	14 (9.6% / 1.6%)	3 (2.1% / 0.3%)	56 (38.4% / 6.4%)	73 (50.0% / 8.3%)

Table 4.2c Cross-tabulation of offending statuses between full adulthood and mature adulthood (n = 408)

Full adulthood offending status	*Mature adulthood offending status*			
	Abstainers	*Non-recidivists*	*Recidivists*	*Chronic offending*
Abstainers	139 (83.2% / 34.1%)	17 (10.2% / 4.2%)	9 (5.4% / 2.2%)	2 (1.2% / 0.5%)
Non-recidivists	35 (66.0% / 8.6%)	4 (7.5% / 1.0%)	13 (24.5% / 3.2%)	1 (1.9% / 0.2%)
Recidivists	40 (32.0% / 9.8%)	6 (4.8% / 1.5%)	66 (52.8% / 16.2%)	13 (10.4% / 3.2%)
Chronic offending	6 (9.5% / 1.5%)	3 (4.8% / 0.7%)	41 (65.1% / 10.0%)	13 (20.6% / 3.2%)

Comparing longer-term retrospective and prospective prediction, Robins' (1978) paradox was especially evident. This paradox suggests that virtually all adults involved in crime will have a history of offending in adolescence (i.e., retrospective prediction), but most involved in crime in adolescence will not go on to offend in adulthood (i.e., prospective prediction). For retrospective prediction, for individuals showing a pattern of chronic offending in full adulthood (ages 24–29), 5.8% had fewer than two convictions in adolescence whereas 60.9% showed a pattern of chronic offending in adolescence as well. The magnitude of the association was greater in mature adulthood (ages 30–35). None of the individuals showing a pattern of chronic offending in mature adulthood had fewer than two convictions in adolescence whereas 62.1% of this group showed a pattern of chronic offending in adolescence. Prospective prediction tells a different story. Only about 25% of individuals who showed a pattern of chronic offending in adolescence did so in full adulthood and only about 10% of individuals who showed a pattern of chronic offending in adolescence did so in mature adulthood.

In sum, this examination of chronic offending reiterated the importance of longitudinal research (Cullen, 2011). Looking only at chronic offending in adolescence ignores much heterogeneity that is to come. Findings also reinforced Moffitt's (1993) assertion that it is difficult to make distinctions between AL and LCP offending trajectories when looking only at criminal behavior in adolescence. Cross-tabulation methods are limited in that they only allow comparisons across two time points and do not account for exposure time. This cross-tabulation approach, therefore, cannot measure CPO because only the volume of offending is considered. The aggregation of offending at each age-stage masks what is occurring *during* these age stages. For example, between ages 18–23, one individual may incur 12 convictions at age 18 but none thereafter. Another individual may incur two convictions at each age from 18–23. Cross-tabulation methods helped build a bridge to the examination of CPO trajectories by highlighting that there is heterogeneity even among those associated with chronic offending (e.g., some continue the behavior, some do not). Examining CPO allows for a more nuanced description of offending over the life-course (see Chapter 5).

Dimension 3: Severity of offending

Especially compared to chronic offending, there is a lack of research that defines and measures the severity of offending (Snyder, 1999).[9] In developmental criminology, offending versatility is one of the most common indicators of the severity of a person's criminal career (Basto-Pereira & Farrington, 2020). We measured offending versatility as a count of the number of different crime-types for which sample members were convicted. Seven crime types were examined: violent, property, violation, drug, miscellaneous, weapon, and sexual. There was a significant and positive correlation between conviction frequency and conviction versatility in adolescence ($r = .673$, $p < .001$). This relationship became stronger with age. When looking within each of the adult age-stages, there was a near-perfect correlation between conviction frequency and versatility (correlation coefficients ranged from $r = .934$ to $.955$, $p < .001$). In adulthood, frequency and seriousness, at least based on offense versatility, were two sides of the same coin.

The justice system's response to criminal behavior is also informative of offense severity. A key principle of Canadian sentencing guidelines is that a person's sentence should be proportional to the severity of their offense. A similar argument was proposed by Warr (1989), who conceptualized severity as a combination of the harmfulness and wrongfulness of an act. Harmfulness refers to the extent to which a victim suffers negative consequences as the result of an individual's actions. Wrongfulness refers to the moral blameworthiness of the action (e.g., evidence of planning) and the person associated with that action (e.g., age, cognitive ability). One way to account for the harmfulness and wrongfulness of an act is to investigate the amount of time a person is incarcerated. In Canada, although sentencing is individualized, sentences are bound by principles of parity. Specifically, s. 718.2(b) of the *Canadian Criminal Code* (1985) specifies that "a sentence should be similar to sentences imposed on similar offenders for similar offenses committed in similar circumstances." Thus, while individual circumstances can be used as aggravating or mitigating circumstances, judges must also consider precedent (i.e., decisions made in similar cases) and sentencing guidelines.[10]

Looking at the correlation between time incarcerated and frequency of convictions at each age-stage revealed a different trend compared to what was observed for the examination of offending versatility. Days incarcerated and frequency of convictions were strongly correlated in adolescence (r = .667, p < .001), but the magnitude of this correlation decreased from emerging adulthood (r = .555, p < .001) to full adulthood (r = .502, p < .001) to mature adulthood (r = .421, p < .001). The weaker association between convictions and incarceration length reflected the possibility that a low number of convictions did not preclude a high number of days spent incarcerated. It may be that at older age-stages the courts were less tolerant of certain behaviors, especially serious offenses, and responded more punitively. By mature adulthood, individuals may have lengthy histories of justice system involvement that act as aggravating circumstances in sentencing decisions. What this also suggests is that, with age, the failure to account for exposure becomes an even greater threat to the reliability of research findings. That is, with age, there is a greater amount of time spent incarcerated per each conviction incurred, precluding opportunities for future offending. Sampson and Laub's (2003) analysis of offending trajectories did not control for exposure time from age 32 onward. In the ISVYOS, this period was the point at which accounting for exposure time was most critical. Taken together with Figure 4.1 showing that there is stability in the prevalence of incarceration during the first two decades of adulthood, we believe that these findings reiterate the importance of intervention during adolescence, perhaps even earlier in their life-course, given that we can see the negative outcomes of failed interventions and missed turning points later in the life-course.

Dimension 4: Criminal career length

The fourth criminal career dimension, length, is useful for accounting for heterogeneity in offending patterns among individuals with the same number of crimes. The primary indicator of the length of a person's criminal career, referred to as duration, refers to the time between first and last offense (Piquero et al., 2004). Duration is simple to measure but can be underestimated with an insufficient follow-up period (Jolliffe et al., 2017; Kazemian & Farrington, 2006). Thus, we focused solely on 404 individuals with complete data at each year of age between ages 12 through 35 (e.g., were not deceased, did not emigrate, their record was not sealed).

Two indicators of duration were measured: years between first and last conviction and years between first and last justice system involvement (i.e., either conviction or incarceration). We refer to these as conviction duration and justice system duration. Farrington et al. (2014) found that official data were more accurate than self-report data in estimating when individuals committed their last offense because individuals tended to underestimate their age at last offense. Whether the starting point for duration was measured by first conviction age (M = 14.61; SD = 2.00) or first justice system involvement age (M = 14.41; SD = 1.49) made little difference. However, individuals' average age at last justice system involvement (M = 27.80; SD = 6.87) was approximately one year older compared to age at last conviction (M = 26.84; SD = 6.93). Putting together the start and end ages, the average conviction duration for the sample was 12.23 years (SD = 7.51) and the average justice system duration was 13.38 years (SD = 7.40). This duration is underestimated as at least some individuals in the sample remained active after the most recent data collection period.

What constitutes a long criminal career? Jolliffe et al. (2017) identified seven community-based studies where self-report or official data were used to examine long-term criminal careers, which they defined as instances in which a person perpetrated at least one crime by age 20 and another at age 30 or older. By this criteria, long-term patterns of offending were relatively rare in community-based studies, including the PYS (13.5% of the sample), the Seattle Social Development Project (3%), the CSDD (12.1%), and boys from the 1945 and 1958 Philadelphia Birth cohorts (3.7% and 2.8%, respectively). For the Transfivestudy of Dutch Nationals, prevalence of long-term offending among boys was 11.4% in the G3 cohort and 17.2% in the G4 cohort. For girls, it was 0.8% in the G3 cohort and 1.2% in the G4 cohort. Although comparisons are complicated by the fact that these other studies tended to have longer follow-up periods, 49.7% (n = 272) of participants in this ISVYOS subsample examined from ages 12–35 met Jolliffe et al.'s (2017) criteria for a long-term criminal career. Approximately 55% of male participants and 30% of female participants met this criteria.

Piquero et al. (2004) conducted one of the few examinations of criminal career length among persons involved in the justice system. Data from the CYA Study were used to measure criminal career duration as the number of years between first and last arrest. Participants were followed until an average of approximately age 37. Criminal career length ranged from 4–30 years with an average of 17.27 years (SD = 4.62) between first and last arrest. Piquero et al. (2004) observed a clear link between an earlier age of onset of offending and a longer criminal career. Similarly, for the ISVYOS, age of onset of first conviction was significantly and negatively associated with criminal career conviction duration ($r = -.434$, $p < .001$).

Piquero et al. (2004) found that the more time an individual spent incarcerated, the shorter the length of their criminal career (i.e., the two parameters were negatively correlated). The opposite was observed in the current study ($r = .615$, $p < .001$). For the CYA data, it was possible that lengthy periods of incarceration deterred individuals from offending. Another possibility was that individuals incarcerated for a lengthy period of time averaged an older age of release from custody and thus were unlikely to reoffend due to the typical decline in offending with age. A third possibility was that, whereas the Canadian system punished individuals based on the severity of their offenses, sentencing decisions under the California system were not necessarily indicative of the harmfulness and wrongfulness of the crimes that individuals perpetrated. Accordingly, differences between the two studies may be related to differences in the justice systems in place at the time.

Summary

The criminal career framework is useful for reflecting on how patterns of justice system involvement for ISVYOS participants conformed (or did not) to expectations from developmental, propensity, and life-course theoretical perspectives. Developmental criminology is often focused on the age of onset and the information it provides in terms of risk for future offending (e.g., Loeber & Le Blanc, 1990). For ISVYOS participants, the passage of time was necessary before age of onset was informative of future offending. As most participants were involved in high rates of offending in adolescence and emerging adulthood, the age onset of first conviction provided little insight into variations in convictions at these age-stages. However, by full adulthood and mature adulthood, onset was significantly and negatively associated with the frequency of convictions. This supported developmental criminology perspectives and runs counter to claims made by some propensity theorists (e.g., Gottfredson & Hirschi, 1990). It also runs counter to Laub and Sampson's (2003) assertion that the relationship between past and future offending grew weaker with age. For ISVYOS participants, the relationship between onset and future offending grew stronger with age. More than half the sample were still active in the justice system during their 30s. The process of desistance may be extremely slow for this sample as opposed to the simple kniffing-off from past mistakes and negative peers when entering adulthood.

Others suggested that the age-crime curve was invariant (e.g., Gottfredson & Hirschi, 1990; Laub & Sampson, 2003), meaning that individuals' levels of offending in adulthood should always be lower compared to their levels of offending in adolescence. We found that to be associated with chronic offending in mature adulthood (ages 30–35) implied a similar frequency of offending to those associated with chronic offending during adolescence (ages 12–17). For this sample, the notion of the inexorable effect of aging was not observed for all participants. This did not mean that aging was irrelevant or that chronic offending in adolescence always led to chronic offending at other age-stages. Cross-tabulation analyses showed that although chronic offending at an earlier age-stage was significantly associated with chronic offending at the next age-stage, there were also examples of discontinuity in offending. It is undeniable that there is continuity for this group, which aligns with propensity theories. However, propensity theories are too general to explain the diversity of criminal career outcomes observed in this sample. There is a dynamic aspect of offending that highlights some instances of transitions from non-chronic criminal careers to chronic offending but especially highlights transitions from chronic to non-chronic offending. These shifts could reflect life-course theoretical perspectives on desistance or the intermittency associated with offending (e.g., Piquero, 2013). Clarifying whether this is desistance or just intermittency requires looking beyond static indicators of chronic offending at two age-stages and instead looking at CPO as part of a specific trajectory (Chapter 5). Laub and Sampson (2003) anticipated that the randomness of life events would expose all, even the highest-risk youth, to informal social controls in adulthood that weakened the relationship between past and future offending. However, their notion of desistance by default was not the case when looking at criminal career parameters within the ISVYOS sample, at least in terms of the follow-up period through age 35.

The four pillars that frame DLC criminology have given relatively little attention to sociolegal responses to crime and how adjudicated persons react, adapt, or learn from these responses (e.g., arrest, trial, incarceration). The justice system may not make explicit reference to criminal career parameters, but the information we had on participants' criminal histories was known to the justice system and is regularly included in risk assessment tools (e.g., Borum et al., 2002) used to make decisions about, for example, the type of sentence a person should receive and how to intervene with this person (Viljoen et al., 2010). This implies that the justice system draws connections between past and future offending and attempts to directly intervene with, and allocate disproportionate resources to, the individuals scoring highest on these criminal history items from risk assessment tools.

Despite efforts by the justice system to identify individuals involved in early onset, frequent, and serious offending and disrupt the link between these parameters and future offending, for the ISVYOS sample, criminal career parameters in adolescence were informative of criminal career parameters through different stages of adulthood. This is possible evidence that past and current strategies to reduce offending for those in the deep-end of the justice system were unable to break developmental criminology and propensity principles of offending without providing the specific interventions and services that help bring about significant turning points that are part of life-course principles. An alternative perspective is that by having, for example, an early onset of offending, these youth, from a young age, were well-known to police and other agents of the justice system and thus were more likely to be targeted or considered a suspect in criminal investigations. Either way, the justice system applied to this sample various sentencing principles to justify greater periods of incarceration, more intensive community restrictions/probation conditions, and treatment and intervention services, but this approach was not fully successful in interrupting the path from early, frequent, and serious offending in adolescence to a similar pattern of offending in adulthood. For a better understanding of how volume and persistence intersected, Chapter 5 looked at conviction trajectories for ISVYOS participants.

Notes

1 Morselli et al. (2006) pointed out that the long-standing disagreements between the Gluecks and Sutherland included the fact that the Gluecks saw maturation as a facilitator of desistance whereas Sutherland viewed maturation as the crystallization of a person's criminal identity. In effect, at the time, the Gluecks were more open to discussions of desistance than Sutherland.

2 Official data on criminal behavior is criticized on the grounds that they reflect the work of the justice system (e.g., law enforcement work, the courts) and social reactions to crime (e.g., reporting crime to the police). Self-reports of criminal behavior are advantageous for several reasons, including the fact that crime is often undetected by the justice system (Farrington et al., 2003). The data from the ISVYOS are useful for understanding the types of problems that practitioners within the justice system are tasked with dealing with. This is especially true because individuals may be less likely to self-report the most serious and violent forms of criminal behavior that are most likely to bring a person into contact with the justice system (Stouthamer-Loeber et al., 2008). There may also be some advantages to official records. For example, individuals appear to be less forthcoming about self-reported offending later in adulthood; analyses of data from the CSDD showed that desistance occurred later in the life-course when interpreting official versus self-report data (Farrington et al., 2014). As well, self-reported offending is consistently higher among those with a history of formal justice system involvement compared to those without (Basto-Pereira & Farrington, 2020; Gilman et al., 2014; Jolliffe et al., 2003). Subgroups with the highest rate of official offending and subgroups with the highest rate of self-report offending tend to be composed of the same individuals (Fontaine et al., 2014), meaning that while relying on official data underestimated offending among ISVYOS participants, the individuals associated with the highest rates of official offending are commonly the same individuals associated with the highest rates of self-report offending.

3 For Cohort I, fewer than 10 participants were at least age 40 and so the figure excludes this age and above for this cohort. For Cohort II, fewer than 10 participants were at least age 32 and so the figure excludes data on this age and above for this cohort.

4 Persons were excluded from these analyses if (a) criminal history data were unavailable, (b) the person emigrated or died during the developmental stage under investigation, or (c) the person was younger than the upper-bound of the age range examined. The sample size for each age-stage was as follows: (1) adolescence (ages 12–17; n = 1,528), emerging adulthood (ages 18–23; n = 1,535), full adulthood (ages 24–29; n = 880), and mature adulthood (ages 30–35; n = 410). There were more participants with available data in emerging adulthood compared to adolescence because of the sealing of youth records.

5 None of the Cohort II participants were followed through age 35.

6 Prevalence was less than 100% because some participants perpetrated their crime in adolescence but were not caught and adjudicated until adulthood. In Canada, individuals can be held in youth custody even between the ages of 18–20 provided the date of their crime was prior to age 18 (i.e., prior to adulthood).

7 This was contrary to Piquero et al.'s (2009) findings using data from the Philadelphia Birth Cohort, where onset was related to offending early in the life-course, but once looking beyond the first few years of adulthood, onset of offending was not related to continued offending.

8 Within each age-stage, the total number of convictions incurred for the sample was divided by two; chronic offending represented the point at which the fewest

number of participants was needed to reach this number (i.e., 50+% of all convictions).

9 Most of this research provided rankings of the severity of types of offenses (e.g., Barrett et al. 2015; Oudekerk et al., 2012; Sellin & Wolfgang, 1964) but this included limited rating scales (e.g., 0–5) that cannot fully capture heterogeneity in offense severity, included offenses that are not crimes today (e.g., homosexuality), included offenses that are no longer considered as serious (e.g., marijuana possession), and excluded more contemporary offenses (e.g., distribution of child pornography over the internet). Moreover, focusing only on specific types of offenses ignores heterogeneity within different crime types. Certain circumstances can aggravate the severity of an offense, such as whether it caused personal injury, involved use of threats or intimidation (e.g., verbal, physical, or weapon intimidation), and the value of the property stolen or damaged. Sebba (1980, 1984) argued that severity indexes fail to account for mens rea (e.g., intent, recklessness, negligence). Cohen (1988) and Lesieur and Lehman (1975) argued that seriousness indexes do not account for the full scope of offense characteristics that impact perceptions of harmfulness (e.g., offender, victim, and social context characteristics, costs of physical and mental victimization).

10 A fundamental principle of justice, though certainly not necessarily always carried out in practice (Bushway & Piehl, 2001; Mitchell, 2005; Steffensmeier & Demuth, 2000), is that a person's sentence must be proportionate to the harmfulness and wrongfulness of the act committed. In Canada during the era in which participants were adjudicated, there is evidence that this principle was carried out in practice. Brantingham (1985) found that the strongest predictors of sentence length were the number of prior convictions and the use of a weapon. Sociodemographic characteristics did not affect sentence length (also see Carrington & Moyer, 1995; Doob & Sprott, 2007).

5 Capturing trajectories through the justice system

Introduction

Developmental criminology, propensity theories, and life-course criminology are built on distinct assumptions about longitudinal sequences of offending. In order of parsimony, propensity models recognize a continuum of patterns of offending that differ in degree (e.g., high versus low rate of offending) but not in kind (e.g., shape, timing of onset). This is more intuitive when considering that propensity theories view offending as a single dimension (e.g., frequency) caused by a single factor (e.g., antisocial propensity). Life-course criminology suggests that the longitudinal sequence of offending is characterized by zig-zags and random variations due to the intricacies of life events and the unpredictability of turning points. This is more intuitive when offending is examined over a long period of time. Developmental criminology is based on the idea that patterns of offending vary in degree and kind. This is more intuitive when considering Moffitt's (1993) distinction between AL and LCP offending.

Looking at individual criminal career parameters provides limited insight into the accuracy of propensity, life-course, and developmental criminology hypotheses about offending patterns. Similarly, chronic offending is a static indicator that cannot provide information about the accuracy of developmental and life-course criminology perspectives on the potentially dynamic nature of offending. Even though propensity theories tend to reduce offending to a single parameter, evaluating the accuracy of propensity theories requires examining whether multiple parameters provide only redundant information about offending over the life-course.

In Chapter 4 we found a relationship between parameters from different dimensions of the criminal career (e.g., the relationship between age of onset of first conviction and frequency of convictions). The observed relationship between past and future offending suggests the presence of offending *trajectories*. Trajectories can be statistically modeled. While the computation of trajectories is more complex than the measurement of any single criminal career parameter, it is also quite efficient in its ability to summarize multiple parameters of the criminal career in a single analysis. Analytic strategies like SPGM can also account for exposure time (e.g., time spent in the community as opposed to in custody) when modeling offending trajectories (for limitations of this approach, see McCuish, 2020).

Whereas initial measurement strategies defined chronic offending solely based on meeting some frequency threshold, more recent perspectives have discussed chronic offending as frequent offending that persists over time (Moffitt, 1993; Remschmidt & Walter, 2010; Wikström & Treiber, 2009). To avoid confusing the two different definitions for the same term, we refer to frequent offending that persists over time as CPO. SPGM can be used to measure CPO as a specific type of offending trajectory or *types* of offending trajectories. Unlike strategies used to measure chronic offending that have predefined thresholds, SPGM allows CPO to emerge from the data, if such a pattern even exists. Simply counting the number of crimes over a specific time period, as is the case with chronic offending, ignores potential differences in how these crimes unfold. Figure 5.1 illustrates the consequences of looking only at the volume of offending. Three offending trajectories are shown. Each individual incurred 23 convictions between ages 12–23 and could be considered to have met some threshold definition of chronic offending. Yet, how these convictions unfolded over age are dissimilar. Furthermore, aggregating these trajectories into a single pattern does not reflect any individual pattern particularly well.

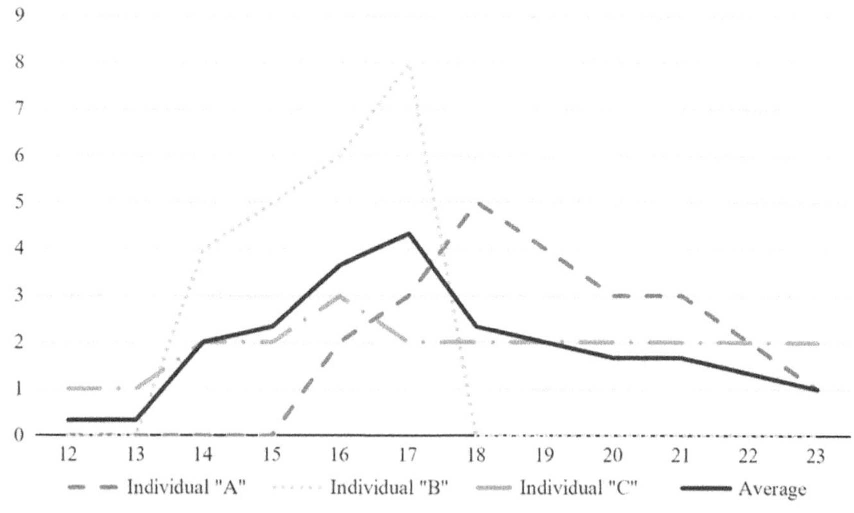

Figure 5.1 The consequences of taking the average offending trajectory when the average trajectory poorly fits the observed trajectories of all individuals.

Notes: x-axis = age. y-axis = number of observed convictions.

Contribution to research on CPO trajectories

It is difficult to make theoretical contributions to criminology simply by modeling trajectories (Skardhamar, 2010). The main issue is that the statistical modeling of offending trajectories has been used to address a very narrow set of theoretical questions mostly related to verifying Moffitt's AL/LCP patterns. Focusing solely on whether CPO is present or absent ignores the question of whether CPO captures a homogenous group and should be labeled as such in the first place (e.g., LCP). Prior research examined trajectories, not so much for the purpose of theoretical development, but rather to confirm or reject assumptions about the longitudinal sequence of offending. We depart from the endeavor of searching for a specific number of offending trajectories by instead interpreting the underlying stories that these trajectories reveal, including risk and protective factors associated with offending trajectories over the life-course (Blokland et al., 2005; van der Geest et al., 2009; Piquero et al., 2010).

The analyses in this chapter focused on modeling conviction trajectories across different developmental stages to examine (1) if there was a trajectory or multiple trajectories associated with CPO, (2) what justice system involvement looks like for these different trajectories, and (3) whether risk factors in childhood/adolescence were informative of trajectory group membership.

CPO as a particular trajectory

Researchers often mean different things when discussing chronic offending (Jolliffe et al., 2017; Whitten et al., 2017, 2019). Traditional measures of chronic offending relied on different ways of identifying a critical threshold in the volume of convictions for sample members that justified the 'chronic' label. Moffitt (1993) expanded researchers' interests by looking at CPO. Although Moffitt (1993) described the interaction between frequency and persistence as LCP offending, we do not use this term to describe offending trajectories for the ISVYOS sample given that the follow-up period did not cover the full life-course. As another point of clarification, a high rate of convictions means that the rate of convictions is atypical of other trajectories identified for the sample. A CPO trajectory does not need to demonstrate the same rate of offending over the entire life-course. McCuish (2020) demonstrated that it was likely impossible for individuals who incurred a high-rate of convictions to maintain the same frequency of offending over the life-course because the justice system responds most punitively (e.g., lengthy custody sentences) to individuals associated with particularly high rates of past offending, which restricts the ability to continue offending. Given that Sampson and Laub (2003) felt that early mortality for individuals associated with a high rate of offending was evidence against the policy utility of Moffitt's

LCP offending trajectory, they might feel similarly about incarceration. Our perspective is that criminologists should not relieve themselves of the responsibility of helping develop evidence-based means of intervening with high-risk persons simply because eventually they will be incarcerated or deceased and thus unable to offend.

The analyses in this chapter included trajectory models between ages 12–23, ages 12–29, and ages 12–35. Measuring trajectories through the three different adulthood age-stages allowed for an inspection of whether the length of the follow-up period was important for the nature and prevalence of CPO trajectories (Cullen, 2011). We also modeled trajectories over different age-stages so that we could use these models in future chapters to address different research questions.

Trajectories were modeled using the traj Stata plugin (Jones & Nagin, 2013). SPGM allows the number and shape of trajectories to emerge from the data (Nagin, 2005). The zero-inflated Poisson model with quadratic functional form was used to estimate the distribution of offending trajectories, which is appropriate for modeling periods of inactivity that are common when examining longitudinal patterns of offending (Piquero, 2013). For each of the three follow-up periods examined, we began with a one-group trajectory solution and then fit additional trajectories to the data. Four criteria were considered when selecting the number of trajectories that best fit the data (1) Bayesian Information Criteria (BIC) values closest to zero, (2) posterior probabilities of at least 0.70 for all trajectories, (3) parsimony (e.g., the absence of trajectory splitting), and (4) at least 5% of the sample assigned to each trajectory in the model (Nagin, 2005).

All trajectory models accounted for exposure time, which was defined as the proportion of each age-period in which a participant was free in the community (i.e., not incarcerated). Participants were excluded from trajectory models if their death or emigration outside of the province resulted in missing data during any year of age in which convictions were modeled (4.6% of the emerging adulthood subsample, 9.7% of the full adulthood subsample, and 12.4% of the mature adulthood subsample). Each model had excellent fit (see Table 5.1). Odds of correctly classifying an individual to the trajectory best describing their pattern of offending was high (i.e., greater than five; Nagin, 2005) for all trajectories.

Description of offending trajectories

The trajectory model covering emerging adulthood (n = 1,452) is shown in Figure 5.2 Although a seven-group solution had BIC values closest to zero of the eight models tested, when moving from a five-group solution to a six-group solution, as opposed to an additional trajectory with unique shape, there were simply two trajectories of nearly identical shape and height (i.e., splitting). For the purpose of parsimony we therefore retained the five-group

Table 5.1 Model fit indices for the three trajectory analyses

	Offending trajectories				
	Group 1	*Group 2*	*Group 3*	*Group 4*	*Group 5*
Emerging Adulthood (Ages 12–23)					
Label	Low Rate	Stable Chronic	AL	EOFD	HRP
n (%)	445 (30.6%)	362 (24.9%)	284 (19.6%)	158 (10.9%)	203 (14.0%)
Mean probability: G1	0.96 (0.11)	0.02 (0.06)	0.03 (0.08)	0.00 (0.00)	0.00 (0.00)
Mean probability: G2	0.02 (0.08)	0.94 (0.12)	0.01 (0.04)	0.01 (0.06)	0.01 (0.06)
Mean probability: G3	0.03 (0.09)	0.01 (0.06)	0.94 (0.11)	0.01 (0.05)	0.00 (0.00)
Mean probability: G4	0.00 (0.00)	0.01 (0.04)	0.01 (0.06)	0.96 (0.09)	0.02 (0.06)
Mean probability: G5	0.00 (0.00)	0.03 (0.08)	0.00 (0.00)	0.02 (0.07)	0.95 (0.11)
OCC	48.31	47.47	69.39	194.76	124.09
Full Adulthood (Ages 12–29)					
Label	AL	EOFD	Stable Chronic	HRP	
n (%)	342 (41.4%)	141 (17.1%)	162 (19.6%)	181 (21.9%)	-
Mean probability: G1	0.99 (0.06)	0.01 (0.05)	0.01 (0.04)	0.00 (0.00)	-
Mean probability: G2	0.01 (0.05)	0.97 (0.09)	0.01 (0.06)	0.01 (0.04)	-
Mean probability: G3	0.01 (0.05)	0.02 (0.07)	0.97 (0.10)	0.01 (0.05)	-
Mean probability: G4	0.00 (0.00)	0.01 (0.03)	0.01 (0.03)	0.99 (0.05)	-
OCC	96.41	143.53	115.55	250.29	-
Mature Adulthood (Ages 12–35)					
Label	Low Rate	EOSD	AL	EOFD	HRP
n (%)	113 (28.0%)	57 (14.1%)	117 (29.0%)	48 (11.9%)	69 (17.1%)
Mean probability: G1	0.99 (0.05)	0.00 (0.02)	0.01 (0.04)	0.00 (0.01)	0.00 (0.02)
Mean probability: G2	0.00 (0.03)	0.96 (0.09)	0.00 (0.00)	0.01 (0.03)	0.03 (0.08)
Mean probability: G3	0.02 (0.06)	0.00 (0.00)	0.98 (0.07)	0.00 (0.03)	0.00 (0.00)
Mean probability: G4	0.00 (0.01)	0.01 (0.03)	0.01 (0.04)	0.98 (0.06)	0.00 (0.00)
Mean probability: G5	0.01 (0.04)	0.02 (0.07)	0.00 (0.00)	0.00 (0.00)	0.97 (0.08)
OCC	189.58	138.31	115.86	306.52	152.77

Notes: AL = adolescence-limited conviction trajectory; EOFD = early onset-fast desistance conviction trajectory; SRP = slow rising persistent conviction trajectory; EOSD = early onset-slow desistance conviction trajectory; HRP = high rate persistent conviction trajectory. Odds of correct classification (OCC) based on the weighted posterior probability.

model. In this model there were two CPO trajectories, representing 38.9% of the sample. For some (i.e., the high rate persistent (HRP) trajectory), their CPO trajectory was defined by convictions that started off high in adolescence and remained high through emerging adulthood. For others (i.e., the slow rising persistent (SRP) trajectory), their CPO trajectory was defined by the lack of a decline in convictions following adulthood that is typically seen as part of the traditional age-crime curve.

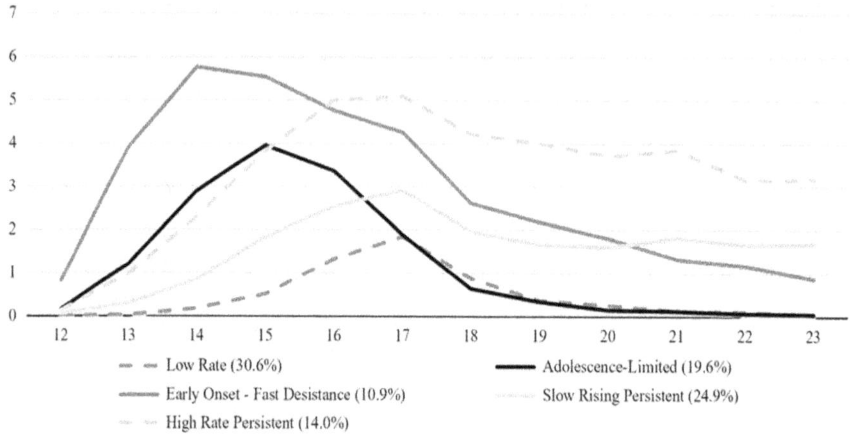

Figure 5.2 Trajectories defined by observed convictions through emerging adulthood (n = 1,452).

Notes: Time incarcerated accounted for as an exposure variable. x-axis = age. y-axis = number of observed convictions.

For the full adulthood analysis (n = 826), splitting occurred between a four-group solution and five-group solution and therefore a four-group solution was retained (Figure 5.3). There were two CPO trajectories that comprised 41.5% of the sample. The shapes of these trajectories resembled those of the HRP and SRP trajectories from the emerging adulthood analysis and were labeled as such. Cross-tabulating the association between emerging adulthood trajectory assignment and full adulthood trajectory assignment revealed important details about the continuity of convictions. For example, over 80% of individuals in the HRP trajectory in emerging adulthood were associated with the HRP trajectory in full adulthood. Half of the individuals in the EOFD trajectory in emerging adulthood were associated with the two CPO trajectories in full adulthood, showing that initial declines in patterns of convictions through ages 18–23 did not mean that this trend continued through ages 24–29. In effect, a longer follow-up period revealed that what initially appeared to be a pattern of desistance, for some individuals, was just a pattern of offending intermittency.

For the mature adulthood analysis (n = 404), splitting occurred between a five- and six-group solution and therefore the five-group model was retained (Figure 5.4). One CPO trajectory, referred to as HRP, comprised 17.1% of the sample. Once again, the addition of an extra six years of follow-up data provided important details about the continuity of offending over the life-course. Only about half of individuals in the HRP trajectory in full adulthood were associated with the HRP trajectory in mature adulthood. Thus, this age-stage was particularly important for the timing of desistance,

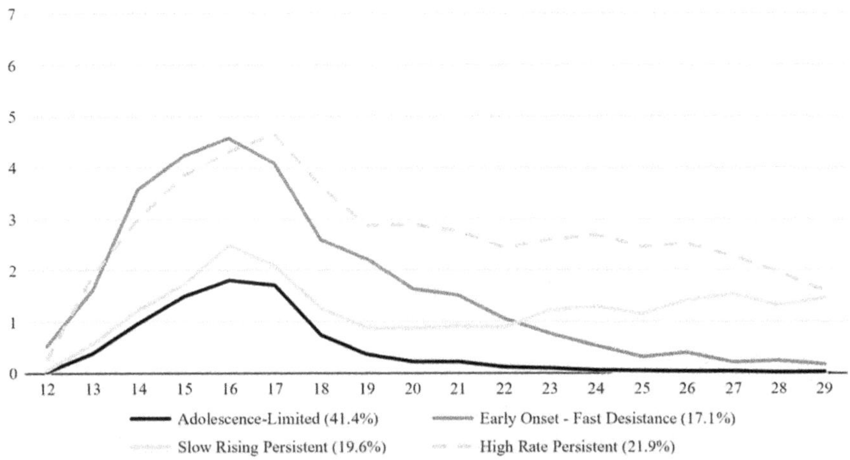

Figure 5.3 Trajectories defined by observed convictions through full adulthood (n = 826).

Notes: Time incarcerated accounted for as an exposure variable. x-axis = age. y-axis = number of observed convictions.

although for at least some individuals, the association with a less frequent/persistent offending trajectory when moving from full adulthood to mature adulthood may have been related to experiencing particularly lengthy periods of incarceration that gave the impression of desistance, even though time incarcerated was used to account for exposure time (McCuish, 2020). As we show below, there is some evidence to suggest that the early onset-slow desistance (EOSD) and early onset-fast desistance (EOFD) trajectories included individuals defined by CPO, it is just that the length of time incarcerated precluded their ability to continue to offend at a high rate through the later stages of adulthood.

The trajectories identified across all models can be summarized as different variations of two meta-trajectories reminiscent of Moffitt's dual taxonomy. The first meta-trajectory is characterized by a pattern of offending that peaks in adolescence and reaches a near-zero level of offending in adulthood. There are two variations to this meta-trajectory, which we labeled as the adolescence-limited (AL) trajectory and the low-rate trajectory. For the AL trajectory, adolescence marks the last point of contact with the justice system. For the low-rate trajectory, it seemed possible that individuals experienced snares (McGee et al., 2015; Petkovsek et al., 2016) that pulled them back into the justice system intermittently throughout adulthood.

The second meta-trajectory is characterized by a high-rate of offending that begins in adolescence and continues at least through emerging adulthood and thus is reminiscent of CPO. Four trajectories identified from the three analyses are part of this meta-trajectory: the EOFD trajectory, the

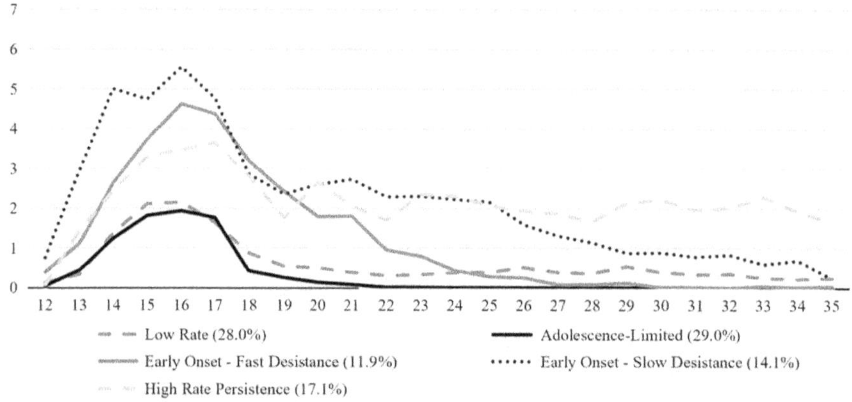

Figure 5.4 Trajectories defined by convictions through mature adulthood (n = 404).
Notes: Time incarcerated accounted for as an exposure variable. x-axis = age. y-axis = number of observed convictions.

EOSD trajectory, the SRP trajectory, and the HRP trajectory. Each of these trajectories indicates a similar pattern of early and high-rate offending in adolescence. However, by adulthood, their trajectories take different shapes. It might seem like an oxymoron to suggest that this CPO meta-trajectory includes trajectories defined by desistance. However, for those in the EOFD and EOSD trajectories, the desistance process takes a long time, even decades. For these trajectories, the slowing down process associated with desistance still involved rates of offending that would be considered especially high relative to (a) other trajectories in the sample and (b) CPO trajectories in other studies. For example, the EOSD trajectory was still averaging 0.5 convictions a year through ages 30–35. For some in this trajectory, this might be evidence of a slow path to redemption. For others, their declining convictions may have resulted from the justice system's punitive response to their behavior via a lengthy custody sentence (McCuish, 2020).

Importantly, while SPGM adjusts for time incarcerated when assigning individuals to specific trajectories, Figures 5.2–5.4 present observed convictions rather than expected convictions. Expected convictions can be calculated by dividing a person's observed number of convictions by the proportion of time that they spent in the community. This provides a person's expected number of convictions had they spent an entire year in the community as opposed to being incarcerated. For example, if an individual were convicted of five crimes and spent six months in custody at age 16, they would have 10 expected convictions (i.e., 5 ÷ 0.5).

For the analysis of trajectories through mature adulthood, the AL group averaged 38.55 (SD = 116.33) expected (or prorated) convictions between ages 12 to 35. The low rate group averaged 95.99 (SD = 222.21) expected convictions.

The EOFD group averaged 228.38 (*SD* = 361.44) expected convictions. The EOSD group averaged 545.55 (*SD* = 611.98) expected convictions. Finally, the HRP group averaged 705.43 (*SD* = 744.70) expected convictions. Thus, when incarceration was used to calculate expected convictions, the volume of convictions for the AL trajectory increased by a factor of approximately 4.7 (i.e., 8.19 observed against 38.55 expected). When this was done for the HRP trajectory, the volume of convictions increased by a factor of approximately 13.7. Figure 5.5 shows the average number of expected convictions at each year of age within each trajectory from the mature adulthood analysis. Relying on Figure 5.4's depiction of observed convictions underestimates CPO. For example, between ages 30–35, the EOSD trajectory averaged nearly 10 expected convictions at *each* year of age (i.e., about 20 times the number of observed convictions during this period). Accordingly, it is appropriate to consider this a CPO trajectory.

The difference between observed and expected convictions should not be interpreted as the number of convictions that the justice system prevented by using incarceration as a sentencing option. We simply wanted to illustrate that the failure to consider the impact of incarceration on future convictions can result in misinterpreting declines in convictions as evidence of desistance. Incarceration at least may have a variable impact on individuals associated with different trajectories. For example, the shape of conviction trajectories is most greatly impacted by incarceration for individuals associated with CPO.

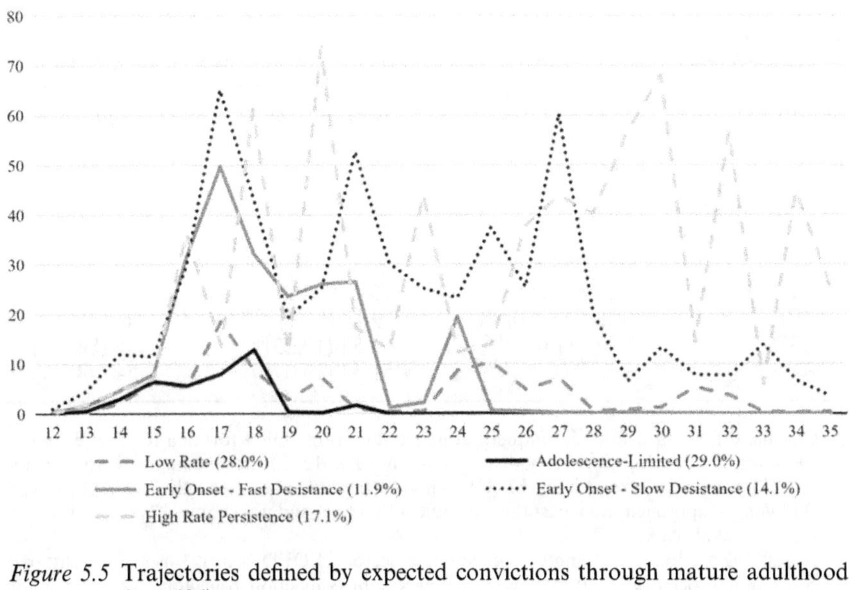

Figure 5.5 Trajectories defined by expected convictions through mature adulthood (n = 404).

Notes: Time incarcerated accounted for as an exposure variable. x-axis = age. y-axis = number of expected convictions

Offending trajectories and their association with criminal career parameters

Table 5.2 outlines the relationship between conviction trajectories and other criminal career parameters. Like the relationship between onset and frequency in Chapter 4, the relationship between conviction trajectories and the age of onset of first conviction varied depending on the length of the follow-up period. If only measuring trajectories through emerging adulthood, the HRP trajectory had a significantly *older* average age of onset of first conviction compared to the AL trajectory. However, by mature adulthood, the HRP trajectory had a significantly *younger* average age of

Table 5.2 Comparison of criminal career parameters across offending trajectories

	Criminal career parameters		
	Conviction age of onset M (SD)	*Conviction frequency M (SD)*	*Chronic offending*† *n (%)*
Emerging Adulthood (Ages 12–23)			
[a]Low Rate	16.15 (1.87)[b,c,d,e]	5.62 (3.64)[b,c,d,e]	0 (0.0%)
[b]AL	13.88 (0.93)[a,c,d,e]	15.02 (5.92)[a,c,d,e]	5 (1.8%)
[c]EOFD	13.16 (0.92)[a,b,d,e,]	35.22 (9.58)[a,b,d,e]	110 (69.6%)
[d]SRP	15.16 (1.43)[a,b,c,e]	19.03 (7.08)[a,b,c,e]	27 (7.5%)
[e]HRP	14.43 (1.25)[a,b,c,d]	39.43 (12.35)[a,b,c,d]	166 (81.8%)
Full Adulthood (Ages 12–29)			
[a]AL	15.32 (1.88)[b,d]	8.43 (5.33)[b,c,d]	0 (0.0%)
[b]EOFD	13.86 (1.28)[a,c]	30.38 (9.28)[a,c,d]	12 (8.5%)
[c]SRP	15.19 (2.27)[b,d]	22.46 (9.70)[a,b,d]	4 (2.5%)
[d]HRP	14.18 (1.47)[a,d]	48.75 (12.46)[a,b,c]	130 (71.8%)
Mature Adulthood (Ages 12–35)			
[a]AL	15.09 (1.63)[c,d,e]	8.19 (5.72)[b,c,d,e]	0 (0.0%)
[b]Low Rate	15.26 (2.77)[c,d,e]	15.29 (9.02)[a,c,d,e]	0 (0.0%)
[c]EOFD	14.19 (1.23)[a,b,d]	29.17 (8.76)[a,b,d,e]	6 (12.5%)
[d]EOSD	13.37 (1.06)[a,b,c,e]	52.53 (12.23)[a,b,c]	48 (84.2%)
[e]HRP	14.08 (1.29)[a,b,d]	51.52 (19.07)[a,b,c]	54 (78.3%)

† Chronic offending defined by Piquero et al.'s (2007) probability formula for the respective age-stages (e.g., trajectories modeled between ages 12–23 were compared to chronic offending modeled from ages 12–23). This measure almost perfectly overlapped with Wolfgang's approach to measuring chronic offending and thus only Piquero's formula was presented here.

Notes: AL = adolescence-limited conviction trajectory; EOFD = early onset-fast desistance conviction trajectory; SRP = slow rising persistent conviction trajectory; EOSD = early onset-slow desistance conviction trajectory; HRP = high rate persistent conviction trajectory. Superscripts indicate significant differences per Tamhane post-hoc comparison.

onset of first conviction compared to the AL trajectory. In effect, the relationship between onset and CPO trajectories became stronger with the passage of time. The examination of onset also showed that there was variability within CPO trajectories. For example, the HRP trajectory in mature adulthood averaged a significantly older age of onset of first conviction compared to the EOSD trajectory.

The last column in Table 5.2 shows whether the measurement of CPO (i.e., volume and persistence) was redundant from the measurement of chronic offending (i.e., volume only). It was quite clear that talking about chronic offending does not mean talking about just one specific pattern of convictions. For example, less than 10% of individuals in the SRP trajectory in emerging adulthood met the criteria for chronic offending. In mature adulthood, 84% of individuals in the EOSD trajectory met the criteria for chronic offending and only 78.3% of individuals in the HRP trajectory did so. In effect, not all individuals associated with a CPO trajectory were also associated with chronic offending. This was likely due to such individuals being incarcerated for lengthy periods of time; their expected convictions were much higher than their observed convictions, but only observed convictions were used to measure chronic offending.

In Table 5.3, additional criminal career parameters were compared across the mature adulthood trajectory analysis as it represented the longest follow-up period, providing a clearer picture of conviction trajectories over the life-course. We looked at the total length of time that each participant spent incarcerated as an indication of criminal career severity (Warr, 1989). Individuals in the HRP trajectory averaged approximately 100 months incarcerated, which was significantly greater than the AL, low rate, and EOFD trajectories. This represented one third of the period between ages 12–35 (i.e., approximately 8 years in custody over the 24-year follow-up period). With the cost of incarceration being approximately $100,000 CAD per year, the average cost of incarceration for a single person in the HRP trajectory was nearly $1,000,000 CAD.

Individuals associated with the EOSD trajectory also spent a substantial amount of time in custody (e.g., nearly eight years). The decline in convictions during the last 10 years of the follow-up period may have indicated that custody functioned as a positive turning point in their life-course (McCuish et al., 2018b). Addressing the rehabilitative needs of justice-involved persons has been one of the main goals of Canada's prison system (Gendreau, 1996). This has included the creation of the risk-need-responsivity (RNR) model (Bonta & Andrews, 2007) and the development of tools for maximizing custody-based treatment efficacy (Viljoen et al., 2019). An alternative interpretation is that the decline in convictions for members of the EOSD trajectory was because they spent so much time in custody that they lacked opportunities to incur new convictions. This can occur even when exposure time is accounted for in the trajectory model McCuish, 2020). Although we were unable to directly assess the

Table 5.3 Different measures of offense severity compared across conviction trajectories in mature adulthood (n = 404)

	Mature adulthood offending trajectories					
	AL (n = 117) *M (SD) / n (%)*	*Low Rate (n = 113)* *M (SD) / n (%)*	*EOFD (n = 48)* *M (SD) / n (%)*	*EOSD (n = 57)* *M (SD) / n (%)*	*HRP (n = 69)* *M (SD) / n (%)*	χ^2/F, *df*, *p*, φ/η
Offending Severity						
Months Incarcerated	13.78 (29.98)^{b,c,d,e}	27.45 (37.73)^{a,d,e}	39.50 (27.66)^{a,d,e}	95.39 (37.60)^{a,b,c}	101.26 (44.27)^{a,b,c}	$F^{\dagger}[304] = 97.0$, $p < .001$, $\eta = 0.50$
Offending Versatility	2.96 (1.20)^{b,c,d,e}	3.89 (1.15)^{a,c,d,e}	4.60 (0.82)^{a,b,d,e}	5.32 (0.74)^{a,b,c}	5.32 (1.02)^{a,b,c}	$F^{\dagger}[385] = 91.2$, $p < .001$, $\eta = 0.44$
# of Violent Offenses	1.24 (1.55)^{b,c,d,e}	2.48 (2.39)^{a,d,e}	3.17 (2.57)^{a,d,e}	4.95 (2.77)^{a,b,c}	4.75 (3.34)^{a,b,c}	$F^{\dagger}[258] = 29.9$, $p < .001$, $\eta = 0.25$
# of Weapon Offenses	0.09 (0.32)^{b,c,d,e}	0.40 (0.87)^{a,d,e}	0.52 (0.82)^{a,e}	1.04 (1.19)^{a,b}	1.67 (2.06)^{a,b,c}	$F^{\dagger}[163] = 20.8$, $p < .001$, $\eta = 0.20$
Any Homicide Offense	6 (5.1%)	15 (13.3%)	5 (10.4%)	5 (8.8%)	9 (13.0%)	χ^2 [4] = 5.29, $p = .259$, $\varphi = 0.11$
Any Sexual Offense	10 (8.5%)	13 (11.5%)	5 (10.4%)	9 (15.8%)	14 (20.3%)	χ^2 [4] = 6.30, $p = .178$, $\varphi = 0.13$
Criminal Career Length						
Conviction Duration	2.68 (2.29)^{b,c,d,e}	14.85 (4.76)^{a,c,d,e}	10.81 (4.13)^{a,b,d,e}	18.72 (2.90)^{a,b,c}	19.75 (2.51)^{a,b,c}	$F^{\dagger}[261] = 375.83$, $p < .001$, $\eta = 0.79$

Justice System Duration	4.40 (4.55)[b,c,d,e]	15.97 (4.27)[a,c,d,e]	11.46 (3.99)[a,b,d,e]	19.77 (2.70)[a,b,c]	20.49 (1.80)[a,b,c]	$F^{\dagger}[307] = 316.87$, $p < .001$, $\eta = 0.74$
Conviction Persistence	0 (0.0%)	37 (32.7%)	1 (2.1%)	45 (78.9%)	65 (94.2%)	χ^2 [4] = 235, $p < .001$, $\varphi = 0.76$
Justice System Persistence	2 (1.7%)	50 (44.2%)	4 (8.3%)	52 (91.2%)	67 (97.1%)	χ^2 [4] = 241, $p < .001$, $\varphi = 0.77$

† Levene's test of the assumption of equal variance violated. Brown-Forsythe test statistic shown.
a Significantly different from AL
b Significantly different from Low Rate
c Significantly different from EOFD
d Significantly different from EOSD
e Significantly different from HRP.

Notes: Differences detected using the Tamhane post-hoc test for ANOVA. AL = adolescence limited conviction trajectory; EOFD = early onset-fast desistance conviction trajectory; EOSD = early onset-slow desistance conviction trajectory; HRP = high rate persistent conviction trajectory. φ = phi effect size. η = eta squared effect size.

rehabilitative impact of incarceration, the purpose of our analysis was to highlight that the justice system's use of incarceration has implications for how a person's pattern of convictions takes shape over the life-course.

In terms of conviction versatility, the EOSD and HRP trajectories averaged just over five of the seven crime types measured (see Chapter 3), which was significantly higher compared to the other three trajectories. Single item indicators of serious crimes (e.g., homicide, sexual offenses) were not associated with conviction trajectories. However, frequency of convictions for violence and weapons were significantly higher for the HRP and EOSD trajectories compared to the lower-rate conviction trajectories. It may be that perpetrating a single serious offense is more of a random event than a sign of a particular pattern of offending. The association between offending frequency and severity only emerged in this study when serious offenses were repeatedly perpetrated.

The bottom of Table 5.3 shows the relationship between trajectories and criminal career duration. Notably, there were no significant differences in criminal career duration between the EOSD and HRP trajectories, regardless of how criminal career duration was measured. This aligned with the description of desistance as a process of slowing down (e.g., Laub & Sampson, 2003) as well as with our depiction of the EOSD trajectory as part of the CPO meta-trajectory. Similarly, the EOFD trajectory averaged three times as many convictions as the AL trajectory (Table 5.2) and an average criminal career duration that was approximately eight years longer compared to the AL trajectory.

We used an indicator of criminal career persistence to verify the appropriateness of such a label for the HRP trajectory. Persistence was defined in two different ways: (1) whether an individual had at least one conviction in all four age-stages and (2) whether an individual had justice system involvement (e.g., conviction or incarcerations) in all four age-stages. The effect size for the relationship between trajectories and average conviction duration was slightly stronger than for the relationship between trajectories and average number of total convictions ($\eta = 0.79$ versus $\eta = 0.73$). The correlation coefficient between conviction duration and total convictions was .693, suggesting that (a) these parameters were not measuring the same aspect of offending and (b) both were important to the development of conviction trajectories. Almost 100% of individuals in the EOSD and HRP trajectories were involved in the justice system at each of the four age-stages. For the EOSD trajectory, the prevalence of conviction persistence was 15% lower than justice system persistence, which reiterated the importance of looking at time incarcerated to avoid overestimating desistance. As well, almost half of participants in the low rate conviction trajectory were associated with justice system involvement at each age-stage, which was substantially higher compared to the EOFD trajectory, despite averaging half the number of convictions as the EOFD trajectory. The low rate trajectory might be defined in other studies as a CPO trajectory, but in this study, their rate of offending was too low compared to other trajectories in the sample to be considered high rate. Thus, frequent and persistent offending were not measuring the same aspect of the criminal career, highlighting the value of examining their intersection through CPO trajectories.

Offending trajectories and their association with individual-level characteristics

Chapter 2 touched on Sampson and Laub's (2003) argument that risk factors in childhood and adolescence were not informative of CPO. We felt that their conclusions needed to be revisited given issues with (1) a lack of CPO within their sample, (2) the measurement of status offenses and their impact on underestimating persistence, (3) failure to control for exposure time, and (4) unreliable measures of risk factors. Table 5.4 looks at whether risk/needs factors in childhood/adolescence were related to conviction trajectories between ages 12–29. We focused on this age-stage so that we could include participants from both cohorts (only Cohort I was followed into mature adulthood at the time of data collection). There were three examples of CPO trajectories in this model: the EOFD trajectory, the SRP trajectory, and the HRP trajectory. We focused on the following domains: (1) school behavior, (2) substance use, (3) aggression, (4) self-reported offending, (5) family functioning, (6) self-identity, and (7) mental health.[1]

Beginning with the HRP trajectory, nearly all individuals assigned to the HRP trajectory were male participants. It was also extremely rare for the HRP trajectory to include persons from a non-Indigenous minority ethnic group. Nearly two-thirds of the HRP trajectory included persons with a history of hard drug use. By comparison, just under 50% of persons in the AL trajectory had a history of hard drug use. The HRP trajectory's high rate of convictions in adolescence mirrored its high self-reported offending versatility in adolescence. The HRP group averaged a significantly higher number of different types of self-reported offenses compared to the AL trajectory. The HRP trajectory also averaged a significantly higher level of family dysfunction (e.g., alcohol problems, drug problems, experience of physical abuse, experience of sexual abuse, criminal record, mental health issues) compared to the AL trajectory. About three quarters of the HRP trajectory were placed in foster care in adolescence compared to 50% of the AL trajectory.

The SRP trajectory averaged a significantly greater number of school behavior problems, a significantly higher number of different types of self-reported offenses, and a significantly higher number of different self-reported mental health concerns compared to the AL trajectory. Foster care placement was also higher in this trajectory compared to the AL trajectory.

The EOFD trajectory was more likely to include male participants compared to the AL trajectory. The EOFD trajectory averaged a significantly higher number of different types of self-reported offenses compared to the AL trajectory. The EOFD trajectory also included the highest proportion of

Table 5.4 Association between participant characteristics and offending trajectories through full adulthood (n = 826)

	Offending trajectories (ages 12–29)				
	AL (*n* = 342) *M (SD) / n (%)*	*EOFD* (*n* = 141) *M (SD) / n (%)*	*SRP* (*n* = 162) *M (SD) / n (%)*	*HRP* (*n* = 181) *M (SD) / n (%)*	χ^2/F, *df*, *p*, φ/η
Demographics					
Gender					
Male Participants	236 (69.0%)	119 (84.4%)	122 (75.3%)	176 (97.2%)	χ^2 [3] = 60.8, $p < .001$, $\varphi_c = 0.27$
Ethnicity					
White	179 (56.6%)	88 (64.4%)	85 (56.0%)	107 (61.6%)	χ^2 [6] = 37.53 $p < .001$, $\varphi = 0.16$
Indigenous	68 (21.5%)	35 (25.2%)	49 (32.0%)	59 (34.3%)	
Non-Indigenous Minority	69 (21.8%)	14 (10.4%)	19 (12.0%)	7 (4.1%)	
School Functioning					
School Behavioral Problems	5.95 (4.36)[c]	6.23 (4.27)	7.55 (4.29)[a]	6.72 (3.98)	F[553] = 3.64, $p = .013$, $\eta = 0.02$
Substance Use					
Substance Use Versatility	4.63 (2.25)	4.70 (2.38)	5.11 (2.24)	5.07 (2.10)	F[743] = 2.26, $p = .082$, $\eta = 0.01$
Hard Drug User	144 (46.6%)	61 (46.9%)	82 (58.2%)	103 (62.8%)	χ^2 [3] = 14.72 $p = .002$, $\varphi = 0.14$
Self-Reported Offending					
Offending Versatility	4.12 (3.49)[b,c,d]	5.39 (3.11)[a]	5.38 (3.35)[a]	5.27 (3.02)[a]	F[601] = 6.67, $p < .001$, $\eta = 0.03$

Family					
Family Dysfunction	3.18 (2.85)[d]	3.92 (2.80)	3.66 (3.36)	4.03 (3.16)[a]	$F[601] = 3.38$, $p = .018$, $\eta = 0.01$
Foster Care Placement	48 (50.0%)	34 (79.1%)	39 (63.9%)	41 (71.2%)	$\chi^2[3] = 11.99$ $p = .007$, $\varphi = 0.21$
Identity					
Positive Self-Identity	72.45 (9.75)	69.73 (9.97)	72.16 (9.73)	70.31 (10.27)	$F[711] = 3.23$, $p = .022$, $\eta = 0.01$
Positive "Other-Defined" Identity	67.44 (12.24)	63.87 (13.59)	66.65 (11.70)	64.71 (13.15)	$F[676] = 3.03$, $p = .029$, $\eta = 0.01$
Mental Health					
Total Mental Health Problems	1.54 (2.14)[c]	1.82 (1.98)	2.22 (2.33)[a]	1.99 (2.13)	$F[580] = 2.84$, $p = .037$, $\eta = 0.02$

a Significantly different from AL
b Significantly different from EOFD
c Significantly different from SRP
d Significantly different from HRP.

Notes: The Bonferroni correction used to interpret significant post-hoc differences in self-identity did not reveal any significant differences in identity between particular trajectories. φ = phi effect size. η = eta squared effect size. There are missing data on participant characteristics (see Chapter 3). AL = adolescence limited conviction trajectory; EOFD = early onset-fast desistance conviction trajectory; SRP = slow rising persistent conviction trajectory; HRP = high-rate persistent conviction trajectory.

participants who were placed in foster care during adolescence. Finally, the EOFD trajectory averaged the lowest scores on each measure of positive identity.

In sum, not only were CPO trajectories different from the AL trajectory, but they also differed from the AL trajectory in unique ways (e.g., hard drug use for the HRP trajectory, mental health concerns and school behavior problems for the SRP trajectory, identity for the EOFD trajectory). The three CPO trajectories also shared some similarities, including high levels of self-reported offending versatility and a history of foster care placement.

One of the robust findings from research using ISVYOS data was that foster care was especially informative of CPO (see Yang et al., 2017, 2020). To better understand *why* foster care was statistically related to offending, we asked a subsample of Cohort II (n = 120) open-ended questions about whether foster care placement influenced their involvement in crime. Of the participants we interviewed, only 28.6% answered "yes". Some described foster care as a break from their "real world" (e.g., substance abuse, abusive parents, homelessness), others indicated that they were involved in criminal behavior well-before their placement in foster care. Indeed, three quarters of participants indicated that they were placed in foster care after justice system involvement and 60% indicated that they were placed in foster care *because* of their justice system involvement. However, at least some youth had particularly negative reflections on their foster care experience. One participant said that their foster parents "fucked up my life and put me on pills (Ritalin)". Another noted that "in foster care I was living with other youth who were criminals and they taught me things and now I'm a criminal." Other participants explained that traumatic events that precipitated their placement in care were responsible for their offending. For example, one youth indicated that the death of their mother resulted in being placed into the care of MCFD at age nine and it was the death of their mother that really impacted their justice system involvement. In sum, for certain individuals, foster care appeared to directly influence their justice system involvement. For others, traumatic events that resulted in foster care placement influenced their criminal behavior. The findings reported here reflect the foster care experiences of incarcerated youth and should not be generalized to the foster care experiences of youth more broadly.

Summary

This chapter described the nature of conviction trajectories, including CPO conviction trajectories (i.e., the intersection of frequent and persistent offending), for ISVYOS participants followed through different phases of adulthood. We identified two meta-trajectories. One was associated with AL offending or extremely low levels of offending in adulthood, the latter of which may represent individuals who were associated with an AL-type path but experienced snares in adulthood. The second meta-trajectory was associated with CPO. Importantly, there was heterogeneity in CPO trajectories. CPO could be characterized by (a) an explosive pattern of convictions during adolescence that quickly decreased thereafter (e.g., the EOFD trajectory); (b) a more constant and stable pattern of convictions from adolescence through the late 20s (e.g., the SRP trajectory), (c) an early onset of convictions that continued at a high rate into the late 20s followed by a slow decline (e.g., the EOSD trajectory); or (d) a constantly high pattern of convictions throughout adolescence and adulthood, irrespective of multiple contacts with the justice system and lengthy periods of incarceration (e.g., the HRP trajectory). Desistance and persistence were not mutually exclusive parameters for this sample because individuals were involved in such a high rate of convictions in adolescence that their desistance process extended across multiple stages of adulthood. That is, we saw declines in convictions that began in emerging adulthood (e.g., EOFD and EOSD trajectories), but participants associated with these patterns were still active throughout later stages of adulthood. This type of pattern may be less common in community-based studies where the process of desistance is shorter because peak levels of offending are not as high.

Chronic offending and CPO do not describe the same pattern of offending (see Table 5.2) and we also do not think that CPO means just one thing. While it is important to avoid the reification of trajectories, there is at least some evidence that CPO can manifest through trajectories that can be distinguished across different criminal career parameters and vary in shape, especially in adulthood (see Figure 5.6).

The persistence and frequency aspects of CPO can be underestimated when looking only at observed convictions. Figure 5.5 shows that expected convictions (i.e., the number of convictions expected if a participant was free

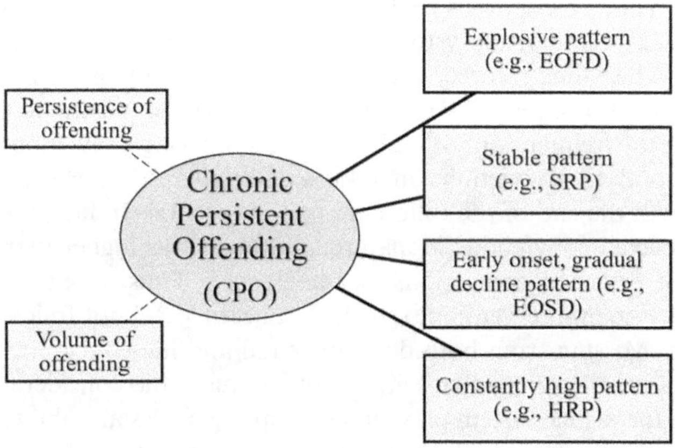

Figure 5.6 Variations in the nature of chronic and persistent offending.
Notes: Volume and persistence of offending define CPO, but the interaction between these two paramaeters can lead to multiple different trajectory patterns.

in the community for an entire year of age and not incarcerated) can be upwards of ten times higher in a given year compared to observed convictions. Justice system involvement is typically thought of as an *indicator* of CPO, but our analyses showed that justice system involvement characterized by lengthy periods of incarceration masks a person's involvement in CPO.

Confusion can develop when comparing CPO trajectories across studies that use different samples (e.g., community versus justice-involved), that include boys only or boys and girls, that define offending in different ways (e.g., self-report versus official offending, arrest versus convictions), that have different follow-up periods, that use different analytic strategies, or that do or do not account for exposure time. As such, different conclusions can easily be made depending on the study interpreted. This has perhaps contributed to variations in the description of CPO trajectories and differences in the types of conclusions drawn about common characteristics of persons associated with CPO trajectories. Table 5.5 highlights inter-study variation in the prevalence and nature of CPO. Criminal career researchers should be explicit with respect to what is meant by terms like *CPO*, not just in terms of how it varies from chronic offending as an indicator of a single parameter (i.e., frequency), but also in terms of how CPO trajectories are commonly given similar names in different studies (e.g., HRP, high-level chronic) even though inspection of these trajectories shows that they look quite different across studies. A trajectory labeled 'high-level chronic' in one study might equate with "low rate offending" in another.

For the HRP trajectory identified in the mature adulthood analysis, convictions begin in early adolescence and peak at the end of adolescence but nevertheless remain relatively high (i.e., approximately two convictions per year) through the early 30s. The justice system was aware that individuals in the HRP trajectory had a long history of frequent and serious offending. Accordingly, persons from the HRP trajectory received lengthy custody sentences. That convictions peaked in adolescence was at least partly due to the lack of opportunity to offend at a similarly high rate in adulthood. Indeed, when time incarcerated was considered in the measurement of expected convictions, the HRP conviction trajectory demonstrated a threefold increase in the frequency of offending when comparing convictions in emerging adulthood to convictions in adolescence; this difference remained stable through the end of the follow-up period (age 35). In fact, the peak number of expected convictions in mature adulthood was higher than the peak number of expected convictions in adolescence. Thus, when accounting for justice system intervention, the HRP trajectory did not follow the age-crime curve. Missing from both developmental and life-course theoretical perspectives on change and stability in offending is the consideration of the role that the justice system plays in interrupting a person's ability to remain involved in crime at a high rate. While our examination of conviction trajectories through mature adulthood meant that our follow-up period was 35 years shorter than the longest follow-up period for

Table 5.5 The definition of CPO and its prevalence across major longitudinal studies compared to the ISVYOS

Study	*Measurement of CPO trajectory*	*Length of follow-up*	*Description*	*CPO prevalence in original study*	*CPO Prevalence in the ISVYOS (Ages 12–35)*
CSDD (Nagin et al., 1995).	SPGM analysis of convictions.	Ages 10–32.	One CPO trajectory (12.9%; n = 52) described as "high level chronic" that peaked at 1.7 convictions during a 2-year window (ages 18–19). Another CPO trajectory (10.4%; n = 42) described as "low level chronic" that peaked at 0.4 convictions during a 2-year window (ages 20–21).	23.3% total; n = 94.	HRP trajectory (17.1%, n = 69) that peaked at 3.5 convictions and EOSD trajectory (14.1%, n = 57) that peaked at ~6 convictions (31.2% total; n = 126).
UJD Study (Laub et al., 1998).	SPGM analysis of arrests.	Ages 7–32.	One CPO trajectory (2.8%; n = 11) that peaked at approximately 3 arrests and another (25.7%; n = 95) that peaked at 1.25 arrests.	27.5% total; n = 106.	HRP trajectory (17.1%, n = 69) that peaked at 3.5 convictions and EOSD trajectory (14.1%, n = 57) that peaked at ~6 convictions (31.2% total; n = 126).
UJD Study (Sampson & Laub, 2003).	SPGM analysis of arrests.	Ages 7–70.	CPO trajectory that peaked at approximately 2.5 arrests.	~3.2% (n = 15).	HRP trajectory (17.1%, n = 69) that peaked at 3.5 convictions.
Pathways to Desistance Study (Monahan et al., 2013).	SPGM of self-reported offending versatility.	Ages 14–25.	One CPO trajectory with approximately six different self-reported offenses at each year of age from 14–25.	7.5% (n = ~82).	HRP trajectory (17.1%, n = 69) that averaged approximately two convictions at each year of age from 12–35.

(*Continued*)

Table 5.5 (Continued)

Study	*Measurement of CPO trajectory*	*Length of follow-up*	*Description*	*CPO prevalence in original study*	*CPO Prevalence in the ISVYOS (Ages 12–35)*
CYA Project (Piquero et al., 2001).	SPGM of arrests.	Ages 18–33.	One CPO trajectory defined by continued arrests at a high rate between ages 18–33 that peaked at approximately 7.5 arrests.	7.1% (n = ~19).	HRP trajectory (17.1%, n = 69) that peaked at 3.5 convictions.
CCLCS (Blokland et al., 2005).	SPGM of convictions.	Ages 12–72.	One CPO trajectory defined as high rate-persistent (1.6%; n = ~5) and one trajectory defined as moderate-rate desisters (5.7%; n = ~17). The HRP group averaged 127.6 convictions and the moderate-rate desisters averaged 32.9 convictions.	7.3% (n = ~22).	HRP trajectory (17.1%, n = 69) averaged 51.52 convictions. EOSD trajectory (14.1%; n = 57) averaged 52.53 convictions.
Harreveld Study (van der Geest et al., 2009).	SPGM of convictions.	Ages 12–32.	One CPO trajectory defined as high-frequency chronic (5.9%; n = 16) that averaged 77 convictions, and another defined as high-frequency desister (15.2%; n = 41) that averaged 26.9 convictions.	21.1% (n = 57).	HRP trajectory (17.1%, n = 69) averaged 51.52 convictions. EOSD trajectory (14.1%; n = 57) averaged 52.53 convictions.

Notes: CPO = Chronic and persistent offending. CSDD = Cambridge Study in Delinquent Development. UJD = Unraveling Juvenile Delinquency. CYA = California Youth Authority. CCLCS = Criminal Career and Life Course Study. SPGM = semi-parametric group-based modeling. HRP = high rate persistent. EOSD = early onset-slow desistance.

participants from the UJD Study, there is at least some evidence that there is a group of individuals in the ISVYOS whose offending remains high and stable for multiple decades.

The second purpose of the current chapter was to investigate claims made by Sampson and Laub (2005b) that "we cannot predict long-term trajectories of offending … the childhood (developmental) paradigm cannot provide the answer" (p. 75). First, we think that developmental criminology is more than just prediction. The hallmark of developmental criminology is intervention. Second, prediction does not need to be equated with destiny. We do not believe that there are certain risk factors that dictate with 100% certainty that someone will be associated with, for example, the HRP conviction trajectory. However, there are certain risk/needs factors in adolescence that are associated with this trajectory, and even if not associated with this trajectory, they may nevertheless influence other severe forms of disadvantage (e.g., early mortality, adult substance use addiction or mental health problems) and therefore are worthy of attention and intervention. Developmental criminology research is not conducted in a vacuum. Youth in the study participated in evidence-based intervention and treatment programs that have been shown to help reduce offending (e.g., cognitive behavioral therapy).

When compared against the AL trajectory, several characteristics in childhood/adolescence were associated with the EOFD, SRP, and HRP trajectories. Characteristics that distinguished membership in these two trajectories from the AL trajectory came from different domains of functioning (e.g., substance use, family dysfunction, school behavior problems, mental health). That characteristics in childhood/adolescence were associated with the HRP trajectory (and others not characterized by AL offending) does not mean that individuals with such characteristics are locked into this trajectory. There is a balance to be struck between (a) ignoring the importance of characteristics in childhood/adolescence based on the assumption that random life events and human agency will alter such individuals' trajectory and (b) using such characteristics to make claims about the need for deterrence, punishment, and selective incapacitation. While imperfect, the Canadian model focuses on the rehabilitation of individuals involved in serious and violent offenses through, for example, establishing safe, secure, and treatment-focused custody centers that use trauma-informed practices to ensure youth are in the right climate to benefit from interventions, including those that focus on a person's strengths and not just their risk factors (Penner et al., 2011). The RNR model may not be appropriate for all incarcerated youth, especially in Canada, because of their multi-need risk factor profiles. This model may be more appropriate for youth characterized by an AL pattern of offending. This model emphasizes cognitive-behavioral aspects of offending (e.g., Andrews et al., 2006). It is unclear how this model accounts for CPO trajectories where trauma and mental health factors play a key role.

One risk factor especially important to CPO trajectories is foster care placement (also see Yang et al., 2017, 2020). Our conviction trajectories reflect the justice system's response to the behavior of ISVYOS participants. MCFD is responsible for the administration of both the youth justice system and child welfare services, including foster care. In some ways, placement in foster care is another way in which the justice system responded to ISVYOS participants. Youth who are dually involved in the justice system and child welfare system come from extremely disadvantaged circumstances at the earliest stages of the life-course. Justice system sanctions include telling the young person that they must reside in a particular group-home or foster home as part of the conditions of their release from custody. In effect, the foster care system *can* be used as another arm of the justice system. Persons associated with CPO trajectories are faced with life adversities at a very early age and the extent of their adversities leads them on a path where they are known to the child welfare and youth justice systems. The tendency for such individuals to be associated with CPO trajectories is a testament to the challenges that these systems have in coordinating their efforts to address the multiple needs that these individuals present with.

Over time, there is both continuity and change in convictions for this sample. There is also variability in the nature/shape of CPO trajectories. Heterogeneity *within* CPO is not something that has been given a great deal of consideration by the DLC paradigm. Can risk/needs factors in childhood/adolescence as well as adult social outcomes help make sense of this variability? The next three chapters focus on better understanding: (a) what happens before official justice system involvement (Chapter 6), (b) the long-term predictive validity of psychopathy as an indicator of a childhood/adolescence propensity for offending (Chapter 7), and (c) why desistance happens for some but not others (Chapter 8).

Note

1 See Chapter 3 for a description of these measures. Measures not described in Chapter 3 include aggression, which reflected participants' endorsement of 12 aggressive behaviors of varying levels of severity, from throwing objects and minor fistfights to using weapons while fighting, group fights, and beating up others without reason. Mental health needs represented the sum of 14 different types of mental health issues that participants endorsed as applicable to them (e.g., depression, anxiety, suicidal ideation, conduct disorder, learning disability).

6 The development of antisocial behavior among serious and violent youth

Introduction

So far, we have focused on participants' official criminal behavior. There are many hypotheses about the backgrounds of youth involved in serious and violent crimes. To some, these are vulnerable youth who fell through the cracks of the system (Gonzales, 2011). For others, these are youth who have been labeled in such a way as to promote their serious and violent criminal behavior (Bernburg et al., 2006). Some view these youth as "psychopaths-in-the-making" (Lynam, 1998). To begin to understand the accuracy of these hypotheses requires looking beyond patterns of convictions.

Developmental and propensity theorists alike reminded the field of criminology that criminal behavior is just one element of a person's broader pattern of antisocial behavior (e.g., Loeber & Hay, 1994; Paternoster & Brame, 2000). Propensity theorists and developmentalists agree that antisocial behavior is more than just criminal behavior and is especially more than just those criminal behaviors that are detected by police and adjudicated by the courts. Antisocial behavior consists of different types of rule-breaking transgressions, occurs in different contexts, and manifests in different ways at different age-stages. Where developmentalists and propensity theorists differ is with respect to how antisocial behavior manifests. For propensity theorists, crime and analogous behavior are manifestations of a general antisocial tendency (Gottfredson & Hirschi, 1990). For developmentalists, there are various patterns of antisocial behavior (e.g., Patterson, 1993). For example, some individuals may have a tendency covert or secretive behavior whereas others have a tendency towards overt or aggressive antisocial behavior (Loeber & Hay, 1994).

Understanding the development of antisocial behavior requires attention to when the behavior develops, where it develops, and what type of behavior manifests. Will behavior at certain times, in certain contexts, or of a certain type, help make sense of the pathway from minor forms of antisocial behavior to serious and violent offending? From a developmental perspective, looking at broader patterns of antisocial behavior can help make sense of the contexts and motivations influencing criminal behavior. Antisocial behavior that manifests across various social contexts may have important implications for whether social control mechanisms (e.g., family, schooling) will be useful for influencing desistance. Is there a path from early childhood behavior to a CPO trajectory, and if so, what does this path look like? While research has addressed the nature of antisocial behavior for over 200 years (see Le Blanc, 2012), developmental criminology formalized the study of the type, evolution, and manifestations of antisocial behavior (Le Blanc & Fréchette, 1989; Loeber & Le Blanc, 1990).

Like criminal career research, developmental criminology takes stock of patterns of offending over the life-course. However, developmental criminology is also interested in broader patterns of antisocial behavior and thus examines rule violations and other behaviors not necessarily defined as criminal. Compared to criminal career research, developmental criminology is more precise about the interrelationship between different types of antisocial behavior and how this behavior progresses over the life-course. Developmentalists identified four broad categories of antisocial behavior: authority conflict, covert, overt, and reckless (Le Blanc & Bouthillier, 2003; Loeber & Hay, 1994). Authority conflict behaviors include engaging in stubborn behavior (e.g., refusing to switch tasks), being defiant and disobedient (e.g., disturbing classrooms, refusing to follow rules at home), and avoiding authority (e.g., skipping school). Covert behaviors include minor delinquency (e.g., shoplifting), property damage (e.g., vandalizing a school), and moderate to serious delinquency (e.g., stealing a vehicle). Overt behaviors include minor aggression (e.g., hitting others), physical fighting (e.g., schoolyard fights), and violence (e.g., robbery, instrumental aggression). Reckless behaviors put the individual or others in danger (e.g., substance use, driving without a license). The examination of these patterns of antisocial behavior begins at the activation stage in the progression of antisocial behavior (Loeber & Le Blanc, 1990). Activation starts with the onset of behavior. The timing of onset is informative of how individuals progress through this stage, which also includes the degree to which behavior becomes more frequent, persists over a longer time period, and includes a greater variety of antisocial/criminal behavior.

Contribution to developmental criminology

Intake interviews with Cohort II participants included an English adaptation of Le Blanc et al.'s (1996) MASPAQ,[1] which measures self-reported authority conflict, covert, overt, and reckless antisocial behaviors. It also includes questions about the timing of such behaviors and whether the behaviors were perpetrated in different contexts (e.g., behaviors at school, at home). The self-report aspect of this instrument allowed for the examination of participants' antisocial behavior from their own perspective during adolescence. This perspective is important given it is a time in which the young person demonstrates autonomy from parents and teachers.

One problem with the cross-sectional measurement of self-reported antisocial behavior is that youth who were older at the time of the interview had more opportunity to engage in different behaviors under examination. We therefore focused only on participants who were age 16 or 17 at the time they were interviewed. This accounted for 60% of the Cohort II sample (n = 574) and included 478 boys and 96 girls. Over half the sample were White, 32.9% were Indigenous, and 14.7% self-identified as a non-Indigenous minority group (e.g., Black, Asian, South East Asian). Participants were asked about (a) lifetime engagement in certain behaviors, (b) the age of onset of such behaviors, and (c) for certain types of behavior, the age at which they last engaged in such behavior (i.e., age of offset). Behavioral dimensions referred to two scales measuring antisocial behavior perpetrated in a specific context (school behavioral problems, home behavioral problems) and four scales measuring manifestations of different types of antisocial behavior (substance use, aggression, self-reported delinquency (SRD), and self-reported offending (SRO)).

To understand the broader contexts that facilitate the emergence of involvement in serious and violent behavior, ISVYOS data were used to address the following questions:

1. What is the prevalence of different antisocial behaviors across different dimensions? Are certain behaviors more likely to manifest before age 12 or from age 12 onwards?
2. Are different antisocial behavior dimensions correlated?
3. What is the correlation between antisocial behavior before age 12 and from age 12 onward?
4. Are there different latent profiles within a given dimension of antisocial behavior? For example, do some individuals tend to be involved in covert types of antisocial behavior and others involved in overt types of antisocial behavior?
5. What is the relationship between latent profiles of self-reported antisocial behavior and CPO trajectories?
6. What does antisocial and criminal behavior versatility look like in a single case?

Prevalence of antisocial behavior across different dimensions

This section described the prevalence of antisocial behavior across different domains and settings. For some domains, ISVYOS participants were asked to self-report both the age of onset of the behavior as well as the age of offset of the behavior. This allowed for an inspection of whether certain behaviors were more or less likely to be endorsed at different age-stages. Looking at raw values of age of onset means that individuals who did not endorse a particular behavior were not included in the description of the average age of onset. To avoid loss of participants, age of onset was dichotomized to indicate whether a participant did or did not endorse a particular behavior before age 12. Age 12 was used as the cut-point because this is the age of criminal responsibility in Canada.

Self-reported school behavioral problems

Participants were asked about 21 antisocial behaviors specifically occurring at school (see Figure 6.1). Participants were also asked to identify the age of onset of each behavior. Participants averaged 3.52 (*SD* = 3.16) school behavioral problems before age 12 and 10.12 (*SD* = 3.69) school behavioral problems over their lifetime (i.e., at the time of their interview at age 16 or 17). Nearly 100% of the sample endorsed their involvement in authority conflict behaviors like skipping school and being impolite towards teachers. The behaviors most common over participants' lifetimes (up to age 17) were not also most common prior to age 12, which was in line with developmental criminology descriptions of escalation in the severity of antisocial behavior and developmental psychology descriptions of heterotypic continuity (i.e., the latent trait of antisocial behavior will manifest in different ways at different ages). Over 50% of participants had been in trouble for disturbing their class before age 12, but the prevalence of disturbing the classroom by the time participants reached age 17 was just 70%. In other words, if individuals were not in trouble for disturbing their class before age 12, it was unlikely that this behavior would emerge at all. On the other hand, skipping class and using drugs at school was extremely rare prior to age 12 but particularly common by the time sample members were age 17.

Self-reported substance use

Participants were asked about their use of nine substances (see Figure 6.2): alcohol, marijuana, ecstasy, hallucinogens, cocaine, crack cocaine, heroin, crystal methamphetamine, and the non-prescribed use of prescription pills. Participants averaged using 0.90 (*SD* = 1.01) different substances prior to age 12 and 5.43 (*SD* = 2.04) different substances by the time they were as old as 17. Nearly all members of the sample reported using alcohol and marijuana. Drugs like cocaine and ecstasy were also common. Exactly half the sample used at least one of crack cocaine, heroin, or crystal meth by age 17.

Self-reported home behavioral problems

Endorsement of each of 19 different home behavioral problems required that the participant be punished by their parent for that behavior (Figure 6.3). Behaviors included authority conflict problems such as not listening to parents, covert behavioral problems such as stealing the family

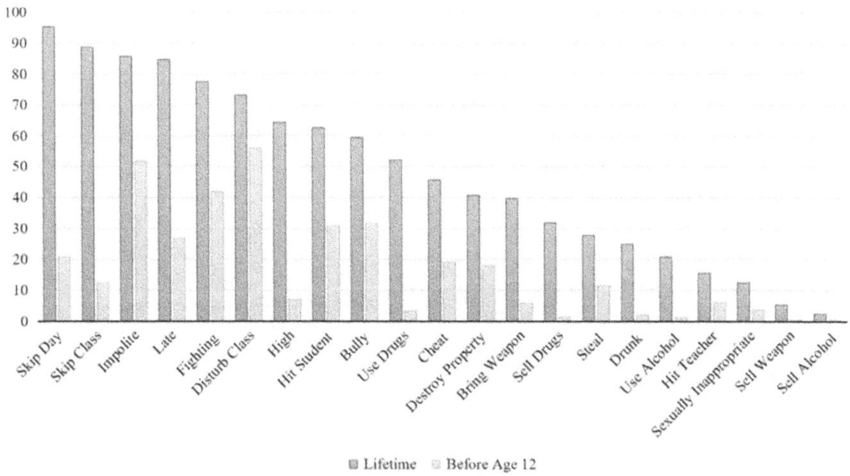

Figure 6.1 Prevalence of self-reported school behavioral problems.
Notes: Lifetime prevalence reflects an endorsement of behavior between birth and age 17. The y-axis indicates the percent of the sample endorsing a particular behavior.

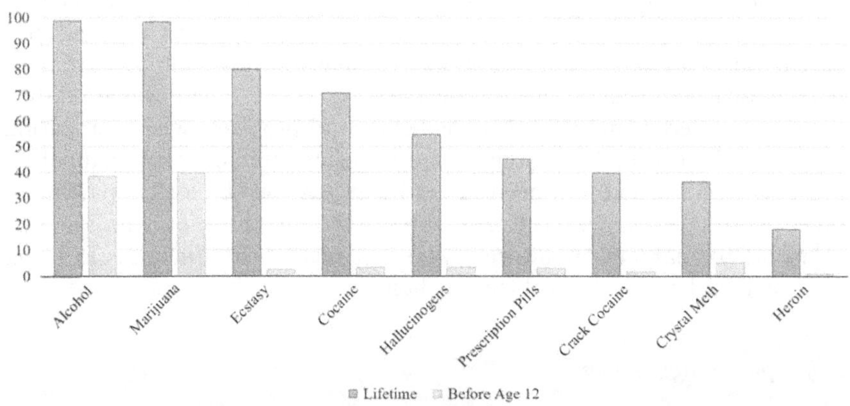

Figure 6.2 Prevalence of self-reported substance use.
Notes: Lifetime prevalence reflects an endorsement of behavior between birth and age 17. The y-axis indicates the percent of the sample endorsing a particular behavior.

car, and overt behavioral problems such as fighting with siblings. On average, participants endorsed 11.54 (*SD* = 5.12) of these home behavioral problems. There was relatively little variation in most behaviors; approximately half of all items were endorsed by 65–80% of the sample. Some

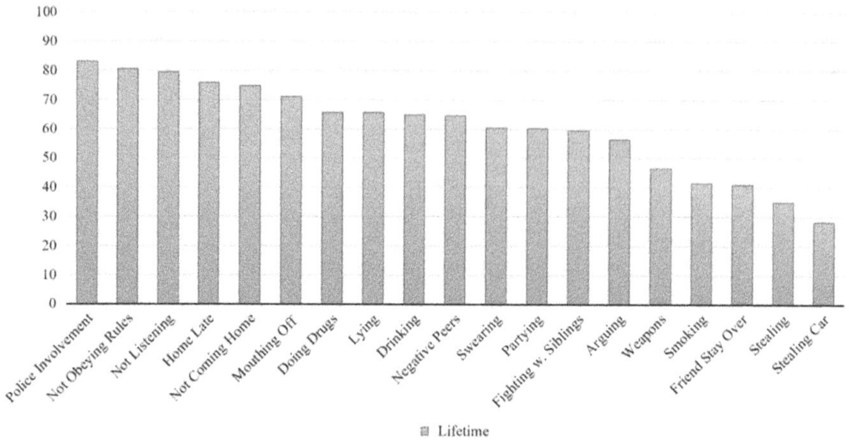

Figure 6.3 Prevalence of self-reported home behavioral problems.
Notes: Lifetime prevalence reflects an endorsement of behavior between birth and age 17. The y-axis indicates the percent of the sample endorsing a particular behavior.

behaviors like smoking may have been less typical, not because smoking was rare for the sample, but because participants were not punished for such behavior. It was possible that individuals were involved in an even greater number of problem behaviors at home, but because of lax or neglectful parents or caregivers they did not endorse items in this scale because their parents or caregivers did not punish these behaviors. There was no difference in the average number of home behavioral problems when comparing those who had or had not been placed in foster care and when comparing those who had or had not been raised by at least one biological parent. In other words, differences between participants in terms of who was responsible for parental monitoring were not related to differences in being punished for behavioral problems at home.

Self-reported aggression

The MASPAQ included items measuring various forms of aggression, from throwing objects and minor fist fights to using weapons while fighting, group fights, and beating up others without reason (Figure 6.4). Participants were also asked about their age of onset for each behavior. Before age 12, participants averaged 2.07 (SD = 2.37) different types of aggressive behavior. Approximately 65% of the sample endorsed at least one aggressive behavior prior to age 12. At the time of their interview at age 16 or 17, participants averaged 7.22 (SD = 3.10) different types of aggressive behavior. Bullying was among the most common types of aggression perpetrated prior to age

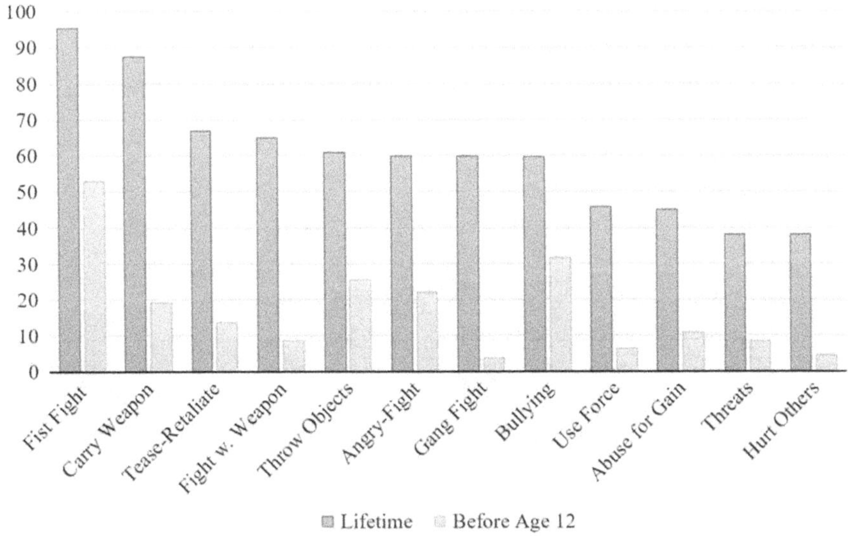

Figure 6.4 Prevalence of self-reported aggressive behaviors.
Notes: Lifetime prevalence reflects an endorsement of behavior between birth and age 17. The y-axis indicates the percent of the sample endorsing a particular behavior.

12 but was one of the least prevalent types of aggression overall. Like disrupting the classroom, bullying appeared to be a behavior that, if not initiated by childhood, was unlikely to emerge in the teenage years. Involvement in gang fights were extremely rare prior to age 12 but 60% of the sample reported involvement in this type of aggression by the time they were age 16 or 17.

Self-reported delinquency

SRD included 15 items mostly specific to the childhood or adolescence age-stages and often not applicable to adulthood (see Figure 6.5), such as vandalizing schools, taking cars without permission, sneaking into movie theatres, and using a fake ID. In addition to asking about age of onset, participants were also asked about the age of offset (i.e., the age that they last engaged in each behavior). Prior to age 12, participants averaged 1.88 (*SD* = 2.40) different forms of delinquency. From age 12 onwards they averaged 9.13 (*SD* = 3.43) different forms of delinquency. Over the full follow-up period the sample averaged 9.28 (*SD* = 3.41) different types of SRD. Property-related delinquency reflecting covert antisocial behavior was most common before age 12 and from age 12 onward. Taking vehicles without permission and using a fake ID were especially atypical in

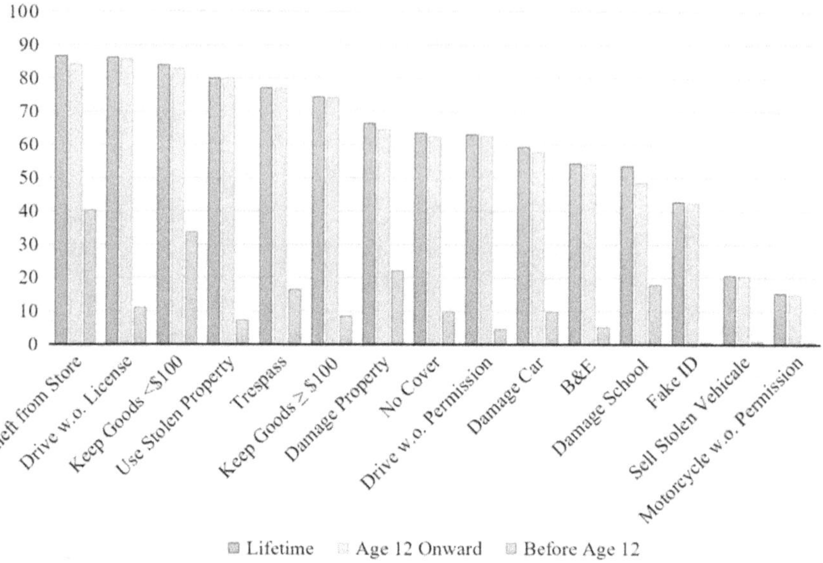

Figure 6.5 Prevalence of self-reported delinquency.

Notes: Lifetime prevalence reflects an endorsement of behavior between birth and age 17. Age 12 onward prevalence reflects an endorsement of behavior between ages 12–17. B&E = Break and Enter. The y-axis indicates the percent of the sample endorsing a particular behavior.

childhood. Heterotypic continuity tended to be one-directional; certain behaviors were extremely rare before age 12 yet common from age 12 onward. However, we did not find behaviors that were common before age 12 yet rare from age 12 onward. This contrasted with, for example, our examination of school behavioral problems that showed that bullying was a more childhood-specific behavioral problem.

Self-reported offending

Participants were asked about 17 different types of SRO (see Figure 6.6), whether detected by police or not. These behaviors included violations of court orders, possession or trafficking of drugs, theft, break and enter, robbery, various forms of assault, different types of sexual assault, and different types of homicide. Due to low base rates, we aggregated all forms of sexual assault (sexual assault with threats, sexual assault with physical force) and all forms of homicide (attempted homicide, manslaughter, criminal negligence causing death, murder). Typically, a strength of self-reported measures of offending is that they help account for the dark figure of crime. However, this may not be true for certain crime types that are especially stigmatizing, like sexual offenses (Lussier et al., 2020a). Only four

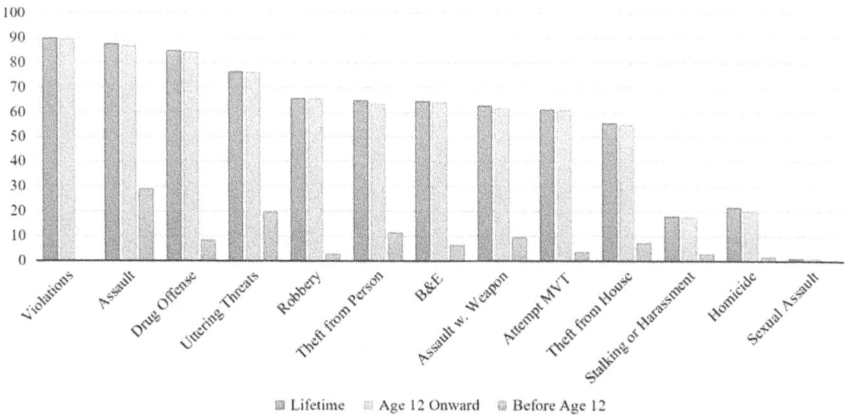

Figure 6.6 Prevalence of self-reported offending.

Notes: Lifetime prevalence reflects an endorsement of behavior between birth and age 17. Age 12 onward prevalence reflects an endorsement of behavior between ages 12–17. B&E = break and enter. MVT = motor vehicle theft. The y-axis indicates the percent of the sample endorsing a particular behavior.

participants self-reported involvement in a sexual offense, yet 30 participants (5.9% of the sample; 6.7% of all boys) incurred an official charge for a sexual offense between ages 12–17 (also see Stouthamer-Loeber et al., 2008).

Participants were asked about both the age of onset and offset of each offense. Prior to age 12, participants averaged 1.00 (*SD* = 1.55) different types of criminal behavior. From age 12 onward they averaged 7.48 (*SD* = 2.77) different types of criminal behavior. In total, participants averaged 7.57 (*SD* = 2.75) different types of criminal behavior by the time of their interview at age 16 or 17. Prior to age 12, the two most common types of SRO were assault and uttering threats. Drug offenses, robbery, and motor vehicle theft were three examples of SRO that were rare before age 12 but relatively common from age 12 onward.

Correlations between antisocial behavior dimensions

This section addressed questions about the correlation *between* different dimensions of antisocial behavior as well as questions regarding correlations *within* a single dimension of antisocial behavior between different age-stages. In Table 6.1, correlation coefficients above the diagonal are specific to boys. Coefficients below the diagonal are specific to girls. For boys, all dimensions of antisocial behavior were significantly and positively correlated with each other. For girls, significant correlations across all antisocial behavior dimensions were slightly less common. For example, for girls, home behavioral problems were not significantly correlated with measures of school

Table 6.1 Bivariate correlations between different measures of self-reported antisocial behavior

	(1)	*(2)*	*(3)*	*(4)*	*(5)*	*(6)*	*(7)*	*(8)*	*(9)*	(10)	*(11)*	*(12)*	*(13)*
SBP Through Age 17 (1)	-	.550***	.349***	.256***	.348***	.628***	.420***	.589***	.292***	.586***	.567***	.363***	.563***
SBP Before Age 12 (2)	.608***		.261***	.441***	.199***	.451***	.658***	.411***	.526***	.390***	.382***	.579***	.368***
Substance Use Through Age 17 (3)	.412***	.313**	-	.310***	.221***	.294***	.176***	.381***	.209***	.382***	.416***	.216***	.412***
Substance Use Before Age 12 (4)	.354***	.572***	.375***	-	.097*	.198***	.398***	.260***	.431***	.238***	.230***	.433***	.222***
HBP Through Age 17 (5)	.240*	.049	.217	.057	-	.334***	.192***	.312***	.129*	.310***	.281***	.105*	.295***
Aggression Through Age 17 (6)	.612***	.441***	.362**	.293**	.217	-	.491***	.623***	.348***	.611***	.692***	.363***	.697***
Aggression Before Age 12 (7)	.342**	.540***	.142	.373**	.026	.474***	-	.382***	.569***	.369***	.401***	.695***	.397***
SRD Through Age 17 (8)	.583***	.404***	.479***	.461***	.372**	.547***	.196	-	.403***	.991***	.720***	.336***	.719***
SRD Before Age 12 (9)	.350**	.598***	.181	.562***	-.188	.375**	.642***	.266**	-	.364***	.350***	.659***	.335***
SRD Age 12 Through 17 (10)	.570***	.377**	.469***	.417***	.435***	.530***	.191	.990***	.217	-	.719***	.309***	.720***
SRO Through Age 17 (11)	.595***	.516***	.547***	.385***	.381**	.739***	.316**	.695***	.262**	.676***	-	.388***	.993***
SRO Before Age 12 (12)	.267**	.512***	.111	.377***	-.178	.312**	.676***	-.003	.610***	-.050	.250*	-	.364***
SRO Age 12 Through 17 (13)	.589***	.511***	.558***	.378***	.400***	.724***	.312**	.691***	.234*	.679***	.997***	.226*	-

* $p < .05$
** $p < .01$
*** $p < .001$

Notes: Correlation coefficients above the diagonal are for boys. Correlation coefficients below the diagonal are for girls.
SBP = School behavioral problems; HBP = Home behavioral problems; SRD = Self-reported delinquency; SRO = Self-reported offending.

behavioral problems, substance use, and aggression. For boys, home behavioral problems also had relatively weak, albeit significant, correlations with all other antisocial dimensions. This may have to do with norms, rules, and parental attitudes towards appropriate versus inappropriate behavior. Certain antisocial behaviors may have been unnoticed or overlooked by parents. A rival plausible explanation is that some participants avoided antisocial behavior at home for fear of their parents' coercive responses to their behavior. Of note, the relationship between home behavioral problems and SRO in adolescence was stronger for girls (r = .400) than boys (r = .295). This may relate to observations from Chapter 3 that girls come from significantly more traumatic and difficult family environments and are significantly more likely to leave home before age 12 compared to boys.

There was a strong correlation between the aggression scale and the school behavioral problems scale. It is possible that generally aggressive youth have difficulty with the behavioral constraints of school (e.g., sitting still, following direction, remaining quiet, complying with authority). Such behavior is consistent with clinical descriptions of oppositional defiant disorder and conduct disorder (e.g., Robins, 1991). SRO and SRD tended to be most strongly correlated with each other. Moreover, other antisocial dimensions tended to be most strongly correlated with SRO or SRD. For example, early substance use versatility was most strongly associated with early SRO and SRD, which possibly reflected that at early developmental stages, antisocial behavior of different types (e.g., drug use, delinquency, and offending) is part of a general antisocial tendency (Gottfredson & Hirschi, 1990). The next set of analyses more directly compared propensity theory assertions about the generality of antisocial behavior versus developmental criminology assertions that some individuals confined their antisocial behavior to a certain type (e.g., authority conflict, covert, overt, and reckless behavioral patterns).

Unraveling patterns of antisocial behavior

The aggregate scales examined above obfuscate potential patterns of item endorsement underlying each scale. Items that reflect different forms of authority conflict, covert, overt, and reckless behavior can be found in each scale. Are some individuals characterized by a tendency towards one type of behavior? Are others likely to engage in all forms of such behavior? Latent class analysis (LCA) is useful for identifying qualitatively unique profiles of antisocial behavior (e.g., McCuish et al., 2015a). Aggregate scales ignore different behavioral configurations (e.g., tendency towards behaviors of a similar type). Aggregate scales also rarely weight their items to account for differences in severity. For example, when examining substance use, aggregate scales do not capture the difference between two individuals both using three substances, the first using alcohol, marijuana, and hallucinogens and the second using heroin, crack cocaine, and crystal methamphetamine.

Arguably, these are two different types of substance users with different intervention needs. An aggregate scale does not capture this difference, but person-oriented analyses like LCA are useful in this regard (e.g., Magnusson & Bergman, 1988).

LCA identifies subgroups that are, at least conceptually, composed of individuals with similar scores on the variables used to define the latent classes (Collins & Lanza, 2010). The appropriate number of latent classes is determined by running successive models, beginning with a one class solution, and then comparing changes in model fit. For a given solution, individuals are assigned to the latent class that most closely resembles their own pattern of behavior.[2] Analyses were conducted using PROC LCA 1.2.6 for SAS 9.4. For each figure, the y-axis shows the probability that an individual within a given latent class endorsed the behavior listed on the x-axis. In PROC LCA, missing data are handled via full-information maximum likelihood except in scenarios where a given participant is missing data on all items (Lanza et al., 2015). For the substance use items, two participants had completely missing data (0.3% of the sample). For the home behavioral problem items, 54 participants had completely missing data (9.4% of the sample), likely because of a lack of contact with parents. For the aggression items, 28 participants had completely missing data (4.9% of the sample). For the SRD items, 72 participants had completely missing data (12.5% of the sample). For the SRO items before age 12 and from age 12 onward, 52 participants had completely missing data (9.1% of the sample). Typically, data were missing because the participant did not finish the interview.

Latent profiles of lifetime school behavioral problems

The LCA of school behavioral problems looked at all behavioral problems endorsed over the lifetime at the time of a participant's interview at either age 16 or 17. Rare behaviors that were conceptually similar (e.g., selling weapons, selling alcohol, selling drugs) and commonly endorsed behaviors that were conceptually similar (e.g., skipping class for a day and skipping a single class) were aggregated. The LCA revealed four profiles (see Figure 6.7). Group 1 (19.9% of the sample; "authority conflict behavioral problems") represented individuals involved in only authority conflict behaviors (e.g., skipping school, talking back to teachers). Group 2 (33.3% of the sample; "overt behavioral problems") represented individuals who were involved in authority conflict behavior as well as overt behaviors such as fighting and hitting another student. Group 3 (27.4% of the sample; "substance use behavioral problems") included individuals who were involved in authority conflict behaviors and reckless behavior (e.g., substance use). Group 4 (19.5% of the sample; "versatile behavioral problems") was characterized by high probabilities of authority conflict, substance use, aggressive, and property-related behaviors.

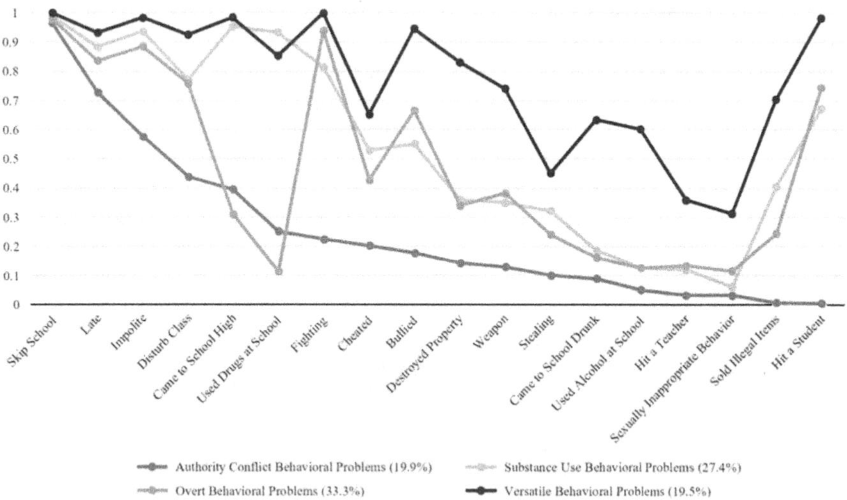

Figure 6.7 Latent class analysis of school behavioral problems through age 17.
Notes: The y-axis represents the probability that a given individual within a given latent class endorsed the behavior indicated on the x-axis

Latent profiles of substance use

The LCA of substance use looked at nine different substances endorsed at the time of a participant's interview at either age 16 or 17. The LCA identified three profiles (see Figure 6.8). Group 1 (19.2% of the sample; "minor use") was characterized by high probabilities of using alcohol and marijuana but low probabilities of having used all other substances. The second group (51.4% of the sample; "recreational drug use") was defined by their use of alcohol and marijuana and also recreational drugs like cocaine and ecstasy. Group 3 (29.4% of the sample; "hard drug use") was characterized by the highest probabilities on all nine substances; 100% of individuals in this group had used at least one of crack cocaine, crystal meth, or heroin (compared to 8.2% of Group 1 and 37.0% of Group 2).

Latent profiles of home behavioral problems

The LCA of home behavioral problems examined whether there were subgroups of individuals who experienced getting into trouble for qualitatively distinct types of behaviors. For this analysis, conceptually similar behaviors of coming home late and not coming home were combined into a single item regarding breaking curfew. Five items were aggregated (not listening to parents, not obeying house rules, mouthing off to parents, swearing, and arguing too much) to create a single indicator of parent-child conflict. Three groups emerged from the LCA (see Figure 6.9). Group

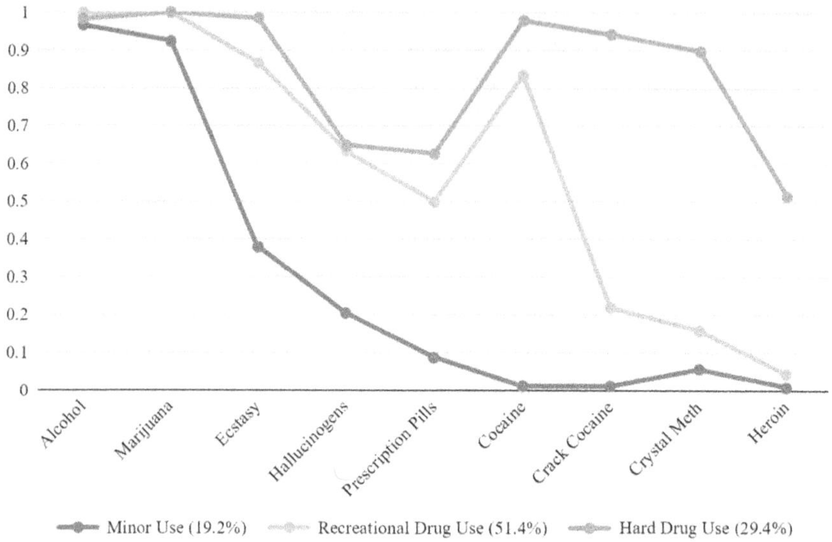

Figure 6.8 Latent class analysis of substance use through age 17.
Notes: The y-axis represents the probability that a given individual within a given latent class endorsed the behavior indicated on the x-axis.

1 (11.2% of the sample; "low family conflict") was associated with a relatively low probability of engaging in any of the home behavioral problems examined. Group 2 (41.0% of the sample; "rule violations") was primarily involved in rule-breaking behaviors, including conflict with parents, getting into trouble with the law, and breaking curfew. Group 3 (47.9% of the sample; "substance use problems") experienced minor conflicts with parents but were also in trouble for drug and alcohol use in the home.

Latent profiles of aggressive behavior

The LCA of aggressive behavior looked at all forms of aggression endorsed at the time of a participant's interview at either age 16 or 17. The LCA revealed four different profiles (see Figure 6.10). Group 1 (18.1% of the sample; "minor aggression") had a high probability of involvement in fist fights but relatively low probabilities of all other aggressive behaviors. Group 2 (39.2% of the sample; "peer-based aggression") was defined by group/gang fights and mutual conflicts with peers (e.g., physically retaliating after being teased). Group 3 (12.5% of the sample; "instrumental aggression") was characterized by instrumental aggression; they tended to bully and abuse others for personal gain. Group 4 (30.2% of the sample; "versatile aggression") was defined by relatively high probabilities of all 12 aggressive behaviors. The versatility of

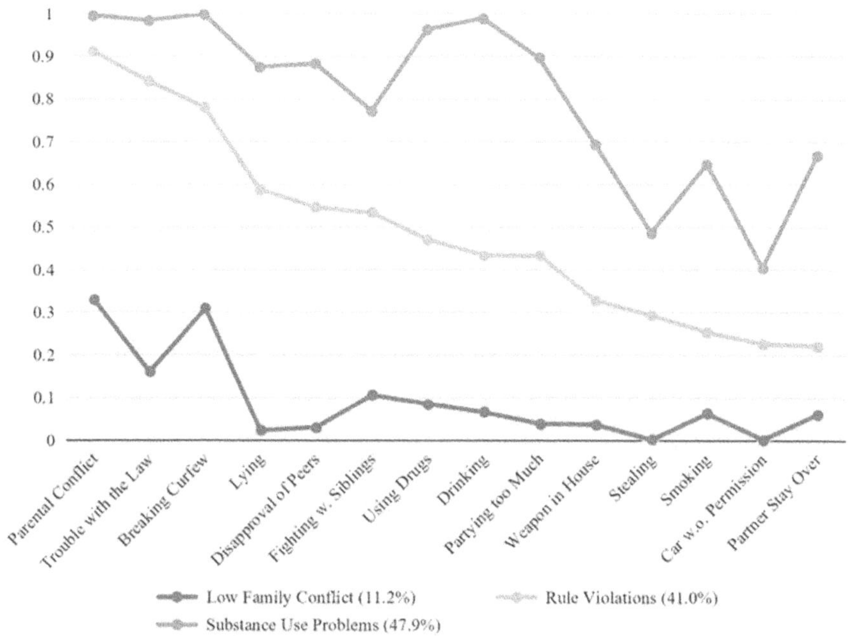

Figure 6.9 Latent class analysis of home behavioral problems through age 17.
Notes: The y-axis represents the probability that a given individual within a given latent class endorsed the behavior indicated on the x-axis.

aggressive behavior was related to the frequency of such behavior. In total, 49.1% of individuals who self-reported getting into fights on a weekly basis were associated with the versatile aggression pattern compared to 3.5% in the low aggression profile and 14.0% in the instrumental profile.

What might be the reason for different patterns of aggressive behavior? During the intake interview, participants were asked to report their motivations for aggressive behavior. Figure 6.11 shows the prevalence of different motivations across the full sample (line) and each latent class (columns). The full sample was more likely to endorse reactive motivations compared to instrumental motivations. For the LCA profiles, regardless of the different types of motivation examined, such motivations were more prevalent among the versatile aggression latent class. For the low aggression latent class, instrumental motivations were especially rare. Interestingly, individuals involved in instrumental forms of aggression (e.g., using force to dominate others) did not vary from individuals involved in peer-influenced aggression with respect to the endorsement of instrumental motivations.

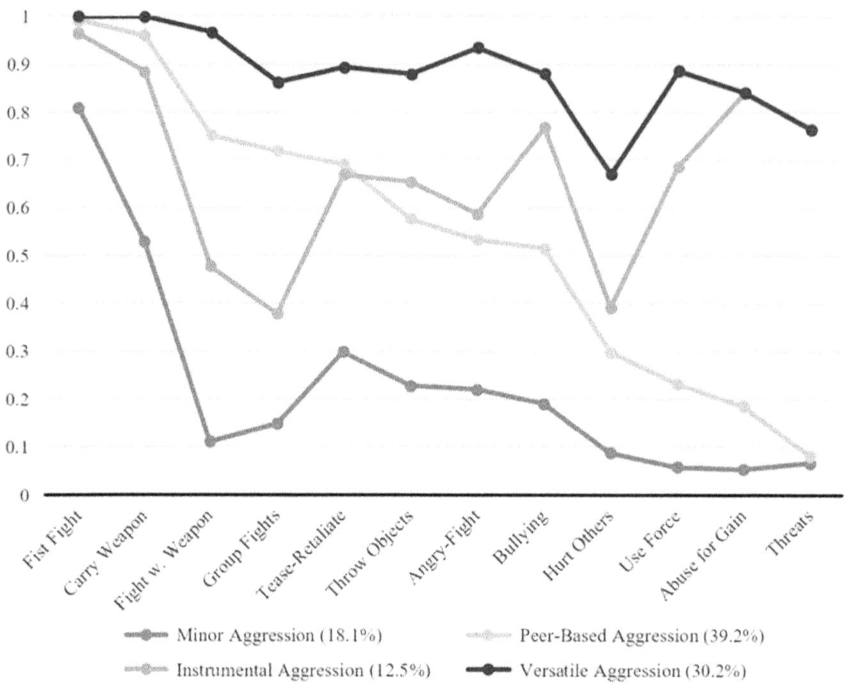

Figure 6.10 Latent class analysis of aggressive behaviors through age 17.

Notes: The y-axis represents the probability that a given individual within a given latent class endorsed the behavior indicated on the x-axis

Latent profiles of self-reported delinquency

Separate LCAs were conducted for SRD before age 12 and for SRD from age 12 onwards (see Figure 6.12a and 6.12b, respectively).[3] The LCA of SRD before age 12 revealed two groups. Group 1 (21.5% of the sample; "early onset") was characterized by an early onset of SRD, though the types of SRD engaged in were not especially serious. Group 2 (78.5% of the sample; "low delinquency") included individuals with no or very low probabilities of delinquent behavior. Unsurprisingly, there was greater heterogeneity in latent profiles of SRD between age 12 and age 17. Four groups best fit the data. Group 1 (13.7% of the sample; "low delinquency") was characterized by relatively low probabilities of all delinquent behaviors. Group 2 (21.1% of the sample; "property delinquency") was characterized by its high probabilities of involvement in property offenses. Group 3 (20.3% of the sample; "vehicle-related delinquency") had high probabilities of stealing vehicles and driving vehicles without a license. Group 4 (44.8% of the sample; "versatile delinquency") had a high probability of endorsing nearly all delinquent behaviors.

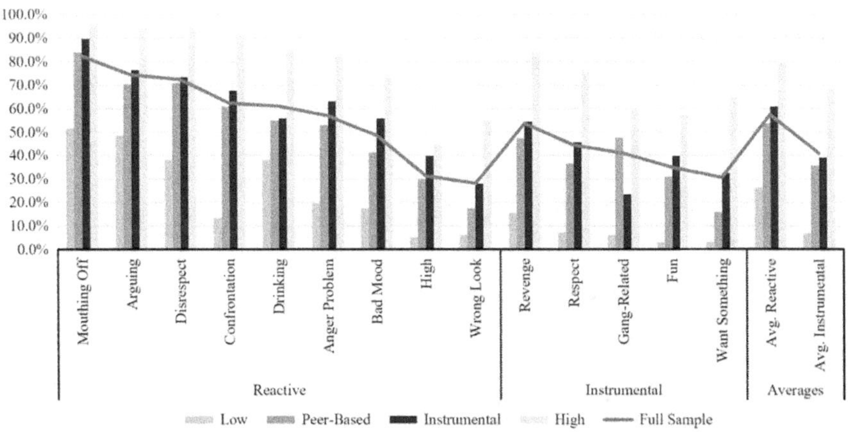

Figure 6.11 The prevalence of different motivations for aggression across the full sample and across latent profiles of aggressive behavior through age 17.

There was a significant association between the two LCAs at different age-stages (χ^2 [3] = 21.95, p < .001, φ = .209). Less than 2% of the "early onset" group before age 12 were associated with the 'low delinquency' group from age 12 onwards, which indicated that de-escalation in SRD was rare. Escalation was more common. Approximately 40% of those in the "low delinquency" group before age 12 were associated with the 'versatile delinquency' group from age 12 onwards.

Latent profiles of self-reported offending

Separate LCAs were conducted that examined SRO before age 12 and from age 12 onwards (see Figure 6.13a and 6.13b, respectively). Violations of court orders were not included in the LCA of SRO before age 12 as it was not possible for individuals to violate court orders prior to age 12. Sexual (0.0%) and homicide offenses (1.4%) were also excluded from this LCA because of their low base rate. The LCA of SRO before age 12 identified three groups. Group 1 (76.6% of the sample; "non-offenders") was unlikely to endorse any particular behavior. Group 2 (14.9% of the sample; "overt offending") was involved in overt behaviors like assault and uttering threats. Group 3 (8.4% of the sample; 'versatile offending') showed a versatile pattern of overt (e.g., assault) and covert (e.g., theft from house) offenses. A series of ANOVA analyses (not shown) indicated that individuals in the overt and versatile groups averaged a significantly earlier self-reported age of first contact with police, more self-reported arrests, and an earlier self-reported age at first incarceration compared to the non-offending group.

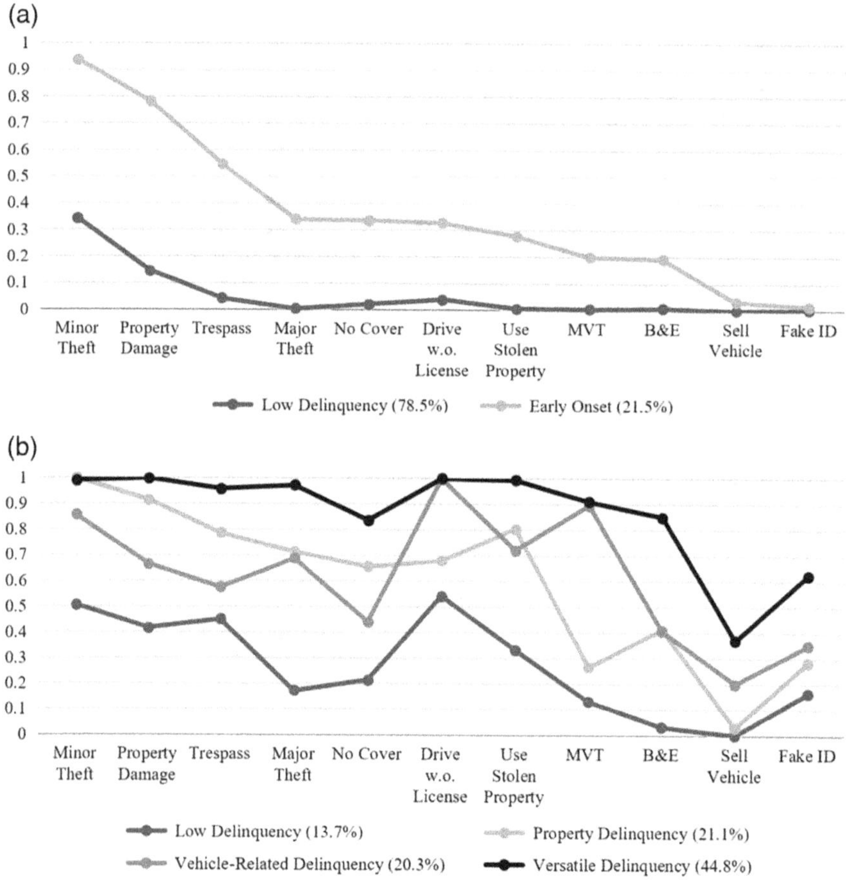

Figure 6.12 a) Latent class analysis of self-reported delinquency before age 12; b) Latent class analysis of self-reported delinquency from age 12 through age 17.

Notes: The y-axis represents the probability that a given individual within a given latent class endorsed the behavior indicated on the x-axis. MVT = motor vehicle theft. B&E = Break and Enter.

For the latent class analysis of SRO from age 12 onwards, four unique profiles were identified. For Group 1 (14.0% of the sample; "authority conflict"), aside from violations of court orders, probabilities of involvement in all other offenses were less than 0.50. Group 2 (17.8% of the sample; "covert offending") showed a proclivity for drug and property-based offenses. Group 3 (27.6% of the sample; "overt offending") tended to endorse behaviors like assault and uttering threats. Group 4 (40.6% of the sample; "versatile offending") had item-response probabilities that were greater than 0.80 for all but the stalking, homicide, and sexual assault items.

There was a significant association between latent profiles across the two age stages (χ^2 [6] = 42.65, p < .001, φ_c = .202). Nearly 80% of individuals

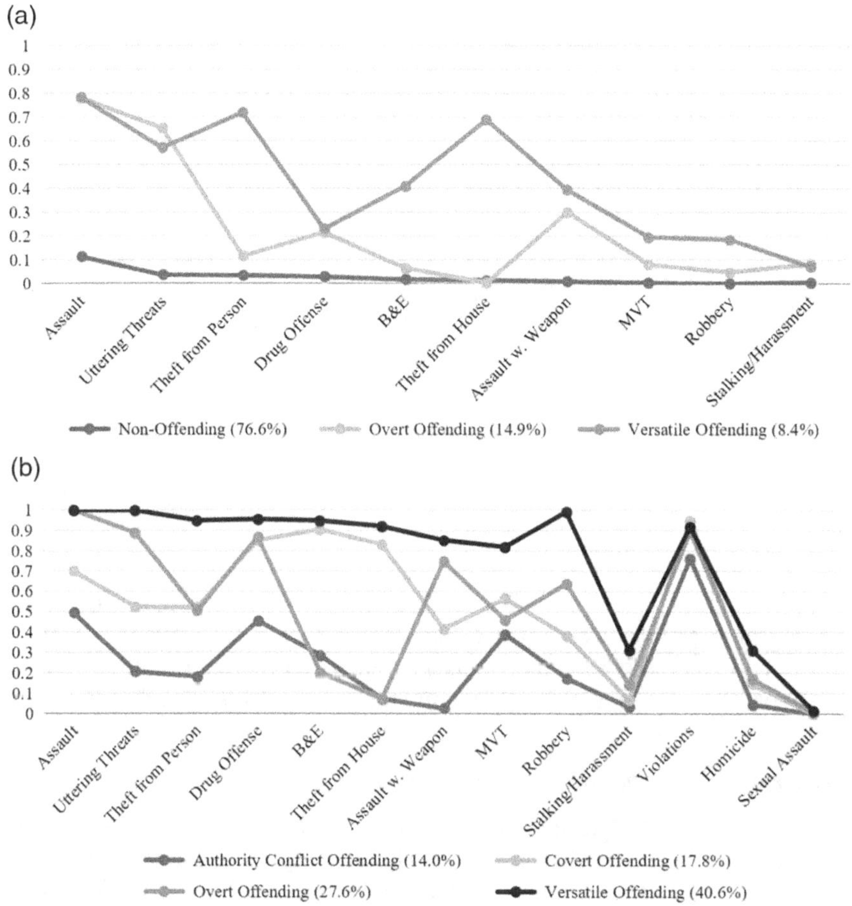

Figure 6.13 a) Latent class analysis of self-reported offending before age 12; b) Latent class analysis of self-reported offending from age 12 through age 17

Notes: The y-axis represents the probability that a given individual within a given latent class endorsed the behavior indicated on the x-axis. B&E = break and enter. MVT = motor vehicle theft.

associated with the versatile pattern of SRO before age 12 were associated with the same pattern from age 12 onwards. However, an individual's lack of offending before age 12 was certainly not an indication that they were destined for a similar pattern from age 12 onwards. One third of all non-offenders prior to age 12 were associated with the versatile offending group identified in the LCA examining SRO from age 12 onwards.

The intake interview also included questions about participants' motivations for offending. As shown in Figure 6.14, for the full sample, reactive and instrumental forms of motivation for offending were equally likely. However, those who showed a versatile pattern of SRO were most likely to

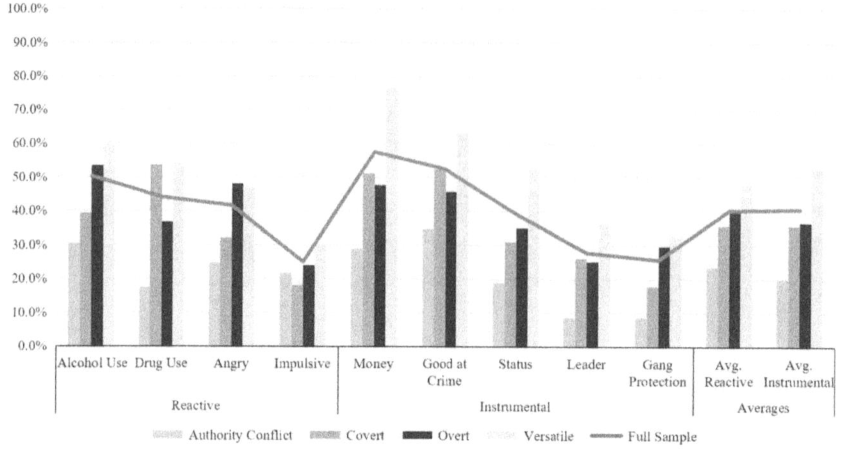

Figure 6.14 The prevalence of different motivations for offending across the full sample and across the latent profiles of self-reported offending from age 12 through age 17.

endorse each type of reactive and instrumental motivation. Distinctions across latent profiles were most evident when looking at instrumental motivations. Compared to other latent classes, the versatile offending group was most likely to endorse money and status as motives for offending.

Gender differences in latent profiles of antisocial behavior

Table 6.2 shows the percentage of boys and girls within each latent class. The general trend was that girls were significantly more likely to be associated with the least concerning pattern of antisocial behavior, regardless of the type of context under examination. There were a couple of exceptions. When it came to SRD, there was no significant association between gender and latent class membership. For the LCA of substance use, girls were approximately twice as likely to be in the hard drug use group compared to boys. Chapter 3 showed that, compared to boys, girls experienced significantly greater levels of family dysfunction (e.g., parents with drinking and drug problems, criminal records, mental health issues) and were significantly more likely to be placed in foster care, leave home before age 12, experience physical abuse, and experience sexual abuse. It was possible that for girls, hard drug use was not just a manifestation of a general antisocial tendency and "reckless" behavior. It may also represent self-medicating behavior stemming from traumatic experiences and transient circumstances (e.g., homelessness). As further evidence that girls' substance use may not be a manifestation of a general antisocial tendency, Table 6.1 shows that girls' substance use versatility was less strongly correlated with other forms of antisocial behavior compared to boys' substance use versatility. To be sure, patterns of self-medication in response to traumatic experiences may be true for boys as well, but the hard drug use pattern was more common among girls (57.3%) than boys (23.7%). Table 6.1 also shows that girls' SRO is more strongly correlated with home behavioral problems compared to the correlation for boys. For girls especially, their antisocial behavior may be less predatory/instrumental and more a response to difficult life circumstances, including a difficult home environment.

Summary of latent class analyses

Each LCA of each antisocial behavior dimension identified a group of participants showing a versatile pattern of behavior. It was not just that this group had a moderate probability of each behavior; compared to other latent profiles, the versatile latent classes had the highest probability of endorsing each behavior included in the LCA. Each LCA also identified a group of individuals who rarely endorsed any of the included behaviors. In effect, despite the sample being recruited under similar circumstances (i.e., incarcerated during adolescence), their antisocial behavior and behavior across different social environments was heterogeneous. This may be truer for boys than girls given that girls were more likely to show a lack of involvement in most forms of antisocial behavior. In between versatility and low levels of antisocial behavior, some participants showed a tendency towards a particular type of behavior. Some individuals confined themselves to authority conflict behaviors, others to covert behaviors, others to overt behaviors. This resembled early developmental criminology perspectives about different behavioral pathways (e.g., Loeber & Hay, 1994).

Despite ending up in custody for involvement in either serious or violent offenses, it was certainly not the case that all participants showed early signs of involvement in particularly serious and violent offenses (per the LCAs of SRD and SRO prior to age 12). This suggested to us that participants' behavior escalated quite rapidly after they turned twelve years old. Clearly, following the transition from elementary school to middle school, their behavior quickly became more and more concerning. The childhood-onset pattern of crime and delinquency commonly discussed as a gateway to the deep-end of the justice system (Loeber & Farrington, 2001) was not the only gateway for this sample. Anecdotally, we interviewed participants involved in some of the most serious offenses imaginable who reported little involvement in antisocial behavior, especially beyond what might be considered normative for boys in late-adolescence. These were persons that found themselves in the wrong situation or with the wrong people and tragic consequences emerged. For one youth we interviewed, their first and only offense involved a retributive homicide that resulted from the encouragement of peers to take back a stolen item. The offense was not the final manifestation of an increasingly serious pattern of aggressive behavior.

Table 6.2 Percentage of boys and girls in each latent class

	Participant gender		
	Girls (n = 96) *n (%)*	*Boys (n = 478)* *n (%)*	χ^2, *df, p,* φ
School Behavioral Problems			
Authority Conflict Behavioral Problems	31 (32.3%)	83 (17.4%)	χ2 [3] = 11.26, p = .010, φ = .140
Overt Behavioral Problems	26 (27.1%)	165 (34.5%)	
Substance Use Behavioral Problems	23 (24.0%)	134 (28.0%)	
Versatile Behavioral Problems	16 (16.7%)	96 (20.1%)	
Substance Use			
Minor Use	14 (14.6%)	96 (20.2%)	χ^2 [2] = 44.07, $p <$ .001, φ = .278
Recreational Drug Use	27 (28.1%)	267 (56.1%)	
Hard Drug Use	55 (57.3%)	113 (23.7%)	
Trouble at Home			
Low Family Conflict	16 (19.8%)	42 (9.6%)	χ^2 [2] = 7.74, $p =$ .021, φ = .122
Rule Violations	27 (33.3%)	186 (42.4%)	
Substance Use Problems	38 (46.9%)	211 (48.1%)	
Aggression			
Minor Aggression	27 (30.3%)	72 (15.8%)	χ^2 [3] = 16.24, $p =$ .001, φ = .172
Peer-Based Aggression	27 (30.3%)	187 (40.9%)	
Instrumental Aggression	16 (18.0%)	52 (11.4%)	
Versatile Aggression	19 (21.3%)	146 (31.9%)	
Self-Report Delinquency Before Age 12			
Low Delinquency	65 (85.5%)	329 (77.2%)	χ^2 [1] = 2.63, $p =$ .105, φ = .072
Early Onset	11 (14.5%)	97 (22.8%)	
Self-Report Delinquency from Ages 12–17			
Low Delinquency	15 (19.7%)	54 (12.7%)	χ^2 [3] = 5.56, $p =$ .135, φ = .105
Property Delinquency	16 (21.1%)	90 (21.1%)	
Vehicle-Related Delinquency	19 (25.0%)	83 (19.5%)	
Versatile Delinquency	26 (34.2%)	199 (46.7%)	
Self-Report Offending Before Age 12			
Non-Offending	72 (86.7%)	328 (74.7%)	χ^2 [2] = 5.89, $p =$ .053, φ = .106
Overt Offending	8 (9.6%)	70 (15.9%)	
Versatile Offending	3 (3.6%)	41 (9.3%)	
Self-Report Offending from Ages 12–17			
Authority Conflict Offending	19 (22.9%)	54 (12.3%)	χ^2 [2] = 8.05, $p =$ .045, φ = .124
Covert Offending	12 (14.5%)	81 (18.5%)	
Overt Offending	25 (30.1%)	119 (27.1%)	
Versatile Offending	27 (32.5%)	185 (42.1%)	

Notes: There are missing data because some participants had completely missing data for all antisocial behavior items. Unless otherwise noted, self-reported antisocial behavior examined through age 17. φ = phi effect size.

From a developmental criminology perspective, early childhood antisocial behavior is considered an important stepping-stone to CPO trajectories (Loeber & Farrington, 2001). Moffitt considered antisocial behavior before age five as an important warning sign for LCP offending. We next examined the association between different latent profiles of different antisocial behavior dimensions and the emerging adulthood conviction trajectory model (see Figure 5.1 of Chapter 5).

Boys' self-reported antisocial behavior and official offending[4]

We will not repeat each result here, but when investigating the relationship between latent profiles and criminal career parameters, across each of the eight LCAs, the more versatile/high pattern of antisocial behavior was associated with an earlier onset of self-reported age at first arrest. The strongest association was with respect to the LCA of SRO from age 12 onwards. Individuals in the versatile SRO latent class became involved in criminal behavior by about age 10, which was significantly earlier compared to the authority conflict and covert SRO latent classes. This also indicated that such individuals were having negative contacts with police before the justice system was able to formally intervene.

Table 6.3 presents the percentage of boys from a given trajectory (see Figure 5.1 of Chapter 5) associated with a given latent profile. We examined the findings from a retrospective point-of-view given that this is the perspective of the clinician or practitioner working with a particular client; they do not have the benefit of knowledge of the future. Looking into the past of individuals associated with a particular trajectory, is there evidence of a particular behavioral pattern that may have been a stepping-stone towards this type of trajectory? Chi-square analyses indicated that five of the eight measures of self-reported antisocial behavior were significantly associated with the conviction trajectories through emerging adulthood. Generally, the trajectories characterized by some evidence of CPO were more strongly associated with the more versatile latent class from each antisocial behavior dimension.

Perhaps what was more interesting was that individuals who showed a versatile pattern of early antisocial behavior were not destined for a CPO trajectory. Further, individuals characterized by a CPO trajectory were not always those who showed that most versatile pattern of antisocial behavior in childhood and adolescence. In effect, individuals showing early signs of antisocial behavior experienced divergent outcomes. The path to CPO through emerging adulthood did not require starting with a versatile pattern of antisocial behavior in childhood and adolescence. This contrasted with Moffitt's (1993) suggestion that individuals associated with an LCP offending trajectory always showed signs of early antisocial behavior and that individuals showing signs of early antisocial behavior were always on the path to LCP offending.

Table 6.3 The relationship between latent profiles of self-reported antisocial behavior and trajectories of official convictions between ages 12–23 (boys only)

	Emerging adulthood conviction trajectories					
	AL (*n* = 39) *n* (%)	*Low rate* (*n* = 139) *n* (%)	*EOFD* (*n* = 27) *n* (%)	*SRP* (*n* = 137) *n* (%)	*HRP* (*n* = 61) *n* (%)	χ^2, *df*, *p*, φ_c
School Behavioral Problems						
Authority Conflict Behavioral Problems	8 (20.5%)	28 (20.1%)	4 (14.8%)	15 (10.9%)	16 (26.2%)	χ^2 [12] = 18.63, $p = .098$, $\varphi_c = .124$
Overt Behavioral Problems	12 (30.8%)	51 (36.7%)	8 (29.6%)	49 (35.8%)	23 (37.7%)	
Substance Use Behavioral Problems	9 (23.1%)	41 (29.5%)	12 (44.4%)	39 (28.5%)	12 (19.7%)	
Versatile Behavioral Problems	10 (25.6%)	19 (13.7%)	3 (11.1%)	34 (24.8%)	10 (16.4%)	
Substance Use						
Minor Use	8 (20.5%)	39 (28.1%)	2 (7.4%)	25 (18.2%)	7 (11.5%)	χ^2 [8] = 16.87, $p = .032$, $\varphi_c = .145$
Recreational Drug Use	21 (53.8%)	79 (56.8%)	17 (63.0%)	75 (54.7%)	34 (55.7%)	
Hard Drug Use	10 (25.6%)	21 (15.1%)	8 (29.6%)	37 (27.0%)	20 (32.8%)	
Trouble at Home						
Low Family Conflict	4 (11.1%)	13 (10.4%)	2 (8.0%)	9 (7.1%)	10 (16.9%)	χ^2 [8] = 9.73, $p = .284$, $\varphi_c = .114$
Rule Violations	10 (27.8%)	59 (47.2%)	10 (40.0%)	55 (43.3%)	26 (44.1%)	
Substance Use Problems	22 (61.1%)	53 (42.4%)	13 (52.0%)	63 (49.6%)	23 (39.0%)	
Aggression						
Minor Aggression	6 (15.8%)	28 (21.4%)	1 (3.7%)	16 (12.2%)	8 (13.6%)	χ^2 [12] = 21.71, $p = .041$, $\varphi_c = .137$
Peer-Based Aggression	18 (47.4%)	51 (38.9%)	11 (40.7%)	48 (36.6%)	34 (57.6%)	
Instrumental Aggression	7 (18.4%)	13 (9.9%)	5 (18.5%)	17 (13.0%)	6 (10.2%)	
Versatile Aggression	7 (18.4%)	39 (29.8%)	10 (37.0)	50 (38.2%)	11 (18.6%)	

Self-Report Delinquency Before Age 12						
Low Delinquency	23 (63.9%)	100 (85.5%)	15 (57.7%)	98 (80.3%)	44 (74.6%)	χ^2 [6] = 14.90,
Early Onset	13 (36.1%)	17 (14.5%)	11 (42.3%)	24 (19.7%)	15 (25.4%)	$p = .005$, $\varphi = .203$
Self-Report Delinquency from Ages 12–17						
Low Delinquency	2 (5.6%)	26 (22.2%)	1 (3.8%)	8 (6.6%)	9 (15.3%)	χ^2 [12] = 35.10,
Property Delinquency	4 (11.1%)	25 (21.4%)	1 (3.8%)	34 (27.9%)	8 (13.6%)	$p < .001$, $\varphi_c = .180$
Vehicle-Related Delinquency	8 (22.2%)	19 (16.2%)	5 (19.2%)	25 (20.5%)	17 (28.8%)	
Versatile Delinquency	22 (61.1%)	47 (40.2%)	19 (73.1%)	55 (45.1%)	25 (42.4%)	
Self-Report Offending Before Age 12						
Non-Offending	28 (75.7%)	96 (78.7%)	18 (66.7%)	101 (79.5%)	43 (72.9%)	χ^2 [8] = 8.88,
Overt Offending	4 (10.8%)	19 (15.6%)	4 (14.8%)	18 (14.2%)	12 (20.3%)	$p = .352$, $\varphi_c = .109$
Versatile Offending	5 (13.5%)	7 (5.7%)	5 (18.5%)	8 (6.3%)	4 (6.8%)	
Self-Report Offending from Ages 12–17						
Authority Conflict Offending	2 (5.4%)	23 (18.9%)	0 (0.0%)	14 (11.0%)	4 (6.8%)	χ^2 [12] = 23.53, $p = .024$, $\varphi_c = .145$
Covert Offending	10 (27.0%)	19 (15.6%)	6 (22.2%)	25 (19.7%)	14 (23.7%)	
Overt Offending	6 (16.2%)	40 (32.8%)	6 (22.2%)	31 (24.4%)	20 (33.9%)	
Versatile Offending	19 (51.4%)	40 (32.8%)	15 (55.6%)	57 (44.9%)	21 (35.6%)	

Notes: There are missing data because some participants had completely missing data for all antisocial behavior items. Unless otherwise noted, self-reported antisocial behavior examined through age 17. AL = Adolescence-limited conviction trajectory; EOFD = Early onset-fast desistance conviction trajectory; SRP = Slow rising persistent conviction trajectory; HRP = High-rate persistent conviction trajectory. φ_c = Cramer's V.

What does antisocial behavior versatility look like?

Table 6.3 showed that individuals associated with a versatile pattern of antisocial behavior in childhood and adolescence were more likely to be associated with a CPO trajectory. To supplement this purely statistical depiction, we provided a more nuanced angle through the review of the background of a single case, whom we refer to as "Allen". For each of the eight LCAs performed above, Allen was assigned to the most versatile/severe group. Allen was also associated with the HRP conviction trajectory. Describing Allen's background will hopefully convey the challenges facing the young person, his family, and the practitioners tasked with trying to help Allen.

Allen came from a chaotic family background. His mother and father drank heavily and used crack cocaine. Their home sometimes lacked heat and hot water. Allen's father, older brother, and several other family members were well-known to the justice system. The father allowed Allen and his sibling to use drugs in the house and often drank with them. This reiterates a problem with relying on measures of whether participants were punished for home behavioral problems and may explain the lack of a correlation between this measure and other domains of antisocial behavior. Allen was rarely punished by his parents for his antisocial behavior.

Although Allen's antisocial behavior was also present prior to age 15, we begin at age 15 because of an important life event that appeared to influence the severity and diversity of Allen's antisocial behavior. The first major incident at age 15 involved Allen's mother discovering a gun in the house. When she explained that she was going to turn it over to police, Allen kicked several holes in the walls of the family home. Allen's mother informed him that he was no longer welcome there and Allen was placed into the care of MCFD. As discussed in Chapter 5, foster care placement is one of the most important correlates of CPO in the sample. Days after being asked to leave the family home, Allen was arrested for a robbery that involved him holding a knife against the throat of a peer and demanding money. Police reported that Allen was suspected of using cocaine. In his interview, Allen confirmed that he used alcohol, marijuana, ecstasy, cocaine, crack cocaine, and crystal methamphetamine. Allen's probation officer (PO) noted Allen's grandmother referred to him as an extremely violent young man and that there was "something wrong with him", especially because he was illiterate. One month after the initial robbery offense, Allen was found drinking alcohol in a stolen vehicle. Just days later, teachers reported that Allen was suspected of inciting his friends to threaten the victim of his robbery offense to keep the victim from testifying.

Allen's bail conditions required him to attend school. Allen refused to do this and so he was regularly charged with violating a court order. When Allen did attend school, his behavior was problematic. In his interview,

Allen endorsed 17 different items from the measure of school behavioral problems, six of which were perpetrated before age 12. Teachers reported that Allen was frequently late for school and arrived looking tired. Allen admitted to his PO that he regularly snuck out of his window to wander the streets late at night. On one of these occasions, he set someone on fire with gasoline because they informed police that someone else was involved in selling drugs. Still at just age 15, Allen was hospitalized after overdosing on ecstasy. Days later he broke his hand in a fight. He refused school, counseling, and substance use treatment and stated that he would rather go to jail.

It was difficult to provide appropriate services to Allen because his parents regularly enabled him, lied to his PO about where he was and what he was doing, and refused to give consent for an assessment for fetal alcohol spectrum disorder. On the rarer occasions that Allen did attend treatment programs, he encouraged others to not participate and threatened those who did. Practitioners noted that Allen would punch walls when angry or use a pen to make stabbing motions directed at staff. In the span of one week, still at age 15, Allen was arrested for being in a stolen vehicle, arrested for assaulting a youth, and had further police contact after throwing rocks at a bus. Days later he was brought to his PO's office by police as he had had an argument with his mother, and in response, punched holes in the walls of the home and broke a window. He was moved to a group home that same day. One hour after arriving at the group home, Allen was arrested by police for driving a stolen vehicle.

After age 15, Allen's behavior continued to escalate in severity. He hit his mother on one occasion and on another occasion he struck his father in the head, which required a hospital visit. He began using pepper spray to rob other youth in his community. At 17 he was noted to have threatened to have witnesses to one of his offenses killed. Shortly before age 18, he noted that he wanted to set a better example for his younger brother. As a step towards this aim, he found a job. However, he continued to deny the need for substance use treatment and felt that he could drink and smoke as much marijuana as he liked without impacting his antisocial behavior. After a short period of abstention from antisocial behavior he started to again argue with his parents. This escalated into physically fighting with his father. He moved in with his grandmother and resumed his alcohol use. While drinking he broke into a random home, which led to new charges of breaking and entering.

Allen's adult justice system involvement was characterized by the perpetration of violence against his mother and various intimate partners. He lived such an unhealthy lifestyle that there were fears that he suffered from tuberculosis. This could not be confirmed because he refused to go to the hospital. Allen took part in the 2011 Stanley Cup Riot in Vancouver.[5] He admitted to his PO that "he did some stupid things" and that he thought the riot was “wicked”. During the same week, while drinking, he hit someone over the head with a hockey stick, rendering the victim unconscious. He was regularly breached for violating no-contact orders that were instituted due to his assaults against intimate partners. He was also involved in a break and enter of a former partner’s residence. By age 30, Allen had incurred 61 convictions and had spent approximately five years of his life in custody.

Allen’s negative behavior was not just criminal. He neglected his son, was behind on child support, and refused to seek treatment for alcohol use despite acknowledging that virtually all of his offenses resulted from an inability to control his anger when he was drinking. He also had difficulty managing emotions, had engaged in self-harm, and experienced suicidal ideation. During periods of depression and low self-esteem he used heroin and cocaine. These instances of depression were in response to, among other life events, the death of a friend due to a motor vehicle accident, the death of another friend due to suicide, and the death of a family member who passed away after a night of drinking with Allen (Allen discovered the family member the next morning). At the time of this book, Allen was living in a shelter. In sum, while there is a clear pattern of versatile forms of antisocial behavior that emerged from an early age, these antisocial behaviors cannot be separated from the difficult family environment, mental health issues, residential instability, and traumatic life events experienced by Allen.

Summary

Data from boys and girls from Cohort II, all of whom were either age 16 or 17 at the time of their interview, were used to address questions from three overarching themes: (1) the prevalence of antisocial behavior across different dimensions and correlations between these dimensions; (2) qualitative patterns of antisocial behavior, and (3) the relationship between self-reported antisocial behavior and official offending. The examination of the prevalence of antisocial behavior helped reveal the severity of the risk/needs factors of these youth. Examining the timing of these behaviors showed that an individual’s antisocial behavior often develops before the age at which the justice system can formally intervene. While the school system is one area in which early intervention can take place, individuals in this sample did not have positive connections with their schools and regularly were required to leave school due to behavioral problems (also see Chapter 3). The child welfare system is another institution that can intervene, but as noted in Chapter 5, welfare system intervention (e.g., foster care placement) is associated with CPO for this sample.

Across each antisocial behavior dimension, there was at least one versatile pattern of behavior. Each LCA also identified a subgroup of individuals who rarely engaged in any of the behaviors measured. Although boys generally showed a more versatile pattern of antisocial behavior compared to girls, when it came to substance use, girls were about twice as likely as boys to be associated with a substance use profile defined by the use of hard drugs like heroin, crack cocaine, and crystal meth. These findings bring to light at least some evidence that boys and girls may be associated with different patterns of behavioral problems, which may have implications for criminal behavior. For example, girls' antisocial behavior may be more closely tied to a negative family/social environment (Table 6.1) and offending may be a response to this environment.

Another trend was the tendency for some individuals to engage in either authority conflict, covert, or overt behavior (also see Loeber & Hay, 1994). Participants from the ISVYOS, despite all being incarcerated in adolescence, were associated with different behavioral pathways to their official involvement in the justice system. It was not as if all youth showed a versatile pattern of antisocial behavior. In fact, the analyses of SRD and SRO early in the life-course showed that although most participants committed at least one type of delinquent or criminal behavior, for approximately three-quarters of the sample, such behavior was quite limited in degree and rarely were such behaviors particularly serious. The analyses could be characterized by problems with telescoping and retrospective biases, but there was some evidence of the validity of the retrospective reports of behavior prior to age 12 given that these reports were associated with similar patterns of behavior from age 12 onwards.

Boys who showed an early onset of SRD were associated with a pattern of frequent and persistent convictions between ages 12 and 23. To move away from stigmatization associated with early interventions for behavioral problems, researchers and clinicians recommended framing intervention as part of public health strategies (e.g., Toumbourou et al., 2019). It is not clear that the justice system is the most appropriate system for responding to this behavior. Considering public health responses is particularly important given that problem behaviors emerged prior to the age of criminal responsibility. Given that individuals in this sample often come from disrupted families, a focus on early family/parent training programs, which are effective for preventing antisocial behavior (Piquero et al., 2016), may be a particularly useful way forward. Indeed, both school and home-based developmental prevention programs are effective in reducing the prevalence of antisocial behavior (Farrington et al., 2017). Our review of Allen's background showed significant family trauma and difficult home circumstances that contributed to foster care placement and a clear escalation in his antisocial behavior.

Despite our examination of a wide range of behaviors from different dimensions, we still failed to measure certain antisocial behaviors. Future research may need to be attuned to antisocial behavior perpetrated through social media and other emerging technologies. To illustrate this, we will describe the antisocial behavior involvement of "Tyler".

Tyler was not involved in a high level of antisocial behavior, at least based on items included in the MASPAQ. He reported only two instances of school behavioral problems, which was well below the sample average. Yet, Tyler's index offense was for an offense perpetrated against one of his teachers in which he used a cell phone and voice-masking software to present himself as a work colleague of the teacher's husband. Tyler, impersonating this work colleague, informed his teacher that her husband had died in a work-related accident. File information noted that Tyler was highly intelligent. He was assessed for Asperger syndrome and although the assessment was negative, the justification for the assessment was Tyler's exceptional ability to focus on his computer. At age five he learned to illegally download films and burn them onto DVDs. He attempted to sell these DVDs at his father's workplace. When employees refused to purchase them, Tyler informed the employees that if they did not buy them, he would tell his father that they gave him the DVDs. Some of these DVDs included pornography. At age eight, Tyler tied his mother to a chair when she refused to cook him a special meal for dinner. Similar to the incident with his teacher, after an argument with his father, Tyler called 911 and, impersonating his father using the same voice-masking technology described above, informed police that he had a gun and was going to shoot his employees. This retributive behavior extended to other family members as well. After a disagreement with his grandfather, Tyler defecated in his grandfather's suitcase as he was about to leave for the airport.

By failing to capture more specific forms of antisocial behavior, especially those perpetrated using new (at the time) technology, we underestimated the severity of Tyler's behavior. Tyler's scores on our self-report measures of antisocial behavior resembled the scores of individuals whose convictions in adulthood tended to be less frequent. Tyler, however, was associated with the HRP conviction trajectory. Tyler's official offending in adulthood was particularly serious. This was not surprising, as RAs left comments in Tyler's intake interview noting that they believed that Tyler was likely to commit serious offenses in the future because of his tendency to hold grudges over trivial arguments. In adulthood, Tyler assaulted someone using bear mace. He then confined a woman to his apartment and held a gun to her and demanded that she repay him for a drug debt. Recently, Tyler was charged for inciting fear by posing as a health care worker and contacting a business to inform them that a COVID-19 outbreak had occurred at their facility. Most recently, Tyler was charged with sexual assault. In sum, Tyler's antisocial behavior was quite versatile, but our closed-ended instruments measuring antisocial behavior were not diverse enough to capture Tyler's behavior. The consequence was a false negative (i.e., Tyler was associated with an antisocial behavior profile anticipated to be related to a non-CPO trajectory). Including space in interviews for open-ended questions about involvement in other forms of antisocial behavior may be helpful for addressing this limitation.

Notes

1 The MASPAQ was not available at the time Cohort I participants were interviewed. Accordingly, data in the current chapter reflected participants from Cohort II only.
2 Model fit is assessed using several criteria, including penalized log likelihood values represented by Akaike Information Criterion (AIC) and BIC values. When comparing models, AIC and BIC values closer to zero indicate an improvement in model fit (Lanza et al., 2007). Assignment is made using the maximum probability of assignment rule. For each group, a given individual has an estimated probability of that group best characterizing their underlying pattern of behavior. The sum of these probabilities equals one. The individual is assigned to whichever group they have the highest probability of being correctly assigned to.
3 Conceptually similar items were aggregated and the presence of any one item indicated the presence of that behavioral type. Items measuring a history of damaging property, damaging a school, and damaging a car were aggregated into a single item (property damage). Theft from a store and stealing something less than $100 were aggregated into a single item (minor theft). Taking a car and taking a motorbike were aggregated into a single item (motor vehicle theft).
4 We focused on boys for the examination of the relationship between self-report and official offending because our subsample of girls was too small (e.g., only one girl was associated with the HRP conviction trajectory).
5 Following the Vancouver Canucks' Game 7 loss to the Boston Bruins in the Stanley Cup Final (National Hockey League), persons in the Greater Vancouver Regional District engaged in looting and property damage to various businesses and public areas in Downtown Vancouver (Davies & Dawson, 2015).

7 Psychopathy and the propensity for chronic and persistent offending

Introduction

In this chapter we take another look at Sampson and Laub's (2005b) claim that "we cannot predict long-term trajectories of offending … the childhood (developmental) paradigm cannot provide the answer" (p. 75). We do so through the lens of hypotheses regarding antisocial and criminal propensity. Propensity theories, sometimes described as population heterogeneity perspectives (Nagin & Paternoster, 2000), explain offending as the result of time-stable between-person differences in the propensity for criminal behavior. A common characteristic of propensity theories is the identification of a single construct that when present in adolescence or earlier increases the risk of offending over the life-course. The identification of specific indicators of propensity in childhood/adolescence provides helpful information about intervention needs early in the life-course (Bushway, 2013). Constructs specified as indicators of criminal propensity include low self-control, which consists of several personality traits, including impulsivity, a desire for immediate gratification, disinterest in long-term goals, and a preference for physical rather than verbal communication (Gottfredson & Hirschi, 1990; Wilson & Hernstein, 1985). Other indicators of antisocial propensity include negative child temperament (e.g., lack of prosocial attitudes, negative emotionality, and boldness/daring; Lahey & Waldman, 2003). These different constructs are not especially atypical among the general population (Mathesius et al., 2017; Nagin et al., 1995). However, CPO trajectories are quite rare in the general population and even in some adjudicated samples (e.g., Laub & Sampson, 2003). In effect, traditional indicators of criminal propensity are too broad to explain CPO trajectories (Corrado et al., 2015).

Propensity theories must consider whether the underlying construct of interest is both sensitive and specific with respect to its association with chronic offending and/or CPO trajectories.[1] Sensitivity refers to whether the indicator of propensity is common to the offending outcome of interest. Low self-control and negative child temperament meet this criterion (e.g., van der Geest et al., 2009). Specificity refers to whether the indicator of propensity for chronic offending and/or CPO trajectories is also *not* common among other offending outcomes (e.g., non-chronic offending). Low self-control and negative child temperament do not meet the specificity criterion because they are also commonly found among individuals who engage in non-chronic offending (Corrado et al., 2015; see Pratt & Cullen, 2000).

Some have suggested that psychopathy is a more appropriate indicator of criminal propensity (DeLisi, 2016; Farrington, 2005). In line with conceptual descriptions of propensity, features of psychopathy emerge early in the life-course (Seagrave & Grisso, 2002) and are sensitive and specific to chronic offending. In line with the sensitivity component, some theorized that those with strong features of psychopathy and those defined by chronic offending were the same group of individuals (DeLisi & Piquero, 2011; Vaughn & DeLisi, 2008). In line with specificity, strong features of psychopathy comprise only approximately 1% of the general population (Skeem & Mulvey, 2001) and 30% of the prison population (Cooke & Michie, 1999), implying that these features are not so prevalent as to be much more common than CPO/chronic offending.

Features of psychopathy include deficits in behavioral, interpersonal, and affective functioning. Behavioral features of psychopathy resemble low self-control (Cleckley, 1976; Lynam, 1996) and can influence offending through the desire for immediate gratification and sensation-seeking tendencies (Corrado et al., 2015). Interpersonal features include manipulativeness, deceitfulness, and the exertion of interpersonal dominance over others. These negative interactions with others can increase the likelihood of offending (Corrado et al., 2015). Affective features include callous-unemotional traits, a disregard for the well-being of others, and a lack of empathy. Such features are associated with poorer responses to treatment (Olver et al., 2013) and less sensitivity to the feelings of others (Salekin, 2016), both of which imply that an individual may be at a stronger risk of offending. Thus, features of psychopathy seem to meet some of the criteria for criminal propensity and its core features are theoretically associated with involvement in criminal behavior (see Fox et al., 2015).

Contribution to propensity theories

In forensic psychology, psychopathy is considered one of the most important individual-level risk factors for future offending (Hart, 1998). It is routinely assessed among adjudicated adults and youth, both on its own and as part of broader risk assessment protocols (e.g., Viljoen et al., 2010), and is commonly considered in justice system decisions regarding sentencing, level of security, eligibility for parole, and release conditions (Hart, 2016). However, criminology has overlooked the role of psychopathy in the development of offending over the life-course (Farrington, 2005; Fox et al., 2015), which may be partly related to the ALC paradigm's almost exclusive focus on an individual's social environment as part of this paradigm's attempt to discredit personality-based explanations of offending (Kornhauser, 1978). The examination of psychopathy and chronic offending has been mostly conceptual or based on cross-sectional research (DeLisi & Piquero, 2011; Vaughn & DeLisi, 2008). Research on whether psychopathy is informative of HRP offending or other CPO trajectories has been less common. This chapter examined whether there was support for the propensity theory notion that an antisocial or criminal propensity in adolescence, represented by features of psychopathy, was associated with chronic offending or CPO trajectories through adulthood.

Psychopathy in criminology

The DLC paradigm's inattention to features of psychopathy makes sense in light of criminology's problematic history with this construct. Principles of construct validity (Cronbach & Meehl, 1955) emphasize beginning with the development of a clear definition of the construct of interest, discerning how to measure it in ways that match its definition, and, among other things, evaluating its predictive validity. This is not the way criminological research initially approached the study of psychopathy. The psychiatrization of offending paradigm regularly referred to psychopathy with the goal of furthering the eugenics movement (Rafter, 1997). Bernard Glueck described the most dangerous criminals as psychopaths and William Healy referred to criminality *as* psychopathy (Rafter, 1997). In the 1930s, individuals involved in sex crimes were adjudicated under Sexual Psychopath Laws (Karpman, 1951). Such laws arbitrarily labeled the person as a "psychopath" (Lussier et al., 2020a). What these different examples of the usage of psychopathy have in common is that they are all tautological. Psychopathy was never defined because the construct was not yet fully understood. Instruments to measure psychopathy were never developed. Instead, criminology's use of the psychopathy construct involved waiting until a person perpetrated a particular type of crime and then labeling that person a "psychopath". For decades in criminology, psychopathy served as an amoebic placeholder for whichever group researchers wanted to label as deserving of punishment (Rafter, 1997).

Sociologists studying crime raised justified concerns with the psychiatrization of offending paradigm and its use of terms like psychopathy to designate certain persons as dangerous and beyond rehabilitation (Sutherland, 1949). Sociologists from the Chicago School highlighted that research during the psychiatrization of offending paradigm lacked control groups, failed to consider temporal order, and used highly specific samples (Kornhauser, 1978; Tennenbaum, 1977). To distance itself from this work, Sutherland (1947) rejected psychological/biological explanations of crime and forged a path for sociology to become the "intellectual center" of criminology in the United States (Akers, 1992, 1). This led to sociologically based formal traditions of theory development, research design, measurement, and analysis (Sutherland, 1937). Graduate student training for decades to come was characterized by sociological theoretical traditions, which included discrediting the utility of personality constructs on the basis that their assessment was too subjective (Sutherland, 1947). East Coast sociology held perspectives similar to the Chicago School regarding the subjective nature of personality measurement and asserted that the origins of personality were a product of social systems rather than biological ones, and therefore attention should be given only to a person's social environment (Parsons, 1958). It is safe to say that sociocriminologists' skepticism about criminology's past use of psychopathy was warranted. However, the field of forensic psychology, especially in the latter half of the 20th century, worked diligently to refine the definition and measurement of psychopathy. Criminology did not take much notice.

Psychopathy in forensic psychology

It took nearly 200 years after Pinel's (1806) "manie sans délire" description of psychopathy for forensic psychology to formally define and measure this construct. Cleckley (1941) was one of the first to describe the prototypical symptoms of psychopathy. After several years of refinement, Cleckley (1976) used a series of clinical cases to identify and describe 16 personality traits that were prototypical features of psychopathy (e.g., absence of emotion, callousness, superficial charm, self-centeredness, pathological lying). Unlike Sexual Psychopath Laws and initial criminological research, Cleckley (1976) did not equate psychopathy with offending except to suggest that individuals with strong features of psychopathy would be less responsive to punishment. To such individuals, crime was an expedient means to an end.

It was not until several decades later that Robert Hare and David Cox (1978) initiated the formal measurement of Cleckley's definition of psychopathy by developing a "7-point scale of psychopathy, the conceptual framework for the ratings being typified best by Cleckley's (1976) *The Mask of Sanity*" (Hare, 1980, p. 111; emphasis in original). This scale underwent a series of revisions which culminated in the 20 items of the Psychopathy Checklist-Revised (PCL-R; Hare, 1991). Subsequent studies using confirmatory factor analysis identified that underlying the PCL-R were four facets consisting of deficits in interpersonal, affective, lifestyle, and antisocial functioning.[2] Forth et al. (2003) modified some PCL-R items and adapted the scoring of others so that they were developmentally appropriate for youth. This resulted in the creation of the PCL:YV.

A criticism of the PCL-R was that it did not resemble Cleckley's conceptualization of psychopathy as a personality disorder because it was too heavily-based on the measurement of behavioral indicators (Cooke et al., 2012; Dawson et al., 2012). Cleckley described offending as an outcome of psychopathy, whereas the PCL-R included criminal and antisocial behavior items as if they were symptoms of psychopathy. The inclusion of such items contrasts with studies using prototypicality analyses, item-response theory, and network analysis. These studies showed that behavioral items were among the least relevant to the construct (Cooke & Michie, 1997; Kreis et al., 2012; McCuish et al., 2019b; Verschuere et al., 2018). As well, the inclusion of criminal and antisocial behavior items created a potential tautology; PCL-R scores were used to predict offending, but offending was used to help determine PCL-R scores (Skeem & Cooke, 2010). Studies examining the predictive validity of the PCL-R and PCL:YV typically found that the antisocial facet was the strongest predictor, and sometimes the only predictor, of recidivism among the four facets (Edens et al., 2007; Kennealy et al., 2010; Leistico et al., 2008). Although not without its faults, the PCL-R and PCL:YV are routinely referred to as the gold standard for the measurement of features of psychopathy (Skeem & Cooke, 2010). Our point here is that forensic psychology's careful attention to, and debate about, the measurement of psychopathy sharply contrasts with how early criminological research referenced this construct.

Another distinction between forensic psychology's approach to psychopathy research and the approach used by the psychiatrization of offending paradigm relates to attention to ethical concerns about the use of psychopathy in different contexts. Concerns have been expressed about extending measures of psychopathy to different populations, including youth (Seagrave & Grisso, 2002), Indigenous Persons, and other persons underrepresented in reliability and validity studies (Hart, 2016). Others raised concerns about whether the assessment of psychopathy was relevant to death penalty sentencing decisions (DeMatteo et al., 2020). Others raised concerns about the influence of the term on juror perceptions (Kelley et al., 2019). Attention has been given to sociological principles pertaining to the importance of considering culture, systems, and communities when evaluating the reliability and validity of measurement tools assessing personality (Hart, 2016). In effect, the contemporary assessment of psychopathy has addressed or at least considered many of the concerns raised during the ALC paradigm.

The re-introduction of psychopathy to criminological research

With the emergence of the DLC paradigm came renewed interest in psychopathy as a potentially useful risk factor for understanding crime over the life-course (McCuish, 2016). Criminological theories such as Moffitt's dual taxonomy, Thornberry's interactional theory, Nagin and Paternoster's propensity theory, Wikstrom's situational action theory, Le Blanc's control theory, and Lahey and Waldman's developmental propensity model all implicitly or explicitly referenced features of psychopathy (Fox et al., 2015). While the importance of psychopathy was acknowledged, it made limited appearances in empirical research because many DLC studies were initiated before formal measures of psychopathy were developed (McCuish, 2016). While criminologists were late to identify the importance of psychopathy, the tendency of forensic psychology to emphasize specific research questions meant that there was still room for criminology to contribute to research on the relationship between psychopathy and offending. Specifically, studies in forensic psychology almost always focus on the prediction of recidivism (c.f., Colins et al., 2015), which on its own is a poor indicator of the CPO trajectories that some developmental and some propensity theories seek to explain (Lussier & Davies, 2011). For example, as shown in Chapter 5, over 75% of ISVYOS participants recidivated in emerging adulthood. Recidivism is too ubiquitous to distinguish between trajectories of offending over the life-course.

The PYS was perhaps the first study that gave attention to both DLC principles and measures of psychopathy (Loeber et al., 2001). The PYS found that features of psychopathy in childhood and adolescence predicted offending versatility in adulthood (Lynam et al., 2009). This helped initiate a body of research that looked beyond the relationship between psychopathy and recidivism. Dyck et al.'s (2013) examination of a Canadian sample of justice-involved youth indicated that stronger features of psychopathy were associated with more frequent and versatile offending between ages 12–23. Although only examining offending into early adulthood, various studies using data from the Pathways to Desistance Study observed that psychopathy was prospectively associated with a more versatile pattern of self-reported offending (e.g., Altikriti et al., 2020; Baskin-Sommers & Baskin, 2016; McCuish et al., 2020a). A major goal of the ISVYOS was to build on this research.

The ISVYOS and the PCL:YV

When Professor Raymond Corrado was asked by MCFD to conduct a review of its custody facilities in the early 1990s, his committee informally identified concerns with personality traits of some young persons in custody that represented possible barriers to successful rehabilitation (also see, Olver et al. 2013). The major question of this time was whether these personality traits resembled features of psychopathy and whether they could be reliably measured among youth. A subsample of participants from Cohort I of the ISVYOS was used to help establish the reliability and validity of the PCL:YV (see the PCL:YV manual; Forth, 1995, Forth et al., 2003). The PCL:YV is a symptom rating scale coded using information from a 60–90-minute semi-structured interview and a review of file-based collateral information. The 20 items comprising the PCL:YV were identified as traits important to the construct of psychopathy in adolescence (Forth et al., 2003) and are rated from 0–2 (0 = *item does not apply*; 1 = *item applies somewhat*; 2 = *item definitely applies*).

Graduate and undergraduate RAs were involved in scoring the PCL:YV. All RAs had prior experience administering the intake interview. Training was conducted primarily by the lead developer of the Psychopathy Checklist: Screening Version (Stephen Hart). Training sessions involved defining and explaining the meaning of items from the PCL:YV, explaining the purpose of different interview questions, and reviewing and discussing video recordings of interviews conducted for the assessment of psychopathy. RAs were also trained to review file-based information (e.g., index offense, family history) to better understand the participant's background, to help contextualize participant responses, and to assist with PCL:YV ratings. Interrater reliability was conducted using a subsample of raters (see Vincent, 2002). Per Cicchetti and Sparrow's (1981) rankings, the intraclass correlation coefficient (ICC) value for PCL:YV total scores was excellent (0.92). ICC values for each of the four facets were not available, but ICC values were excellent for the combination of interpersonal and affective facets (ICC = 0.82) and the combination of lifestyle and antisocial facets (ICC = 0.89). Confirmatory factor analysis of the PCL:YV using these data (McCuish et al., 2018c) supported a four-factor model defined by Interpersonal (four items), Affective (four items), Lifestyle (five items), and Antisocial (five items) facets. Two items, short-term relationships and sexual promiscuity, do not load onto any facet.

Given that this chapter focused on the long-term predictive validity of features of psychopathy in adolescence, we only included participants with a PCL:YV who were followed through age 35 (n = 273; 77.8% of all Cohort I participants with a PCL:YV assessment). Among this group, 16 died (6.8% of the sample) and 19 had missing criminal history data due to moving outside the province (8.0% of the sample).

The 20 items of the PCL:YV (Table 7.1) had strong internal reliability (Cronbach's alpha = 0.80). For the four facets, polychoric ordinal alpha values,[3] which are more appropriate than Cronbach's alpha values given the limited number of items and the lack of range when it comes to the scoring of each item (Cortina, 1993), were 0.77 for the Interpersonal facet, 0.74 for the Affective facet, 0.63 for the Lifestyle facet, and 0.77 for the Antisocial facet. The average PCL:YV test score was 21.46 (SD = 6.55; R = 4 to 37), which was higher compared to formerly incarcerated youth from the Pathways to Desistance Study (M = 15.91; SD = 7.73; Cauffman et al., 2009). While cut-scores are not recommended given evidence that psychopathy is a dimensional construct (Murrie et al., 2007) and also because the "psychopathy" label should be avoided for youth (Seagrave & Grisso, 2002), 21.1% of the sample scored 30 or greater on the PCL:YV, which is typically used to denote high scores on the PCL-R (Hare, 2003). This was also close to the prevalence of the mature adulthood HRP conviction trajectory identified in Chapter 5.

Chronic offending and chronic and persistent offending

Table 5.2 in Chapter 5 showed that the group associated with chronic offending and the group associated with CPO were not comprised of the same persons. Chronic offending is a static indicator of whether a person's

Table 7.1 PCL:YV scores and conviction outcomes for ISVYOS participants followed through mature adulthood (n = 273)

	M (SD) / n (%)
PCL:YV	
PCL:YV Total Score	21.46 (6.55)
PCL:YV Facets	
Interpersonal Facet	3.08 (2.06)
Affective Facet	4.46 (2.00)
Lifestyle Facet	5.09 (2.10)
Antisocial Facet	7.05 (2.31)
PCL:YV Items	
Impression Management	0.65 (0.69)
Grandiose Sense of Self	0.75 (0.76)
Pathological Lying	0.59 (0.67)
Manipulation for Personal Gain	1.12 (0.73)
Lack of Remorse	1.35 (0.66)
Shallow Affect	0.83 (0.72)
Callous/Lacking Empathy	1.12 (0.72)
Failure to Accept Responsibility	1.15 (0.74)
Stimulation Seeking	1.19 (0.70)
Parasitic Orientation	0.79 (0.66)
Lacks Goals	0.89 (0.74)
Impulsivity	1.14 (0.68)
Irresponsibility	1.06 (0.65)
Poor Anger Control	1.38 (0.70)
Early Behavioral Problems	1.03 (0.81)
Serious Criminal Behavior	1.77 (0.44)
Revocation of Conditional Release	1.51 (0.70)
Criminal Versatility	1.36 (0.77)
Interpersonal Sexual Behavior	1.08 (0.83)
Unstable Interpersonal Relationships	0.57 (0.74)
Chronic Offending	
Reconviction Probabilities (Ages 12–35)	43 (18.1%)
Reconviction Probabilities (Ages 30–35)	23 (9.6%)
Chronic and Persistent Offending	
High-rate Persistent Conviction Trajectory (Ages 12–35)	51 (21.4%)
High-rate Persistent Conviction Trajectory (Ages 30–35)	30 (12.5%)

Notes: Chronic offending based on Piquero et al.'s (2007) reconviction probability formula (see Chapters 2 and 5). Among participants with a PCL:YV, 12.8% of the sample (n = 35) had missing data on offending between ages 12–35 and 12.1% of the sample (n = 33) had missing data on offending between ages 30–35. The two main reasons for missingness were mortality (n = 16) and living outside the provinde during the follow-up period (n = 19 between ages 12–35 and n = 17 between ages 30–35).

frequency of offending meets a particular threshold. CPO builds upon this measure by examining whether a high-rate of offending persists across time. Initial propensity theories on the relationship between psychopathy and offending had static indicators of chronic offending in mind (Vaughn & DeLisi, 2008). Indeed, propensity perspectives give little attention to the dynamic nature of offending (Gottfredson & Hirschi, 1990). However, developmental perspectives have argued that psychopathy is suited to understanding dynamic measures of CPO trajectories as well (e.g., Lussier et al., 2020b). Is psychopathy informative of both static and dynamic measures of offending? Do different features of psychopathy differentially relate to static and dynamic measures of offending? We measured chronic offending and CPO trajectories between ages 12–35 to maximize the duration of the period in which convictions were examined. However, examining convictions between ages 12–35 means that the initial shape of a person's trajectory emerged *before* a participant's rating on the PCL:YV. Given that the PCL:YV includes items measuring prior criminal behavior, there was the possibility of a tautological issue in that PCL:YV scores were predicting past offenses that formed part of a person's PCL:YV score. This was addressed by also measuring chronic offending and CPO trajectories that looked at convictions incurred between ages 30–35 (see Table 7.1).

For chronic offending between ages 12–35, using Piquero et al.'s probability formula[4], 18.1% of the sample met the threshold for chronic offending, which was set as at least 41 convictions (*M* = 56.06; *SD* = 14.93). For chronic offending between ages 30–35, using the same formula, 9.6% of the sample met the threshold of 13 convictions needed to be defined by chronic offending (*M* = 18.26; *SD* = 5.83).

For CPO between ages 12–35, we used the five-group trajectory model originally presented in Figure 5.3 from Chapter 5. The most prototypical CPO trajectory in this model was the HRP trajectory, which comprised 21.4% of the sample in this chapter. Individuals assigned to the HRP trajectory averaged 53.04 (*SD* = 19.90) convictions between ages 12–35. The EOSD trajectory, which comprised 14.7% of the sample, averaged 51.34 (*SD* = 10.58) convictions during the follow-up period. The nearly identical number of convictions despite variability in the shape of the two trajectories reiterated that there may be different pathways to CPO. Looking at static indicators of chronic offending may mask this variability.

A second analysis using SPGM was performed (controlling for exposure time) to model trajectories between ages 30–35. A four-group model was retained[5] (see Figure 7.1). The HRP trajectory represented the prototypical example of a CPO trajectory and averaged 15.37 (*SD* = 7.29) convictions between ages 30–35. The slow rising group was fairly inactive for the first two years of the follow-up period and the slow desistance group was fairly inactive for the last two years of the follow-up period. These two trajectories each averaged more than 400 days incarcerated during the six-year window, which may have contributed to offending inactivity. These two trajectories still averaged nearly one conviction per year. Even though we examined just one developmental stage, the reason why we consider these examples of CPO trajectories is because each of these trajectories had a high rate of convictions in earlier developmental periods as well. For example, between ages 12–29 (i.e., the years prior to the measurement of the trajectories), the HRP trajectory averaged 44.60 (*SD* = 19.04) convictions. Between ages

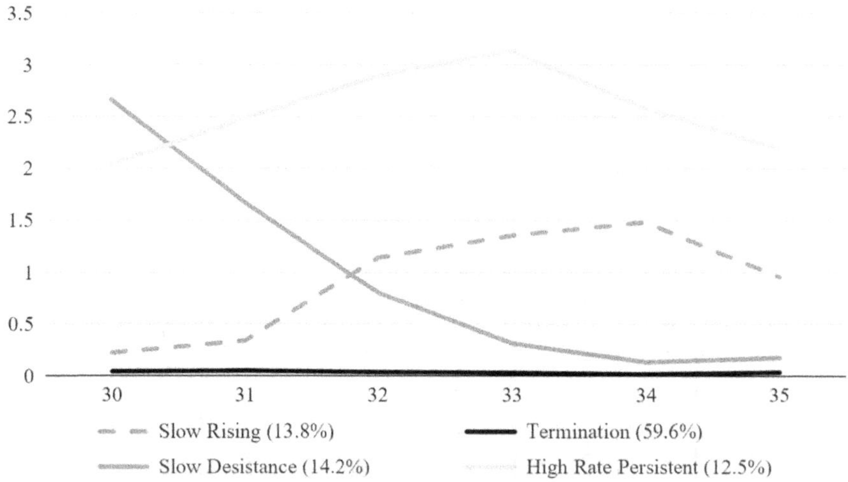

Figure 7.1 Trajectories of convictions between ages 30–35.
Notes: Time incarcerated accounted for as an exposure variable. x-axis = age. y-axis = number of observed convictions.

12–29 the slow desistance and slow rising trajectories averaged approximately 30 convictions each. In other words, these trajectories did not represent patterns of offending that emerged out of the blue. Even the "termination" trajectory averaged more than 15 convictions between ages 12–29, meaning that it was not as if the other trajectories were being compared to a trajectory characterized by the absence of convictions during earlier age-stages.

The PCL:YV and chronic offending

The relationship between PCL:YV scores and chronic offending between ages 12–35 is shown at the left-hand side of Table 7.2. Individuals defined by chronic offending scored significantly higher on the PCL:YV. Their total scores were three points higher when compared to those associated with non-chronic offending. However, at the facet level, only the lifestyle and antisocial facets were significantly higher for those defined by chronic offending compared to those defined by non-chronic offending. This may be evidence of the earlier-mentioned tautological concerns with the PCL:YV, which would cast doubt on the utility of features of psychopathy as an indicator of criminal propensity. Were features of psychopathy related to chronic offending, or was it simply the case that early and high rates of convictions contributed to higher PCL:YV scores and higher scores on the antisocial facet? Looking at chronic offending between ages 30–35 addressed this question.

Table 7.2 Mean differences in PCL:YV scores across chronic offending outcomes

	Chronic offending between ages 12 and 35			*Chronic offending between ages 30 and 35*		
	Non-chronic offending M (SD)	*Chronic offending M (SD)*	*t,df, p, d*	*Non-chronic offending M (SD)*	*Chronic offending M (SD)*	*t,df, p, d*
PCL:YV						
PCL:YV Total Score	20.87 (6.49)	23.13 (5.43)	$t = 2.13$ (236), $p = .035$, $d = 0.38$	20.85 (6.36)	24.64 (5.54)	$t = 2.75$ (238), $p = .006$, $d = 0.64$
Interpersonal Facet	2.93 (1.97)	3.27 (2.01)	$t = 0.98$ (220), $p = .328$, $d = 0.17$	2.88 (1.88)	3.96 (2.42)	$t = 2.53$ (222), $p = .012$, $d = 0.50$
Affective Facet	4.44 (2.02)	4.48 (1.91)	$t = 0.12$ (235), $p = .904$, $d = 0.02$	4.40 (2.01)	4.71 (1.99)	$t = 0.71$ (237), $p = .477$, $d = 0.38$
Lifestyle Facet	4.91 (2.14)	5.73 (1.91)	$t = 2.31$ (236), $p = .022$, $d = 0.40$	4.96 (2.10)	5.88 (2.18)	$t = 2.00$ (238), $p = .046$, $d = 0.16$
Antisocial Facet	6.75 (2.34)	8.12 (1.75)	$t^{\dagger} = 4.35$ (79.08), $p < .001$, $d = 0.66$	6.83 (2.31)	8.45 (1.66)	$t^{\dagger} = 4.26$ (31.8), $p < .001$, $d = 0.81$

† Levene's test of equal variance violated. d = Cohen's d effect size.

For offending between ages 30–35 (right-hand side of Table 7.2), the magnitude of the difference between PCL:YV total scores across chronic versus non-chronic offending was greater compared to the magnitude of the difference observed when looking at offending between ages 12–35. This suggested that the relationship between PC:YV scores and chronic offending was not due to tautological concerns. Of additional importance, individuals defined by chronic offending between ages 30–35 averaged a significantly higher score on the interpersonal facet compared to individuals not defined by chronic offending. These interpersonal deficits described youth who were manipulative, domineering, deceitful, and grandiose. Much like the relationship we found between the onset of offending and frequency of offending (Chapter 4), the importance of interpersonal features of psychopathy to offending emerged once a longer follow-up period was used.

Table 7.3 examined whether the findings described above held when controlling for demographic characteristics. For the measure of chronic offending at each age-stage, two logistic regression models were conducted. The first examined whether PCL:YV total scores predicted chronic offending. The second examined whether PCL:YV facets predicted chronic offending. For chronic offending between ages 12–35, a one-unit increase in PCL:YV total scores increased the odds of chronic offending by 110% ($p < .001$). Like the bivariate analyses, only the lifestyle and antisocial facets were significantly associated with chronic offending. When looking at chronic offending between ages 30–35, convictions between ages 12–29 were controlled for to account for the relationship between past and future offending. PCL:YV total scores were not a significant predictor of chronic offending between ages 30–35.[6] While this might be interpreted as evidence that PCL:YV scores only relate to offending through measures of criminal behavior captured by the antisocial and lifestyle facets, Model 2 showed that, controlling for convictions between ages 12–29, a one-unit increase in the interpersonal facet increased the odds of chronic offending compared to non-chronic offending by 141% ($p = .015$).

The PCL:YV and chronic and persistent offending trajectories

The analyses that follow investigated whether psychopathy was associated with a more dynamic measure of offending over the life-course. Table 7.4 shows the bivariate relationship between PCL:YV scores and conviction trajectories between ages 12–35. The three trajectories associated with some form of CPO (e.g., EOFD, EOSD, and HRP) averaged significantly higher PCL:YV scores compared to the AL trajectory. The EOFD and HRP trajectories also averaged significantly higher PCL:YV scores compared to the low rate trajectory. In terms of PCL:YV facets, the EOFD, EOSD, and HRP trajectories averaged significantly higher scores on the lifestyle and antisocial facets compared to the AL trajectory. The HRP trajectory also

Table 7.3 Logistic regression analyses using PCL:YV scores to predict chronic offending

	Chronic offending between ages 12 and 35		*Chronic offending between ages 30–35*	
	Model 1 (PCL:YV total scores) OR (95% CI)	*Model 2 (PCL:YV facet scores)* OR (95% CI)	*Model 1 (PCL:YV total scores)* OR (95% CI)	*Model 2 (PCL:YV facet scores)* OR (95% CI)
Demographics				
Male Participants	**9.62 (2.80–33.04)***	**10.79 (2.99–39.01)***	.	.
Ethnicity				
White	.	.	.	.
Indigenous	1.43 (0.69–2.95)	1.67 (0.75–3.72)	1.91 (0.68–5.35)	2.12 (0.68–6.61)
Non-Indigenous Minority	**0.33 (0.12–0.93)***	0.46 (0.15–1.41)	0.33 (0.04–3.13)	0.23 (0.02–2.48)
Criminal History				
Convictions (Ages 12–29)	.	.	**1.06 (1.03–1.08)***	**1.06 (1.03–1.09)***
PCL:YV				
PCL:YV Total Score	**1.10 (1.05–1.16)***	.	1.07 (0.98–11.7)	.
Interpersonal Facet	.	1.14 (0.95–1.37)	.	**1.41 (1.07–1.87)***
Affective Facet	.	0.88 (0.73–1.06)	.	0.89 (0.66–1.18)
Lifestyle Facet	.	**1.25 (1.04–1.50)***	.	0.95 (0.71–1.27)
Antisocial Facet	.	**1.33 (1.11–1.58)****	.	1.22 (0.90–1.65)

* $p < .05$
** $p < .01$
*** $p < .001$.

Notes: OR = odds ratio. Gender was not controlled for in the analysis of chronic offending between ages 30–35 because low base-rates of female participants associated with chronic offending resulted in inordinately high ORs.

averaged a significantly higher score on the lifestyle and antisocial facets compared to the low rate trajectory. Interpersonal and affective facets were unrelated to CPO trajectories between ages 12–35.

Table 7.5 shows the bivariate relationship between PCL:YV scores and conviction trajectories measured between ages 30–35. The HRP trajectory averaged significantly higher PCL:YV total scores compared to the termination trajectory. The slow rising trajectory, which averaged more than five

Table 7.4 Mean differences in PCL:YV scores across conviction trajectories (ages 12–35)

	Trajectory groups					
	AL *M (SD)*	*Low rate* *M (SD)*	*EOFD* *M (SD)*	*EOSD* *M (SD)*	*HRP* *M (SD)*	*F, df, p, η*
PCL:YV						
PCL:YV Total Score	18.51 (6.44)^{c,d,e}	20.09 (5.76)^{c,e}	24.26 (6.34)^{a,b}	23.15 (5.18)^{a}	23.67 (6.07)^{a,b}	F (233) = 8.39, $p < .001$, $\eta = 0.13$
Interpersonal Facet	2.76 (1.91)	2.71 (1.82)	3.32 (2.29)	2.94 (1.90)	3.60 (2.10)	F (217) = 1.80, $p = .130$, $\eta = 0.03$
Affective Facet	4.01 (2.20)	4.44 (1.83)	5.13 (1.77)	4.49 (1.84)	4.68 (2.09)	F (232) = 1.64, $p = .165$, $\eta = 0.03$
Lifestyle Facet	4.31 (2.16)^{c,d,e}	4.63 (1.95)^{c,e}	6.14 (2.26)^{a,b}	5.60 (1.74)^{a}	5.69 (2.04)^{a,b}	F (233) = 6.43, $p < .001$, $\eta = 0.10$
Antisocial Facet	5.86 (2.59)^{c,d,e}	6.47 (2.18)^{d,e}	7.86 (1.93)^{a}	8.20 (1.71)^{a,b}	7.88 (1.66)^{a,b}	$F^{\dagger}$ (197.79) = 12.73, $p < .001$, $\eta = 0.17$

† Levene's assumption of equal variance violated. Browne-Forsythe test statistic shown.
Notes: [a]Significantly different from adolescence-limited (AL) trajectory; [b]significantly different from low rate trajectory; [c]significantly different from early onset-fast desistance (EOFD) trajectory; [d]significantly different from early onset-slow desistance (EOSD) trajectory; [e]significantly different from high rate persistent (HRP) trajectory. η = eta squared effect size.

convictions during the follow-up period, also averaged a significantly higher PCL:YV score compared to the termination trajectory. The HRP, slow rising, and slow desistance trajectories each averaged significantly higher scores on the antisocial facet compared to the termination trajectory. Where the HRP trajectory stood out was that its average score on the interpersonal facet was significantly higher compared to the termination trajectory. Once again, it is through the passage of time that the relationship between core features of psychopathy in adolescence and adult offending outcomes emerges.

Table 7.6 shows the results of two multinomial logistic regression analyses that examined the relationship between PCL:YV scores and conviction trajectories between ages 12–35, controlling for demographic characteristics. The HRP trajectory averaged the highest scores on the PCL:YV and was treated as the reference category to allow for (a) the comparison of PCL:YV scores between a CPO trajectory and non-CPO trajectories as well as (b) comparisons *among* CPO trajectories to examine heterogeneity that may

Table 7.5 Mean differences in PCL:YV scores across conviction trajectories (ages 30–35)

	Trajectory groups				
	Termination	*Slow desistance*	*Slow rising*	*High-rate persistent*	*F, df, p, η*
	M (SD)	*M (SD)*	*M (SD)*	*M (SD)*	
PCL:YV					
PCL:YV Total Score	20.01 (6.21)[c,d]	21.74 (6.83)	23.24 (6.68)[a]	24.09 (4.81)[a]	F (236) = 5.18, $p = .002$, $\eta = 0.06$
Interpersonal Facet	2.83 (1.84)	2.43 (1.96)[d]	3.39 (2.19)	3.83 (2.05)[b]	F (220) = 3.48, $p = .017$, $\eta = 0.05$
Affective Facet	4.30 (2.03)	4.71 (2.04)	4.49 (2.09)	4.66 (1.79)	F (235) = 0.55, $p = .648$, $\eta = 0.01$
Lifestyle Facet	4.82 (2.15)	4.89 (2.08)	5.55 (2.07)	5.77 (1.93)	F (236) = 2.46, $p = .063$, $\eta = 0.03$
Antisocial Facet	6.37 (2.42)[b,c,d]	7.56 (1.77)[a]	7.80 (1.93)[a]	8.36 (1.52)[a]	F (236) = 10.11, $p < .001$, $\eta = 0.11$

Notes: [a]Significantly different from termination trajectory; [b]significantly different from slow desistance trajectory; [c]significantly different from slow rising trajectory; [d]significantly different from high-rate persistent trajectory. η = eta squared effect size.

exist between CPO trajectories. Model 1 shows that a one-unit increase in PCL:YV score significantly decreased the odds of being in the AL and low rate trajectories compared to the HRP trajectory. Differences were not observed between the HRP trajectory and other CPO trajectories. With respect to PCL:YV facets, increases in the interpersonal facet significantly decreased the odds of being in the low rate and EOFD trajectories compared to the HRP trajectory. The EOFD trajectory averaged 29 convictions between ages 12–35 and was associated with a particularly high rate of convictions in adolescence and included individuals defined by a pattern of chronic offending. Thus, core interpersonal features of psychopathy were informative of differences *among* CPO trajectories and not just between CPO and non-CPO trajectories.

Table 7.7 focuses on conviction trajectories between ages 30–35. All analyses controlled Table 7.7 for total convictions between ages 12–29 to account for the relationship between past and future offending. Model 1 shows that the bivariate relationship between PCL:YV scores and conviction trajectories was accounted for by past convictions.[7] A one-unit increase

Table 7.6 Multinomial logistic regression models using PCL:YV scores to predict CPO (ages 12–35)

	Trajectory groups†							
	Model 1 (PCL:YV total scores)				*Model 2 (PCL:YV facet scores)*			
	AL RRR (95% CI)	*Low Rate RRR (95% CI)*	*EOFD RRR (95% CI)*	*EOSD RRR (95% CI)*	*AL RRR (95% CI)*	*Low Rate RRR (95% CI)*	*EOFD RRR (95% CI)*	*EOSD RRR (95% CI)*
Demographics								
Male Participants	**0.08 (0.02–0.31)*****	**0.12 (0.03–0.47)****	0.58 (0.09–3.89)	1.92 (0.19–19.49)	**0.07 (0.02–0.28)****	**0.11 (0.03–0.46)****	0.48 (0.07–3.62)	1.71 (0.16–17.88)
Ethnicity								
White	.	.	.	.	.	.	.	.
Indigenous	**0.31 (0.11–0.87)***	0.92 (0.37–2.24)	0.43 (0.11–1.74)	0.44 (0.15–1.28)	**0.23 (0.07–0.70)***	0.61 (0.23–1.66)	0.41 (0.09–1.80)	**0.31 (0.10–0.96)***
Non-Indigenous Minority	2.64 (0.65–10.80)	**4.37 (1.10–17.36)***	**4.80 (1.03–22.25)***	0.74 (0.11–4.82)	1.66 (0.38–7.23)	3.62 (0.87–15.09)	**6.32 (1.13–35.45)***	0.89 (0.13–6.11)
PCL:YV								
PCL:YV Total Score	**0.85 (0.79–0.92)*****	**0.90 (0.84–0.97)****	1.02 (0.94–1.11)	0.98 (0.91–1.06)	.	.	.	.
Interpersonal Facet	.	.	.		0.81 (0.63–1.04)	**0.78 (0.61–0.99)***	**0.70 (0.50–0.98)***	0.78 (0.60–1.01)
Affective Facet	.	.	.	.	1.14 (0.89–1.45)	1.21 (0.95–1.54)	1.26 (0.91–1.74)	1.05 (0.81–1.36)
Lifestyle Facet	.	.	.	.	**0.74 (0.58–0.94)***	**0.78 (0.620.98)****	1.30 (0.93-0.80)	0.95 (0.73–1.25)
Antisocial Facet	.	.	.	.	**0.73 (0.58–0.91)****	0.82 (0.66–1.01)	1.04 (0.75–1.43)	1.18 (0.90–1.54)

† The high-rate persistent trajectory is the reference group.

Notes: CPO = chronic and persistent offending. RRR = relative risk ratio. AL = adolescence-limited; EOFD = early onset–fast desistance; EOSD = early onset–slow desistance.

Table 7.7 Multinomial logistic regression models using PCL:YV scores to predict CPO (ages 30–35)

	Trajectory groups†					
	Model 1 (PCL:YV total scores)			*Model 2 (PCL:YV facet scores)*		
	Termination RRR (95% CI)	*Slow desistance RRR (95% CI)*	*Slow rising RRR (95% CI)*	*Termination RRR (95% CI)*	*Slow desistance RRR (95% CI)*	*Slow rising RRR (95% CI)*
Demographics						
Ethnicity						
White	.	.	.	.	.	.
Indigenous	**0.23 (0.08–0.70)****	0.62 (0.20–1.94)	0.63 (0.20–1.95)	**0.20 (0.06–0.67)****	0.50 (0.14–1.80)	0.52 (0.15–1.80)
Non-Indigenous Minority	3.26 (0.31–34.83)	3.34 (0.29–39.20)	3.84 (0.35–42.06)	5.39 (0.41–70.31)	7.44 (0.52–106.81)	6.06 (0.48–76.17)
Criminal History						
Convictions (Ages 12–29)	**0.90 (0.87–0.93)*****	**0.96 (0.93–0.99)****	**0.97 (0.94–0.99)***	**0.89 (0.86–0.93)*****	**0.95 (0.92–0.99)***	0.97 (0.94–1.00)
PCL:YV						
PCL:YV Total Score	0.95 (0.87–1.04)	0.95 (0.86–1.04)	0.98 (0.89–1.08)	.	.	.
Interpersonal Facet	.	.	.	**0.64 (0.47–0.87)****	**0.58 (0.41–0.83)****	0.80 (0.59–1.10)
Affective Facet	.	.	.	1.19 (0.88–1.61)	1.29 (0.92–1.80)	1.05 (0.77–1.44)
Lifestyle Facet	.	.	.	1.19 (0.88–1.60)	0.99 (0.71–1.37)	1.09 (0.79–1.49)
Antisocial Facet	.	.	.	0.80 (0.59–1.09)	0.90 (0.65–1.26)	0.89 (0.64–1.23)

† The high-rate persistent trajectory is the reference group.
Notes. CPO = chronic and persistent offending. RRR = relative risk ratio. Gender was not controlled for because low base-rates of female participants associated with the HRP trajectory resulted in inordinately low risk ratios.

in number of convictions between ages 12–29 was associated with a significantly lower odds of being in each of the termination, slow desistance, and slow rising trajectories compared to the HRP trajectory. However, as shown in Model 2, controlling for prior number of convictions, a one-unit increase in interpersonal features of psychopathy significantly decreased the odds of membership in the termination trajectory and slow desistance trajectory compared to the HRP trajectory. This illustrated the importance of looking beyond dichotomous and static indicators of chronic offending. Interpersonal features of psychopathy were not just useful for making distinctions between persons in terms of the volume of convictions (e.g., chronic versus non-chronic). They were also useful for making distinctions among persons whose high rates of offending took on different shapes during the follow-up period. In sum, interpersonal features of psychopathy in adolescence helped distinguish, nearly 20 years later, a CPO trajectory from a non-offending trajectory (termination trajectory) and a CPO trajectory from a trajectory that still showed some signs of CPO (slow desistance trajectory).

Psychopathy and propensity theory

This chapter addressed theoretical questions about psychopathy as an indicator of criminal propensity informative of chronic offending (DeLisi, 2016) and as an indicator of criminal propensity informative of the type of CPO trajectories described by Moffitt (1993). Different propensity theories identified psychopathy as important to a person's propensity for chronic offending (DeLisi, 2016; Nagin & Paternoster, 2000). Similarly, although Moffitt's dual taxonomy is categorized as a developmental theory, her description of neuropsychological deficits as an indicator of a person's risk for LCP offending aligns with propensity theory principles. McCuish et al. (2014) suggested that youth features of psychopathy were ideal for operationalizing Moffitt's description of neuropsychological deficits because, aside from being conceptually related to criminal behavior in a variety of ways (McCuish, 2016), psychopathy was both sensitive (i.e., likely to be found among individuals associated with a CPO trajectory) and specific (i.e., unlikely to be found in non-CPO trajectories).

Our examination of conviction trajectories between ages 12–35 showed that higher PCL:YV total scores decreased the odds of being in the AL and low rate trajectories compared to the HRP trajectory. This analysis also showed that the interpersonal facet from the PCL:YV helped distinguish, not only between the low rate trajectory and HRP trajectory, but also between the HRP trajectory and another CPO trajectory, the EOFD trajectory. This highlighted the value of not reducing measures of offending to static indicators of total convictions. Among those associated with a high number of convictions, especially in adolescence and emerging adulthood, there are differences in interpersonal features of psychopathy. These interpersonal features helped make sense of why some youth involved in extremely high rates of convictions in adolescence and emerging adulthood experienced declines in convictions later in the life-course (i.e., the EOFD trajectory) whereas others remained stable in their high levels of convictions later in the life-course (i.e., the HRP trajectory). In fact, between ages 12–23, there were virtually no differences in the frequency of convictions between the EOFD trajectory ($M = 27.61$; $SD = 7.43$) and HRP trajectory ($M = 28.33$; $SD = 11.78$). From a static perspective, where all that matters is volume of offending, these two trajectories were indistinguishable. However, from a more dynamic viewpoint of the life-course, with a longer follow-up period and an understanding of what happens during the transition to adulthood, some individuals will experience adulthood differently. They will get jobs, find healthy relationships, move away from negative ones, and take care of their children (Laub & Sampson, 2003). For others, they will maintain their path that started in adolescence; interpersonal features of psychopathy seem to have a role in this stability. Static propensity theories do not consider these divergent pathways.

We also examined whether putting 20 years between the measurement of psychopathy and the measurement of offending resulted in an end to the usefulness of youth features of psychopathy for understanding offending. PCL:YV total scores were not significantly related to conviction outcomes between ages 30–35 once accounting for the number convictions incurred between ages 12–29. This may be evidence of the process of cumulative continuity whereby early risk factors have cascading consequences on other life domains. Higher PCL:YV scores influenced convictions in the short-term, and this high-rate of involvement in the justice system may have had state dependent effects (e.g., labeling, cutting the individual off from family and the job market) that influenced a continued high rate of convictions through ages 30–35. However, when looking at specific facets of the PCL:YV, we saw evidence of contemporary continuity. Interpersonal features of psychopathy measured in adolescence predicted convictions between ages 30–35 even when controlling for convictions incurred between ages 12–29.

Why might interpersonal features of psychopathy be important for long-term patterns of offending? First, individuals with such features show, from an early age, a tendency towards manipulation, grandiosity, pathological lying, and superficial charm. To score high on the interpersonal facet of the PCL:YV requires demonstrating these tendencies across time and social domains and in ways that go beyond normative youth egocentricity. Although interpersonal facets of psychopathy significantly increased the odds of being associated with a CPO trajectory, we also know that members of the sample are typically characterized by a wide range of other risk factors as well (see Chapter 3). Thus, this style of interpersonal interaction, when in the presence of a social environment associated with a wealth of challenges (e.g., substance use, family dysfunction, abuse), may facilitate a long-term pattern of negative or criminogenic interactions leading to the accumulation of numerous convictions through adulthood. We are not saying that this environment *accounts* for the relationship between interpersonal features of psychopathy and CPO, only that we cannot ignore that almost all members of our sample also faced adverse social environments. Negative interpersonal interactions may have been more rewarding in this environment.

The HRP trajectory also averaged significantly higher scores on the interpersonal facet compared to the EOFD trajectory. The EOFD and HRP trajectories showed a nearly identical pattern of convictions in adolescence, but only the EOFD trajectory experienced sharp declines in the frequency of offending upon entering adulthood. It is possible that individuals with a long-term pattern of interpersonal domination, deceitfulness, and manipulativeness may not respond to normative life events and maturational development in ways anticipated by life-course theorists (Lussier et al., 2020b). Instead, work, marriage, and parenthood may result in opportunities for further offending. A case study presented in Chapter 8 illustrated how a long history of bullying, interpersonal dominance, and pathological lying resulted in an individual's intimate relationships acting as a risk factor for continued offending as opposed to a turning point for desistance.

Not all individuals associated with the HRP trajectory were characterized by strong features of psychopathy. As shown in Chapter 5, hard drug use and family dysfunction were significantly related to the HRP trajectory. This reiterated Lalumière et al.'s (2005) perspective that cumulative disadvantage and psychopathy were two unique pathways to a CPO trajectory[8]. Therefore, although psychopathy appears sensitive to chronic offending and CPO, we are hesitant to suggest that groups of individuals associated with chronic offending and groups of individuals associated with strong features of psychopathy are composed of the same persons. While psychopathy may be sensitive to chronic offending and CPO, not all individuals with strong features of psychopathy were associated with the HRP trajectory, highlighting that the specificity criterion of criminal propensity was not fully met. To provide further insight into why a high PCL:YV rating was sometimes associated with a non-CPO trajectory, the section below examines instances of false positives in the sample.

An exploration of false positives through case studies

For the data used in this chapter, 4 of 33 participants with a PCL:YV score of at least 30 were associated with a non-CPO trajectory. Why did individuals who appeared callous and unemotional, manipulative, deceitful, impulsive, and sensation-seeking nevertheless cease their involvement in the justice system for the better part of adulthood? Perhaps PCL:YV scores were overestimated. For example, raters may have confused features of low self-control or psychosocial immaturity with features of psychopathy (Seagrave & Grisso, 2002). A second possibility is that individuals successfully avoided being detected by

Table 7.8 Description of false positive cases

	Participant			
	Melissa	*Bill*	*Michael*	*Rachelle*
Ethnicity	White	White	White	White
PCL:YV Score	30.53	30	31.58	30.53
Trajectory (Ages 12–35)	AL	AL	AL	Low Rate
Trajectory (Ages 30–35)	Termination	Termination	Termination	Termination
Justice System Involvement Onset	Age 14	Age 15	Age 13	Age 14
Convictions (Ages 12–17)	11	8	4	11
Convictions (Ages 18–23)	0	0	0	1
Convictions (Ages 24–29)	0	0	0	7
Convictions (Ages 30–35)	0	0	0	0
Days Incarcerated (Ages 12–17)	362	204	471	433
Days Incarcerated (Ages 18–23)	0	1	1	7
Days Incarcerated (Ages 24–29)	0	0	0	57
Days Incarcerated (Ages 30–35)	0	0	0	0
PCL:YV Rating Accuracy	Accurate	**Inaccurate**	**Inaccurate**	Accurate
Detection Avoidance	Detected	Detected	Detected	**Avoided Detection**
Changes in Adulthood	**Change**	**Change**	No Change†	No Change

† While *Michael* experienced stability in functioning between adolescence and adulthood, this represented stability in other mental health issues rather than stability in features of psychopathy (i.e., results of traumatic brain injury/poor executive functioning.

Notes: Boldface type indicates reason for false positive. False positive defined as a case with a score of 30+ on the PCL:YV but was assigned to a non-CPO trajectory. PCL:YV scores do not always equal whole numbers due to prorating instructions specified in the PCL:YV manual (Forth et al., 2003).

the justice system (Gao & Raine, 2010). A third possibility is that features of psychopathy declined with age, which in turn decreased the risk for continued offending (see McCuish & Lussier, 2018). Each of these possibilities was investigated for the four false positive cases[9] by reviewing each participant's PCL:YV rating, interview information, and CORNET file. Our review (see Table 7.8 for a summary) indicates a fair degree of variability regarding the reasons for why these false positives occurred.

Melissa: In adolescence, Melissa engaged in violence towards others, manipulated others for money, justified her actions by arguing that she needed drugs, fabricated stories, and was noted by the RA responsible for scoring her PCL:YV that she tried to charm and manipulate the RA into bringing cigarettes into the custody center for her. She often intruded the RA's personal space, which is a characteristic of interpersonal dominance. She blamed her mom for her involvement in crime, stole from her mom, ended relationships because she felt bored, and urinated into a spray bottle to antagonize others in custody. She was described as solving personal problems in ways that showed a disregard for social rules. In adolescence she was involved in violent crimes and stalking/harassment. Overall, features of psychopathy were observed across multiple domains (e.g., with friends, family, strangers, peers) and thus Melissa's PCL:YV rating appeared accurate.

Melissa appeared to have truly desisted as opposed to having simply avoided detection by the justice system. Melissa was arrested at ages 25, 27, and 29 for separate assaults. All three assaults were perpetrated against the father of her children. In all three arrests, charges were either not approved or dropped prior to trial. These assaults appeared to be the result of an escalation in mutual conflicts with the father of her children. Melissa was seeking to have the father charged with fraud. Practitioners rated Melissa low on various risk assessment tools and were not suspicious of ongoing criminal activity. In sum, while there was evidence of violence that did not result in formal convictions, this violence was confined to a very specific context.

Melissa's false positive result seemed to stem from changes in features of psychopathy that occurred between adolescence and adulthood. This change reduced her risk for offending. Changes in features of psychopathy between adolescence and adulthood are fairly common (McCuish & Lussier, 2018). Melissa abstained from drugs and alcohol. She cared for her three children who were in her custody. Although her employment was sporadic, this was likely related to the fact that she was the full-time caregiver for three children. In effect, while Melissa's adulthood was still characterized by certain challenges, by all accounts, considering her experiences as a youth, Melissa's story is relatively positive compared to other ISVYOS participants.

Bill: The false positive result for Bill appeared to stem from an inaccurate PCL:YV assessment. Bill was a braggadocious youth whose endorsement of criminogenic attitudes and related subculture may have given the impression of someone with strong features of psychopathy. During his interview, Bill boasted about the perpetration of brutally violent offenses as well as an assault against a police officer. Bill routinely switched schools or skipped school because he was bored. He also reported that boredom motivated his involvement in criminal behavior. In contrast to Bill's portrayal of himself, practitioners suggested that Bill tried to come across as more violent than in reality. Practitioners were more optimistic about Bill's future in adulthood. Although Bill claimed to regularly get into fights in custody, there was no record of this in his file. It is possible that such fights went undetected, but given collateral information from practitioners, it is possible that Bill wanted to portray himself in a certain light during his interview. In sum, Bill's score may have been more consistent with criminogenic attitudes and low self-control than strong features of psychopathy. The low levels of psychosocial maturity and high levels of moral disengagement that Bill showed in adolescence are known to improve during the transition to emerging adulthood (McCuish et al., 2020b), and this may have been true for Bill as well.

Bill incurred no new charges as an adult. At age 18 he was held in sheriff's cells for one day for violating conditions of his probation on a prior offense committed in adolescence. It did not appear that he was involved in offenses undetected or unpunished. Practitioners were more concerned about Bill's substance use issues and mental health. On one occasion in adulthood, he attempted to commit suicide. It appeared that Bill, now age 39, had not been involved in the justice system in any capacity for 20 years.

Michael: Michael's high score on the PCL:YV may have reflected symptoms of mental health problems unrelated to psychopathy. This is not to say that an RA inaccurately scored the PCL:YV, only that PCL:V items may have been too broad to exclude other metal health problems[10]. In adolescence, Michael was involved in especially serious offenses, including robberies, kidnappings, and arson. There were conflicting reports about his behavior in custody. Sometimes he was polite and compliant and other times loud, disrespectful, and oppositional to staff. His father visited Michael in custody, which Michael was very excited about (i.e., not in line with affective features of psychopathy). Collateral information supported Michael's assertion that he had few friends. While in custody he attempted suicide and engaged in self-mutilation. On one occasion he lit a fire in his room, refused to leave, and had to be rescued by staff. A psychological assessment indicated that Michael suffered from a traumatic brain injury and that this injury may have contributed to his negative behavior. In effect, the traits he displayed that comported with PCL:YV items were possibly not features of psychopathy but rather the result of trauma to the brain and poor executive functioning. This reiterates Hart and Cook's (2012) point that scores on an instrument should not always be equated with the true disorder (i.e., the analogy of the map versus the terrain).

In adulthood, Michael spent just one day in custody (age 20) and then was never again involved in the justice system. For the reasons detailed below, we do not believe that Michael remained involved in crime and was simply able to avoid detection by the justice system. In line with the principle of heterotypic continuity, the ways that Michael's mental health influenced behavioral outcomes in adolescence was different from how it influenced behavioral outcomes in adulthood. After one day in adult custody, Michael was transferred to a mental health facility better suited for his needs. His file indicated that he suffered from a severe mental disability (not otherwise specified) and that he was unpredictable. He was noted to have an "odd presentation" and staff had difficulty understanding him. Staff noted Michael was constantly thinking about suicide. We believe that this was why he was transferred to a mental health facility. The last entry in Michael's file came when he was 25 years old. It appeared that he wrote a suicide letter to his child. It was not possible to confirm whether Michael committed suicide and so he was not included in the ISVYOS' subsample of participants who were deceased. In sum, it seemed that the features of psychopathy that Michael presented with may have been manifestations of the traumatic brain injury that he experienced as well as other unspecified mental health problems. These issues continued in adulthood, but it seemed to negatively impact Michael's ability to transition to adult roles as opposed to continuing to influence his involvement in crime.

Rachelle: In adolescence, Rachelle engaged in cruelty to animals, fire setting, sexually inappropriate behavior, aggression towards her younger brother, and intimidating and threatening behavior towards a wide range of different people, including family, peers, and teachers. She was noted to show poor insight into how these behaviors were problematic. She regularly failed to comply with rules established by her mother, school, and the justice system. She did not accept responsibility for her crimes. While incarcerated, Rachelle smuggled a knife onto her living unit following a family visit. During the same period in custody, she fashioned a bedsheet into a noose and hung it on a wall to serve as a threat to another resident. Mental health professionals suggested that Rachelle was unlikely to respond to treatment. Her mother described Rachelle as desperately needing help and that she was unable to help her. Overall, Rachelle's PCL:YV rating appeared justified.

Rachelle's false positive result appeared related to her ability to avoid detection by the justice system. When she was detected, she was able to avoid punishment. Rachelle's official criminal history in adulthood was more severe compared to the other three cases, but still trivial compared to the average ISVYOS participant. Rachelle spent 64 days incarcerated during adulthood and incurred eight new convictions (i.e., an average of 8 days incarcerated per conviction). For the sample in this chapter, the average number of days incarcerated per single conviction was 120.53 ($SD = 331.16$). Thus, Rachelle was able to avoid more punitive sanctions. The below-average length of time incarcerated per conviction was not a result of Rachelle engaging in minor offenses typically associated with non-punitive sanctions. At age 24, she was convicted of two counts of drug trafficking and one count of resisting arrest. From then on, Rachelle was able to avoid punishment following arrest. At age 28 she was arrested for perpetrating an assault against an intimate partner and stealing from them. She was not convicted. At age 31 she was involved in a series of thefts but once again was not convicted. This pattern was replicated again at age 34, 35, and 37 despite engaging in threats and harassment against former partners. In total, Rachelle incurred charges for 10 different offenses but was not convicted of any of them. Thus, our reliance on convictions clearly underestimated Rachelle's involvement in crime. Moreover, reports from various justice system practitioners suggested that Rachelle's involvement in criminal behavior was much more pervasive than indicated by her arrest record.

A probation officer noted that another client referred to Rachelle as "one of the biggest drug dealers" in the town she lived in. Her family was known to be involved in organized crime. The family business included running an escort agency. In Canada, depending on how the agency is run, this is not necessarily a crime. However, Rachelle admitted to her PO that she sold drugs to the women working at the agency. Several of the family businesses appeared to be potential hubs for money laundering. At age 26, Rachelle's grandmother accused her of stealing from her.

Rachelle's features of psychopathy also appeared to persist into adulthood. During the times at which she was incarcerated she was noted by custody staff to fake sick to get out of work. In response to accusations of stealing from her grandmother, Rachelle claimed that her grandmother suffered from dementia and should be ignored. Practitioners described Rachelle as manipulative and presented as less mature than her age. Rachelle would remind justice system officials that her grandfather was a prominent member of the community. Practitioners interpreted this as Rachelle insinuating that bad things could happen if the justice system did not treat her favorably. Rachelle told the court that her offenses stemmed from a drug addiction. This resulted in her receiving house arrest rather than a custody sentence. She then told her PO that she did not have a substance use problem. She simply told the judge this to mitigate the severity of her sentence. She suggested to her PO that she was addicted to money and not drugs. She claimed that this addiction was due to her former partner giving her thousands of dollars per week and that she was now used to living a specific lifestyle. Rachelle's involvement in selling drugs to women working at her family's escort agency may be evidence of the parasitic orientation feature of psychopathy (Hare, 2003).

In sum, Rachelle's initial PCL:YV assessment appeared accurate, features of psychopathy continued to influence her involvement in offending, and a different approach to measuring offending (e.g., self-report interviews in adulthood) would have revealed a more pervasive pattern of offending (i.e., a true positive result).

Summary

Forensic psychology has helped promote, not just a more scientific process of defining and measuring psychopathy, but also a more ethical approach to the use of the term in research and legal settings (De Matteo et al., 2020; Seagrave & Grisso, 2002). Instead of reducing the term *psychopathy* to whichever group of persons criminologists wanted to issue more punitive justice system responses to (see Rafter, 1997), criminologists more recently have used forensic psychology definitions and measures of psychopathy to propose that this construct is the best indicator of a person's propensity for chronic offending (e.g., DeLisi, 2016). In support of this type of propensity theoretical perspective, we found that PCL:YV scores in adolescence were associated with chronic offending through mature adulthood. This included the prediction of chronic offending nearly 20 years after the PCL:YV assessment. The examination of conviction trajectories built on this finding by showing that PCL:YV scores were related to certain forms of CPO but not others. The HRP conviction trajectory represented a specific subtype of chronic offending where convictions were both frequent and persistent, and this was the type of CPO pattern that was most strongly associated with features of psychopathy. Unlike descriptions of desistance by default and assertions that risk factors in adolescence do not matter for adult offending (Laub & Sampson, 2003), features of psychopathy in adolescence had important implications for CPO measured nearly 20 years later.

Researchers have criticized the PCL:YV because its interpersonal and affective facets lacked predictive validity (Edens et al., 2007; Kennealy et al., 2010; Leistico et al., 2008). Analyses in the current study showed that the interpersonal facet was significantly associated with the HRP trajectory. This discrepancy when compared against past research may be because earlier studies focused on recidivism over relatively short follow-up periods. Early in the life-course, low self-control and maturational difficulties resembling the lifestyle and antisocial facets of the PCL:YV may leave little room for distinctions from persons displaying interpersonal deficits. Whereas low self-control and maturation improve with age (Monahan et al.,

2013), the tendency to be manipulative, domineering, and deceitful may persist over time and influence continued offending over the life-course. In this chapter, the affective facet was consistently unrelated to chronic offending and CPO. Affective deficits may still be important to practitioners because they are associated with poorer responsivity to treatment (Olver et al., 2013) and thus may indirectly impact offending. Another possibility is that the PCL:YV does a poor job of measuring affective facets (McCuish et al., 2019b). Other studies using different instruments showed that affective features of psychopathy were significantly related to a young person's offending (McCuish et al., 2020a). McCuish et al. (2015) found that the PCL:YV's affective facet was significantly associated with a pattern of official offending disproportionately characterized by violent convictions relative to other types of offenses. Thus, affective facets may be specific to the perpetration of serious offenses but unrelated to more general patterns of frequent offending.

Relative to the late 1980s, there is much more optimism about the efficacy of treatment strategies emphasizing the reduction of negative behaviors perpetrated by individuals with strong features of psychopathy (Polaschek & Skeem, 2018). Part of the challenge is getting individuals with strong features of psychopathy to successfully complete treatment; when they do, it is associated with similar levels of therapeutic change experienced by those with lower features of psychopathy as well as a reduced likelihood of recidivism (Sewall & Olver, 2019). Cognitive behavioral therapy for youth with strong features of psychopathy is one therapeutic approach that appears effective in reducing both features of psychopathy and negative outcomes associated with the disorder (see Hecht et al., 2018 for a review). Interventions may be particularly effective if they begin early in the life-course and involve parent-training (da Silva et al., 2020). The malleability of features of psychopathy contrasts with some descriptions of criminal propensity as something that is stable across the full life-course (Nagin & Paternoster, 2000).

Our analyses reported group-level differences. This means we are confident in saying that the group of individuals with higher PCL:YV scores were more likely to be assigned to the HRP conviction trajectory compared to the group of individuals with lower PCL:YV scores. We do not know whether this conclusion is accurate when making claims about the risk of CPO for specific persons. We have been contacted by justice system practitioners asking about whether our findings regarding the relationship between psychopathy and offending could be used to, for example, justify a lengthier sentence for a particular adjudicated person. We caution against this. Making predictions about what a single individual might do does not carry the same level of accuracy as our group-level predictions (Hart & Cooke, 2013). Hart et al. (2007) showed that using risk assessment scores to make an accurate prediction of whether a given individual will reoffend in the future results in extremely imprecise forecasting. They provided a quote from Sir Arthur Conan Doyle's "The Sign of the Four" to contextualize their findings

> [W]hile the individual man is an insoluble puzzle, in the aggregate he becomes a mathematical certainty. You can, for example, never foretell what any one man will do, but you can say with precision what an average number will be up to. Individuals vary, but percentages remain constant.

Our findings contribute to knowledge about the development of offending over the life-course. We caution against using such findings to make conclusions about any specific individual. Our examination of false positive cases showed that sometimes the assessment of psychopathy is inaccurate. Other analyses have shown that individuals' strong features of psychopathy in adolescence can dissipate as they go through a process of maturation (McCuish & Lussier, 2018). Others pointed to how the individual defined by a high level of risk in adolescence can experience, even at random, positive social outcomes that lead to desistance (Laub & Sampson, 2003). These social outcomes were investigated in Chapter 8.

Notes

1. Not all propensity theories suggested that the construct of interest influenced chronic offending. Gottfredson and Hirschi (1990) suggested that low self-control was an indicator of criminal propensity but aging reduced opportunities for offending among such individuals in such a way as to lead to desistance from criminal behavior.
2. Others raised concerns that these facets simply reflect the underlying structure of the PCL-R and that it is incorrect to conclude that there are four facets of psychopathy (e.g., Cooke et al., 2012).
3. $\alpha = (k * r_{avg}) / (1 + (k - 1) - r_{avg})$ where k is the number of items in the scale and r_{avg} represents the average correlation between items in the scale (Gadermann et al., 2012).
4. We did not examine Wolfgang's approach to measuring chronic offending because 100% of those defined by chronic offending per Wolfgang's approach were also defined by chronic offending per reconviction probabilities.
5. BIC values were closer to zero for the four-group model compared to a three-group model. A five-group model failed to converge and thus the four-group model was retained.
6. When past convictions were not controlled for, a one-unit increase in PCL:YV scores significantly increased the odds of chronic offending by a factor of 1.10.
7. A separate model with past convictions not controlled for showed that a one-unit increase in PCL:YV total scores significantly ($p = .003$) lowered the odds of being in the termination trajectory compared to the HRP trajectory (OR = 0.90 [95% CI = 0.84–0.96]).
8. While these authors focused on sexual offending, sexual offending is typically part of a broader pattern of general offending (Lussier et al., 2020) and therefore

their theoretical perspective may be useful for understanding general offending as well.

9 The prevalence of false positives would have been lower if we had not accounted for early mortality. Six individuals with a high score on the PCL:YV were deceased. Future research should examine the association between psychopathy and other negative outcomes (e.g., early mortality, car accidents, tax evasion, substance abuse, etc.).

10 As another example, one of our participants from Cohort II scored greater than 30 on the PCL:YV, but this was possibly due to the consequences of chronic traumatic encephalopathy as opposed to psychopathy. This reiterates that while the PCL:YV/PCL-R may be the gold standard for the measurement of psychopathy, they are not the gold standard definition of psychopathy (e.g., Skeem & Cooke, 2010).

8 Desistance among youth involved in serious and violent offenses

Introduction

Chapter 6 used a developmental criminology perspective to describe the early initiation of antisocial behavior. Chapter 7 used a propensity perspective to describe the persistence of criminal behavior. Chapter 8 uses a life-course perspective to describe desistance from criminal behavior. Criminal career research initially defined desistance as the absence of re-offending. This is an event-based definition of desistance and requires that individuals remain crime-free for some specified length of time. This definition created debate regarding how long an individual needed to remain crime-free before they were considered to have desisted. Was five years the "magic number" to indicate desistance? Why not seven years? Or ten? Event-based measurement approaches defined desistance as the absence of offending for as many as 4,015 days (Farrington & Hawkins, 1991) or as little as 30 (Healy, 2010). Especially if we are interested in change, event-based definitions of desistance are limited because they ignore the progress that an individual makes to reach this stage (Kazemian, 2007).

Life-course criminology influenced the reconceptualization of desistance as a process that describes an individual's decline from their previous rate of offending and ultimately their maintenance of a state of non-offending. Bushway et al. (2001), for example, defined desistance as the process of a reduction in the rate of offending from a nonzero level to a stable rate empirically indistinguishable from zero. Termination from offending is an outcome of desistance; the experiences and changes that individuals have as they move from higher to lower levels of offending is what helps to understand why individuals stop offending (Laub & Sampson, 2001). Unlike event-based definitions, recidivism may be *part* of the desistance process. Life-course criminology also influenced major theoretical perspectives on why desistance occurs. Sampson and Laub's (1993) reanalysis of the UJD Study helped initiate their theory of desistance as a process, referred to as the age-graded theory of informal social control.

The age-graded theory of informal social control, based on Elder's life-course principles, is one of the most prominent theoretical explanations of desistance. Briefly, the transition from adolescence to adulthood provides access to informal social control in the form of social roles, responsibilities, and constraints, all of which discourage offending (Laub & Sampson, 2003). Often referred to as turning points, or events that alter an individual's offending trajectory, marriage, parenthood, and employment are three adult roles that are hypothesized to promote desistance. For example, employment alters a person's life circumstances in several ways: it structures a person's daily routine; it influences the types of people they interact with; it creates expectations about the person's attitude and behavior; it provides opportunities to develop relationships with prosocial persons and feel appreciated by others. In effect, turning points impact desistance by reducing an individual's willingness to jeopardize their new social roles (Mulvey et al., 2004) and by limiting their exposure to offending opportunities (Warr, 1998).

Contribution to life-course criminology

In this chapter we examined whether informal social controls influenced desistance for persons with a history of serious and violent offending in adolescence. Until recently, one of the biggest limitations of the ISVYOS was the lack of data on adult outcomes other than offending and mortality. Ideally, we would have followed Sampson and Laub's lead by re-interviewing participants in adulthood. Unfortunately, for several reasons (see Chapters 3 and 10), this was not possible. To gather data regarding adult outcomes, we relied on various sources of information completed by practitioners and stored on CORNET. This information included risk assessment tools that measured the quality of different sources of informal social control. This chapter presents preliminary results regarding justice system practitioners' ratings of the quality of different sources of informal social control among a subsample of 644 participants. Informal social controls included family relationships, living arrangements, relationships with intimate partners, academic/vocational skills, and employment patterns. Focusing on the quality of informal social control helped address, not just whether an informal social control was present or absent, but its likelihood of being meaningfully related to desistance (see Nguyen & Loughran, 2018).

The analyses in this chapter proceeded in three stages. The first stage used ISVYOS data to address: (1) whether characteristics in adolescence were informative of the quality of informal social controls in adulthood (i.e., selection effects), (2) whether different sources of adult informal social control were prospectively associated with adult convictions, and (3) whether characteristics in adolescence moderated the relationship between positive sources of informal social control and desistance. This last scenario describes treatment effect heterogeneity, which is where the informal social control treatment effect is associated with heterogeneous outcomes depending on an individual's level of risk in adolescence. The second analytic stage changed the focus from between-person differences to within-individual change by looking at whether within-individual change in informal social control mattered for within-individual change in convictions. The third stage used a case study to illustrate the importance of examining the quality and not just the presence of informal social controls.

An informal social control perspective on desistance

Sampson and Laub's (1993; also see Laub & Sampson, 2003) life-course theoretical perspective was formalized over a decade-long period in which they conducted additional research on participants from the UJD Study. They referred to their life-course theory as an age-graded theory of informal social control. Sampson and Laub did not ignore offending onset and persistence. However, in line with Elder's (1998) emphasis on the dynamic nature of human development across the life-course, they primarily focused on change, which naturally involved explaining desistance. Sampson and Laub believed that developmental criminology painted individuals as easily predictable organisms with a specific and well-defined life path. Whether this portrayal was accurate is debatable given that change is routinely discussed in developmental criminology (Loeber & Le Blanc, 1990). Nevertheless, Sampson and Laub argued that human agency and the randomness of life events make prediction messy and therefore developmental criminology is of limited value.[1] From Sampson and Laub's perspective, the environment directly influences an individual and has implications for offending over the life-course. The environment is more than just family and peers, it includes macro-level structural forces that funnel individuals into adult roles. These structural forces help explain why desistance occurs even for individuals from particularly disadvantaged circumstances. Drawing from this sociogenic perspective, Laub and Sampson raised the idea that desistance was the natural path for all persons involved in crime (i.e., "desistance by default") because of the inevitable acquisition of sources of informal social control.

Informal social controls refer to factors that help bond an individual to society. As Sampson and Laub focused on adults, they primarily referred to the bonds of work, marriage, and parenthood. Other informal social controls include a person's living situation, including neighborhood quality (e.g., collective efficacy), stable/adequate housing (Kirk, 2009; Sharkey & Sampson, 2010), and peer networks (Lussier & McCuish, 2016). Initially, Sampson and Laub (1997) acknowledged the relevance of cumulative disadvantage to the acquisition of informal social control. Delinquency in adolescence mortgaged the future in ways that precluded opportunities for turning points later in the life-course. For example, a criminal record was a barrier to conventional opportunities like employment. However, following further examination of participants from the UJD Study, Laub and Sampson (2003) revised their theory and asserted that at the macro-level, the nature of the United States' social structure meant that, with age, individuals were funneled into adult roles even if not actively pursuing such roles. At the micro-level, human agency allowed individuals to, through sheer willpower, overcome disadvantage. Together, the impact of social structure and human agency implied that turning points were typical for everyone.

How do informal social controls influence desistance?

Laub and Sampson's (2003) update to their theory included clarifying the mechanisms by which informal social controls influenced desistance. It was not as simple as to say that individuals want to stop offending and so they seek to become married. Rather, individuals involved in crime seek out, or experience through happenstance, adult social roles in the same ways as individuals not involved in crime. For example, individuals seek employment to rent a house, purchase a car, and buy groceries. In the process of being employed, an individual becomes embedded within a workplace culture (e.g., employee camaraderie, respect from a boss, pay raises) that favors desistance because offending now carries even greater social costs.

By creating these side-bets that increase the social costs of offending, informal social controls influence desistance in four ways. First, individuals may "knife off" from their past behavior, peer group, and life circumstances to further diminish possible rewards from crime. In doing so, individuals become embedded within a social network that provides positive social capital. Second, informal social controls generally involve spending time with other people, implying that individuals are more often in the presence of a capable guardian who can deter offending (Warr, 1998). In adolescence, especially for boys, the mere presence of a romantic partner can reduce the likelihood of risk-taking behavior (Silva et al., 2020). Third, informal social controls create obligations that occupy a person's unstructured free time. Hours spent at work reduce opportunities to offend (Warr, 1998). Fourth, new roles can bring about new attitudes and beliefs about the value of offending. This can create a more prosocial self-identity and a renewed purpose in life that inspires a desire to maintain a pattern of non-offending.

Unresolved questions from the age-graded theory

Although the age-graded theory of informal social control is arguably the most influential theory of desistance (Laub et al., 2018), there are at least three unresolved questions about the relationship between informal social controls and desistance (see Nguyen & Loughran, 2018). These questions relate to (1) the importance of turning points at different age-stages, (2) whether turning points are actually a consequence of desistance, and (3) whether certain characteristics in adolescence influence which individuals experience, or benefit from, informal social control.

Regarding the first unresolved question, Sampson and Laub (1997) described informal social controls as age-graded. Timing matters (Ouimet & Le Blanc, 1996). For example, Uggen (2000) found that those employed at age 26 and younger were less likely to terminate their involvement in offending compared to those who were employed and were older than 26. It is not just that the person is old enough; it is that they are mature and more likely to value these different sources of informal social control (Nguyen & Loughran, 2018). An individual does not necessarily fully value an adult social role the moment they enter that role. Becoming employed before passing through other key life stages may increase the risk of offending (Bachman & Schulenberg, 1993). Similarly, parenthood early in the life-course before the development of different elements of maturation may leave individuals poorly equipped, both in terms of maturation and financial stability, to manage in a prosocial way stressful events that come with parenting (Na, 2016).

Regarding the second unresolved question, recognizing that informal social controls act as turning points at certain developmental stages but not others introduces a paradox. If informal social controls do not begin to matter until later in adulthood, why are nearly all desistance trajectories characterized by a decline in offending that starts in late adolescence or early adulthood (Piquero, 2008)? Indeed, each trajectory in the UJD Study resembled the age-crime curve (Sampson & Laub, 2003) yet Laub and Sampson (2003) pointed to factors that were critical for desistance that did not emerge until middle adulthood (i.e., after the process of desistance was underway). Skardhamar and Savolainen (2014) showed that the process of desistance typically preceded entry into adult roles. As an individual's offending declines, do they become more likely to enter adult roles? Given that the process of desistance is typically underway by emerging adulthood (Piquero, 2008), research must look earlier in the life-course to identify the factors that initiated this process. This does not mean that informal social controls later in life are irrelevant, only that it may be a misnomer to describe them as "turning" points. It may be more accurate to consider informal social controls later in the life-course as factors that speed up the desistance process. Figure 8.1 illustrates this point by showing conviction trajectories through mature adulthood for ISVYOS participants (see Chapter 5 for a description of the model). For all trajectories, convictions peaked in adolescence. Over a decade later at age 27 (i.e., the age at which Uggen (2000) found employment to be helpful for desistance), the two trajectories characterized by desistance were already at a near-zero rate of offending. Thus, if employment were to be a literal turning point, it would need to occur, and matter, much earlier in the life-course than age 27.

Regarding the third unresolved question, research is needed to address whether individuals involved in crime are equally likely to experience and benefit from informal social control. Differences in the likelihood of experiencing informal social control is referred to as selection effects.

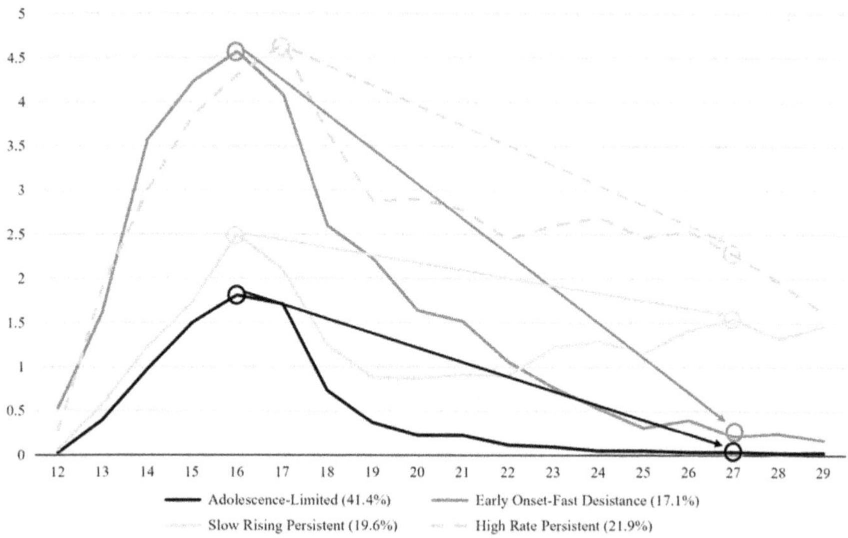

Figure 8.1 Demonstrating the timing of desistance relative to when previous research (Uggen, 2000) found employment helpful for desistance. The arrows illustrate that the process of desistance for the adolescence-limited and early-onset fast desistance trajectories was essentially complete by age 27.

Differences in the likelihood of benefiting from informal social controls is referred to as treatment effect heterogeneity. For example, would the individual who experienced a high level of family conflict in adolescence benefit from informal social controls in adulthood in the same way as individuals with low levels of family conflict in adolescence? State dependence and cumulative disadvantage are two developmental principles explaining why selection effects and treatment effect heterogeneity may occur. State dependence refers to a process whereby prior offending negatively alters a person's life circumstances. For example, incarceration may result in a person losing their job, which weakens their sources of informal social control. Cumulative disadvantage refers to a process whereby a person's experience of certain risk factors has a cascading impact on other life domains, including a reduction in the likelihood of experiencing or benefiting from informal social control.

Sampson and Laub's (1997) initial presentation of their age-graded theory acknowledged that interventions by the formal justice system can sever social bonds through state dependent effects. The justice system response to criminal behavior can profoundly impact life circumstances in ways that increase the risk of future offending (Nagin & Paternoster, 2000). For example, the community reentry experiences of persons adjudicated for sexual offenses include entering disadvantaged neighborhoods that provide fewer opportunities for housing and employment (Mustaine et al., 2006) and minimal social support (e.g., Bohmert et al., 2016). Similarly, developmentalists pointed to the combination of neuropsychological deficits and family adversity in childhood as factors that interfere with normative progression through developmental stages and make turning points less likely (Moffitt, 1993). Consequently, the likelihood of acquiring informal social controls (i.e., selection effects) and benefiting from these informal social controls (i.e., treatment effect heterogeneity) is reduced. Laub and Sampson's (2003) updated version of their age-graded theory gave less credence to state dependence and cumulative disadvantage principles. Instead, they considered desistance as the default state for all involved in crime because informal social controls were a normative aspect of the life-course. There was simply too much random variation over the life-course, in part because of human agency and macro-level social structures, for a person's upbringing in adolescence to preclude experiencing the beneficial impact of informal social control.

Empirical evidence for selection effects and treatment effect heterogeneity is mixed. Laub and Sampson (2003) presented qualitative evidence that men with criminogenic backgrounds had quality marriages that helped promote desistance (also see quantitative analyses in Laub et al., 1998; Sampson et al., 2006). On the other hand, research using data from the Toledo Adolescent Relationships Study found that levels of violence were higher for men with prior high levels of antisocial behavior who were in relationships with women with low levels of prior antisocial behavior (Cooper et al., 2020). In fact, partner violence was more likely to occur when disparities in risk were present. That is, a highly antisocial man was more likely to engage in partner violence when their partner's risk for antisocial behavior was low. With respect to treatment effect heterogeneity, Blokland and Nieuwbeerta's (2005) long-term study of justice-involved persons from the Netherlands showed that life circumstances like marriage were associated with desistance, but the influence of such circumstances was weaker for individuals who offended more frequently.

ISVYOS data

Data on participants from Cohort I and Cohort II were used to address some of these unresolved questions by examining: (1) whether characteristics in adolescence were informative of the quality of adult informal social controls (i.e., selection effects), (2) whether sources of adult informal social control were prospectively associated with a lower rate of convictions, and (3) whether the relationship between informal social controls and a lower rate of convictions was moderated by characteristics in adolescence (i.e., treatment effect heterogeneity).

Risk and informal social control in adolescence

Several risk/needs factors in adolescence were used to test for selection effects and treatment effect heterogeneity. One of these measures of risk was derived from the Youth Criminal Risk and Needs Assessment (YCRNA), which is an in-house risk assessment tool regularly completed by BC Corrections practitioners (Peters, 2016). Participants were an average of 15.28 years old ($SD = 1.50$) at the time of their baseline YCRNA, which was used in all analyses in this chapter. Three scales were created from YCRNA items. First, to look at the association between past and future informal social control, we summed the ratings of five indicators of informal social control: family relationships, parental supervision, living arrangements, education and employment, and peer relations. Ratings were made on a scale from 0-3. Items were reverse-coded so that higher scores reflected higher levels of informal social control ($M = 9.41$; $SD = 3.02$; Cronbach's alpha = 0.76). To capture cumulative disadvantage, we created a measure of individual-level risk based on the sum of 32 dichotomous risk factors concerning, for example, mental health, adverse childhood experiences, peer delinquency, and criminal behavior ($M = 7.75$; $SD = 5.35$; Cronbach's alpha = 0.85). We also created a measure of family-level risk based on the sum of 11 dichotomous risk factors ($M = 2.73$; $SD = 2.30$; Cronbach's alpha = 0.70). Participants with higher scores on the family-level risk scale tended to have uninvolved caregivers with substance use issues and histories of their own abuse experiences. This scale also included an item measuring parents' uncooperativeness with the justice system, meaning that the family did not help probation officers and social workers with facilitating access to intervention and treatment strategies aimed to benefit the young person. To measure state dependence, we calculated the number of months participants spent incarcerated between ages 12–17 ($M = 8.50$; $SD = 8.63$).

Emerging adulthood informal social control

Informal social control was measured using data from the Adult Community Risk Needs Assessment (ACRNA), which is regularly completed as part of case management practices (Hannah-Moffatt & Maurutto, 2003). At the most recent stage of data collection (December 2019), ACRNA data were searched for 972 participants, 241 of whom did not have an ACRNA (24.8% of all persons searched). This was because their record was sealed (77.6% of such cases) or because an ACRNA was never completed (22.4% of such cases). For the remaining 731 participants, 644 (88.1%) had an ACRNA between ages 18–23. This included 538 men (83.5%), 101 women (15.7%), and 5 participants whose gender was unknown (0.8%). On average, participants were 21.98 years old ($SD = 1.36$; R = 18.42–23.92) at the time their ACRNA was completed. Focusing on this age-stage was important given that it often coincided with the timing of desistance for this sample. Focusing on informal social controls too far in the future may mean that declines in convictions predicted informal social control rather than vice-versa (i.e., the first unresolved question associated with the age-graded theory).

The ACRNA included five indicators of informal social control: family relationships, living arrangements, intimate partner relationships, vocational skills, and employment patterns. Justice system practitioners rated the quality of each informal social control on a 0–3 scale that we reverse-coded so that higher scores reflected more positive indications of informal social control. Thus, "0" indicated that the informal social control in question was causing major interference in the background of the individual, "1" indicated that it was causing some interference, "2" indicated that it was not causing interference, and "3" indicated that the informal social control was a strength.

Figure 8.2 shows the ratings for each informal social control from the ACRNA. Practitioners rarely rated an informal social control as a strength. Accordingly, for analyses examining each type of informal social control, we recoded each item by merging the "0" and "1" scores and "2" and "3" scores to create a dichotomous variable where "0" reflected an informal social control that was causing interference and "1" reflected a positive informal social control (i.e., one that at least was not resulting in dysfunction). For each source of informal social control, more than half the sample experienced this adult outcome in a negative way (i.e., it caused at least minor interference in the participant's life). Slightly less than 15% of participants experienced a positive intimate partner relationship according to justice system practitioners. There was strong concordance between having one type of positive informal social control and another type of informal social control (see Table 8.1). For example, 73.8% of individuals with a positive connection to family also had a positive living arrangement. Positive sources of informal social control were least informative of having a positive intimate partner relationship. For example, only 23.8% of individuals with a positive connection to family also had a positive intimate partner relationship. There were no gender differences in the prevalence of each of the five informal social controls.

To create an informal social control scale in adulthood, similar to our youth-based measure, the five items (scored on the 0-3 scale) were summed so that higher scores reflected more positive levels of informal social control ($M = 10.47$; $SD = 2.71$; Cronbach's alpha = 0.76). There were no gender differences in the average level of informal social control despite women incurring a much lower rate of convictions compared to men (Chapter 5).

Desistance

Unlike past chapters, we did not look at conviction trajectories because informal social controls were assessed at different points in adulthood and the number of years of follow-up was not as extensive. For this chapter, we measured the number of convictions incurred following each individual's

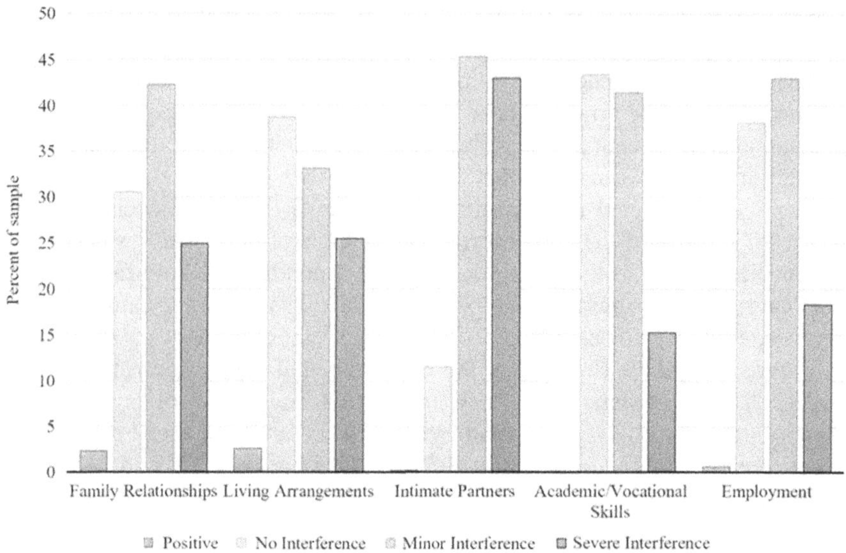

Figure 8.2 The quality of emerging adulthood informal social control for the sample.

ACRNA. Participants averaged 7.08 convictions ($SD = 9.45$; $R = 0–75$) during the follow-up period, which ran for an average of 2,588.69 days ($SD = 1459.33$), or about seven years. We accounted for variation in the length of the follow-up period among participants by creating an offset variable. We first identified the number of days between a person's ACRNA ($M = 21.98$ years old; $SD = 1.36$) and their age at the time that their criminal history was most recently coded ($M = 29.02$; $SD = 3.81$). We calculated for each participant the number of days they spent incarcerated during their follow-up period ($M = 415.33$; $SD = 620.19$). For each participant, we subtracted days incarcerated from days followed-up to identify the number of days they were free in the community ($M = 2{,}173.35$; $SD = 1{,}392.89$). For each participant, their number of days free in the community was divided by 6,879, which represented the number of days free for the individual with the most days free in the community. All individuals in the sample, therefore, had an exposure value between 0.00 and 1.00. This exposure value was accounted for in subsequent analyses. Individuals who were free for less than 0.5% of the total follow-up period ($n = 8$) and those who were deceased ($n = 10$) were excluded from analyses predicting the number of convictions incurred during the follow-up period.

Table 8.1 Concordance between measures of informal social control in emerging adulthood

	Family relationships	*Living arrangements*	*Intimate partners*	*Academic/vocational skills*	*Employment*
Family Relationships	-	73.8%***	23.8%***	67.9%***	60.0%***
Living Arrangements	58.5%***	-	20.7%***	60.4%***	58.3%***
Intimate Partners	66.7%***	73.3%***	-	61.3%**	60.0%***
Academic/Vocational Skills	51.4%***	57.8%***	16.7%**	-	68.2%***
Employment	51.0%***	62.5%***	18.1%***	76.5%***	-

** $p < .01$
*** $p < .001$.
* $p < .05$
Notes: Significance based on chi-square statistic. The percentage in each cell reflects the percentage within a particular row that were also characterized by the positive informal social control in a given column.

Between-group analyses

First, to address the debate about the importance of selection effects (Moffitt, 1993) versus the randomness of turning points (Laub & Sampson, 2003) we examined whether indicators in adolescence of individual-level and family-level risk (i.e., cumulative disadvantage) and time incarcerated (i.e., state dependence) predicted quality of informal social controls in adulthood. Second, in line with expectations from the age-graded theory of informal social control, we examined whether experiencing quality informal social controls in emerging adulthood was related to a lower rate of convictions later in the life-course. Third, in consideration of treatment effect heterogeneity, we examined whether the impact of positive informal social control on conviction outcomes varied based on a person's level of cumulative disadvantage and state dependence in adolescence.

Informal social control in adulthood: Selection effects?

Table 8.2 presents a series of logistic regression analyses where five different informal social controls in emerging adulthood (family relationships, living arrangements, intimate partner relationships, academic/vocational skills, and employment) were regressed onto measures in adolescence of informal social control, individual-level risk, family-level risk, and days incarcerated between ages 12–17. Approximately six years elapsed between these measures and measures of informal social control in emerging adulthood.

Beginning with the measure of informal social control in adolescence, a one-unit increase in this scale significantly increased the odds of having a positive family relationship in emerging adulthood. A one-unit increase in individual-level risk significantly decreased the odds of having a positive family relationship in emerging adulthood. Contrary to theoretical expectation, a one-unit increase in family-level risk significantly increased the odds of having a positive living arrangement in emerging adulthood. It is possible that high levels of family risk influenced individuals to avoid living with family and to seek independent living, which was seen by practitioners as a positive outcome. A one-unit increase in months incarcerated in adolescence significantly decreased the odds of having a positive living arrangement in emerging adulthood, of having a positive intimate partner relationship in emerging adulthood, and of having a positive employment status in emerging adulthood.[2] The relationship between incarceration in adolescence and the lack of positive sources of informal social control in emerging adulthood may be evidence of state dependent effects in which incarceration isolated the young person from opportunities to bond to family or enter the workforce. Another possibility is that time incarcerated was a proxy for a person's underlying risk for offending. Of the two

Table 8.2 Logistic regression analyses of characteristics in adolescence predicting quality of adult informal social control

	Family relationships OR (95% CI)	*Living arrangements OR (95% CI)*	*Intimate partners OR (95% CI)*	*Academic & vocational skills OR (95% CI)*	*Employment OR (95% CI)*
Control Variables					
Male Participants	0.90 (0.46–1.76)	1.86 (0.97–3.56)	1.12 (0.40–3.19)	0.88 (0.48–1.59)	0.81 (0.44–1.49)
Ethnicity					
White	–	–	–	–	–
Indigenous	0.62 (0.36–1.07)	0.96 (0.58–1.58)	**0.38 (0.16–0.94)***	**1.66 (1.04–2.66)***	1.61 (0.99–2.61)
Non-Indigenous Minority	0.99 (0.49–2.01)	1.04 (0.52–2.11)	0.89 (0.32–2.46)	1.37 (0.70–2.68)	1.43 (0.72–2.86)
Adolescence Characteristics					
Months Incarcerated	0.97 (0.94–1.00)	**0.95 (0.92–0.98)****	**0.92 (0.86–0.98)***	0.98 (0.96–1.01)	**0.96 (0.93–0.99)***
Individual-Level Risk	**0.91 (0.86–0.97)****	0.97 (0.92–1.01)	0.99 (0.91–1.07)	0.97 (0.93–1.02)	1.01 (0.97–1.06)
Family-Level Risk	1.08 (0.96–1.22)	**1.13 (1.01–1.27)***	0.92 (0.76–1.12)	1.04 (0.93–1.16)	1.05 (0.94–1.17)
ISC Scale	**1.13 (1.03–1.23)****	**1.16 (1.06–1.26)****	1.10 (0.98–1.25)	1.01 (0.93–1.10)	1.05 (0.97–1.15)
Model Fit					
-2LL	401.16	437.04	210.93	471.29	445.91
χ^2 (df)	30.67(7)***	32.59(7)***	21.21(7)**	9.40(7)	15.99(7)*

* $p < .05$
** $p < .01$
*** $p < .001$.

Notes: OR = odds ratio; CI = confidence interval. For the adolescence informal social control (ISC) scale, higher scores indicated more positive levels of informal social control. For the risk factor scales, higher scores reflected higher levels of risk.

possible explanations, state dependent effects seemed more plausible given that direct measures of individual-level risk were controlled for in the analyses.

Informal social control and adult offending outcomes

Negative binomial analyses were conducted to examine whether informal social control measured in emerging adulthood was informative of future convictions after controlling for differences in exposure time. The follow-up period covered an average of seven years between the ACRNA and the date that convictions were most recently recorded. In Model 1 of Table 8.3, a positive family relationship was associated with a 31% decrease in the incidence rate of convictions. This aligned with Boman and Mowen's (2018) finding that family support was associated with lower levels of self-reported reoffending among persons from the Serious and Violent Offender Reentry Initiative Study. Additionally, a positive intimate partner relationship was associated with a 46% decrease in the incidence rate of convictions. Model 2 in Table 8.3 indicated that a one-unit increase in the emerging adulthood informal social control scale (i.e., the sum of the five indicators of informal

Table 8.3 Negative binomial analysis using adult informal social controls in emerging adulthood to predict future convictions

	Model 1 *Convictions* *IRR (SE)*	*Model 2* *Convictions* *IRR (SE)*
Control Variables		
Male Participants	**2.54 (0.53)*****	**2.67 (0.53)*****
Ethnicity		
White	-	-
Indigenous	1.32 (0.21)	1.32 (0.21)
Non-Indigenous Minority	0.87 (0.19)	0.88 (0.19)
Adult Informal Social Control		
Family Relationships	**0.69 (0.13)***	-
Living Arrangements	0.78 (0.13)	-
Intimate Partners	**0.54 (0.12)****	-
Academic/Vocational Skills	1.22 (0.23)	-
Employment	0.72 (0.13)	-
ISC Scale	-	**0.86 (0.03)*****
Model Fit		
LL	−1684.25	−1699.74
χ^2 (df)	52.02(8)***	55.31(4)***

* $p < .05$
** $p < .01$
*** $p < .001$.
Notes: IRR = incidence rate ratio; SE = standard error; ISC = informal social control. The ISC scale represents the sum of the five different types of informal social control examined in Model 1.

social control coded in their original 0–3 scale) was associated with a 14% decrease in the incidence rate of new convictions.

In line with Laub and Sampson's (2003) expectations, informal social controls, in particular family relationships and intimate relationships, were associated with a lower frequency of convictions. Employment and academic/vocational skills were unrelated to a lower incidence rate of new convictions, possibly because they were measured at a point where individuals may be too young or not yet at a point of maturity where they stand to benefit from employment (also see Uggen, 2000). Hill et al. (2017) noted that financial independence at a younger age may be related to increased involvement in offending and so these particular adult roles and skills might not be turning points for this sample at this time. This is not to say that these factors are unimportant for desistance. It is possible that their emergence later in adulthood helps speed up or maintain the desistance process.

The influence of characteristics in adolescence on treatment effect heterogeneity

Tables 8.4–8.7 examined whether certain characteristics in adolescence moderated the relationship between informal social controls in emerging adulthood and future convictions. For example, a positive intimate partner relationship in emerging adulthood was a protective factor against future convictions (see Table 8.3), but would this relationship hold at different levels of different types of risk factors in adolescence? Number of months incarcerated in adolescence (Table 8.4) did not significantly interact with any of the five types of informal social control examined, nor did it moderate the relationship between the informal social control scale in emerging adulthood and future offending. Measures in emerging adulthood of positive family relationships, positive intimate partner relationships, and the informal social control scale each were prospectively and negatively associated with future convictions.

Individual-level risk in adolescence (Table 8.5) moderated the relationship between emerging adulthood living arrangements and future convictions such that living arrangements only protected against future convictions when individual-level risk in adolescence was low. In the same way, individual-level risk in adolescence also moderated the relationship between the emerging adulthood informal social control scale and future convictions.

Family-level risk in adolescence (Table 8.6) moderated the relationship between family relationships and convictions and living arrangements and convictions such that these informal social controls protected against convictions only when family-level risk in adolescence was low. In the same way, family-level risk moderated the relationship between the emerging adulthood informal social control scale and future convictions.

Level of informal social control in adolescence (Table 8.7) moderated the relationship between family relationships and convictions and intimate

Table 8.4 Negative binomial analysis of interactions between emerging adulthood informal social control and months incarcerated in adolescence

	Model 1 *Convictions* IRR (SE)	*Model 2* *Convictions* *IRR (SE)*	*Model 3* *Convictions* *IRR (SE)*	*Model 4* *Convictions* *IRR (SE)*	*Model 5* *Convictions* *IRR (SE)*	*Model 6* *Convictions* *IRR (SE)*
Control Variables						
Male Participants	**2.42 (0.51)*****	**2.44 (0.52)*****	**2.44 (0.52)*****	**2.41 (0.51)*****	**2.41 (0.51)*****	**2.48 (0.51)*****
Ethnicity						
White	-	-	-	-	-	-
Indigenous	1.29 (0.21)	1.28 (0.21)	1.29 (0.21)	1.30 (0.21)	1.30 (0.21)	1.30 (0.20)
Non-Indigenous Minority	0.93 (0.22)	0.94 (0.22)	0.93 (0.22)	0.94 (0.22)	0.96 (0.23)	0.96 (0.22)
Adult Informal Social Control (Main Effect)						
Family Relationships	**0.68 (0.13)***	**0.69 (0.13)***	**0.68 (0.13)***	**0.68 (0.13)***	**0.68 (0.13)***	-
Living Arrangements	0.80 (0.13)	0.80 (0.13)	0.80 (0.13)	0.80 (0.13)	0.78 (0.13)	-
Intimate Partners	**0.61 (0.14)***	**0.61 (0.14)***	**0.56 (0.15)***	**0.61 (0.14)***	**0.62 (0.14)***	-
Academic/Vocational Skills	1.21 (0.23)	1.20 (0.23)	1.21 (0.23)	1.21 (0.23)	1.21 (0.24)	-
Employment	0.72 (0.14)	0.71 (0.14)	0.71 (0.14)	0.72 (0.14)	0.72 (0.14)	-
ISC Scale	-	-	-	-	-	**0.86 (0.03)*****
Moderator (Main Effect)						
Months Incarcerated in Adolescence	1.02 (0.01)	1.02 (0.01)	**1.02 (0.01)***	1.02 (0.01)	1.02 (0.01)	1.02 (0.01)
Interaction						
Family Relationships x Months Incarcerated	1.00 (0.02)	-	-	-	-	-
Living Arrangements x Months Incarcerated	-	1.01 (0.02)	-	-	-	-
Intimate Partner x Months Incarcerated	-	-	0.98 (0.05)	-	-	-
Academic/Vocational x Months Incarcerated	-	-	-	1.01 (0.02)	-	-
Employment x Months Incarcerated	-	-	-	-	1.02 (0.02)	-

ISC Scale x Months Incarcerated	-	-	-	-	-	1.01 (0.00)
Model Fit						
LL	−1631.78	−1631.64	−1631.70	−1631.72	−1631.39	−1645.26
χ^2 (df)	54.57(10)***	54.85(10))***	54.73(10))***	54.69(10))***	55.35(10))***	59.52(6))***

* $p < .05$
*** $p < .001$.
** $p < .01$
Notes: IRR = incidence rate ratio; SE = standard error; ISC = informal social control. The ISC scale represents the sum of the five different types of informal social control.

Table 8.5 Negative binomial analysis of interactions between emerging adulthood informal social control and individual-level risk in adolescence

	Model 1 Convictions IRR (SE)	*Model 2 Convictions IRR (SE)*	*Model 3 Convictions IRR (SE)*	*Model 4 Convictions IRR (SE)*	*Model 5 Convictions IRR (SE)*	*Model 6 Convictions IRR (SE)*
Control Variables						
Male Participants	**2.70 (0.68)*****	**2.55 (0.64)*****	**2.83 (0.71)*****	**2.84 (0.72)*****	**2.79 (0.70)*****	**2.57 (0.64)*****
Ethnicity						
White	-	-	-	-	-	-
Indigenous	1.45 (0.29)	**1.50 (0.29)***	**1.54 (0.30)***	**1.56 (0.30)***	1.53 (0.30)	1.41 (0.26)
Non-Indigenous Minority	0.93 (0.28)	0.94 (0.28)	0.95 (0.28)	0.89 (0.27)	0.96 (0.29)	0.91 (0.25)
Adult Informal Social Control (Main Effect)						
Family Relationships	0.72 (0.17)	0.73 (0.17)	0.69 (0.16)	0.69 (0.16)	0.68 (0.16)	-
Living Arrangements	0.93 (0.19)	0.90 (0.18)	0.91 (0.18)	0.91 (0.18)	0.90 (0.18)	-
Intimate Partners	0.75 (0.21)	0.78 (0.22)	0.78 (0.23)	0.75 (0.21)	0.75 (0.21)	-
Academic/Vocational Skills	1.25 (0.29)	1.23 (0.29)	1.24 (0.29)	1.23 (0.29)	1.25 (0.30)	-
Employment	0.63 (0.14)	**0.60 (0.14)***	0.66 (0.15)	0.68 (0.16)	0.66 (0.15)	-
ISC Scale	-	-	-	-	-	**0.87 (0.03)*****
Moderator (Main Effect)						
Individual Risk in Adolescence	0.99 (0.02)	0.97 (0.02)	1.00 (0.02)	1.10 (0.02)	1.00 (0.02)	1.01 (0.02)
Interaction						
Family Relationships x Individual Risk	1.06 (0.04)	-	-	-	-	-
Living Arrangements x Individual Risk	-	**1.10 (0.04)****	-	-	-	-
Intimate Partners x Individual Risk	-	-	1.04 (0.06)	-	-	-
Academic/Vocational Skills x Individual Risk	-	-	-	0.97 (0.04)	-	-
Employment x Individual Risk	-	-	-	-	1.01 (0.03)	-

ISC Scale x Individual Risk	–	–	–	–	–	**1.02 (0.01)***
Model Fit						
LL	−1142.63	−1139.97	−1143.56	−1143.42	−1143.72	−1155.52
χ^2 (df)	35.25(10)***	40.56(10)***	33.40(10)***	33.68(10)***	33.09(10)***	38.15(6)***

* $p < .05$
** $p < .01$
*** $p < .001$.
Notes: IRR = incidence rate ratio; SE = standard error; ISC = informal social control. The ISC scale represents the sum of the five different types of informal social control.

Table 8.6 Negative binomial analysis of interactions between emerging adulthood informal social control and family-level risk in adolescence

	Model 1 Convictions IRR (SE)	*Model 2 Convictions IRR (SE)*	*Model 3 Convictions IRR (SE)*	*Model 4 Convictions IRR (SE)*	*Model 5 Convictions IRR (SE)*	*Model 6 Convictions IRR (SE)*
Control Variables						
Male Participants	**2.79 (0.74)*****	**2.75 (0.72)*****	**2.91 (0.78)*****	**2.92 (0.78)*****	**2.92 (0.78)*****	**2.92 (0.85)*****
Ethnicity						
White	-	-	-	-	-	-
Indigenous	1.31 (0.27)	1.36 (0.28)	**1.53 (0.31)***	1.52 (0.31)	**1.53 (0.31)***	1.32 (0.27)
Non-Indigenous Minority	0.87 (0.27)	0.79 (0.25)	0.90 (0.29)	0.93 (0.31)	0.95 (0.31)	0.84 (0.25)
Adult Informal Social Control (Main Effect)						
Family Relationships	0.63 (0.15)	0.70 (0.17)	0.67 (0.17)	0.66 (0.16)	0.66 (0.16)	-
Living Arrangements	1.01 (0.22)	0.92 (0.20)	0.96 (0.21)	0.95 (0.21)	0.96 (0.21)	-
Intimate Partners	0.98 (0.30)	0.87 (0.27)	0.86 (0.27)	0.85 (0.26)	0.85 (0.26)	-
Academic/Vocational Skills	1.29 (0.33)	1.20 (0.30)	1.36 (0.36)	1.38 (0.36)	1.36 (0.36)	-
Employment	**0.58 (0.14)***	**0.61 (0.15)***	**0.61 (0.15)***	**0.60 (0.15)***	**0.60 (0.15)***	-
ISC Scale	-	-	-	-	-	**0.88 (0.03)****
Moderator (Main Effect)						
Family Risk in Adolescence	0.92 (0.04)	**0.85 (0.05)****	0.99 (0.04)	0.97 (0.05)	0.96 (0.05)	1.00 (0.04)
Interaction						
Family Relationships x Family Risk	**1.34 (0.13)****	-	-	-	-	-
Living Arrangements x Family Risk	-	**1.35 (0.11)*****	-	-	-	-
Intimate Partners x Family Risk	-	-	1.04 (0.16)	-	-	-
Academic/Vocational Skills x Family Risk	-	-	-	1.05 (0.09)	-	-
Employment x Family Risk	-	-	-	-	1.07 (0.09)	-
ISC Scale x Family Risk	-	-	-	-	-	**1.05 (0.02)****

Model Fit						
LL	−994.14	−992.37	−998.89	−994.14	−998.53	-1006.18
χ^2 (df)	39.52(10)***	43.06(10)***	30.01(10)***	39.52(10)***	30.73(10)***	38.01(6)***

* $p < .05$
** $p < .01$
*** $p < .001$.
Notes: IRR = incidence rate ratio; SE = standard error; ISC = informal social control. The ISC scale represents the sum of the five different types of informal social control.

Table 8.7 Negative binomial analysis of interactions between emerging adulthood informal social control and level of informal social control in adolescence

	Model 1 Convictions IRR (SE)	*Model 2 Convictions IRR (SE)*	*Model 3 Convictions IRR (SE)*	*Model 4 Convictions IRR (SE)*	*Model 5 Convictions IRR (SE)*	*Model 6 Convictions IRR (SE)*
Control Variables†††						
Male Participants	**2.49 (0.58)*****	**2.57 (0.61)*****	**3.10 (0.70)*****	**2.74 (0.64)*****	**2.80 (0.66)*****	**2.75 (0.62)*****
Ethnicity						
White	-	-	-	-	-	-
Indigenous	1.28 (0.22)	1.38 (0.24)	1.35 (0.23)	1.41 (0.25)	1.33 (0.23)	1.30 (0.22)
Non-Indigenous Minority	1.00 (0.26)	0.97 (0.25)	0.94 (0.24)	0.97 (0.25)	1.02 (0.27)	0.93 (0.23)
Adult Informal Social Control (Main Effect)						
Family Relationships	**0.67 (0.14)***	0.68 (0.14)	0.71 (0.14)	0.70 (0.14)	**0.67 (0.14)***	-
Living Arrangements	0.90 (0.16)	0.85 (0.15)	0.98 (0.18)	0.85 (0.15)	0.84 (0.15)	-
Intimate Partners	**0.57 (0.14)***	0.61 (0.16)	**0.45 (0.11)****	**0.60 (0.16)***	**0.57 (0.14)***	-
Academic/Vocational Skills	1.20 (0.25)	1.22 (0.26)	1.08 (0.22)	1.20 (0.25)	1.20 (0.25)	-
Employment	**0.63 (0.13)***	**0.65 (0.14)***	**0.70 (0.14)***	0.69 (0.14)	0.69 (0.14)	-
Emerging Adulthood ISC Scale	-	-	-	-	-	**0.86 (0.03)*****
Moderator (Main Effect)						
Adolescence ISC Scale	1.00 (0.03)	0.99 (0.04)	0.99 (0.03)	**0.94 (0.03)***	0.97 (0.03)	0.97 (0.03)
Interaction Effect						
Family Relationships x Adolescence ISC Scale	**0.86 (0.05)****	-	-	-	-	-
Living Arrangements x Adolescence ISC Scale	-	0.93 (0.05)	-	-	-	-
Intimate Partners x Adolescence ISC Scale	-	-	**0.70 (0.06)*****	-	-	-
Academic/Vocational Skills x Adolescence ISC Scale	-	-	-	1.05 (0.06)	-	-
Employment x Adolescence ISC Scale	-	-	-	-	0.95 (0.05)	-
	-	-	-	-	-	**0.97 (0.01)****

Emerging Adulthood ISC Scale x Adolescence ISC Scale						
Model Fit						
LL	-1385.11	-1387.64	-1378.41	-1388.23	-1388.15	-1006.18
χ^2 (df)	49.98(10)***	44.92(10)***	63.38(10)***	43.74(10)***	43.91(10)***	38.01(6)***

* $p < .05$
** $p < .01$
*** $p < .001$.
Notes: IRR = incidence rate ratio; SE = standard error; ISC = informal social control. The ISC scale represents the sum of the five different types of informal social control.

partner relationships and convictions such that these sources of informal social control in emerging adulthood protected against convictions only if the participant came from a background characterized by high levels of positive informal social control in adolescence. This was also observed when looking at how levels of informal social control in adolescence moderated the relationship between the emerging adulthood informal social control scale and future convictions.

In sum, it is notable that the informal social controls that were significant predictors of convictions in the analysis of main effects (see Table 8.3) were consistently moderated by different measures of risk in adolescence. Thus, treatment effect heterogeneity was present. That is, positive sources of informal social control in emerging adulthood were not associated with a lower frequency of future convictions when individuals were also characterized by a greater level of risk factors in adolescence. To illustrate the above findings, Figure 8.3 presents plots that show the interactive effect on convictions between each measure of risk in adolescence and the emerging adulthood informal social control scale.

Months incarcerated in adolescence did not significantly impact the relationship between informal social control and convictions (top-left panel of Figure 8.3). Individuals with high levels of informal social control in emerging adulthood but also high individual-level risk in adolescence had a predicted rate of convictions that looked similar to individuals with average levels of informal social control and individual-level risk (top-right panel). The same observation was made for the moderating effect of family-level risk (bottom-left panel). Lastly, individuals benefited from high levels of informal social control in emerging adulthood only if they also had high levels of informal social control in adolescence (bottom-right). In other words, if an individual's experience of positive informal social control in emerging adulthood was not a continuation of their level of positive informal social control in adolescence, then it was less likely to influence a lower incidence rate of new convictions.

Informal social control among serious and violent youth grown up

There are a few caveats to mention before interpreting these between-group analyses. A limitation of these analyses is that parenthood was not measured despite it being a particular important source of informal social control (Laub & Sampson, 2003). Our findings might differ from Laub and Sampson (2003) because we measured informal social control in emerging adulthood across male and female participants from different ethnic backgrounds. Laub and Sampson focused on informal social control for White males in later stages of adulthood. As well, Laub and Sampson relied on self-reported informal social control whereas the current study relied on reports from justice system practitioners regarding the quality of informal social control. While this may be a limitation, practitioners' ratings of

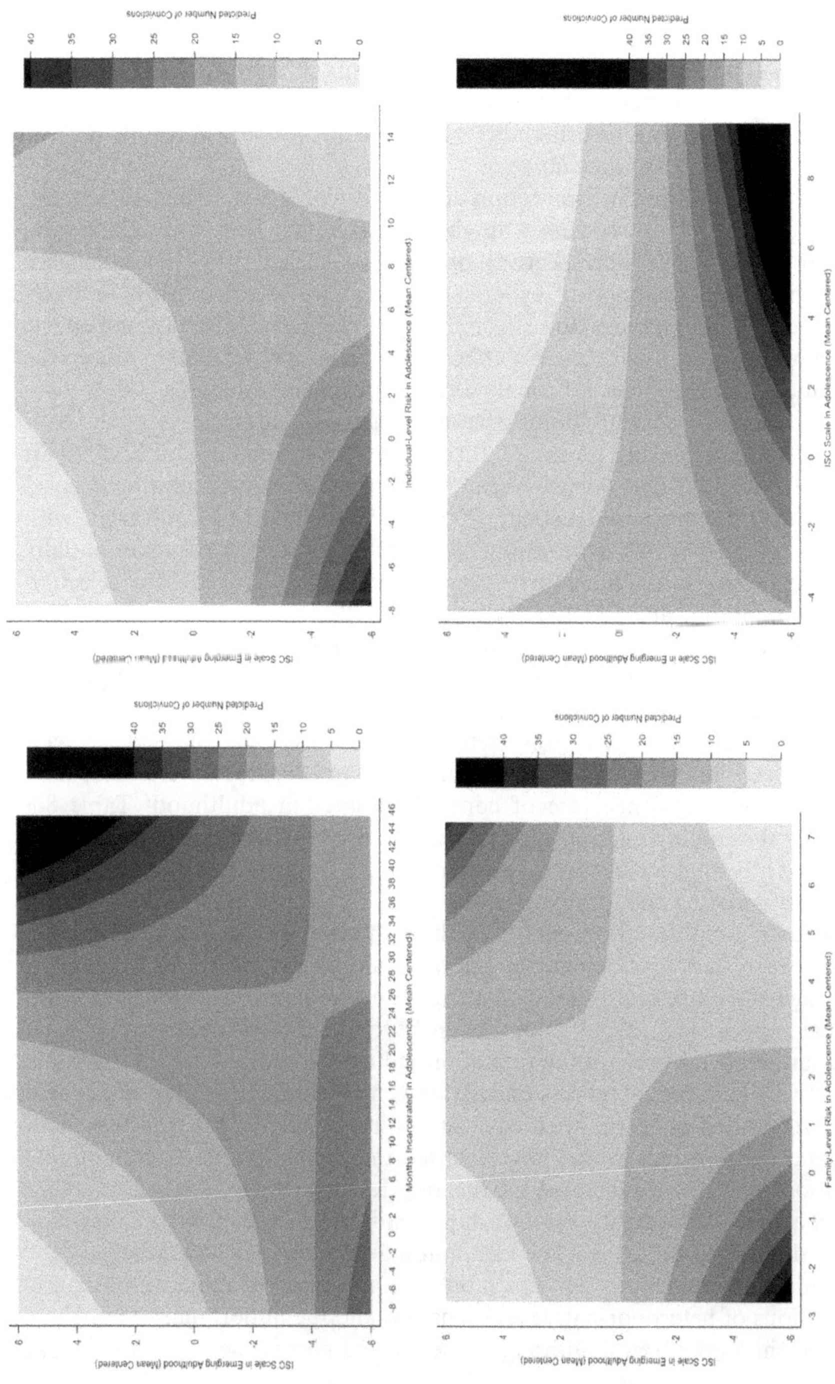

Figure 8.3 Continuous by continuous interactions between adult informal social controls and characteristics in adolescence.
Notes: Variables comprising the interaction term were mean-centered. The mean ("0") does not appear in the center of the x-axis because characteristics in adolescence were non-normally distributed. See Tables 8.4–8.7 for the coefficients associated with each interaction.

informal social control were based on their interviews with our participants as opposed to guesswork or relying on court reports. Moreover, one of the benefits of measuring informal social control quality is that practitioners cannot exactly help their client enter a relationship, but they can find ways to help support or provide resources for existing relationships (e.g., couples counseling). Identifying, for example, intimate partners as a source of strength and helping to bring about the best in these relationships may be useful for promoting desistance.

The first question in this section addressed whether informal social controls occurred for everyone, at random (i.e., in line with Laub and Sampson's life-course perspective), or whether characteristics in adolescence influenced the likelihood of experiencing informal social controls in emerging adulthood (i.e., selection effects). Table 8.2 showed that selection effects were present, albeit with modest effect sizes. Various risk factors reduced the likelihood of positive informal social control in emerging adulthood. Months incarcerated in adolescence was especially informative of the likelihood of experiencing positive informal social controls in adulthood. This aligned with state dependence research that found that incarceration delayed entry into adult roles (Huebner, 2005, 2007). While this contrasted with Laub and Sampson's description of informal social control as essentially unpredictable, other life-course perspectives acknowledged that selection effects are important. Elder (1994) noted that "less is known about the effect of personality and life patterns on social structure" and acknowledged that individuals are constrained by their environment and that this is important to understand life-course development (p. 5).

The second question in this section addressed whether individuals who experienced informal social control in emerging adulthood were associated with a lower incidence rate of convictions later in adulthood. Table 8.3 showed that family relationships and intimate partner relationships were the types of informal social control most important for improving the likelihood of desistance. At this developmental stage, family referred more so to an individual's biological parents than their children/spouse. This reflects the idea of arrested development in emerging adulthood, where individuals in this age-stage are still reliant on their parents for instrumental and emotional support (e.g., Côté, 2000). Even beyond adolescence, ties to parents play an important role in the rate of offending. Of course, it is also possible that the role of family reflects underlying genetic differences. Past life-course research raised concerns with equating intimate partner relationships with marital relationships. Some have asserted that being in a non-common law relationship can even increase the risk of offending. More recent scholarship emphasized that quality relationships tend to emerge prior to marriage (Skardhamar et al., 2015). The idea that marriage is somehow necessary for a quality relationship is perhaps more so a reflection of religious-based expectations of heteronormative relationships and the importance of marriage before children. Overall, although experiencing positive sources of informal social control in emerging adulthood was relatively rare for individuals incarcerated during adolescence, when such factors were present, they were associated with lower levels of convictions later in the life-course.

The third question in this section addressed whether there was evidence of treatment effect heterogeneity by examining whether individuals benefited from informal social controls differently according to their characteristics in adolescence. A series of moderation analyses (Tables 8.4–8.7) revealed that it was important to consider an individual's underlying level of risk to offend to understand how informal social controls in emerging adulthood operated. The ways in which positive life events impacted an individual's trajectory through the justice system varied according to level of risk in adolescence. This reiterated the importance of rehabilitation-focused interventions to help address underlying risk factors, many of which were beyond the young person's control. These results aligned with van der Geest et al.'s (2011) finding that the impact of employment on desistance varied according to whether employment was stable or temporary. Doherty and Ensminger (2013) found that marriage had a weaker association with desistance for men compared to women. Cooper et al. (2020) found that for men with high levels of antisocial behavior, an intimate relationship with women characterized by low levels of antisocial behavior (i.e., a relationship characterized by risk asymmetry) was more likely to result in the perpetration of partner violence. In sum, informal social controls do not have a uniform impact on desistance. We also found that the impact of emerging adulthood informal social control on a lower incidence rate of future convictions only occurred when these informal social controls represented the continuation of high levels of informal social control in adolescence. Informal social controls were not so much 'turning points' but rather a positive environment in adolescence that continued into adulthood.

Within-individual change in informal social control

The analyses thus far neglected important DLC questions about within-individual change in informal social control and its relationship with within-individual change in convictions. Analyses examining within-individual change are more in line with conceptualizations of desistance as a process (e.g., Bushway et al., 2001) Analyses of within-individual change are also useful because each participant acts as their own control, which means that the model controls for all time-invariant characteristics (Allison, 2015). For a subsample of 324 participants, a series of analyses were performed that examined the contemporary (i.e., within the same year of age) and prospective (i.e., one year later) relationship between within-individual change in the emerging adulthood informal social control scale and within-individual change in convictions. The inclusion criteria were that all individuals had an ACRNA for at least three of the six years that covered emerging adulthood (e.g., ages 18–23)[3].

We used the cross-lagged dynamic panel model in Stata (*xtdpdml*), which allows for the inclusion of a lagged dependent variable, lagged time-variant variables, and time invariant variables (Allison, 2015). There are several benefits of this analytic strategy. First, we were interested not just in within-individual change but also the direct effects of between-person differences in risk in adolescence on within-individual changes in convictions. Individuals may experience an identical degree of change in a qualitatively different way depending on their underlying level of risk (Boman & Mowen, 2018). Given the evidence shown earlier for treatment effect heterogeneity, it was important to examine whether baseline levels of risk in adolescence moderated the impact of within-individual change in informal social control on within-individual change in convictions. For example, a within-individual decrease in level of informal social control in emerging adulthood may be experienced in different ways for individuals characterized by high levels of informal social control in adolescence compared to individuals whose level of informal social control in adolescence was low. Individuals in the latter scenario are in a more precarious position where small changes in informal social control could have a larger impact on offending (see Boman & Mowen, 2018). Another strength of cross-lagged dynamic panel models is that they can control for the relationship between past and future offending. In traditional fixed-effects models, controlling for the lagged effect of convictions at time *t-1* violates assumptions of the model (Allison, 2015).[4]

Cross-lagged dynamic panel models were used to examine whether within-individual change in the emerging adulthood informal social control scale related to within-individual change in convictions when controlling for a lagged indicator of convictions and a series of invariant characteristics (e.g., demographics, risk factors in adolescence).[5] Two different analyses were conducted.[6] The first replicated Boman and Mowen's (2018) examination of the contemporaneous relationship between their exogenous variables (family support and criminogenic peers) and outcome variable (offending). For the second analysis, to establish temporal order, we applied a 1-year lag to the informal social control scale. All analyses controlled for exposure time and for baseline differences in four types of risk/protective factors in adolescence: (1) time spent incarcerated, (2) individual-level risk, (3) family-level risk, and (4) the adolescence informal social control scale (all measures described above). In line with Boman and Mowen (2018), we specified interaction terms to explore whether the impact of within-individual change in informal social control on within-individual change in convictions varied according to a person's level of risk/protective factors in adolescence.

The contemporaneous analysis (Table 8.8) indicated that within-individual increases in informal social control were associated with, within the same year of age, within-individual decreases in convictions (Model 1). This relationship was not moderated by any of the baseline measures (Models 2–5). Across all models, within-individual increases in exposure time were negatively associated with within-individual changes in convictions. This does not necessarily mean that being in the community reduced involvement in crime. Instead, convictions may have increased the likelihood of being incarcerated and spending more time incarcerated. Baseline indicators of individual-level risk in adolescence were positively associated with within-individual increases in convictions (i.e., higher levels of risk were associated with within-individual increases in convictions). The lagged measure of convictions at time *t*-1 was unrelated to within-individual change in convictions at time *t*. This could be because within-individual increases in convictions resulted in within-individual decreases in exposure time at time *t*. Accordingly, individuals would have less opportunity at time *t* to incur new convictions.

Once establishing temporal order by lagging the emerging adulthood measure of informal social control (Table 8.9), a different story emerged compared to the contemporaneous analysis. Within-individual changes in informal social control were unrelated to within-individual changes in convictions at the next year of age. Interactions between baseline indicators of risk in adolescence and within-individual change in informal social control at time *t*-1 were also unrelated to within-individual changes in convictions at time *t*. Once again, baseline indicators of individual-level risk in adolescence were positively associated with within-individual increases in convictions. In effect, characteristics established in adolescence were informative of the rate of change in convictions in emerging adulthood, but changes in informal social control in emerging adulthood were not associated with changes in convictions at the next year of age.

The importance of quality informal social controls

The analyses conducted thus far were not suitable for illustrating the complexity of the developmental histories, including informal social control experiences, of ISVYOS participants. To contextualize the quantitative analyses presented in this chapter, and to reiterate the importance of investigating the quality of informal social controls, we outlined James' (pseudonym) history of violence and how this transmitted to his relationships. We begin by discussing James' broader developmental history and criminal involvement to set the backdrop for the nature of his intimate partner relationships. James was characterized by a host of unresolved risk factors from his adolescence that appeared to directly impact how he performed in his role as a family member and as an intimate partner. Failing to acknowledge these factors in adolescence and, instead, making assumptions about desistance by default may create barriers to desistance. For James, adult roles, intimate relationships, and family relationships exacerbated his involvement in the justice system. James' case demonstrated the importance of considering treatment effect heterogeneity and avoiding assumptions that turning points are a normative process of the life-course. Making assumptions that individuals in adulthood will desist by default due to structurally

Table 8.8 Cross-lagged dynamic panel model focusing on the contemporaneous relationship between informal social control and convictions

Variable	*Model 1* *b coef. (SE)*	*Model 2* *b coef. (SE)*	*Model 3* *b coef. (SE)*	*Model 4* *b coef. (SE)*	*Model 5* *b coef. (SE)*
Independent variables					
Emerging Adulthood ISC Scale	**-0.14 (0.05)****	**-0.14 (0.05)****	**-0.14 (0.05)****	**-0.14 (0.05)****	**-0.13 (0.05)***
Control measures (Time variant)					
Lagged Convictions	-0.01 (0.03)	-0.01 (0.03)	-0.01 (0.03)	-0.004 (0.03)	-0.003 (0.03)
Exposure	**-3.68 (0.42)*****	**-3.62 (0.42)*****	**-3.71 (0.42)*****	**-3.69 (0.42)*****	**-3.70 (0.42)*****
Control measures in adolescence (Time invariant)					
Incarceration	-0.02 (0.05)	-0.11 (0.24)	-0.02 (0.05)	-0.02 (0.05)	-0.02 (0.05)
Individual Risk	**0.04 (0.02)***	**0.04 (0.02)***	-0.05 (0.10)	**0.04 (0.02)***	**0.04 (0.02)***
Family Risk	-0.04 (0.04)	-0.05 (0.04)	-0.04 (0.04)	-0.07 (0.26)	-0.05 (0.04)
ISC Scale	-0.01 (0.03)	-0.02 (0.03)	-0.01 (0.03)	-0.01 (0.03)	-0.03 (0.19)
Interaction Terms					
Emerging Adulthood ISC Scale x Incarceration in Adolescence	.	0.01 (0.02)	.	.	.
Emerging Adulthood ISC Scale x Individual Risk in Adolescence	.	.	0.01 (0.01)	.	.
Emerging Adulthood ISC Scale x Family Risk in Adolescence	.	.	.	0.003 (0.03)	.
Emerging Adulthood ISC Scale x Adolescence ISC Scale	.	.	.	.	0.001 (0.02)

Fit indices					
χ^2 (Model versus saturated)	61.031$^{(ns)}$	79.74$^{(ns)}$	74.542$^{(ns)}$	77.957$^{(ns)}$	82.892$^{(ns)}$
RMSEA	0.017	0.014	0.000	0.011	0.018
CFI	0.985	0.986	1.000	0.991	0.977

* $p < .05$
** $p < .01$
*** $p < .001$.
Notes: Model 1 examined main effects of each time-invariant control measure. Models 2–5 looked at interaction effects for each of the four time-invariant control measures. SE = standard error; RMSEA = Root mean square error of approximation; CFI = comparative fit index; ^{ns} = the estimated model fits the data as closely as a saturated model (i.e., the model is a good fit to the data); ISC = informal social control. The ISC scale represents the sum of five different types of informal social control.

Table 8.9 Cross-lagged dynamic panel model focusing on the lagged relationship between informal social control and convictions

Variable	*Model 1* *b coef. (SE)*	*Model 2* *b coef. (SE)*	*Model 3* *b coef. (SE)*	*Model 4* *b coef. (SE)*	*Model 5* *b coef. (SE)*
Independent variables					
Lagged Emerging Adulthood ISC Scale	0.02 (0.05)	0.02 (0.05)	0.02 (0.04)	0.04 (0.04)	0.01 (0.05)
Control measures (Time variant)					
Lagged Convictions	0.01 (0.03)	0.01 (0.03)	0.01 (0.03)	0.02 (0.03)	0.01 (0.03)
Exposure	**-3.97 (0.42)*****	**-3.90 (0.42)*****	**-3.96 (0.42)*****	**-0.44 (0.05)*****	**-3.85 (0.43)*****
Control measures in adolescence (Time invariant)					
Incarceration	0.01 (0.05)	-0.07 (0.22)	0.01 (0.05)	0.01 (0.03)	0.01 (0.05)
Individual Risk	**0.05 (0.02)****	**0.05 (0.02)****	-0.01 (0.09)	**0.10 (0.04)****	**0.05 (0.02)****
Family Risk	-0.06 (0.04)	-0.06 (0.04)	-0.06 (0.04)	-0.29 (0.18)	-0.07 (0.04)
ISC Scale	-0.02 (0.03)	-0.02 (0.03)	-0.02 (0.03)	-0.03 (0.03)	0.05 (0.16)
Interaction Terms					
Lagged Emerging Adulthood ISC Scale x Incarceration in Adolescence	.	0.01 (0.020	.	.	.
Lagged Emerging Adulthood ISC Scale x Individual Risk in Adolescence	.	.	0.01 (0.01)	.	.
Lagged Emerging Adulthood ISC Scale x Family Risk in Adolescence	.	.	.	0.25 (0.18)	.
Lagged Emerging Adulthood ISC Scale x Adolescence ISC Scale	.	.	.	.	-0.01 (0.02)

Fit indices					
χ^2 (Model versus saturated)	$70.681^{(ns)}$	$95.434^{(ns)}$	$86.904^{(ns)}$	$91.791^{(ns)}$	97.561^{*}
RMSEA	0.028	0.029	0.022	0.026	0.031
CFI	0.957	0.942	0.965	0.951	0.935

† Variables were standardized to help with model convergence.
* $p < .05$
** $p < .01$
*** $p < .001$.
Notes: Model 1 examined main effects of each time-invariant control measure. Models 2–5 looked at interaction effects for each of the four time-invariant control measures. SE = standard error; RMSEA = Root mean square error of approximation; CFI = comparative fit index; ^{ns} = the estimated model fits the data as closely as a saturated model (i.e., the model is a good fit to the data); ISC = informal social control. The ISC scale represents the sum of five different types of informal social control.

induced turning points ignores the possibility of both continued offending and continued victimization among individuals with a history of incarceration in adolescence.

James' developmental history

James' developmental history was atypical for the sample because his biological parents were married and remained together. Only 11.1% of ISVYOS participants reported that both their biological parents raised them after the age of 13. James' father worked while his mother cared for James and his two younger sisters. James reported to his probation officer (PO) that his father would drink and become violent towards him and his mother. James' mother confirmed that her husband slapped her on numerous occasions because he blamed her for James' poor behavior, which included biting his grandmother, cutting his mom's hand with a knife, and stealing from neighbors. James' mother reported that he angered easily and argued often, which made it difficult for him to make friends. She worried that he would be recruited by drug dealers as he was constantly looking for acceptance. Neither of James' parents spoke English, but they communicated with James' PO through an interpreter. The PO believed the mother to be supportive, caring, and patient, but also mentioned that James' parents sometimes enabled him. That said, James' mother reported to James' PO that she found drugs and large sums of money in his bedroom, showing that she was willing to communicate James' negative behavior to persons in the justice system.

James entered the justice system at age 15 following an assault against his sister. He was ordered by the court to not be in the upstairs portion of his home to keep his two younger sisters safe. Still at age 15, he again assaulted his mother and was placed in a transition bed for a short period before returning home. Less than a month after assaulting his mother, he assaulted his grandmother. James was referred for a psychological assessment and was diagnosed with conduct disorder and oppositional defiant disorder. Another incident occurred in which he pushed his mother after arguing about the use of a video game console.

James' violent behavior eventually extended beyond his family. His fights at school were believed to result from James' hyperactivity and so he was prescribed Ritalin. Still at age 15, James' violence escalated to street-fights, including fighting a man in his mid-twenties. The severity of James' violence in the family home escalated as well. On one occasion, James threatened to kill his father and punched him in the face. Multiple family members were required to restrain James. The assault occurred because his parents told him he was not allowed to go to a party because of his court-ordered curfew. Following this event, his sister reported to his PO that their family lives in fear of James.

By age 17, James was involved in drug trafficking. His family observed him with large amounts of money, multiple cell phones, and drug paraphernalia. At age 18, James' mother reported that James was a bully at home and suspected that he was regularly using ecstasy and steroids. James was stabbed shortly before his 19th birthday. A few days later he was hospitalized due to alcohol poisoning. At age 19, James was expelled due to regularly fighting at the alternative high school program he attended. He claimed to his PO that rival drug dealers kidnapped him. He considered this to be exciting and just part of his lifestyle. Still at age 19, James was jumped at a party and beaten so severely that he required stitches.

At age 20, James' demeanour briefly changed. While incarcerated at an adult facility, his cellmate was a gang member who received a long-term sentence. James reported to his PO that he did not want to go down this same path, that he had been upsetting his family, that his family wanted him to change, and that he wanted to change. This attitude did not last long. By age 21, James' PO described James as a master at deflecting and minimizing. He claimed to go to work with his father, but it was discovered that James was involved in drug trafficking and his father covered for him by saying that James was at work with him. Although James attended group treatment for violent offending, his presence there was harmful. He was described as disruptive, manipulative, and controlling. He bullied and intimidated other members of the treatment group. By age 22, James was the subject of a "Roger's Order", which meant that James was identified as dependent on treatment for substance abuse and/or a mental illness and was legally required to inform his PO if he was *not* seeking treatment.

At age 23, James received a lengthy sentence for assault and kidnapping. He did not return to his community until age 25. James made disparaging remarks about the victim of this offense and indicated that he would do it again. Although he claimed to be working construction, he was unable to provide his PO with paystubs. While living with his parents and sisters, James gained employment working six days a week for a unionized construction company. One evening after work, he entered his sister's room, started screaming at her, took of his shirt, and said that he would punch her in the face. He then spat on his sister's face.

James' intimate partner relationships

From a life-course perspective, ties to family and intimate partners are considered turning points that facilitate desistance (Laub & Sampson, 2003). The following background information on James highlighted that his relationships were not turning points. Rather, they provided additional opportunities to offend, especially when underlying risk factors remained untreated. Although we focused on intimate partners and not marital partners, it is difficult to see how circumstances would be different if James' risk factors remained present. James became involved in a relationship with "Jill" when he was 25. James told his PO that Jill experienced severe abuse growing up and that this abuse continued with her previous intimate partners. James suggested that he was committed to helping her and giving her a sense of family. One month into their relationship, police were called to attend a domestic dispute. Jill was observed with multiple injuries on her face, her cellphone was broken, and she advised that James had forcibly confined her in her apartment and assaulted her.

At age 26, James felt ashamed that his sisters were afraid of him and blamed his steroid use. He was no longer employed and suffered from anxiety. He resumed his relationship with Jill and they began living together. Shortly thereafter, he explained to his PO that he did not like living with her and that he found her annoying because she kept telling him who to not hang out with (i.e., the sort of influence that is typically considered a turning point; Laub & Sampson, 2003; Warr, 1998). Two weeks later he told his PO that Jill was smothering him and getting on his nerve and that he does not want to go back to jail because of her. The PO believed that James was insinuating that he would assault Jill if she continued this behavior. The PO informed James that he was responsible for managing his behavior and emotions. James responded by muttering that he would break Jill's legs. One week later, James and Jill purchased a dog. The next day they got into another argument and Jill informed James that he was no longer welcome in her apartment. That same evening, James moved in with "Sarah" and her child.

Less than a week later, James was back with Jill. Within a day of reconciling, Jill informed James' PO that he was not allowed to stay at her place because he was threatening her. The PO contacted the police, who were dispatched to Jill's residence and arrested James. The next day, Jill called James' PO to say that James had pushed her and threatened to destroy her car. James attended the PO's office the next day with a former gang member who wanted to mentor James (the same person he met in custody). However, within a week, James got tired of living with the former gang member, reconciled with Jill, and was back living with her.

After another breakdown in his relationship with Jill, James moved back in with Sarah and her child. Shortly thereafter, James attended Jill's residence and initiated an argument that resulted in neighbors calling the police. Police observed James repeatedly punching Jill. She suffered a broken nose, broken phone, and several of her belongings were missing. James was once again arrested, but this time he was held in custody. When released on bail several months later, James complained to his PO about being perceived as "some horrible woman beater". He moved back in with Sarah and her child. Police indicated that Sarah was active in the drug trade and associated with gang members. Sarah was asked to find a safe place for her child to live if James was to remain in her apartment. Sarah indicated that she would give her child back to the child's father rather than ask James to leave. The PO suspected that this decision was motivated by James paying Sarah's rent and supplying her with drugs. James and Sarah were eventually arrested by police for drug trafficking. The child was placed into the custody of social services. Police investigated James for assault and sexual assault against both Sarah and her child. Charges were not brought forward.

Two days after the abovementioned arrest, James told his PO that he was no longer going to live with Sarah because she was "misinterpreting their relationship". Six days after this, he reported to his PO that he was back living with Sarah. Two weeks into this arrangement, police were called as Sarah was threatening to commit suicide. James moved into a new apartment. Within a month, police were called to Jill's residence because a neighbor heard screaming coming from the apartment unit. Police attended, where they found Jill bleeding and her face swollen. Her roommates reported that James had choked Jill, confined her to a bedroom, choked the dog that they had previously purchased, and held the dog over the balcony of the apartment and threatened to kill it. James was arrested and placed in custody, which is where he currently resides at the time of this writing.

In sum, James was sometimes employed, but this employment was used as a cover for his involvement in drug trafficking. His employment did not prevent him from engaging in criminal behavior, including assaults against partners and family members. While James always had places to live, those who he lived with were commonly the target of his violence. Most of James' convictions came from perpetrating intimate partner violence (IPV). A justice system practitioner who completed the Spousal Assault Risk Assessment (SARA; Kropp et al., 1994) indicated that James displayed traits of jealousy and obsession and engaged in victim-blaming and displacement of responsibility. At age 27, James claimed that he wanted to get married, start a family, and find a job, but when asked about why he wanted these things, he mentioned that it would look good to the judge presiding over his IPV charges. James' perpetration of IPV appeared to stem from his own exposure to family violence. Indeed, he stated that he hit his mother because his father hit him. Notably, James' father hit James' mother for allowing James to hit her, revealing a clear cycle of violence within the family dynamic. James continued this pattern in his intimate relationships, making such informal social controls, not a turning point, but rather an additional outlet for violence. The notion of desistance by default does not seem applicable to James. He abused steroids and ecstasy, suffered from severe symptoms of ADHD, had poor anger control, and idolized a criminogenic lifestyle. Failing to address these underlying risk factors implies that informal social controls will not act as turning points that promote desistance. To be clear, these risk factors were not an anomaly for the sample (see Chapter 3). James' case was used to illustrate the treatment effect heterogeneity trend identified in our earlier analyses.

Summary

The age-graded theory of informal social control has become the predominant theoretical perspective on desistance (Laub et al., 2018). This theory emphasized studying desistance exclusively among individuals involved in chronic, serious, and violent offending (Laub & Sampson, 2003). To help build on research on the desistance experiences of formerly incarcerated youth (also see Schroeder et al., 2007) and adults involved in serious offenses (e.g., Boman & Mowen, 2018), this chapter addressed four questions regarding the development, impact, functioning of, and change in informal social controls in adulthood.

The first question addressed assertions from Laub and Sampson (2003) that the acquisition of informal social control was a random process. Contrary to this, risk factors in adolescence, especially the length of time incarcerated, reduced the likelihood of experiencing quality informal social controls in adulthood. Such selection effects should be considered alongside desistance theories that use human agency to explain why otherwise high-risk persons are able to desist from offending (Giordano et al., 2002; Laub & Sampson, 2003; Paternoster & Bushway, 2009).

Human agency has been used as an individual-level measure of the "American Dream" (Messner & Rosenfeld, 2012); marginalized persons can overcome cumulative disadvantage by "pulling themselves up by their bootstraps". While important to acknowledge that individual motivation and independence can play an important role in the desistance process, there is also an inherent risk of discussing human agency as a catch-all construct to explain why desistance is a normative part of the life-course. Levels of human agency may not be equal across all persons, especially those who are already marginalized or dealing with various forms of oppression. The desistance literature tends to assume that individuals are "super agents" who are free to overcome obstacles through sheer desire (Farrall & Bowling, 1999, p. 258). However, like certain notions of the American Dream (Isaacs et al., 2008), the idea that all individuals have equal access to agency is inaccurate. For example, Black youth are more at risk of experiencing discrimination, which can lead to poorer sleep (Yip et al., 2020), which in turn can lead to lower levels of self-control (Meldrum et al., 2015), which is an important aspect of agency (Bandura, 2006). In general, structural disadvantages are physically and emotionally draining (Boykin et al., 2020) and reduce agency (Levy et al., 2016). Ignoring these experiences may give the wrong impression about desistance as a normative aspect of the life-course. Acknowledging that human agency is not equal across all persons does not imply that desistance research must revert to ontogenic perspectives, but it does require considering how individual-level factors and social/historical situations and contexts may impact between-group differences and within-individual change in agency.

One youth in our study, "Daniel", was raised by his mother, who was addicted to crack cocaine. Daniel recalled knowing the difference between a crack spoon and a regular spoon by age five. He witnessed physical assaults perpetrated against his mother by various men. He recalled going to the community foodbank to pick up food for his sibling and mother. Daniel moved in and out of the child welfare system. On one occasion he moved back with his mother, who eventually became homeless. Daniel was offered crystal methamphetamine by a male associate and became addicted. He reported to his probation officer that he used this drug almost daily between ages 12–19. When young people like this are using energy to look out for family members, find shelter, and avoid victimization, the amount of agency that they have left to abstain from criminal behavior may be limited. It should not be assumed that turning points will be normative for people like Daniel, as it alleviates some responsibility from the justice system and others to help individuals in need of assistance. Dufour et al. (2018) described the importance of identifying formal (e.g., initiated by agents of the justice system) and informal (e.g., initiated by mentors) strategies that help improve, not just the chances of desistance, but improvement in an individual's self-identity and overall quality of life. This idea resembles Giordano et al.'s (2002) description of hooks for change, but encourages the justice system and treatment providers to play a more active role in establishing these hooks or intervening on the underlying risk factors that make establishing these hooks for change difficult.

The second question addressed whether informal social controls in emerging adulthood predicted a lower rate incidence rate of future convictions measured over a seven-year follow-up period that ended when participants were, on average, age 29.02 (*SD* = 3.81). In line with the age-graded theory of informal social control, quality family relationships, quality intimate partner relationships, and overall higher levels of quality sources of informal social control predicted a significantly lower incidence rate of future convictions. Quality informal social control in emerging adulthood was not common for ISVYOS participants, but when present, it helped with desistance. This did not mean individuals with quality informal social controls did not incur any new convictions during the follow-up period. While the presence of offending as evidence of desistance may seem counterintuitive, findings from this chapter matter for framing what constitutes success and failure in the justice system. The youth justice system places a heavy emphasis on risk assessment tools as part of evidence-based practices (Sullivan, 2019; Viljoen et al., 2019). Almost invariably, these risk assessment tools are validated according to whether they help predict recidivism. The justice system perspective that recidivism is a negative outcome ignores the bigger picture when it comes to youth in custody, at least in Canada. As shown in Chapter 4, all but 2% of the ISVYOS sample could be considered recidivists. Does this mean that practitioners failed to help promote desistance for 98% of their clients? We do not think so. Most participants experienced declines in offending between adolescence and emerging adulthood. A car moving at a high rate of speed does not come to an immediate stop just because brakes are applied. It is also unreasonable to expect youth coming from extremely negative circumstances who are involved in a high rate of offending to immediately abstain from crime.

Success need not be evaluated solely based on the absence of recidivism. For some, success can come from a slowing down in their level of offending over time (i.e., desistance). Ignoring declines in offending and only seeing "the new offense" ignores the process, commitment, and hard work by both the individual involved in crime and the justice system practitioners seeking to help them. Failing to acknowledge this within-individual change and instead emphasizing recidivism as evidence against desistance could potentially result in discounting effective treatment programs. Program evaluation should therefore think differently about recidivism as a definitive indicator of failure.

The third question addressed whether informal social control influenced a lower incidence of convictions only when levels of risk in adolescence were low (i.e., treatment effect heterogeneity). Whereas incarceration in adolescence was most important for predicting whether informal social controls were or were not present, we found that individual-level risk, family-level risk, and levels of informal social control in adolescence moderated the relationship between total levels of adult informal social control and the incidence rate of future convictions. Life-course criminology is arguably most responsible for helping to redefine success and failure by emphasizing desistance as a process rather than as an event. However, what we are learning about our sample is that assumptions about "desistance by default" (Laub & Sampson, 2003, 278–9) could reduce the justice system's impetus on helping persons. The UJD Study sample were primarily involved in public nuisance behaviors and status offenses (Sampson & Laub, 2003). Normative processes of maturation may have helped these individuals age out of crime. In fact, based on the trajectories presented by Sampson and Laub (2003), it is unlikely that adult roles like marriage and parenthood were truly turning points given that the process of desistance occurred earlier than when individuals assumed these roles (see Skardhamar & Savolainen, 2014 for a similar argument). With respect to this contemporary sample of formerly incarcerated youth, the magnitude of risk/needs factors and severity of offending seemed too high to assume that desistance will happen by default. For such youth, even when positive informal social controls were present, desistance was no more likely than it was for youth without positive sources of informal social control (see Figure 8.3).

To use a case study to illustrate this point, for "Robert", acquiring a stable job was not sufficient to act as a turning point. Robert worked a steady job as a heavy-duty mechanic. He was paid well above minimum wage. However, he also felt that trafficking drugs was more profitable. He poorly managed his money and regularly used cocaine. He eventually escalated from cocaine use to crack cocaine use, gave up his job, and went on disability. Anger control problems that emerged in adolescence continued in adulthood. Robert incurred 13 convictions in adolescence, 14 in emerging adulthood, 17 in full adulthood, and 16 in mature adulthood. He spent over 3,000 days incarcerated between ages 12–35. For individuals like Robert, making assumptions that they will acquire a job and desist by default overlooks a wide range of treatment and intervention needs. Statements that support notions of desistance by default may be used to justify harmful policies that involve abandoning intervention and treatment programs that help individuals with substance abuse, anger control, and symptoms of mental health disorders on the basis that individuals will desist regardless of any intervention.

As another case study that highlights the importance of avoiding assumptions about informal social control, Tyler (see Yang et al., in progress) reported having a very strong connection with his mother. This could be interpreted as evidence of an important family bond in adolescence that could help promote desistance. However, his mother was involved in the sex trade and used crystal methamphetamine. She also experienced suicidal ideation. Tyler reported that at a young age he began robbing others to give money to his mother to support her drug use. After adjudication by the justice system, Tyler was required to reside in a group home. Tyler frequently left the group home to check in on his mother to make sure she ate and slept. Tyler's mother told him that she would have killed herself if it were not for Tyler's care. Thus, Tyler made sure to frequently check in on her. This repeated absenteeism from his group home led to him losing his placement. This violated conditions of his sentence, and as a consequence, he incurred a new conviction for failing to comply with a court order. Tyler described his relationship with his mother in positive terms. However, this attachment directly influenced his justice system involvement. This reiterated the value of the current study's reliance on independent ratings of participants' informal social controls given that Tyler's family relationships interfered with his ability to avoid justice system involvement even though Tyler described his relationship with his mother in positive terms.

The fourth question addressed whether changes in informal social control impacted changes in offending. To account for potentially important baseline characteristics in adolescence, cross-lagged dynamic panel models were used to examine (a) whether between-person differences impacted within-individual change in convictions and (b) whether the interaction between baseline characteristics in adolescence and within-individual change in informal social controls in emerging adulthood impacted within-individual change in convictions. Participants characterized by a greater number of individual-level risk factors in adolescence were associated with within-individual increases in convictions during emerging adulthood. Within-individual change in total levels of informal social control was negatively associated with within-individual change in convictions during the same window of measurement (i.e., same year of age). However, this relationship disappeared when looking at the lagged effect of change in informal social control on change in convictions. Future research is needed to help clarify whether, for example, it is instead within-individual changes in convictions that bring about within-individual changes in informal social control.

Notes

1 Developmental principles were not focused on using childhood risk factors as an indication of a person's destiny for certain outcomes in adulthood. Developmental criminology's main principle was intervention, not prediction. Developmentalists argued that it was not necessary to be 100% accurate in the prediction of adult outcomes 20 years later to justify the use of psychoeducational intervention strategies.
2 A negative binomial analysis (not shown) indicated that increases in individual-level risk and months incarcerated significantly decreased the incidence rate of positive sources of informal social control.
3 We consider these analyses exploratory because we have yet to complete data collection due to being unable to enter custody centers as a result of policies made in response to COVID-19.
4 Variables in the righthand side of the equation must be independent of the error terms associated with all such variables. This will not be the case if a lagged outcome variable is included in the righthand side of the equation. The cross-lagged panel model estimates a series of progressive chained equations over time that satisfies the assumption of independence between error terms and predictor variables.
5 Because the cross-lagged dynamic panel model assumes normality for endogenous and exogenous variables, we did not examine individual types of informal social control, which were dichotomous, and instead only examined the emerging adulthood informal social control scale as our main exogenous variable. Exogenous variables are those that are not directly influenced by prior values of the outcome variable. Endogenous variables are used to predict the outcome variable but are also influenced by prior levels of the outcome variable. Proportion of a given year of age in the community was treated as a weakly exogenous (or "predetermined") variable because the lagged indicator of convictions influenced amount of time incarcerated. Convictions in emerging adulthood and time incarcerated in adolescence were logged (after adding a constant of 0.01) due to positive skew.
6 Model fit was judged according to three criteria: χ^2 values, root mean square error of approximation (RMSEA) values, and CFI values. The latter two are most important (see Williams et al., 2018 for a full discussion). The χ^2 statistics compare the estimated models with saturated models. Higher p values indicate better fitting models. For RMSEA, values less than 0.05 indicate good model fit. For CFI, values greater than 0.90, ideally greater than 0.95, indicate good model fit (Hu & Bentler, 1999).

Section III

Reflections on the ISVYOS

The final section of this book includes three chapters (Chapters 9–11). Chapter 9 examined whether there were differences in Cohort I and Cohort II participants across risk factors and adult justice system involvement. These analyses allowed for an inspection of whether the profiles and outcomes of incarcerated youth changed between the Young Offender's Act (Cohort I) and Youth Criminal Justice Act (Cohort II). Chapter 10 reflected on the experience of interviewing youth in custody. Chapter 10 was written especially for graduate students and early career researchers collecting data in custody facilities. The chapter highlighted some key points about conducting research and collecting data with youth in custody. Chapter 11 summarized the main findings of the book and described the next phase of data collection for the ISVYOS.

9 The differential impact of youth justice policy

Introduction

This chapter compared Cohort I and Cohort II in terms of their risk profiles and offending outcomes in adolescence and adulthood. There was reason to believe that Cohort I and Cohort II differed because they were included in the ISVYOS during different eras in Canada's youth justice legislation. Cohort I was adjudicated under the YOA, which represented a response to public and Federal government concerns that youth crime was out of control (Bell, 2014; Corrado & Markwart, 1994). Incarceration was regularly used as a response to youth crime, which led to Canada having a rate of youth incarceration higher than most jurisdictions in the United States (Bell, 2014; Smith, 1998). Cohort II was adjudicated under the YCJA, which tried to balance competing aims, including (1) reducing the reliance on incarceration as a sentencing option, (2) using longer-term custody sentences for youth involved in the most serious and violent crimes, and (3) making rehabilitation, rather than deterrence, the outcome desired as the result of incarceration (Bala et al., 2009). Before looking at differences across the two cohorts, we looked at the history of youth justice in the United States and Canada and described principles of the YOA and YCJA in greater detail.

The United States and Canada established youth justice systems based on the belief that children and youth needed saving (Bell, 2014; Feld, 1993). Especially at the turn of the 20th century, with the welfare and rehabilitation of youth in mind, members of the temperance and child saving movements sought to make "other children" like "their children" by correcting problematized behavior. Youth justice systems were therefore designed as a response to a growing movement to regulate the behavior of youth through, for example, compulsory school attendance, child labor laws, and the creation of status offenses like truancy, incorrigibility, vagrancy, and sexual promiscuity (Bell, 2014). Over time, it became clear that this youth justice philosophy regularly violated the rights of youth (Feld, 1993). Youth had poor access to counsel. Proportionate sentencing philosophies were ignored. Little effort was made to adapt judicial processes to ensure that a young person understood their rights. Although recognizing a youth's rights was an important transition from the welfare-based policies of initial youth justice legislation, the youth court experience became more adversarial (Feld, 1993). Treating youth before the court similar to their adult counterparts resulted in the public and some politicians viewing such youth as "hardened criminals". Perspective shifted from the need to save wayward youth to the need to save members of the public from such youth (Feld, 1993).

By the 1980s, especially in the United States, rehabilitative goals of the youth justice system were replaced with a crime control model that focused on responding to perceived out-of-control youth through punishment (Cauffman & Steinberg, 2012). In some parts of the United States, transfers to adult court were mandated for youth of a certain age or youth of any age involved in certain offenses. During the same era, Canada altered its youth justice legislation on several occasions by increasing the maximum sentence length that youth could receive for their involvement in serious crimes and by increasing the use of pretrial detention (Bell, 2014).

By the 21st century, two major research themes from criminology and developmental psychology helped influence the justice system's movement away from punitive philosophies. Criminologists demonstrated that there was a lack of empirical support for assertions that general and specific deterrence reduced crime (Nagin & Snodgrass, 2013). Punitive sanctions, including prosecuting youth as adults, did not appear to reduce offending (Monahan et al., 2015). In Canada, research on youth with no fixed address found that these persons' lives were characterized by poverty, substance use, and associations with peers in similar circumstances; considering the consequences of their behavior was secondary to these needs and lifestyles (Baron & Kennedy, 1998; McCarthy et al., 2002). In the Supreme Court of Canada's (SCC) decision in *R. v. D.B.* (2008), Justice Abella suggested that social science research on the psychosocial maturation and reduced judgment of youth supported the abolishment of deterrence as a sentencing principle.

Developmental psychology research demonstrated that, compared to adults, youth were more risk-taking, more strongly influenced by peers, less aware of the consequences of their behavior, more likely to experience identity changes conducive to desistance, and more negatively impacted by disproportionately punitive sentences (Cauffman & Steinberg, 2012; Roberts, 2004; Steinberg, 2009). These differences implied that youth were also less culpable for their behavior. This research influenced a series of cases from the U.S. Supreme Court that acknowledged that age differences in decision making justified, at the very least, prohibiting the use of certain sentences like the death penalty for youth. The willingness of courts to accept evidence provided by developmental psychology was particularly influential in transitioning back to rehabilitative principles of youth justice (Steinberg, 2009). This research also ensured that youth justice systems' justification for an emphasis on rehabilitation was rooted in developmental science rather than morality and opinions about normative behavior in adolescence (Monahan et al. 2015).[1]

Contribution to juvenile justice policy

Youth and adults differ in many ways (e.g., maturational development, culpability), which justifies having a separate youth justice system (Daftary-Kapur & Zottoli, 2014; Steinberg, 2009). Only rarely do researchers investigate the functioning of the youth justice system. Such research typically focuses on the macro-level impact of new youth justice legislation (e.g., changes in the rate of incarceration, types of offenses processed in court; Moyer, 2005). Instead of looking at changes or differences at the aggregate-level, this chapter examined whether risk/needs factors in adolescence and justice system outcomes varied between ISVYOS participants from Cohort I (YOA) and Cohort II (YCJA). To understand the ways in which these cohorts might vary, we first described differences in youth justice system philosophies. Two main differences included the YCJA's emphasis on (1) reserving the use of custody for only those youth involved in serious or violent offenses and (2) using custody for rehabilitation rather than deterrent purposes.

In terms of the analytic approach, first, we conducted a series of between-group analyses that compared the cohorts across various risk factors and justice system outcomes in adolescence and adulthood. We evaluated whether cohort membership moderated the relationship between youth justice system involvement and adult justice system involvement to see whether the more rehabilitative tone of the YCJA helped break the connection between past and future offending. Second, we examined the impact of within-individual change in the length of time incarcerated on future within-individual change in convictions, including whether this relationship was moderated by cohort membership. In effect, we answered whether increasing a person's length of time incarcerated resulted in an increase or decrease in a person's future convictions and whether this relationship varied by the type of youth justice legislation that a participant was adjudicated under. Findings have implications beyond the Canadian youth justice system because Canada's system was based on models of youth justice germane to the United States, Western and Northern Europe, and Australia, among other regions (Corrado et al., 2010; Roach, 1998). For context, we begin by describing differences in justice system principles between the YOA and YCJA.

Youth justice in Canada

The Juvenile Delinquents Act (JDA) was established in 1908 as Canada's first formal youth justice system. Under the JDA, rehabilitative goals superseded procedural justice ones and thus youth could receive indeterminate sanctions for even minor delinquency. The JDA was associated with Canada's Child Savers Movement, which emphasized placing youth in reformatory schools for truancy, gambling, and incorrigibility (Bell, 2014). In some ways, the youth placed in these reformatories resembled youth from the Gluecks' UJD Study. Canada's contemporary youth justice system, and the youth associated with this system, are much different from the JDA and the Gluecks' sample. The JDA operated as Canada's federal youth justice legislation until 1984. One reason for abandoning the JDA was public perception that serious and violent youth crime was on the rise and that incarceration was needed to protect the public from a new generation who showed little concern for the welfare of others (Corrado & Markwart, 1994).

A second reason for abandoning the JDA related to changes in Canada's legal sphere. In 1982, Canada adopted the Charter of Rights and Freedoms, which established various rights afforded to all persons before the justice system. The JDA was characterized by poor access to legal counsel, status offenses, and indeterminate and disproportionately punitive sanctions, all of which potentially or definitively violated a young person's Charter rights. In 1984, the YOA replaced the JDA and abolished indeterminate sentences and status offenses. For these and other reasons, Canada's Conservative Party (then known as the Progressive Conservative Party) criticized the YOA as soft on crime (Bala et al., 2009). In response, three amendments to the YOA were made between 1986 and 1995 that (1) established age 17 as the maximum age for processing under the youth justice system, (2) raised the maximum sentences for homicide offenses, and (3) eased restrictions on the transfer of youth to adult court (Bell, 2014). Thus, the YOA began to resemble youth justice legislation in the United States.

From the mid-1990s onward, the YOA attempted to balance its goals of rehabilitating youth through diversionary measures and protecting the public by incarcerating youth. The YOA failed to clarify the circumstances in which one goal should be prioritized over the other, which resulted in an overreliance on incarceration under the assumption that it would protect the public by deterring future offending (Bala et al., 2009). Incarceration was regularly used in response to youth who failed to comply with court orders (Doob & Sprott, 2004). Such sentencing practices contributed to Canada incarcerating youth at a rate that was approximately twice as high as the United States (700 youth per 100,000 (Bell, 2014) compared to 350 youth per 100,000 (Smith, 1998)). Some still viewed the act as soft on crime. Others were concerned with the overuse of pretrial detention. Others were concerned that judges had too much discretion (Bell, 2014). With some exceptions (Trépanier, 2004), there was widespread interest in repealing the YOA (Roberts, 2003). The ongoing belief that the YOA was incapable of addressing the issue of youth offending led to another major change to the youth justice system.

The YCJA replaced the YOA in 2003. The YCJA specified several principles of youth justice that at first glance appeared contradictory. Principles included reducing judges' reliance on custody yet also utilizing more punitive sentences for youth involved in serious and violent offenses (Bala et al., 2009). Principles also included an emphasis on crime prevention (e.g., crime control model), introducing meaningful consequences to youth (e.g., proportionality; justice model), and making rehabilitation and reintegration paramount (e.g., welfare model; Corrado et al., 2010). The mistake of the YOA was its failure to explain when judges should invoke which principle. The YCJA clarified the circumstances in which one principle superseded a competing principle.

Essentially, the YCJA identified three different offending profiles and specified which offending profile corresponded with which youth justice principle. First, youth involved in a first-time offense or nonserious offense were to be diverted rather than processed through the formal justice system. Second, for youth not diverted but involved in non-serious offenses, judges were required to consider all alternatives to incarceration as a sentencing option. If a community sentence was deemed sufficient for protecting the public, it must be used. Third, youth involved in serious or violent offenses *could* be sentenced to custody, but it was not *necessary* that they be sentenced to custody. This policy was the inverse of mandatory minimums in the US context that required, without exception, the incarceration of youth involved in certain crimes (Fagan, 2008). Sections 38–39 of the YCJA clarified that before implementing a custody sentence, judges were required to identify that all other sentencing options were insufficient for protecting the public. The goals during incarceration were rehabilitation and service provision. However, s. 39(5) of the YCJA clarified that although rehabilitation was the intended outcome of incarceration, youth could not be sentenced to custody specifically to promote rehabilitation.

An ongoing concern with the YCJA is its inability to address systemic inequalities responsible for the overrepresentation of Indigenous youth in custody (Hogeveen, 2005). Part of this overrepresentation may be due to the failure to establish whether routinely used risk assessment tools were reliable and valid for Indigenous Persons (Hart, 2016). Indigenous youth, girls in particular, may score higher on such tools, but this risk is more strongly associated with harm to the individual's own self rather than to others (Maurutto & Hannah-Moffat, 2007). McCuish and Corrado (2018) found that several risk factors were more prevalent or stronger for Indigenous youth compared to White youth, yet this higher risk did not translate to a higher rate of convictions in adulthood. It is not clear why these factors were not predictive for Indigenous youth. One concern is that if risk assessment tools overestimate the risk of reoffending for Indigenous youth and girls, they will contribute to disproportionately punitive sentences for such youth and thus contribute to their over representation in custody.

Differences in principles and practices across the YOA and YCJA: Implications for the ISVYOS

Table 9.1 summarizes similarities and differences between the YOA and YCJA across six principles of youth justice: (1) philosophy of the youth justice system, (2) use of diversion, (3) use of pre trial detention, (4) sentencing philosophies, (5) use of custody, and (6) extralegal factors. We also considered what the implications are for Cohort I and Cohort II participants when the YOA and YCJA differ on these principles.

Table 9.1 Comparing justice system principles across the YOA and YCJA

Principle	*YOA*	*YCJA*	*Potential meaning*
Youth justice philosophy	Principles without prioritization resulted in too much judicial discretion.[1]	Principle-based legislation with clear hierarchy (e.g., rehabilitation over punitiveness).[1]	Fewer youth from the YCJA incarcerated for reasons that do not align with legislative goals.
Use of alternative measures/ diversion	Recommended and implemented based on offense severity but not required to be considered.	Explicit endorsement of diversion for first-time and non-serious offenses. Implemented based on whether diversion would hold youth accountable. Presumed to be adequate.	YCJA youth more likely to be diverted, including repeatedly diverted. Convictions under the YCJA therefore underestimate offending to a greater degree.
Pre-trial detention	Used for welfare purposes (e.g., protect youth from homelessness, cut off access to drugs).	Only justified if the offense (a) was one that an adult could be incarcerated for and (b) met s. 39 gateways. Welfare purposes expressly prohibited (s. 29). Prosecution must rebut presumption that detention is not necessary if the young person, if found guilty, could not be sentenced to custody.	Less time spent in pre-trial detention for YCJA; implies less overall time incarcerated but also that when incarcerated there was more time for treatment of offense-specific factors[2] that could make time incarcerated more conducive to rehabilitation.
Sentencing philosophies	Vague sentencing provisions. Commonly focused on the welfare of the child. Sentences based on general and specific deterrence. Possible to eclipse sentence lengths for adults perpetrating the same offense (protectionist sentencing philosophies).	The welfare of the child cannot be considered in decisions about the severity of the sentence. General deterrence prohibited. Sentences must be less than what an adult would receive under identical circumstances.	YOA youth incarcerated for offenses that would not result in incarceration for YCJA youth. YOA youth expected to experience lengthier sentences than YCJA youth involved in similar offenses.

(*Continued*)

Table 9.1 (Continued)

Principle	*YOA*	*YCJA*	*Potential meaning*
Custody sentences	Commonly used for welfare purposes. Vague sentencing provisions. Survey of judges indicated their belief in the importance of deterrence.[4]	Long-term protection of the public achieved through rehabilitation and reintegration while incarcerated. A youth cannot be incarcerated longer than an adult would in the same circumstances.	Differences in risk factor profiles; YOA youth defined by health concerns not necessarily important for offending. YCJA youth more likely to be associated with greater severity in (a) risk factor profiles and (b) offending outcomes.
Extralegal factors	Risk assessment implemented at the judge's discretion. Welfare-based decisions especially likely for girls.	Risk assessment included in mandated PSR.[3] YCJA included provisions reminding judges to seek less punitive sentences for Indigenous youth.	Risk assessment may amplify Indigenous overrepresentation under the YCJA.

Notes: [1]Endres (2004). [2]Department of Justice (2007) pointed out that pretrial detention means that offense-specific factors cannot be treated while a person is remanded because they have not been found guilty of that offense. However, pretrial detention counts as time served towards a person's sentence, leaving less time for treatment. [3]Maurutto and Hannah-Moffat (2007). [4]Cesaroni and Bala (2008).

Youth Justice Philosophy. The YOA and YCJA both specified rehabilitation and crime control as goals of the youth justice system. However, the YOA lacked hierarchy in its organizing principles and the result was great variability in sentencing decisions. In contrast, the YCJA clarified when to prioritize diversion over incarceration and vice-versa. As such, we expected Cohort I to have a larger proportion of youth who were incarcerated for less serious offenses compared to Cohort II. Part of the YOA philosophy was that the most appropriate means of protecting the public was by the use of incarceration. The YCJA emphasized that the most appropriate means of protecting the public was through holding youth accountable through meaningful (i.e., proportionate) consequences. These different philosophies should further contribute to a larger proportion of youth incarcerated for less serious offenses in Cohort I compared to Cohort II. Accordingly, the average risk factor profile of Cohort I should be less severe compared to Cohort II.

Diversion. Diversionary options that allowed youth to avoid incurring official charges/convictions were available under both the YOA and YCJA. However, only the YCJA provided explicit direction to police officers and prosecution regarding when diversion was appropriate. Whereas the YOA relied on the nature of the offense when evaluating the appropriateness of diversion, the YCJA indicated that regardless of the offense committed it was necessary to consider the use of diversion if it was appropriate for holding the youth accountable (Bell, 2014). Under the YCJA, diversionary measures were presumed to be an adequate response to minor offenses or a first-time offense. Further, the failure of prior diversionary strategies did not preclude using diversion in the future (i.e., the same youth could be diverted on multiple occasions; Barnhorst, 2004). This created somewhat of a paradox. On the one hand, the YCJA intended to reserve custody for individuals involved in frequent, serious, or violent offending. Thus, Cohort II should be more prolific in their offending compared to Cohort I. On the other hand, because diversion was more likely to be used, and more likely to be used on multiple occasions for Cohort II, official justice system involvement was likely to be underestimated for Cohort II.

Pre trial Detention. One of a judge's first decisions during the adjudication process is whether to deny bail. Judges under the YOA saw pre trial detention as, among other things, a way to protect the welfare of youth in vulnerable circumstances (e.g., homeless). Under the YOA, youth would be remanded in situations where an adult would be granted bail. These types of practices were prohibited per s. 29(1) of the YCJA.[2] This implies that Cohort I was more likely to be remanded for protectionist reasons. Under the YOA, there were concerns that protectionist philosophies resulted in judges placing girls in custody, not because of the severity of their crimes, but rather out of concern that such girls were being exposed to a negative social environment in the community (Corrado et al., 2000).

Sentencing Decisions. The weight given to recidivism sentencing premiums, proportionality, and deterrence varied between the YOA and YCJA. Recidivism sentencing premiums refer to the weight given to a person's criminal history when making sentencing decisions (Roberts, 2008). Doob's (2001) survey of judges under the YOA indicated that half of participants viewed the prior use of a community-based sentence as evidence that it would not be appropriate to use such a sentence for the same person in the future. In contrast, the YCJA explicitly noted that if a youth abided by the conditions of their community-based sentence then it was likely that they would continue to comply and therefore a new community-based sentence was appropriate. This implied that recidivism sentencing premiums were more punitive for Cohort I and therefore Cohort I should have an earlier onset of incarceration relative to Cohort II. Regarding proportionality, the YCJA mandated that youth receive shorter sentences than what an adult would receive in identical circumstances. Welfare-based decision-making under the YOA implied the opposite. Thus, we expected that a Cohort I participant would experience a more punitive sanction than a Cohort II participant involved in the same offense and with the same background. Deterrence was another important sentencing principle under the YOA

(Cesaroni & Bala, 2008). Under the YCJA, deterrence could not be used as part of a judge's reasons for sentencing.[3] This would again contribute to more punitive sentences for Cohort I. In sum, while individuals in Cohort II likely have a more serious background and pattern of offending, this might not be reflected in their official youth record because of the more punitive sentencing practices experienced by Cohort I.

Custody Sentences. Under the YOA, decisions to sentence a young person to custody were largely at the discretion of the presiding judge. Under the YCJA, youth could be incarcerated only if they were involved in one or more of the following "gateways" to a custody sentence: (1) a violent offense, (2) an administrative offense, (3) an indictable offense and prior findings of guilt, or (4) an indicatable offense[4] with aggravating circumstances present. These were necessary but not sufficient conditions for incarceration. Under the YOA, judges regularly used a person's criminal history to justify incarceration (Cesaroni & Bala, 2008). Per s. 39 of the YCJA, a person's criminal record was irrelevant to decisions about custody sentences unless their index offense was an indictable offense. Further, Doob (2001) reported that about a third of surveyed judges under the YOA indicated that in at least half of all cases the welfare of the young person (e.g., their living situation) was used to justify a custody sentence. Under the YCJA, welfare concerns could not factor into the decision to levy a custody sentence. Under the YOA, judges routinely referred to deterrence as a reason for their decision to impose a custody sentence (Cesaroni & Bala, 2008). Under the YCJA, the SCC in *R. v. B.W.P* ruled that deterrence could not be used as a sentencing principle (also see *R. v. D.P*).

Under the YCJA, youth could receive a custody sentence that was to be served in the community (i.e., a deferred custody and supervision order; DCSO). Like other custody sentences, a DCSO could only be administered to youth who met at least one of the four abovementioned gateways. If the youth abided by the conditions of their DCSO, despite technically receiving a custody sentence, they would never spend a day in a custody facility. The YOA had no such sentencing option. Under the YCJA, for youth serving a sentence in custody, the final third of their custody sentence was to be served in the community. This contrasted with the YOA, where youth sentenced to custody generally remained incarcerated until the end of their sentence (Bala, 2003). Taken together, Cohort I should be admitted to custody at an earlier age, be incarcerated for lesser offenses, be incarcerated with greater regularity, and spend more days in custody.

Extralegal Factors. In Canada, pre-sentence reports (PSRs) are completed, typically by a probation officer, to assist with a judge's sentencing decision. The PSR provides judges with information about, for example, a young person's family environment, school performance, substance use, and mental health. Under the YOA, PSRs were only ordered at the judge's discretion. Under the YCJA, PSRs were mandatory for sentencing decisions. In theory, PSRs reduce sentencing disparities between judges by accounting for the facts of the case (e.g., crime perpetrated, attitudes towards the offense) but also the youth's circumstances that contributed to their offense. As a result, it may be possible that through the implementation of PSRs, youth who received custody sentences also shared similar risk/needs profiles. Therefore, Cohort II should include a more homogenous sample compared to Cohort I. However, risk assessment tools included as part of a PSR may exacerbate the marginalization of girls and Indigenous youth as their multi-needs profiles may be used to justify a more punitive sentence (Maurutto & Hannah-Moffat, 2007). It is unclear how much PSRs and risk assessment tools factored into judges' decision to impose one type of sentence over another. Pulis and Sprott (2005) found that the proportion of boys versus girls on probation increased under the YCJA. They suggested that this was evidence that the YCJA was addressing the YOA's protectionist tendencies. Accordingly, girls should comprise a smaller proportion of Cohort II compared to Cohort I. Finally, unlike the YOA, the YCJA included direct reminders to judges to avoid the use of incarceration for Indigenous Persons. If this provision is effective, the overrepresentation of Indigenous youth would be higher in Cohort I compared to Cohort II.

Data

The data used in this chapter highlighted that one of the benefits of conducting a long-term longitudinal project is the ability to inspect and evaluate policy change in a more systematic way. During the course of the ISVYOS, the youth justice model changed in important ways. In this chapter, we examined whether these changes related to differences between Cohort I (adjudicated under the YOA) and Cohort II (adjudicated under the YCJA). Does a change in the philosophy of youth justice legislation have implications with respect to risk factor profiles and justice system outcomes in adolescence and adulthood?

The ISVYOS is not exactly a study of criminal behavior given its focus on official offending. Most offenses perpetrated by youth do not come to the attention of the justice system, let alone result in conviction and incarceration (Sullivan, 2019). Where we think our data are useful is for understanding how persons that reach the deep end of the youth justice system experience involvement in the adult justice system. In this chapter, we compared ISVYOS members from Cohort I ($n = 560$) and Cohort II ($n = 406$) who were at least age 29 at the time criminal history data were most recently coded.[5] We compared Cohort I and Cohort II across demographic characteristics, school functioning, substance use, self-reported offending, family dynamics, identity, mental health, and official offending outcomes in adolescence and adulthood (see Chapters 3 and 5 for descriptions of measures).

Comparing the profiles of Cohort I and Cohort II participants

Bivariate comparisons (Table 9.2) indicated that Cohort II was significantly older at the time of their intake interview compared to Cohort I. This older

Table 9.2 A comparison of cohorts across demographic characteristics, risk factors, and offending in adolescence

	Cohort I (YOA) M (SD) / n (%)	Cohort II (YCJA) M (SD) / n (%)	t/χ^2, df, p, φ/d
Gender			
Male Participant	425 (75.9%)	332 (84.9%)	χ^2 [1] = 11.53, $p = .001$, $\varphi = .110$
Ethnicity			
White	340 (61.3%)	180 (52.9%)	χ^2 [2] = 10.52, $p = .005$, $\varphi = .108$
Indigenous	128 (23.1%)	112 (32.9%)	
Non-Indigenous Minority	87 (15.7%)	48 (14.1%)	
Age at Interview†	16.19 (1.26)	16.70 (0.87)	t [853.64] = −7.03, $p < .001$, $d = 0.47$
School Functioning			
Enrolled in School	278 (52.1%)	134 (40.5%)	χ^2 [1] = 10.98, $p = .001$, $\varphi = .113$
Number of School Changes	6.09 (5.71)	5.87 (5.36)	t [773] = 0.54, $p = .592$, $d = 0.04$
Skip School Before Age 12	90 (21.1%)	61 (18.6%)	χ^2 [1] = 0.74, $p = .390$, $\varphi = .031$
Substance Use			
Substance Use Versatility†	4.48 (2.26)	5.59 (2.00)	t [756.73] = −7.50, $p < .001$, $d = 0.52$
Hard Drug Use	255 (48.6%)	198 (60.4%)	χ^2 [1] = 11.28 $p = .001$, $\varphi = .115$
Family			
Family Dysfunction†	3.47 (2.80)	3.90 (3.53)	t [517.99] = −1.82, $p = .070$, $d = 0.14$
Raised by Ministry of Children and Family Development	20 (4.9%)	67 (20.9%)	χ^2 [1] = 43.76, $p < .001$, $\varphi = .245$
Left Home Before Age 12	86 (19.4%)	42 (13.2%)	χ^2 [1] = 5.18, $p = .023$, $\varphi = .082$
Kicked out of Home Before Age 12	33 (7.5%)	29 (9.1%)	χ^2 [1] = 0.63, $p = .426$, $\varphi = .029$
Identity			
Positive Self-Identity	71.45 (10.00)	70.60 (9.82)	t [812] = 1.18, $p = .238$, $d = 0.09$
Positive "Other-Defined" Identity	66.25 (12.35)	64.21 (13.29)	t [677] = 2.17, $p = .031$, $d = 0.16$
Mental Health			
Self-Reported Mental Health Problems†	0.69 (1.05)	3.45 (2.35)	t [392.86] = −18.82, $p < .001$, $d = 1.52$
Physical Abuse	243 (46.3%)	130 (46.1%)	χ^2 [1] = 0.00, $p = .960$, $\varphi = .000$
Sexual Abuse	118 (22.6%)	25 (9.0%)	χ^2 [1] = 22.97, $p < .001$, $\varphi = .169$

(*Continued*)

Table 9.2 (Continued)

	Cohort I (YOA) M (SD) / n (%)	Cohort II (YCJA) M (SD) / n (%)	t/χ^2, df, p, φ/d
Offending in Adolescence			
Age of Onset	14.28 (1.44)	15.04 (1.55)	t [911] = −7.58, $p < .001$, $d = 0.51$
Days Incarcerated†	354.66 (297.65)	231.05 (254.14)	t [847.11] = 6.71, $p < .001$, $d = 0.45$
Total Convictions	12.24 (8.44)	10.11 (8.11)	t [911] = 3.69, $p < .001$, $d = 0.26$
Incarcerated for Violent Offense	163 (40.3%)	169 (52.5%)	χ^2 [1] = 10.64, $p = .001$, $\varphi = .121$
Incarcerated for Administrative Offense	187 (46.3%)	210 (65.2%)	χ^2 [1] = 25.91, $p < .001$, $\varphi = .189$
Self-Reported Offense Versatility†	2.76 (2.06)	7.69 (2.67)	t [585.87] = −26.95, $p < .001$, $d = 2.07$

† Assumption of equal variance violated.
Notes: φ = phi effect size. d = Cohen's d effect size. Not all participants had data on all measures and some participants moved or were deceased, meaning that the sample sizes for the two cohorts varied depending on the question examined.

age could reflect the YCJA's tendency to use diversionary measures, avoid the use of pretrial detention, and use custody sentences as a last resort. As possible evidence that the YCJA addressed concerns with the YOA's use of incarceration for protectionist purposes, Cohort II had a significantly lower proportion of female participants compared to Cohort I. As mentioned, under the YOA the offenses that brought girls into custody were relatively minor (but still more serious than status offenses and public nuisance behaviors). It was believed that girls were being incarcerated to remove them from negative environments where their offenses were the result of survival-based behaviors (e.g., theft, sex trade, drug use and drug selling; see Corrado et al., 2000). The lower proportion of girls in Cohort II may have been the result of the YCJA prohibiting the use of incarceration for protectionist purposes. Another goal of the YCJA was to reduce the overrepresentation of Indigenous youth in custody. However, Cohort II included a significantly higher proportion of Indigenous youth. This reflected concerns that the YCJA's provisions for reducing the overrepresentation of Indigenous youth lacked practical efficacy (Barnhorst, 2004; Hogeveen, 2005). The overrepresentation of Indigenous youth under the YCJA may have been exacerbated because Indigenous youth were characterized by a greater range of factors traditionally included in risk assessment tools (McCuish & Corrado, 2018). The YCJA's increased reliance on risk assessment when making sentencing decisions (Maurutto & Hannah-Moffatt, 2007) may have contributed to Indigenous youth overrepresentation in custody. Indigenous youth may be particularly negatively impacted by the focus on risk and the neglect of the question “risk of what?” given McCuish and Corrado’s (2018) finding that Indigenous youth, despite being characterized by more risk factors than White youth, did not differ from White youth in terms of offending outcomes. For Indigenous youth, such risk factors may be more strongly associated with negative health consequences as opposed to involvement in criminal behavior (Maurutto & Hannah-Moffat, 2007).

Participants from Cohort II were less likely to be enrolled in school, averaged a greater number of different substances used, were more likely to have used at least one hard drug (crack cocaine, heroin, or crystal methamphetamine), were more likely to report being raised by child welfare services, believed that others viewed them in a more negative light, and self-reported a greater number of mental health problems. This aligned with expectations that individuals under the YCJA would have a more severe risk factor profile. However, Cohort I participants were more likely to have left the family home to live somewhere else before age 12 and were more likely to self-report experiencing sexual abuse. These differences may reflect how judges under the YOA used incarceration for welfare purposes (Doob, 2001). Cohort I may capture a profile more so characterized by risk of victimization and other health concerns than risk of offending. The higher prevalence of sexual abuse for Cohort I may have reflected the higher proportion of girls in this subsample compared to Cohort II.

Regarding youth justice involvement, Cohort I had an earlier age of official justice system contact, incurred a greater number of convictions, and spent more time incarcerated compared to Cohort II. This may be evidence that the YCJA worked as intended. Its goal was to use diversion for first-time offenses and nonserious offenses and avoid the use of pre-trial detention and custody sentences. The DCSO sentencing option under the YCJA meant that an individual from Cohort II could receive a custody sentence but not spend any time in a custody facility.[6] Under the YCJA, youth who received a custody sentence returned to the community after two-thirds of their sentence (e.g., a youth under the YOA and ayouth under the YCJA serving a sentence of six months would not actually spend an equal amount of time incarcerated). Taken together, it may be that youth from Cohort I did not have a more severe offending pattern in adolescence; rather, they were more likely to have their detected offending result in formal sanctions (i.e., count towards their official record), especially at the beginning of their criminal career. As evidence of this, Cohort II self-reported involvement in a significantly greater number of different types of offenses.

During the intake interview for the ISVYOS, participants were asked to report the offense(s) that resulted in their incarceration. Cohort II was significantly more likely to self-report that they were incarcerated for a violent crime (e.g., different forms of homicide, assault, and sexual offenses). This reflected the YCJA’s goal of reserving custody for individuals involved in more serious offenses. Cohort II participants were also significantly more likely to report being incarcerated for administrative offenses (also see Moyer,

2005). We clarified this by comparing Cohort I and Cohort II in terms of their likelihood of being incarcerated for an administrative offense *and* at least one other new offense versus being incarcerated solely for an administrative offense. For Cohort I, 39.0% of participants reported being incarcerated solely for an administrative offense compared to only 20% of Cohort II (χ^2 [1] = 17.42, $p < .001$, $\varphi = .209$). In effect, Cohort II was at an increased likelihood of having an administrative offense at the time of their incarceration, but they were rarely incarcerated solely for such an offense. One interpretation of these findings is that Cohort II committed their serious/violent offense while completing a community-based sentence for another offense, which resulted in an additional administrative offense.

Cohort II's more severe risk factor profile may have also influenced their tendency to be incarcerated for violating administrative conditions. A more extensive risk/needs profile may correlate with a greater number of conditions stipulated as part of their community-based sentences (e.g., orders to attend school, substance use treatment, reside in a particular group home). An extensive number of different conditions may place strain on young persons unfamiliar with strict behavioral expectations; such conditions could be setting the young person up to fail (Sprott & Myers, 2011). Is it possible that the accumulation of judicial consequences carries negative long-term consequences for the adolescence-adulthood transition and the ability to desist from crime?

Adult justice system involvement across cohorts

As shown in Table 9.3, Cohort II incurred a significantly greater number of total convictions and violent convictions. However, time incarcerated in adulthood did not differ between the two groups. This was somewhat surprising; a greater number of convictions, as well as a tendency to be more frequently involved in serious offenses (e.g., violent convictions), was expected to translate to greater amounts of time incarcerated. We also found a significant association between cohort membership and conviction trajectory assignment (based on the conviction trajectory modeled between ages 12–29 in Figure 5.3 of Chapter 5). Cohort II was more likely to be associated with the SRP trajectory compared to Cohort I, although the difference in prevalence was small and the effect size was weak. Compared to other CPO trajectories, the SRP trajectory had a low rate of convictions in adolescence. However, unlike other CPO trajectories, the SRP trajectory showed an increase in the rate of convictions essentially at each year of age from ages 20–29.

There is a clear relationship between past and future offending (Farrington, 2003). We considered whether the link between past and future offending varied according to the type of youth justice system an individual experienced. This section examined whether cohort membership moderated the relationship between youth justice involvement (age of onset, number of convictions, length of incarceration) and adult justice system involvement

Table 9.3 Comparing cohorts across adult offending outcomes

	Cohort I (YOA) M (SD) / n (%)	*Cohort II (YCJA) M (SD) / n (%)*	t/χ^2, df, p, φ/d
Total Convictions (ages 18–29)†	10.95 (12.33)	13.36 (13.60)	t [728.35] = −2.68, p = .007, d = 0.19
Total Violent Convictions (ages 18–29)†	1.31 (1.72)	1.74 (2.13)	t [668.64] = −3.18, p = .002, d = 0.22
Total Days Incarcerated (ages 18–29)†	795.30 (999.60)	742.70 (873.34)	t [834.53] = 0.83, p = .409, d = 0.06
Trajectory Assignment (Ages 12–29)††			
Adolescence-Limited	223 (43.9%)	119 (37.4%)	
Early Onset-Fast Desistance	92 (18.1%)	49 (15.4%)	χ^2 [3] = 8.66, p = .034, φ = .102
Slow Rising Persistent	85 (16.7%)	77 (24.2%)	
High Rate Persistent	108 (21.3%)	73 (23.0%)	

† Assumption of equal variance violated.
†† Based on analyses performed in Chapter 5 (see Figure 5.3).
Notes: d = Cohen's d effect size. Not all participants had criminal history data due to sealed records, moving outside the province, or dying during the follow-up period.

(number of convictions between ages 18–29). The analyses examined whether, for example, the YCJA and its greater emphasis on rehabilitation was able to break or mitigate the association between past and future offending. Risk factors that varied between cohorts (see Table 9.2) were controlled for in all analyses.[7] Model 1 of Table 9.4 looked at the main effects of cohort membership and age of onset of justice system involvement (first conviction or first incarceration, whichever came first) and the interaction between the two. The incidence rate of adult convictions was 1.33 times higher ($p < .05$) for Cohort II compared to Cohort I. A one unit increase in age of onset of justice system involvement was associated with a decrease in the incidence rate of convictions by a factor of 0.16 ($p < .01$). Similar trends were reported in Model 2 (youth convictions) and Model 3 (youth incarceration length).

We were most interested in whether the relationship between past and future justice system involvement functioned differently depending on cohort membership (also see Figure 9.1). Cohort membership moderated the relationship between onset of offending and the incidence rate of adult convictions such that the negative association between onset of offending and the incidence rate of convictions in adulthood was significantly stronger for Cohort I compared to Cohort II. Similarly, the positive association

Table 9.4 Cohort membership and youth justice system involvement as predictors of convictions between ages 18 and 29

	Model 1 (onset interaction) *IRR (95% CI)*	*Model 2 (conviction interaction)* *IRR (95% CI)*	*Model 3 (incarceration interaction)* *IRR (95% CI)*
Male	.	.	.
Female	**0.41 (0.31–0.54)*****	**0.44 (0.33–0.58)*****	**0.44 (0.33–0.58)*****
White	.	.	.
Indigenous	1.16 (0.92–1.46)	1.15 (0.91–1.44)	1.12 (0.89–1.42)
Non-Indigenous Minority	**0.62 (0.46–0.85)****	**0.72 (0.53–0.98)***	**0.58 (0.43–0.79)**
Cohort I	.	.	.
Cohort II	**1.33 (1.03–1.72)***	**1.43 (1.11–1.83)****	**1.42 (1.09–1.83)*****
Onset of Justice System Involvement	**0.84 (0.75–0.93)****	.	.
Onset of Justice System Involvement*Cohort	**1.18 (1.02–1.35)***	.	.
Youth Convictions	.	**1.05 (1.03–1.07)*****	.
Youth Convictions*Cohort	.	**0.97 (0.95–0.996)***	.
Youth Incarceration (Months)	.	.	**1.04 (1.02–1.05)*****
Youth Incarceration (Months)*Cohort	.	.	**0.97 (0.95–0.997)***

* $p < .05$
** $p < .01$
*** $p < .001$.

Notes: IRR = incidence rate ratio. CI = confidence interval. All models controlled for the following variables that significantly differed between Cohort I and Cohort II: Whether the youth was incarcerated for a violent offense at the time of their interview, substance use versatility, raised by MCFD, Enrolled in School, Positive 'Other-Defined' Identity, and Total Mental Health Problems. Onset of justice system involvement represented the age of first conviction or first incarceration, whichever came first. Youth convictions represented total convictions between ages 12–17 and youth incarceration the number of months incarcerated between ages 12–17.

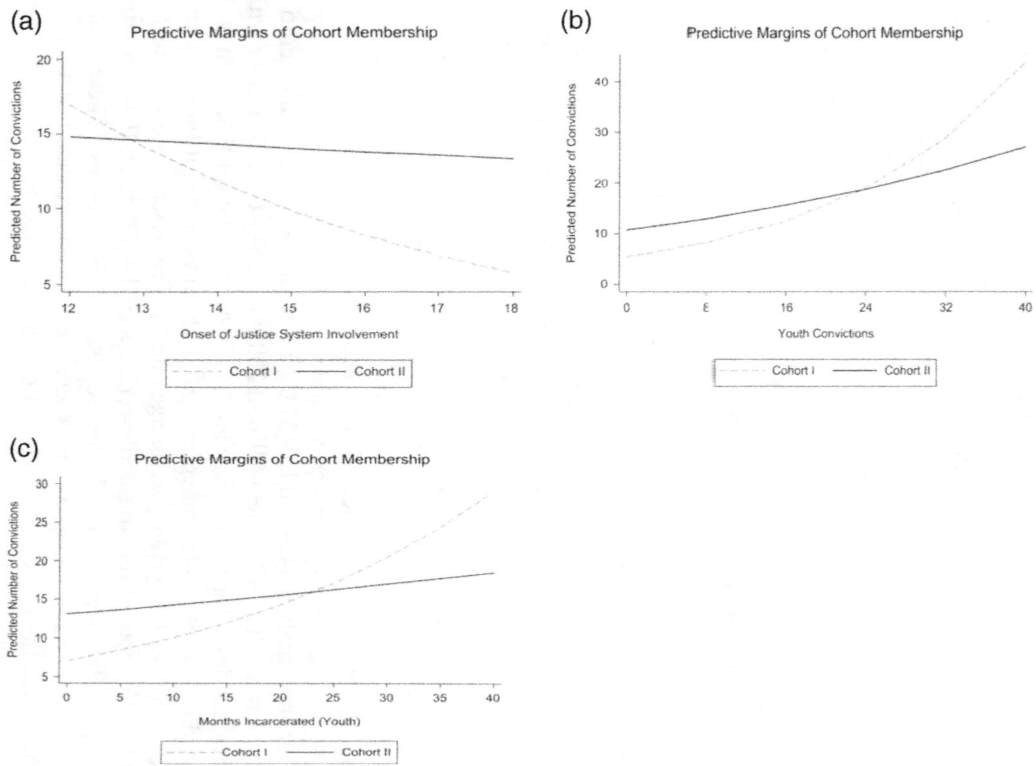

Figure 9.1 Examining whether cohort membership moderates the relationship between past (youth) and future (adulthood) offending.

between youth convictions/youth incarceration and the incidence rate of convictions in adulthood was stronger for Cohort I compared to Cohort II. One interpretation of the interaction plots in Figure 9.1 is that the YCJA was more adept at ensuring that its interventions with youth were rehabilitative and did not result in state dependence effects. This was perhaps most apparent in Panel A, which showed that for youth under the YCJA, the age at which they were brought under the purview of the justice system had no bearing on their rate of convictions in adulthood.

Under the YCJA, youth who spent more time incarcerated did not appear to suffer because of it in the sense that, relative to their peers who spent less time incarcerated, they were not incurring convictions at a higher rate in adulthood. The main effect of cohort membership showed that youth in Cohort II incurred a significantly greater rate of convictions in adulthood, but this did not seem to be related to their justice system experience in adolescence. Rather, it likely reflected their higher level of risk compared to Cohort I. Put differently, Cohort II experienced variability in conviction outcomes in adulthood, but this variability was not well accounted for by official offending in adolescence. A rival explanation is that the YCJA had a more negative impact on youth with less serious offending histories compared to more serious offending histories. As a result, youth with a later age of onset of justice system involvement, fewer convictions, and less time incarcerated were more susceptible to the negative ramifications of the justice system's response to their behavior.

Within-individual change in justice system experiences from adolescence to adulthood

Unobserved factors may account for why an individual received a particular sentence or responded in a particular way to that sentence. Unobserved between-person differences make it challenging to draw firm conclusions about Cohort I and Cohort II differences in youth justice system experiences and adult offending outcomes. Analyses of within-individual change remove biases from these unobserved characteristics. Individuals act as their own control, meaning that models account for time-invariant characteristics (Allison, 2009). This provides greater confidence that relationships observed are not confounded by omitted variables.

Our first analysis (see Table 9.5) used a negative binomial unconditional maximum likelihood model (Allison, 2009) to look at the impact of within-individual deviations in average levels of incarceration (at time t) on within-individual deviations from average levels of convictions (at time t_{+1}). In this case, t represents a given year of age and "$_{+1}$" represents the very next year of age. We focused only on adolescence (ages 12–17) given that our interest was in differences in youth justice system experiences. These analyses showed that when an individual's level of time incarcerated at time t was higher than their average level of time incarcerated for the measurement

Table 9.5 The lagged effect of within-individual changes in time incarcerated (ages 12–17) on within-individual changes in convictions (ages 12–17)

	Convictions (ages 12–17) *IRR (OPG SE)*
Variables in Model	
Age	1.39 (0.03)***
Exposure	0.12 (0.01)***
Incarceration (lagged)	0.99 (0.001)***
Cohort*Incarceration (lagged)	0.99 (0.001)**
Model Fit	
Log likelihood	−7380.64
LR Chi square (917)	3092.43***
Pseudo R^2	0.17

* $p < .05$
** $p < .01$
*** $p < .001$.
Notes: IRR = incidence rate ratio; OPG SE = outer product of the gradient standard error. Coefficients for the main effect of cohort membership and all sample-specific dummy variables excluded from the table.

period (ages 12–17), their number of convictions at time t_{+1} was lower than their average number of convictions for the measurement period. In effect, individuals who experienced more time incarcerated than their average were subsequently convicted of fewer crimes than their average.

We also used these analyses to examine whether cohort membership moderated the relationship between changes in incarceration and changes in convictions. The relationship between changes in incarceration at time t and changes in convictions at time t_{+1} was stronger for Cohort II compared to Cohort I. Essentially, the analysis indicated that within-individual increases in incarceration led to within-individual decreases in convictions and that this relationship was stronger for Cohort II (YCJA) compared to Cohort I (YOA). Whether this represented a deterrent or rehabilitative effect could not be surmised from the data. Although the YCJA was based on rehabilitative principles, it emphasized risk-based interventions similar to the adult RNR model (Bonta & Andrews, 2007).

The negative binomial unconditional maximum likelihood model looked at within-individual change through a process of demeaning, also referred to as person-mean centering (Gunasekara et al., 2014). This means that at each age of measurement, a person's average number of days incarcerated over the entire follow-up period was subtracted from the number of days incarcerated for that particular age. If an individual spent 20 days incarcerated at age 15 and their average number of days incarcerated over the follow-up was 50, their demeaned score would equal "−30". This poses a problem when thinking about whether and how incarceration influences future offending. Person-mean centering examines a person's deviation at time *t* from that person's average over the entirety of the follow-up period. This means that looking at a person's deviation from an average at time *t* involves factoring in events that have yet to transpire. Take for example an individual whose pattern of months incarcerated is as follows: Age 12: 0 months, Age 13: 0 months, Age 14: 1 month, Age 15: 4 months, Age 16: 4 months, Age 17: 8 months. In total, this individual spent 18 months incarcerated over a six-year period (i.e., an average of 3 months incarcerated at each year of age). Accordingly, at age 14, using person-mean centering, the one month they spent in custody was two months *less* than their average across the follow-up period. However, this was also *more* than any amount of incarceration experienced to this point. It is not less than what they *experienced* on average because they have no memory of future incarceration. For this individual, their one month in custody is not experienced as a reduction in the amount of time they are used to spending incarcerated. It is actually an increase. Nevertheless, statistically, their time incarcerated at age 14 is treated as a decrease from their average. In sum, traditional statistical methods for performing within-individual analyses contextualize current events by relying on future events not yet experienced by the person. Unless we are in a Christopher Nolan film, this is not how time works, nor is it how the impact of incarceration works.

We attempted to resolve this issue by using what we term person-prior centering. Instead of looking at whether a person's "score" at time *t* differed from their average "score" across the full study period, this approach looked at whether a person's "score" at time *t* differed from their score at time t_{-1}. For example, this approach looked at change as whether the number of days a person spent incarcerated at a given year of age differed compared to the number of days they spent incarcerated one year earlier. For age 12, the raw value of incarceration was used. For age 13, their days incarcerated was subtracted by their days incarcerated at age 12. For age 14, their days incarcerated was subtracted by their number of days incarcerated at age 13, and so on. The same was done for convictions. Table 9.6 shows correlation coefficients between change in incarceration at time *t* and change in convictions at time t_{+1}, time t_{+2}, and so on. We were most interested in the relationship between change in incarceration length at time *t* and change in number of convictions at the next year of age. For both cohorts, when participants experienced *more* incarceration at time *t* compared to time *t*-1, they subsequently incurred *fewer* convictions at time *t*+1. However, these effects did not last; that is, there was no significant correlation between changes in incarceration at time *t* and changes in convictions at time t_{+2}, t_{+3}, and so on.

Summary

Canada's YOA and YCJA represented two pieces of youth justice legislation that had similar goals. However, the YOA lacked specificity and failed to

Table 9.6 Using person-prior centering to unravel the relationship between changes in incarceration length and changes in convictions

	Change in convictions from year of age					
	Age 13	*Age 14*	*Age 15*	*Age 16*	*Age 17*	*Age 18*
Change in Incarceration Length from Prior Year of Age						
Cohort I						
Age 12	.057	−.148**	−.073	.004	.058	−.104*
Age 13	.402**	−.204**	−.091*	−.081	.033	−.031
Age 14		.357**	−.315**	−.129**	.024	−.019
Age 15			.308**	−.239**	−.034	.042
Age 16				.295**	−.243**	.079
Age 17					.343**	−.310**
Cohort II						
Age 12	.199**	−.101	−.016	−.048	−.006	−.012
Age 13	.708**	−.182**	−.171**	−.026	−.076	−.012
Age 14		.417**	−.266**	−.136**	−.058	.023
Age 15			.381**	−.266**	−.033	−.066
Age 16				.393**	−.333**	−.031
Age 17					.386**	−.220**

* $p < .05$
** $p < .01$
*** $p < .001$.

explain the hierarchy of its guiding principles, and this resulted in incarcerating youth at a disproportionately higher rate relative to other western industrialized nations (Bala et al., 2009; Bell, 2014; Corrado et al., 2010). One goal of the YCJA was to reduce Canada's overreliance on incarceration as a response to young persons in the justice system. This was done by being more precise about when youth should be diverted, when to implement community-based sanctions, and when to impose custody sentences. Data collection for the ISVYOS spanned both the YOA and YCJA, which allowed for a comparison of Cohort I (YOA) and Cohort II (YCJA) across several outcomes. Key findings included:

1. Cohort II risk/need profiles were more severe compared to Cohort I.
2. Patterns of official offending in adolescence were more severe for Cohort I compared to Cohort II.

3. Patterns of official offending in adulthood were more severe for Cohort II compared to Cohort I.
4. The relationship between past youth justice system involvement and future adult justice system involvement was stronger for Cohort I than Cohort II.
5. The impact of changes in the amount of time incarcerated on changes in the frequency of convictions was stronger for Cohort II; within-individual increases in time incarcerated was associated with within-individual decreases in the frequency of convictions at the next year of age.
6. Using a measure of within-individual change that relied on deviations from levels of incarceration/convictions at the immediately prior age-period, for both cohorts, increases in time spent incarcerated were associated with decreases in future convictions.

It was possible that differences in adult justice system outcomes between the two cohorts were attributable to factors other than different youth justice system experiences. For example, was Cohort I subjected to an adult justice system markedly different from the one to which Cohort II was subjected? Cohort I and Cohort II were born in similar eras (1979–1987 and 1986–1990, respectively). Part of the reason why the adult justice system likely cannot account for differences between Cohort I and Cohort II regarding convictions in adulthood is because both cohorts currently experience the same system. Data on conviction outcomes for participants were as recent as December of 2019. When these data were collected, both Cohort I and Cohort II were part of the same adult system, albeit different ages at the time of data collection. Changes to Canada's adult justice system have been relatively slow (Department of Justice, 2019), especially when compared against changes to the youth justice system between the YOA and YCJA (Bala, 2003; Bala et al., 2009). Accordingly, the differences in the type of youth justice system that Cohort I and Cohort II were exposed to were likely greater compared to the differences in the type of adult justice system to which Cohort I and Cohort II were exposed.

In Chapter 4 we discussed how although the justice system is aware of, and tends to try to allocate disproportionate resources to, individuals involved in early-onset, high-rate, and serious offending in adolescence to prevent continued adult offending, these criminal career parameters nevertheless were related to a more serious pattern of adult justice system involvement. In the current chapter, we showed that the YCJA may have been more successful than the YOA in helping to prevent the high-rate, early-onset youth from showing a similarly severe pattern of offending in adulthood. The YCJA's stronger emphasis on treatment and community release planning may have contributed to this finding. However, it is important to avoid sweeping conclusions about the efficacy of the YCJA compared to the YOA given that this was a sample of youth who experienced incarceration (i.e., a small minority of all youth processed by the youth justice system).

For most youth, their first appearance in front of a judge is the last time that they experience formal justice system involvement (Sullivan, 2019). In Canada, only about 15% of all cases resulting in a finding of guilt result in a custody sentence (Statistics Canada, 2015). In effect, we are reporting on one element of the youth justice system that, albeit important, deals with a minority of all youth within this system.

Future research should expand on these findings by measuring justice system experiences from the youth's perspective. The YCJA included a greater number of sentencing options, was more explicit about rehabilitation as its principal goal, and formally emphasized diversion from the youth justice system. However, direct measures of these principles and practices were not available in the ISVYOS data. We do not have direct measures of whether Cohort II was more likely to be diverted, more likely to receive rehabilitative services, or whether the treatment they received was more tailored to their needs. Anecdotally, we did not present results of participants' self-reported sentencing conditions and type of sanction because we did not feel that these data were reliable. Interviews with participants revealed that they regularly had a poor understanding of each charge they were convicted of, let alone the type(s) of sentence(s) they received and the conditions associated with their community release.

A finding that might stand out in this chapter is the observation that within-individual increases in the amount of time spent incarcerated were associated with within-individual decreases in the number of convictions incurred at the next year of age. It might be tempting to conclude that custody can, at least over the short-term, influence reductions in offending. However, it should be kept in mind that once a person was incarcerated under the YCJA, the focus was on rehabilitation and on providing services rather than deterring youth from future offending. Trauma-informed practices, healing circles, substance use treatment, education, health and nutrition, and community reentry planning were all core components of the custody experience for Cohort II. This was not an inexpensive option. In BC, it costs approximately $215,000 to incarcerate a youth for a single year (BC Representative for Children and Youth, 2009). The YCJA also emphasized longer-term sentences compared to the YOA's use of short-term sentences for deterrence (Bell, 2014). This means that practitioners under the YCJA may have had more consecutive days to work with their clients on different risk/needs factors and develop a strong community re-entry plan. The unconditional maximum likelihood negative binomial analysis showed that custody was a stronger short-term deterrent for Cohort II compared to Cohort I. In effect, the impact of custody on future convictions was stronger under a justice system that was far more selective about who was incarcerated. Thus, the findings are not suggesting that using incarceration unilaterally influenced reductions in convictions in the short term.

Notes

1 Roberts (2004) illustrated that some in Canada still assert that "young persons are capable of moral decision making and can distinguish between wrongful acts on the basis of their relative seriousness… if juveniles are capable of taking responsibility for their actions, we should treat them as responsible agents who, inter alia, can and should be called to account for the wrongs that they do" (303).

2 There were still concerns about welfare-based decisions under the YCJA (Department of Justice, 2007). This may be related to the increase in use of risk assessments under the YCJA,which can expose judges to the plethora of different risks/needs factors associated with adolescents before the court. The over-taxed child welfare system may be a reason for why welfare-based decisions persist (Department of Justice, 2007). The overrepresentation of adolescents dually involved in both child welfare and youth justice systems may be amplified under the YCJA. The child welfare system may even see their client's involvement in the youth justice system as a way to dispose of their responsibility for a particularly challenging adolescent with many needs and requiring a multitude of resources (Department of Justice, 2007).

3 Under the YCJA, Justice Abella for the SCC decision in *R v. D.B.* ruled in favor of disregarding deterrence as an explicit aggravating factor in the sentencing of youth. In *R. v. D.P*, Justice Charron in ruling for the majority suggested that specific deterrence was never mentioned in the YCJA and that its omission should be considered purposeful. The Federal Conservative government of Canada enacted legislation to overrule these decisions. This legislation came into effect after the ISVYOS had finished recruiting new participants. It is unlikely that Cohort II participants received a sentence with the (explicit) purpose of specific deterrence in mind.

4 An indicatable offense is an offense for which an adult may receive a custody sentence of two years or longer.

5 Members of Cohort I were born between 1979 and 1987. Members of Cohort II were born between 1986 and 1998. Focusing only on participants followed through age 29 restricted the Cohort II subsample to individuals born between 1986 and 1992. Only two individuals in this subsample from Cohort II were born between 1991 and 1992. The rest were born between 1986 and 1990. This helped minimize differences between Cohort I and Cohort II attributable to contextual factors unrelated to differences in youth justice legislation.

6 When the ISVYOS coded time incarcerated, we relied on actual time incarcerated based on admission and release dates from incarceration facilities as opposed to looking at the specific type of sentence/length of sentence.

7 Some variables were excluded because of overlap with others (e.g., we excluded age of onset because of its correlation with total convictions). Sexual abuse and leaving home before age 12 were excluded because of low base rates.

10 Lessons learned from interviewing incarcerated youth

Introduction

Sociocriminologists during the ALC paradigm primarily used secondary data or data based on the administration of surveys with little interaction with participants, especially when it came to individuals most likely to be involved in chronic offending and/or CPO. The armchair sociocriminology approach espoused by Sutherland's disciples of the ALC paradigm involved sarcastic commentaries about theory principles (e.g., Matsueda, 1997) without attention to measuring theoretical constructs. The DLC paradigm brought in new ways of thinking that required new ways of collecting data. The distribution of surveys to high school or college students was not suitable for studying serious and violent offending over the life-course. New research design approaches required specific knowledge, resources, and skills. This chapter was inspired especially by reviews of lessons learned from the Pathways to Desistance Study (Schubert et al., 2004) and the LoneStar Project (Fahmy et al., 2019; Mitchell et al., 2018) and by descriptions of experiences gaining access to and conducting research in institutional settings (Fox et al., 2011; Trulson et al., 2004). This prior work provided a roadmap for doing research within hard-to-reach populations such as individuals in custody. Our goal was to help contribute to this literature by describing the ISVYOS interview process, from training new RAs, to entering the custody center, to debriefing at the end of interviews. Strong quantitative analyses does not come solely from crunching numbers and running analyses. Getting reliable data to enter into these analyses required a very human and empathic approach. It also required hundreds of hours working with multiple agencies and review boards to ensure that the data were collected ethically.

The ISVYOS was responsible for ensuring the interview process was conducted in accordance with the research ethics agreements between the ISVYOS and MCFD and the ISVYOS and the Simon Fraser University (SFU) Research Ethics Board (REB). Although we will not focus on this process here, many of the project's research decisions and procedures were structured around ensuring that these agreements were upheld. Research Assistants (RAs) were tasked with not merely acting as a transcriber recording responses. They were responsible for establishing assent and maintaining rapport with participants and staff. Data were reliable thanks to participants, but RAs played a key role in ensuring that participants were invested in providing accurate answers. The role of RAs included identifying inconsistent answers and possible confusion or misinterpretation of questions by the participant as well as using follow-up questions to gain clarity. In this chapter, we discussed strategies for interviewing youth with serious behavioral problems who often had poor social skills, inexperience with boundary-setting, and difficulties with attention and comprehension. We ended the chapter with a description of what we would do differently if we were to start the project from the beginning.

Training

Training RAs to administer interviews began at the ISVYOS Research Lab at SFU. Newly-hired RAs were required to read a manual that described the project's purposes and procedures. This manual included a description of appropriate dress and conduct while in youth custody centers. The first training session reviewed each question in the intake interview. New RAs then conducted a mock interview with the ISVYOS project manager or an experienced RA playing the role of participant. For the second training session, the new RA shadowed an experienced RA as they interacted with residents and staff and conducted interviews in the custody center. For the third session, the new RA conducted interviews while being shadowed by an experienced RA. The experienced RA provided feedback to the new RA and to the project manager, who decided whether the RA would continue their training/shadowing or be allowed to recruit and interview participants on their own. A site manager conducted quality assurance checks of interviews to ensure questions were completed and that there was a lack of inconsistent answers. Any inconsistencies that were identified were reviewed with the RA who conducted the interview and, when possible, the RA would re-interview the participant to gain clarity about the answer(s) in question. An example of a possible inconsistency in the interview would be where a participant indicated that they really liked school but also indicated that they regularly skipped school or dropped out of school. This is not always an inconsistent response as some youth may have enjoyed school but dropped out for other reasons (e.g., care for family members, make money selling drugs, etc.), but is the type of answer pattern that warrants following up with the participant.

Entering the custody center

A negative criminal record check was required before RAs were permitted to enter custody centers. Entering the custody center meant adapting to its culture. Staff were referred to as Mr./Mrs./Ms. "Jones". Youth were referred to as "residents" and were called by their last name. In terms of dress, it was better to fit in than to stand out, especially when custody center residents were adept at recognizing who did not fit in. RAs dressed according to common sense and were reminded that they were interviewing youth who had difficulties with behavioral control and appropriate social behavior. It was also possible to be over-professional. Wearing a suit and tie to interview a young person wearing joggers and a sweater exacerbated an already uneven hierarchy/power dynamic. Jewellery was typically not worn, but RAs wore watches to ensure that the interview did not encroach on the time a resident was supposed to spend in a program.

To prevent incarcerated youth from gaining access to valuables, RAs were required to leave keys, phones, purses, wallets, and other items either in their car or in lockers made available to visitors. Knowing that RAs were acting as guests and abiding by the rules of the center also made custody center staff more comfortable with the ISVYOS operating at their institution. RAs signed the center's guest logbook using their first name and last initial. RAs then checked in with "Control". Control represented a group of staff responsible for monitoring all cameras in the institution and allowing access through electronically secured doors throughout the custody centre. Control was responsible for the safety of RAs and the tracking of all people in the institution. There were many different visitors, volunteers, counselors, and lawyers moving throughout custody centers. Checking in with Control helped staff put a face and name to the RA, which facilitated movement throughout the custody center.

After checking in with Control, RAs signed out a personal alarm device (PAD). Pressing a button on the PAD would send a silent alarm to Control. PADs were only introduced for the last five years of data collection. There were no occasions in which an RA was required to activate their PAD. RAs were trained to prioritize their safety by following staff instruction at all times. In the history of the project, there were no instances of a physical assault against an RA. The culture of the custody center was such that visitors and volunteers were deserving of respect from residents. An assault against an RA would be viewed negatively by other residents. Thus, there was not just the threat of justice system punishment, but a loss of social capital. That said, it was not uncommon for residents to make derogatory comments towards RAs. Appropriate responses to such comments were discussed later in the chapter.

After acquiring a PAD, RAs checked in with the manager of the center (referred to as the "Person in Charge" (PIC) or "Assistant Director of Operations" (ADO) to let them know that the SFU interviewers had arrived. The manager provided RAs with a "program sheet" that specified which units would be at which programs and at which times. The interview schedule was built around the program sheet. To ensure the rehabilitative progress of youth was not interrupted, RAs never requested to interview youth if it resulted in that person missing a program. Programs included school, substance misuse (e.g., harm reduction, relapse prevention, fun in recovery), mental health services, religious programs, life skills (e.g., parenting, trades courses, cooking and health), multicultural programs such as Indigenous Awareness, gender-specific programs like "Girls Circle", and fitness/recreation programs.

The check-in process was not only time consuming for RAs but for custody staff as well. For this reason, RAs aimed to arrive at the center at the same time (e.g., travel in the same car, wait in the parking lot for others to arrive) so that Control and the manager would not be interrupted on multiple occasions.

Pre-interview procedures

Residents attended school from morning through mid-afternoon. Since RAs never removed youth from school for an interview, interviews ran from about 3:00 pm to 10:00 pm.[1] RAs arrived approximately one hour before the interview window opened to prepare for the interview. RAs worked out of the "Case Management" section of the custody center where probation officers, social workers, and classification officers had their offices. Connected to Case Management was "Records". Records was responsible for all admissions and releases from custody. Records provided RAs with a copy of the "Location Slate Report", which contained the names of all youth in the custody center and the unit they resided on. Records also provided RAs with a "Face Sheet" for each person admitted to the custody center. The Face Sheet included the youth's demographic information, offense for which they were currently incarcerated, and any alerts (e.g., allergies, mental health problems, contact concerns with other youth).

The Location Slate Report and Face Sheets were used to update an Excel spreadsheet referred to as the "Currently in Institution List". This list included the unit locations of all youth currently in the custody center as well as the interviews that remained to be completed for each youth. The Location Slate Report was used to update the unit that a youth resided on. Youth regularly changed units due to conflict with other youth or to keep them away from individuals who they had co-offended with. Youth on the Currently in Institution List, but not the Location Slate Report, were youth released from the custody center since the last shift and were removed from the spreadsheet. Face Sheets were used to add the youth who were newly admitted to the custody center. The Currently in Institution List was used to identify which RAs would interview which youth.[2] Once an RA identified the individual they expected to interview, they would read the youth's file and complete a one-page file code ("1-Pager") noting important details about the youth, including their offense history, experiences of abuse, mental health, and family relationships. This 1-Pager was reviewed so that the RA was sensitive to the participant's background. It was also important to review files to learn what the youth physically looked like. Sometimes residents would impersonate the individual who the RA was looking to interview.

Determining which resident an RA would interview was mostly random. For the sake of rapport, the ISVYOS tried to ensure that the same RA re-interviewed the same participant. Female RAs were free to interview all youth in the custody center. Male RAs did not interview girls because the interview dealt with sensitive themes, including questions about abuse, and it was believed that talking about such themes in a small, isolated interview room with someone who might resemble the characteristics of the participant's abuser would put the participant in an uncomfortable situation. Neither a person's level of risk, mental health history, offense history, nor placement on separate confinement precluded RAs from approaching that person for an interview.

The introduction

Approximately eight residents were housed on each unit, each with their own room. Most residents were found in the unit's common area watching TV or playing chess or cards. Residents rarely spent much time in their room as this could lead other residents to accuse them of being scared to be on the unit. It was important for RAs to keep in mind that they were not just walking into some unit in some custody center. These units represented the living quarters for residents. Some of these youth spent more time incarcerated than in their home in the community. Treating the unit as someone's home meant entering quietly and showing respect. The first step upon arrival involved asking the line staff (i.e., the staff member in charge of that unit) for permission to speak to a particular resident. When the resident's name was called by the line staff, RAs introduced themselves and informed the resident that they were conducting a research project for SFU and were hoping that they would participate. Establishing that the RA worked for the university and not the custody center avoided being conflated with someone from the justice system. If a youth agreed to participate, they joined the RA in a private interview room where the purpose of the research was explained.

Approximately 90% of residents who were approached agreed to participate in the interview. Sometimes residents asked to be removed from the interview schedule. A week later they would become upset that RAs were ignoring them and interviewing other residents instead. RAs politely reminded such youth that they asked to be removed from the list, but if they had changed their mind, the RA would love to interview them. There were a number of reasons that motivated youth to participate. Some wanted to avoid the boredom on their unit. Others participated because the remuneration (juice and chips) was viewed as currency that they could trade for other things. Some wanted to spend time with a specific RA. We believe that most just wanted to share their story. Participants were altruistic and would express sentiments regarding how "it might be too late for me, but if this information can help develop programs that help other kids, I will do it". Relatedly, it was common for participants to indicate their desire to become drug and alcohol counselors or youth support workers.

If RAs were aware of the unit's social hierarchy, it was advantageous to first provide a simple acknowledgement (e.g., a wave, head nod) to the leaders or "heavies"[3] before seeking to interview new residents. If multiple youth from the same unit were on the interview schedule, RAs prioritized interviewing the longer-term resident first, especially if this person participated in the study on prior occasions. This showed respect for the unit hierarchy and the pre-existing relationship between the participant and the ISVYOS. In general, residents were careful about who they were seen talking to (e.g., stigmatization if observed talking to a social worker, being perceived as a "rat"). For newer residents, to see peers with more experience in the system participate in the interview was a signal that it was safe for them to participate, too.

Once in the closed-door, private interview room that could not be viewed from the unit's common area, RAs tried to reduce a potential power dynamic differential[4] by communicating that the resident was the expert of their own life, that their story was valued by the research team, and that they appreciated the participant's willingness to discuss their story. To encourage openness and minimize impression management (e.g., disingenuous expressions of remorse), RAs explained that they were in a non-judgmental role.[5] Expressions of support can improve participants' willingness to be more forthcoming (Zulawski & Wicklander, 1993). This support must be sincere (Cooke & Logan, 2018). Disingenuous expression of support is as detrimental to rapport as appearing distant (Crewe, 2011). Moreover, considering the prevalence of reactive attachment disorder within incarcerated populations (Abram et al. 2003), being overly friendly instead of letting rapport develop at a more natural pace may arouse suspicion about an RA's motives. Participants typically experienced tumultuous backgrounds that included victimization by persons who were supposed to be responsible for caring for them, and so over-enthusiasm may be perceived by the participant as a disingenuous attempt by the RA to get close to them for the purpose of exploitation. RA sensitivity and sincerity were critical. High levels of enthusiasm worked for some RAs; the key was to find an interview style that was respectful, genuine, and fit the RA's personality.

The final element of the introduction involved obtaining assent by reading an information sheet that described the purpose of the study, how information would be used, and what participants' involvement entailed. RAs explained that involvement in the study would not directly impact participants' experiences in the custody center, but that their involvement might help them gain insight into their own behavior.[6] Youth were often bored by these details and interrupted RAs to say that they did not care and just wanted to sign the information sheet to acknowledge their agreement to participate. RAs explained that they could lose their job if they did not read the information sheet in full. Most participants cared about the wellbeing of RAs. In many cases, residents were denigrated by their peers if they treated persons from outside the institution poorly. One critical reason for reading the information sheet was to communicate rules surrounding confidentiality. In addition to REB-approved statements, concrete examples were useful. RAs explained, for example, that if the youth told them that they had $10,000 underneath their mattress from a bank robbery, the RA was not allowed to inform police. If the RA had rapport with others on the participant's unit, they let the new participant know that they could ask their peers about the study before participating.

Participants were sometimes suspicious about why an RA would be motivated to maintain confidentiality. Explaining this motivation was an opportunity to build rapport. RAs explained that they respected the youth for telling them about their life and wanted to reciprocate that respect by maintaining confidentiality. If participants did not seem convinced, RAs explained that confidentiality was something that they were contracted to uphold and that a violation of confidentiality could jeopardize the project and expose the RA to litigation. RAs also communicated that they were aware of the custody center culture of how residents viewed "rats" as persons who were disloyal and not worthy of respect (also see Mitchell et al., 2018) and that this label would make it difficult for them to work in the custody center and have residents agree to interviews. RAs drew parallels between this custody center subcultural context and research context to establish shared values regarding the importance of keeping your word.

After reading the information sheet, participants were asked if they had questions about the ISVYOS. Participants were mostly interested in how interview information was being used and whether it could help them. RAs explained that the information provided would hopefully help other youth in similar situations. Sometimes participants asked if they could have a copy of the interview to use in court. RAs reminded them that the interview asked about criminal behavior that went undetected by police and thus it would not be in their best interests to disclose interview information. Other questions asked by participants were more personal. RAs were instructed to avoid sharing personal details, but sometimes it was necessary to share mundane personal information to make participants comfortable sharing their own experiences. Personal questions mostly related to what the RA studied in school and why they chose this job. RAs avoided commenting on aspirations for careers in the justice system. Most RAs explained that they wanted to hear the stories of youth in custody so that they could help youth in similar situations. A slightly more personal question related to how much money the RA earned. Rather than directly answer the question, RAs typically explained that this work was part of their graduate school training and that the job interested them. How RAs responded to participant questions (e.g., tone of voice) seemed more important to rapport than the nature of the information included in the response. It was important for RAs to practice patience and understanding. Intrusive questions from participants may be more so a result of inexperience with opportunities to engage in prosocial conversations with young adults than purposefully inappropriate behavior.

Conducting the interview

The intake interview was completed as a pencil-to-paper structured questionnaire. None of the answers required RAs to make inferences or rate participants and thus evaluating interrater reliability was not required. The amount of time needed to complete the interview depended on the participant's cognitive abilities, attention span, and motivation. The average interview required 90 minutes to complete. Follow-up questions were asked for negative behaviors endorsed, which meant that participants with lengthier histories of problem behavior took longer to interview. It was advantageous to complete the interview over at least two sesssions to avoid depleting participants' motivation to provide thoughtful and accurate answers. Interview strategy recommendations were based on our experiences with this interview as well as with a semi-structured interview used for the purpose of assessing and rating features of psychopathy (see McCuish et al., 2019a). Our retrospective reflection on valuable interview strategies is not as ideal as research that systematically investigated which types of strategies were successful (see Fahmy et al., 2019). Nevertheless, the recommendations that follow were based on more than a decade of experience interviewing youth in custody. We are grateful to Dr. Karine Descormiers, Dr. Sarah Kuehn, and Dr. Amy Prevost (former RAs), for their thoughts on conducting successful interviews (see Table 10.1 for a summary).

Interviewing youth as a unique challenge

Compared to adults, youth have lower cognitive abilities and more severe attention deficit problems, both of which can heighten the risk of misunderstanding questions. This risk is amplified when interviewing incarcerated youth given the high rates of learning disorders (Quinn et al., 2005) and attention-deficit disorders (Abram et al., 2003) among this population. RAs were trained to be wary that an answer of "I don't know" was often an indication that the participant did not understand the question and wanted to end an uncomfortable moment of silence. Repeating the original wording of the question could be unhelpful and even further agitate the participant and so RAs were trained to rephrase questions in various ways. Focus and motivation were regular issues for ISVYOS participants. Active listening and observing facial expressions and body language helped identify if a participant was frustrated, bored, or losing motivation. Offering to end the interview early helped ensure that the participant did not become frustrated and provide inaccurate answers. It also helped ensure that the participant did not become disinterested in participating in future interviews and did not have negative things to say about the study, which could influence other residents' hesitancy to participate. In some

Table 10.1 RA perspectives on different aspects of interviewing youth involved in serious and violent offenses

	RA suggestions
Rapport	• Do not rush rapport. Youth can be suspicious; let relationships unfold naturally. Start with small gestures. • Participants can sense when you are nervous/ intimidated. You can lean into it, make a joke of it, or work on being prepared to ease nerves. • Participants appreciate a relaxed interview style. Do not be too uptight or formal. At the same time, it is important to let them know that you are in control of the interview. • Be human; react normally and not as clinical as your training. Be professional but be yourself. • The participant is giving you *their* time. Be grateful. Stories shared by participants can build your entire career. • Not all youth want you to say hi to them inside the custody center. Saying hi requires the youth to explain to others how they know you. If they are clearly avoiding eye contact, take this as a sign to respect their privacy. Never approach participants outside the custody center context. • Individuals you have rapport with can help set the standard/culture of the behavior of other youth on unit. Their endorsement of the interview can be huge for the desire of others to participate. • Accept that not all youth will like you. Be humble. Know when to let the youth be interviewed by someone else. Think about what is best for the reliability of the data. • Good rapport with correctional officers is essential for maintaining access to residents.
Interview(er) Style	• Be aware of the power dynamic; this is not a natural give-and-take conversation. Remind the participant that you are indebted to them (which you are). • You do not need to be the expert in everything. Playing the rookie can make participants feel empowered by teaching you something new. • Being prepared for personal questions means knowing what your answers will be ahead of time. Think about why you are doing this job. Think about what you want to do for a career. Decide how much information you are willing to share. Avoid being dishonest about your personal life; redirect their attention onto themselves instead of fabricating an answer about yourself.

(*Continued*)

Table 10.1 (Continued)

	RA suggestions
	• What works for one RA might not work for you. There are many appropriate interview styles. Wrong interview styles are forced interview styles. Find your style. Adjust your style. Be polyvalent.
Framing, Consent, & Confidentiality	• Keep the explanation of confidentiality and purpose of the study simple. Do not underestimate cognitive or psychological deficits that could affect participants' ability to understand what their participation involves. • When describing the purpose of the study and the need for youth participation, you can reiterate that you have access to the participant's file, which includes probation officer comments, court documents, and so on, but that you are really interested in the participant's answer to these questions. Express that you believe that participants are rarely heard; you want to give them an opportunity to tell their story from their perspective. • Confidentiality can be framed around respect for the young person and keeping your word. Relates to youth offending culture of not being a "rat". Provides a way to develop a shared understanding.
Interview Skills and Conduct	• Participants might get embarrassed if they do not understand a question. Relate by saying something like, "no worries, sometimes I have difficulty understanding what the questions mean. Let me rephrase it for you". Preserve the relationship and reputation. Explain, say sorry, stay calm. • Participants were often raised in environments where disagreements were settled with heated arguments and/or violence. If they get frustrated, give them an opportunity to be exposed to healthy exchanges and prosocial problem-solving. Calmness and positivity can surprise participants but also make them want to return for another interview. • Their unit is their home, and you are walking into it without their permission. Be prepared to not be welcomed with open arms. Some will want you to earn their respect. Keep showing them respect and keep showing up. • If you think the participant is not in the right state of mind, give them a way out of the interview with a promise to return. Saying things like "I see you are upset" may seem empathic, but it can come across as patronizing or identifying the participant as a "victim", which has very negative connotations in the custody center environment.

(*Continued*)

Table 10.1 (Continued)

	RA suggestions
	• Emphasize that they do not need to answer any questions they are uncomfortable with, but in such instances, ask them to let you know. • The goal is not to finish the interview. The goal is to get accurate information. Pay attention to body language to recognize when the youth's energy/motivation is draining. • Interviews sometimes include similar questions. Youth can recognize this and get annoyed and think you are not listening. Once you have asked a similar question a second time, following the youth's answer, acknowledge that the question was similar to past questions and you appreciate them answering the question again (do not acknowledge this *before* their answer, as doing so will inflate the reliability of the tool).
Dishonesty & Antagonism	• Read the participant's file so that you can detect deceit regarding mundane details (e.g., place of residence, name, date of birth). Call them out for it early but make it playful. You are not there to fight with them, you just want to know their perspective. • Dealing with deceit does not need to play out like a bad police interrogation or a confrontational interaction. You do not need to accuse someone of lying. Blame yourself (e.g., "I made a mistake. On question two I have it written down that you have never sold drugs but on question 17 I have it written down that you have sold drugs at school. Where did I go wrong?"). Act like Columbo. Let them have a way out to protect their reputation. It is better for participants to think you are dumb but nice than to think you are smart and always correcting them. • Deceitfulness can be mistaken for the participant's desire to protect you from awful details. Let them know that it is your job, that you are trained for this, and that you are most interested in hearing their perspective. Some may want you to ask for details so that they do not have to volunteer the information. • You are asking questions about intimate aspects of a person's life. It is typical for every participant to be dishonest in some way (e.g., withholding information). Do not take it personally. • Antagonism is about getting a reaction. Some want the attention. Some want to shock you. Be mindful of your reaction to avoid encouraging continued similar behavior.

(*Continued*)

Table 10.1 (Continued)

	RA suggestions
	• Directly address inappropriate comments. Consider the young person's potential inexperience with prosocial interactions and the possibility that boundary-setting was rare in their upbringing. • Some want to prove to you that they are heavily involved in crime; the bravado will be laid on thick. Do not glamorize their criminality but do not judge it nor question the morality of their behavior.
Miscellaneous	• Interviews will be different with different youth. Some want you to earn their respect first, it will take time. Just show up. They will open up. Some want to be left alone, will provide minimal information and you will feel disappointed. Some will never participate; you will never earn their trust. It is okay. Move on. • Leverage connections to help reduce behavioral issues of other residents. You can refuse to meet with someone who is behaving poorly. Choose residents who display proper manners and reinforce this behavior by showing your appreciation. • Say yes when invited to custody center events like a resident's birthday or high school graduation. Be visible, but not too visible. Arrive on your own rather than with custody center staff. Sit by yourself or with other RAs. You may be friendly with staff but consider how participants might perceive this relationship. • Residents can be creative. Juice can be turned into alcohol. It can be used as currency to set up fights with other residents. The tops of soda cans can be used as weapons. The same applies to pens. Paper clips can be turned into needles for making tattoos. Preventing youth from gaining access to such objects keeps everyone safe.

Note. We are grateful to Dr. Karine Descormiers, Dr. Sarah Kuehn, and Dr. Amy Prevost, all former ISVYOS RAs, for sharing their recommendations.

interview rooms there was a ping pong table that RAs used to play a quick game with the participant as a brief distraction from the interview. Letting participants shuffle a deck of cards also helped. Overall, although interviews required the use of more resources, administering surveys without opportunities for one-to-one verification of a participant's understanding of each question and motivation to complete questions accurately would yield less reliable data. We believe that the more resource-intensive interview was necessary.

Compared to adults, youth are more likely to change their answer in response to negative feedback (Richardson et al., 1995) and therefore tone and phrasing of follow-up questions are key. Adversarial phrasing (e.g., "your answer is different from other youth, why is this?") may give participants the impression that they are not "normal", which can influence them to alter their answer to correspond with their perception of the interviewer's expectation. Questions that begin with "how come" rather than "why" may appear less confrontational and elicit a more elaborate response (also see McCuish et al., 2019a). Adults typically engage in impression management by underreporting negative behavior (e.g., Book et al., 2006; Lilienfeld, & Fowler, 2006). The opposite is true for youth (Erikson, 1968; Harter, 1990; Hill & Holmbeck, 1986). However, while youth may exaggerate involvement in antisocial and criminal behavior, they may also minimize the extent to which this behavior creates problems in their life. Youth may be prone to underreporting, for example, reactive forms of aggression that draw attention from the justice system. Participants used the term "heat score" to describe a person with whom they would not want to associate with because that person's behavior was frequently resulting in detection by police. Asking youth about whether their aggression resulted in difficulties with police or other agents of the justice system may result in an attempt to conceal the degree to which the behavior caused functional impairment. In semi-structured interviews conducted for assessing features of psychopathy, RAs asked participants to describe times that they were aggressive. The RA then allowed the details of such incidents to be revealed through natural conversation.

Questions should be specific to the developmental stage of the participant. In semi-structured interviews, when RAs were assessing cognitive inflexibility, as opposed to adult-themed questions involving adherence to employee codes of conduct or willingness to compromise with intimate partners, lines of questioning focused on participants' willingness to abide by rules at school and at home. When assessing intolerant attitudes, because incarcerated youth appeared generally disinterested in political topics (e.g., opinions on immigration, taxes, city planning), questions explored more age-stage specific topics regarding superficial characteristics of different social groups or cliques. Participants regularly referred to other residents with longer hair as "greasy", "skid", "son", and "goof". Regarding cliques, peers not involved in crime were often denigrated as "soft" or "rats". Participants also made distinctions between which drugs were appropriate to use. Alcohol, marijuana, ecstasy, and cocaine use were considered acceptable whereas crack cocaine, heroin, and crystal methamphetamine were referred to as "dirty" drugs and users were admonished as "skids".

Building rapport

Rapport-building should develop throughout the interview and in lock-step with the escalating intrusiveness of the interview process (Cooke & Logan,

2018). Traditional social conventions for building rapport were not appropriate or not allowed in the custody center environment. For example, staff preferred that RAs not make physical contact with youth and so handshakes were avoided unless initiated by the participant.[7] There was also a clear power dynamic. RAs were free to leave the institution at any time. Information flowed in one direction; RAs asked questions and participants answered them. Moreover, the information provided concerned particularly sensitive and personal topics. Participants were not interviewed about a product they purchased or which social media platforms they used. They were asked about some of the worst moments of their life. More typically when such topics are discussed, such as with a friend, there is more of a give-and-take in the conversation. Experiences are shared. RAs needed to be sensitive/appreciative of the disclosure of this information. Empathetic phrasing of questions and related demeanor (e.g., eye contact, nodding of the head; Shepherd, 2007) can make participants more comfortable responding fully and truthfully to sensitive questions.

Participants may become destabilized in different ways (e.g., frustration, hostility, sadness) by questions. Sometimes participants became frustrated because they felt a particular question was unclear. One way that RAs responded to this was by agreeing with the participant about the question lacking clarity. This established a shared experience of "us" (i.e., the participant and RA) versus "them" (i.e., the interview). Sometimes participants became angry if an RA asked them a question that if answered in the affirmative might portray them in a negative light (e.g., hitting a family member). RAs first reminded participants that the interview was not tailored to each participant. The interview was for a much broader range of youth with different experiences and backgrounds and RAs wanted to ask such questions of all youth to avoid making assumptions about who the participant was and what their experiences were like. RAs also let participants know that learning that their answer was "no" was just as helpful as learning that someone else's answer was "yes."

Participants' sadness in discussing certain themes can be addressed via empathetic statements that reflect appreciation for the participant's answer (e.g., "Thank you for sharing your story, we know it is an uncomfortable topic, but this information is really helpful"). RAs were not permitted to provide suggestions for how the young person could improve their situation in case that suggestion interfered with the youth's ongoing treatment plan. Instead, RAs expressed concern and offered to assist with finding support for the participant (e.g., "Thank you for sharing your story with me. If your family situation is causing you a lot of difficulty, I can let a staff member know that you would like to talk to someone about this."). In the custody center, there were on-site social workers and psychiatric nurses available to residents. Also part of BYCC was an in-patient assessment unit where participants received counseling services from forensic psychologists.

The structured nature of the interview could make it difficult to have discussions with participants that help them feel more open and relaxed. It was sometimes necessary to allow residents the freedom to expand on their stories, even if they did not provide information that could be used in the interview. One way to build rapport under more positive circumstances involved allowing participants to demonstrate their knowledge of specific topics. RAs found that acknowledging to the youth that they did not understand a specific term used by the participant (e.g., the RA "playing the rookie") made the interview more enjoyable for the participant as it seemed to give them a sense of empowerment in teaching an "authority figure" new vocabulary. Similarly, Mitchell et al. (2018) found that gang members openly shared experiences especially when the interviewer demonstrated curiosity rather than expertise. Participants enjoyed discussing the meaning of tattoos, slang terms for different drugs, and some would draw gang signs and symbols for RAs to help clarify their meaning and usage.

Breaking confidentiality

The information sheet read aloud to participants indicated that RAs were required to inform custody center staff if the participant made a direct threat to hurt themselves or someone else[8]. If such instances occurred, RAs always let participants know that they were making a disclosure and asked the participant if there was a particular staff member that they would like information disclosed to. If none, RAs informed the director of case management. This was preferred over notifying line staff. Generally, RAs avoided having conversations with line staff to avoid arousing residents' suspicions about the nature of such conversations.

Participants who directly threatened others typically did not care about the RA disclosing this information because they were unconcerned with the consequences (e.g., "staff already know I want to fight him, it doesn't matter if you tell them."). In rarer situations where a participant reacted negatively to an RA's disclosure, future interviews with that participant were conducted with a different RA. It was more common for participants to make comments about self-harm. Participants were typically not bothered by RAs needing to disclose this information because such information was already known by staff. Sometimes participants recanted their statement about self-harm because they felt embarrassed or worried about how this might impact their stay in custody. RAs explained that they still needed to disclose this information but that this would not get the young person in trouble and that they could explain their feelings in private to a mental health practitioner.

Dealing with dishonesty in the interview

Detecting deceit is not necessarily improved through awareness of behavioral cues (Vrij et al., 2006). RA training emphasized interview preparation (e.g., reading previous interviews, reviewing the participant's case file) and attentiveness during the interview (e.g., identifying inconsistent responses).

The goal for RAs was to respond to dishonesty or discrepancies in ways that limited harm to rapport. There are various ways to challenge information provided by participants; it is important that the intensity of the challenge matches the intensity of the deceit (Logan, 2013). RAs were trained to not overreact or take such dishonesty personally as participants often were simply embarrassed about certain life events. The "Columbo" approach is a low-intensity challenge based on the iconic bumbling television series detective whose disheveled appearance and non-threatening questions helped elicit honest answers. This approach involved reacting to the youth's deceptive answers with confusion. For example, the RA may state "I am confused. You just said that prior to your incarceration you were going to school, but in your file, your probation officer noted that you had been expelled. Could you help me understand what is going on here?". This places the participant in an authority position in assisting the confused interviewer with understanding contradictory information. Higher-intensity challenges (e.g., accusation of lying or turning the interview into an interrogation) may threaten rapport, harm the reliability of the interview, and jeopardize the reputation of the study.

In rarer instances, some participants lied or exaggerated for entertainment. Usually this was in the form of egregious statements and thus easy to detect (e.g., "I've committed 30 homicide offenses."). A low intensity challenge can help to ensure that the participant does not treat the interview as a game. Failure to challenge obviously inaccurate information may further embolden a participant's desire to see how much they can get away with. RAs reminded participants that the interview was confidential, that the RA was in a non-judgmental role, and that they wanted to hear the youth's honest perspective. If the behavior persisted, RAs informed participants that the interview would end if they were not truthful. As the interview was the participant's source of entertainment, this threat was typically enough to correct their behavior. It was important to distinguish exaggeration about crimes for entertainment from participants who were genuinely honest about their enjoyment in perpetrating crimes. Some could play up this enjoyment because they wanted to shock or impress RAs.

Questions about involvement in sexual offenses were especially likely to result in dishonesty. Among 1,282 participants, only 2.3% ($n = 30$) acknowledged perpetrating a sexual offense.[9] Among this group, 71.4% ($n = 20$) had been charged with a sexual offense at the time of the interview. In other words, less than 1% of participants ($n = 10$) acknowledged perpetrating a sexual offense undetected by the justice system. This is likely an underestimation of the true prevalence of sexual offenses perpetrated by the sample given findings in self-reported studies using survey-based instruments where there are greater levels of anonymity (Koss et al., 1987). This underestimation may be exacerbated by the custody center culture in which individuals known to be involved in sexual offenses are stigmatized and more at-risk of victimization. Indeed, case managers regularly cautioned their clients to not disclose to anyone their involvement in a sex crime. This may have influenced participant reporting in the intake interview. While it might seem that youth were hesitant to self-report more serious offense types, 16.4% of youth self-reported perpetrating one of attempted murder, manslaughter, or murder ($n = 218$). If a participant was dishonest about the nature of their current offense, as long as there were no concerns that they might be dishonest regarding other topics, it was advantageous to wait until the end of the interview to challenge the participant regarding their current offense in case the challenge negatively influenced the youth's willingness to participate or provide reliable information (also see Cooke & Logan, 2018). To clarify the extent of sexual offending, a more detailed questionnaire was developed by one of the authors of this book. MCFD representatives did not approve of the content of the questionnaire and thus this aspect of the study was abandoned.

Antagonism from participants

Participants' limited social skills, boredom, poor behavioral control, and inexperience with boundary-setting can contribute to antagonistic behavior during the interview. A major motivation for antagonistic behavior is to draw a strong response. Responding defensively or changing the topic might encourage continued antagonization. It is more effective to remain affectively neutral (Kosson et al., 2016) while redirecting the participant's focus from the RA without changing the topic. One participant enjoyed studying niche topics so that he could make others feel inferior for not having the same level of knowledge. He quoted Mark Twain and then extended a phonily sympathetic hand to the RA, and said, condescendingly, "I'm sorry, that might be too esoteric a reference for you". Instead of defensiveness or changing the subject, the RA simply asked the participant what it was that he liked about Mark Twain (see McCuish et al., 2019a).

Some participants asked intrusive questions (e.g., "How much money do you make?"). In isolation, such questions could simply be posed out of curiosity. If such questions persisted despite attempts by RAs to refocus the participant, it may be because the participant wanted to gain information to use against the RA (e.g., "I bet I make more money than you"; also see Kosson et al., 2016). RAs can maintain control over the interview by playing to the egocentricity typical of youth (Selman, 1980) by reiterating that they are interested in the youth's opinions about these topics and that the interview is supposed to be all about them (Kosson et al., 2016).

Ending the interview

Interviews were typically completed over multiple sessions and RAs were trained to avoid ending a session on a sensitive topic (e.g., questions about victimization, family relationships). Talking about a participant's negative family situation, ending the interview abruptly, and then having the participant return to their unit while being visibly upset is insensitive to the participant. It also may place the participant at risk of being bullied by peers for showing emotion. Thus, RAs debriefed with participants before the end of each interview session, regardless of whether the interview was finished. This involved small-talk to change the participant's frame of mind (e.g., asking which types of juice/chips they would prefer for their next interview session, what the youth's unit is doing for the rest of their evening, whether they were watching the Canucks hockey game). Showing interest in the participant's interview experience is another way to improve rapport. Ending the interview by asking participants if there were important topics that remained unaddressed helped ensure that participants felt that their voice was heard. Even if such information could not necessarily be captured in the interview, it could help provide important insight and develop new research questions.

RAs ended shifts by debriefing with each other. Interviews could be challenging for various reasons (e.g., a difficult participant, a participant with a traumatic upbringing, the participant made a disclosure about self-harm). The ISVYOS created a logbook as well as an "interviewer impressions" section of the intake interview to communicate information about a participant that might be helpful for future interviews. The interviewer impressions section allowed RAs to remind themselves to re-ask certain questions if they felt the youth was being dishonest. This section was also used to specify the participant's general demeanor/attitude toward the RA, whether the participant had difficulty listening to or understanding interview questions, rude or intrusive comments, important information disclosed by the participant that was not part of the questionnaire, and information that might help others develop rapport with the youth (e.g., warnings about emotional triggers).

One of the experiences that surprised the ISVYOS team was the level of detachment some participants had following the completion of the interview. Sometimes interviews would be completed off-unit and the RA was required to walk the participant back to their unit. Despite the pleasantness of the interview and not having other residents around to observe the interaction between participant and RA, the participant would walk ahead of the RA with minimal (typically no) conversation. After spending upwards of an hour discussing very intimate details of their life, some participants seemed to disconnect quite swiftly from this process as if they simply ended a routine task and were now moving on. Reactive attachment disorder was regularly listed in the files of participants. It is possible that attachment deficits characterizing features of psychopathy meant that once the interview transaction was complete, there was no further need for social niceties or continued rapport. To be sure, this was not a universal experience, but it was something recognized by multiple team members. It was also experienced by members of the ISVYOS team when conducting different research in adult custody settings.

Reflections on the administration of a 20-year study

Data collection for the ISVYOS has spanned more than two decades and brought about a plethora of unanticipated challenges. The information below details some of these challenges and, when possible, how they were resolved.

Data collection sites

It took approximately six hours, including a two-hour ferry trip, to travel between the Burnaby and Victoria Youth Custody Centres that served as the data collection sites for Cohort II. There were therefore separate RA teams. For most of the data collection period, RAs from the two sites did not communicate with each other. This became problematic because residents were regularly transferred between the two centers. Thus, a youth in Burnaby could be interviewed by RAs, transferred to Victoria, and then re-interviewed by the other RA team as a new participant. Of the 962 members of Cohort II who received an intake interview, 31 (3.2%) were interviewed in Burnaby under the wrongful assumption that they had not been interviewed in Victoria (or vice versa). While we were able to identify these instances and discarded the second of the two interviews, failure to foresee issues with interview duplication resulted in an inefficient use of the study's budget. Towards the end of data collection, there were regular calls between the Burnaby and Victoria sites to update each others' Master Lists with the names of the new youth who were interviewed. The two sites also made more of an effort to communicate whether they were aware of an impending transfer.

Changing the intake interview

The original intake interview was not developed with a 20-year longitudinal study in mind. The funding received was for the purpose of accomplishing shorter-term projects. Thus, acquiring new funding required addressing new research questions. Accordingly, new questions were added to the intake interview and others were removed. These changes could create confusion among readers when looking at different empirical papers based on ISVYOS data. Particular measures were rarely available for all members of the sample and thus the sample size is often different across different papers. When thinking about the importance of open access research, we had to be diligent in saving the syntax, code, and datasets used for each manuscript so that we could explain who was included, who was excluded, and why. Fewer changes to the intake interview would have helped with the clarity of the ISVYOS research design.

Just prior to the end of the recruitment period, social workers affiliated with one of the custody centers expressed to senior officials their concern that the ISVYOS asked residents questions about physical and sexual abuse experiences. Their concern was that these questions would destabilize youth. Even though asking questions about abuse was a common research practice, and even though such questions were even part of in-house risk assessment tools and interviews used by justice system practitioners, the ISVYOS was required to remove questions about abuse from all interviews. Fortunately, because this occurred towards the end of the recruitment of new participants, this only affected approximately 50 interviews. We recognized that the institution was responsible for the safety and well-being of all residents and that we were their guests. Therefore, there was no pushback on their requirements. As mentioned, we were also unable to ask participants about specific sexual experiences, attitudes, and orientations due to the perceived sensitive nature of such topics. In hindsight, it would have been worthwhile to communicate the importance of these questions as well as the fact that such questions were commonly included in various studies and were routinely asked by practitioners. It was somewhat surprising that we could talk to participants about their involvement in homicide offenses not detected by the justice system but could not ask questions about sexual development and victimization experiences.

Questions we wished we included related to social desirability bias and perceptions of the interview. Mitchell et al. (2018) provided some excellent background on what can be learned simply by asking participants about the degree to which they were honest. RAs provided notes regarding their perceptions of a participant's honesty, but systematic questions were not incorporated into the intake interview.

Sensitivities to the custody center subculture

Formulating research questions using the right language is critical for ensuring that participants and RAs have a shared understanding of the question at hand. ISVYOS participants tended to interpret the term "victim" as someone in need of protection because they could not take care of themselves or because they had done something to warrant victimization. "Victims" were equated with people who elected "protective custody", which was a particularly stigmatized status in custody centers in BC. When asking questions like "have you ever experienced victimization while in custody?", some persons may answer in the negative, even if they were seriously assaulted in the past, because the term "victimization" meant something different to them. More specific examples (e.g., have you ever been punched by another resident while in custody?") may be more likely to elicit the desired information. Similarly, if researchers are interested in relationships between staff and residents, asking residents about whether staff "help them" can be misconstrued as the resident ratting out their peers.

Clear examples (e.g., "do you believe that staff care about your safety?") may be more effective. Another important aspect of custody center subculture was the stigmatization against people who "named names". Participants seemed suspicious of RA motives if they were asked specifically about the names of friends, family, and persons they co-offended with.

Data entry

A pencil-to-paper interview was useful because RAs were able to show participants the questions they were answering and how their answers were recorded. Some RAs learned how to read upside down and write checkmarks and numbers upside down so that the participant could follow along and maintain focus. The downside of the pencil-to-paper format was the resources invested in data entry. Volunteer and paid data entry positions were a great way for undergraduate students to gain insight into the process of research. However, the intake interview alone included more than a thousand datapoints, which created the possibility of writing ineligibly and making mistakes recording answers and entering data. A necessary but costly aspect of the ISVYOS involved running descriptives on every variable from every interview to search for impossible values. Computer-assisted interview (CAI) software programs that simultaneously record and store interview answers would have been more efficient. Fahmy et al. (2019) and Mitchell et al. (2018) provided useful recommendations regarding the use of CAI software in prison-based research. Before relying on CAIs, we recommend liaising with officials from the data collection site(s). In our case, staff from the data collection sites were concerned about residents getting hold of and using laptops as weapons. Fights between residents and assaults against residents and staff were common. Riots at BYCC lead to serious concerns about the safety of staff and residents[10] (Crawford, 2016). Further, some residents were incarcerated for "swatting"[11] and other cybercrimes and thus concerns were raised about participants getting access to the laptops and using them for criminal purposes. While we would recommend using CAIs, they were not feasible in our situation.

Summary

Being an RA on the ISVYOS sometimes required interviewing youth with severe behavioral problems, limited social skills, inexperience with boundary-setting, poor attention spans, and difficulties understanding questions and expressing themselves. While this often made the job difficult in the short-term, in the long-term, these experiences helped RAs look at theories and research from a new angle. Interviewing participants was extremely rewarding both personally and professionally. Information provided in interviews led to ideas for theses, dissertations, journal articles, and this book. Our hope is that this chapter will ease some of the pains of conducting research with this population and also enhance the interview experience of participants.

The training process should not be rushed. Mock interviews with RAs posing as participants are different from the unpredictability of youth in the custody center environment. The opportunity to shadow different RAs with different personalities can help new RAs find the approach that works best for them. Reviewing files to gain a better understanding of where the participant was coming from was key to the success of the interview. Before starting the interview, ensuring that participants had a clear understanding of confidentiality was necessary to make them feel comfortable with revealing intimate details of their life. RAs had to read a set script approved by the SFU REB, but it was sometimes useful to go beyond the script to explain to participants what confidentiality entailed.

RAs were trained to understand that their job was not to simply record answers. Youth pose unique challenges because, compared to adults, they tend to have poorer attention spans, abilities to express themselves, social skills, and understanding of personal boundaries. This was amplified when focusing on *incarcerated* youth. It was necessary to adapt research protocols and RA behavior to the unique qualities of this population rather than expect participants to adapt to the interview environment. A successful interview (see Table 10.1) is characterized by rapport-building, reliability, and the ability to clarify answers and respond to dishonesty and antagonism in ways that make the participant and RA comfortable. Interviews should end in ways that allow participants to feel that their time and story were valued.

Looking back across 20 years of ISVYOS data collection thus far, there are many things that we would have done differently. Better communication across data collection sites helps ensure that the same person is not interviewed twice. The use of CAIs could help with both saving resources and improving the reliability of data. Before implementing interviews, pilot studies or informal discussions with custody staff and residents about interview questions could help avoid the use of inappropriate or awkward terminology.

Notes

1 The custody center used a token economy system. One reward for good behavior was a later lockdown time. All residents started at "Level 2" and were required to lockdown at 9:00 pm. Level 3 locked down was at 9:30 pm and Level 4 at 10:00 pm. Youth on Level 1 were downgraded from Level 2, typically due to fighting or vandalism, and were required to lockdown at 8:30 pm.

2 A second spreadsheet was referred to as the "Master List" and included the names and other identifying information of all the youth who had participated in the project in some way. Newly interviewed youth were assigned a code number and added to the Master List along with the date that each interview was completed.

3 Heavies are known as the inmates who have power and prestige inside, whether due to physical size, gang affiliation/connections, or toughness.

4 To be sure, some residents did not feel that there was a power dynamic, or that if there was, that it was in their favor.
5 The employment interview and RA training allowed managers to screen for persons who showed that they understood that they were in a non-judgmental role, were not permitted to offer advice, and viewed the position as a genuine opportunity to learn from participants.
6 Some participants had not reflected on the nature and frequency of their substance use. Some participants expressed shock at the variety of different substances they had used within a short time frame.
7 Handshakes were also not recommended for hygiene reasons (e.g., it was not uncommon for male participants to have their hands down their pants).
8 Past thoughts of self-harm or intention to hurt others was not justification for breaching confidentiality.
9 For the 30 participants who self-reported a sexual offense, several were initially untruthful until challenged by the RA. The typical challenge involved contrasting the youth's statement with file information (i.e., Columbo approach).
10 Staff members were unarmed (e.g., did not carry firearms, mace, batons) and riot gear consisted only of protective shields.
11 Swatting typically involves a call to 911 or police agency to make fraudulent threats (e.g., about an active shooter) to elicit the activation of an emergency response team (Bei Li, 2018).

11 Conclusion

Introduction

The ISVYOS began in 1998 during a time at which there were rich theoretical discussions within the DLC literature regarding patterns of offending over the life-course and underlying risk factors (e.g., Moffitt, 1993; Sampson & Laub, 1993). This was also a time when practitioners were responding to the fallout from Martinson's "nothing works" dogma that called for the revocation of rehabilitation (Gendreau & Ross, 1987). In the province of BC, practitioners and policymakers felt that they lacked a strong understanding of the risk/needs profiles of incarcerated youth. Indeed, the DLC literature at the time focused mostly on community-based samples. Professor Raymond Corrado was asked to join a committee that informally assessed the needs of incarcerated youth in BC. The committee produced an unpublished report that illustrated a gap between what practitioners believed would work (i.e., rehabilitation) and what Federal policymakers and some members of the public wanted to see as the official response to youth crime (i.e., deterrence). The report showed that youth in custody had an array of programming needs due to major trauma and associated negative outcomes, including foster care placement, self-medicating with drugs and alcohol, survival-directed behaviors (e.g., break & enters, drug trafficking, sex work), early/continuous school problems and dropouts, and unstable/unhealthy living conditions. In response to these findings, Professor Corrado was encouraged by senior policymakers in BC to initiate the ISVYOS to develop an understanding of the risk/needs profile of youth in custody.

After over 20 years of data collection made possible by more than 100 undergraduate, MA, and PhD students, we felt that the ISVYOS had produced data that made writing this book warranted. We wrote this book with the hopes of providing a better understanding of the adult justice system outcomes of formerly incarcerated youth while also showing that the different theoretical perspectives under the DLC paradigm were not necessarily competing against each other but rather were providing different approaches to answering different questions. We also felt that this book was warranted because other research on individuals asserted to be involved in serious and violent offenses made claims about offending (in)stability, the relative unimportance of early risk factors, and notions of desistance by default (e.g., Laub & Sampson, 2003), which did not comport with our data. We conclude this book by (1) summarizing the main points from each chapter, (2) reflecting on how empirical findings from the book fit with Farrington's (2003) widely accepted conclusions about the development of offending, and (3) providing some final thoughts on what we have learned about the life-course of youth involved in serious and violent offenses grown up.

Key findings from each chapter

Section I: Context

Chapter 1 outlined how over the last 100 years there have been three research paradigms associated with explanations of crime at the level of the individual: (1) the psychiatrization of offending paradigm, (2) the ALC paradigm, and (3) the DLC paradigm. The psychiatrization of offending paradigm was characterized by the belief that criminal behavior was the result of psychopathology. This research was largely based upon ideological thinking and unreliable measures of undefined or ambiguous constructs like feeblemindedness. The Gluecks' research was somewhat of an exception to other research from this paradigm given its use of control samples and longitudinal methods. However, it would take several decades before the importance of the Gluecks' research became fully realized. Part of the reason for this delay is that the Gluecks' research was Edwin Sutherland's primary target in his successful attempt to discredit non-sociological explanations of criminal behavior (see Laub & Sampson, 1991; Posick & Rocque, 2018). The ALC paradigm emerged from Sutherland's direct response to concerns about the subjective decision-making associated with the psychiatrization of offending paradigm. The ALC paradigm showed a reticence to research on incarcerated persons given mistakes of the past and instead emphasized generalizable samples and testing theories that primarily focused on explaining delinquent behavior during adolescence. The DLC paradigm looked beyond adolescence by, first, establishing through the criminal career pillar of DLC criminology the key parameters of offending to be measured over the life-course (e.g., age of onset, frequency, versatility, desistance). Developmental, propensity, and life-course perspectives, representing three other pillars of DLC criminology, took up the task of formulating and testing theories meant to explain these different parameters. While each theory focused on offending over the life-course, developmental criminology theories were principally concerned with the onset of offending, propensity theories with the continuity and frequency of offending, and life-course theories with desistance from offending.

An emphasis on generalizability helped these four pillars become mainstays of criminological research (Cullen, 2011). We felt that it was necessary to fill in the edges of this research literature that primarily examined community samples of children and youth. How do these four pillars apply to individuals coming from some of the most disadvantaged circumstances imaginable and who find themselves incarcerated during adolescence? In general, DLC research has given insufficient attention to the individuals perhaps most in need of resources and intervention and who represent a familiar face to justice system practitioners. We are not the only ones (Mulvey et al., 2004) and certainly not the first ones (Cernkovich et al., 1985; Le Blanc & Fréchette, 1989) to raise such concerns. When focusing on an adjudicated sample, all individuals have a history of offending. Thus, rather than providing explanations for why justice system involvement does or does not happen for some persons, a more relevant line of analysis for adjudicated samples pertains to within-group heterogeneity in offending outcomes. One of the ways to examine this heterogeneity involves distinguishing chronic from non-chronic offending.

Chapter 2 described Wolfgang et al.'s (1972) discovery that a small proportion of the Philadelphia Birth Cohort was responsible for most of all arrests for this population. Accordingly, Wolfgang et al. defined chronic offending as the minimum number of persons needed to account for at least 50% of all offenses perpetrated by the sample. We considered this approach a static description of chronic offending because once an individual met the threshold of a specific number of offenses, they would always be considered a "chronic offender". With the emergence of theories (Moffitt, 1993) and analytic strategies (Nagin & Land, 1993) regarding the development of offending over the life-course, DLC criminology became focused on measuring the intersection of the volume and persistence of offending. This more dynamic description viewed chronic offending as a phenomenon that could change or take different shape over time. We referred to this pattern as chronic and persistent offending (CPO) to recognize the distinction between static and dynamic measures of chronic offending as well as the distnction between chronic offending that is or is not also persistent. Our data supported these distinctions.

Laub and Sampson's (2003) book and their series of debates with others (e.g., Nagin & Tremblay, 2005; Sampson & Laub, 2005c) made two main conclusions about CPO trajectories. The first was that there was a lack of evidence for CPO trajectories. Sampson and Laub (2003) found that individuals from the UJD Study associated with the highest rate of offending in adolescence were not associated with the highest rate of offending in adulthood. The second main conclusion was that risk factors in childhood/adolescence were not informative of adult offending outcomes. Laub and Sampson (2003) suggested that their UJD Study was best-suited for addressing questions about CPO and that other studies were unlikely to produce different findings. In making such suggestions, they directly challenged the value of developmental criminology and indirectly challenged the research direction of the ISVYOS. We believe that inspection of CPO and its correlates requires addressing, at minimum, four research design needs: (1) the inclusion of individuals at-risk of CPO, (2) the measurement of behaviors that are considered criminal at all stages of the life-course (e.g., measurement does not rely on status offenses only considered criminal in adolescence), (3) the measurement of exposure time, and (4) the specification of appropriate risk factors for the prediction of CPO. Chapter 2 outlined how these research design needs were not addressed in analyses of the UJD Study, which we believed justified skepticism concerning Laub and Sampson's claims about the limited value of developmental criminology.

Regarding the first research design need, Laub and Sampson asserted that to study CPO required sufficient base rates of the phenomenon and, therefore, it was necessary to use a sample of individuals characterized by a frequent pattern of offending in adolescence. While we agree with their assertion, the rate of offending for the UJD Study sample more closely resembled a community-based sample than a sample of contemporary adjudicated youth. The UJD Study was conducted at a time where the youth justice system was more aligned with a child welfare perspective. This has important implications for the nature of the sample used by Laub and Sampson to make their claims, claims that were not generalizable to contemporary contexts. Second, studies of CPO need to be attuned to how criminal behavior is measured to avoid underestimating persistence. The UJD Study sample came from a period in which youth were sent to reform schools for status-based offenses (e.g., truancy, incorrigibility, vagrancy, drinking). Identifying stable patterns of offending between adolescence and adulthood is difficult because behaviors that constitute status offenses are not treated as criminal when perpetrated in adulthood. Thus, minor forms of deviancy, which were the most common crime-type for the youth in the UJD Study, even if repeated in adulthood, were not counted towards offending in adulthood. Third, analyses of the UJD Study did not account for exposure time, sometimes at all, and sometimes not past age 32. Thus, such analyses underestimated the prevalence of CPO (see Eggleston et al., 2004). Individuals involved in a particularly high volume of offenses or serious offenses (or both) are often subjected to lengthy custody sentences that restrict their ability to continue offending (McCuish, 2020) and thus failure to account for exposure time will be especially likely to result in overestimating desistance. Fourth, some of the risk factors that Laub and Sampson used to predict CPO were potentially unreliable (Farrington, 2020) and others were not relevant to the prediction of CPO (Robins, 2005). Further, potentially important risk factors like psychopathy were not examined. Laub and Sampson's conclusions about developmental criminology were somewhat misleading and did not align with contemporary issues and challenges facing youth justice practitioners.

Chapter 3 showed how the ISVYOS was suitable for addressing these four research design needs. At the time the study was initiated (1998), the public and policy sentiment, and the perspective of some researchers, was that incarcerated youth were "superpredators" (DiIulio, 1995). The traditional focus on generalizable samples meant that there were little data available to provide evidence-based responses to these claims. Practitioners in the province of BC felt left in the dark about what to do with youth in custody. The initial purpose of the ISVYOS was to address this knowledge gap. The youth justice system in BC had an extensive filtering process that meant youth were incarcerated almost exclusively due to involvement in serious or violent crimes. During the time participants were recruited, the rate of youth incarceration in BC ranged from approximately 40 to approximately 80 per 100,000 youth (Statistics Canada, 2020a). This meant that researchers would need a sample of approximately 1,500 youth in the community to find just one youth who experienced incarceration.

This first phase of the ISVYOS provided a description of the profile of youth in custody centers throughout BC, including demographic characteristics, family environment, substance use, prior criminal behavior, identity, and victimization. Participants from this first phase, referred to as Cohort I (n = 596), were recruited during Canada's YOA legislation. The second phase of the ISVYOS recruited participants (Cohort II; n = 1,123) during the time of Canada's YCJA, which compared to the YOA, made even more of an effort to keep youth involved in nonserious offenses out of custody. Practitioners noted the complex risk factor profiles of youth in custody, especially in terms of mental health challenges. Accordingly, the second phase of the ISVYOS emphasized, among hundreds of other variables, the measurement of mental health problems within the sample. The third phase of the ISVYOS sought to clarify the adult social and offending outcomes of Cohort I and Cohort II participants. Section Two of the book provided a description of serious and violent youth grown up through the lens of the DLC paradigm's four pillars.

Section II: Empirical answers to core DLC questions

Chapter 4 used the criminal career perspective to examine the adult justice system outcomes of ISVYOS participants. Four different criminal career dimensions were examined: prevalence, frequency, severity, and length. In terms of prevalence, half the sample were still active in the justice system between ages 30–35. We identified the minimum percentage of the sample responsible for at least 50% of all convictions during each of the four age-stages examined in the book (adolescence (ages 12–17), emerging adulthood (ages 18–23), full adulthood (ages 24–29), and mature adulthood (ages 30–35)). Individuals associated with chronic offending during mature adulthood incurred a similar number of convictions compared to individuals associated with chronic offending during adolescence. This finding contrasted with assertions that offending declines with age for all persons (Hirschi & Gottfredson, 1983; Laub & Sampson, 2003). That said, there was also evidence of Robins' (1978) paradox. More than half of participants with a pattern of chronic offending in adolescence were not identified by such a pattern in mature adulthood. We also examined the relationship between past and future criminal career parameters. Age of onset of first conviction was not informative of the number of new convictions incurred during emerging adulthood. However, age of onset was significantly and negatively associated with frequency of convictions during full adulthood and mature adulthood. In effect, through the passage of time, an earlier onset of offending was associated with a greater number of convictions, which contrasted with Sampson and Laub's (2003) assertion that the relationship betwen past and future offending diminished with time. The relationship between severity of offending and frequency of offending varied depending on how severity was measured. Severity as measured by versatility of different crime types was almost perfectly correlated with conviction frequency. However, severity as measured by time incarcerated showed that some individuals in the sample were involved in especially serious offenses that resulted in lengthy periods of incarceration and thus a more limited frequency of convictions. Finally, when looking at criminal career length between ages 12 and 35, the average participant was still active in the justice system at age 27. This is of course underestimated because, for many individuals in the sample, their offending continued after the most recent wave of data collection.

Little is known about the justice system's contribution to the continuity or discontinuity of offending. Despite efforts by the justice system to identify individuals involved in early onset, frequent, and serious offending and disrupt the link between these parameters and future offending, for the ISVYOS sample, criminal career parameters in adolescence were informative of criminal career parameters through different stages of adulthood. This is possible evidence that past and current justice system strategies to reduce offending for incarcerated youth were unable to break developmental criminology and propensity theory principles of offending without providing the specific interventions and services needed to bring about the types of turning points that are part of life-course criminology. An alternative perspective is that by having a pattern of early onset, high-rate, and serious offending in adolescence, certain individuals became well-known to agents of the justice system, which made it easier for them to be targeted or detected by this system. For some of these youth, there was a clear pattern of institutionalization that started with placement in foster care well before their onset of offending. There was some evidence of intermittent offending, but especially considering the amount of time individuals spent incarcerated, their adulthoods were characterized by an accumulation of contacts with various institutions with negative long-term implications that could not be knifed-off with time and some socializing as hypothesized by the age-graded theory of informal social control.

Chapter 5 moved from static indicators of chronic offending that were defined by meeting a threshold for a certain frequency of offending to modeling the rate of an individual's convictions at each year of age to examine CPO trajectories. The fact that the ISVYOS sample is composed of a highly specific subgroup of youth who all experienced incarceration (i.e., an outcome that happened for about 1 in 1,500 youth in BC) may lead to assumptions that there will be little variability in conviction trajectories *within* the sample. After all, the sample should include exactly the types of persons associated with LCP offending, and DLC research has discussed LCP offending as a single type of trajectory. The ISVYOS showed that CPO was not a unidimensional phenomenon; there was heterogeneity, not just in conviction trajectories more generally, but in patterns of CPO trajectories. Studies on youth criminal recidivism usually examined shorter follow-up periods (about 3-4 years), which did not allow for the identification of variability in patterns of CPO that we uncovered with this research design – patience paid off.

ISVYOS participants provided a contrasting image to that of the *classic desister*. Desistance and persistence were not mutually exclusive parameters for this sample. Individuals were involved in such a high rate of convictions in adolescence and emerging adulthood that the process of desistance (i.e., slowing down in level of offending over time) spanned, in some cases, more than a decade (e.g., the EOSD trajectory). This type of pattern may be less common in community-based studies where the process of desistance is shorter because peak levels of offending are not as high. Indeed, trajectories from community-based studies labeled "chronic" or "high-rate" more closely resembled the low rate conviction trajectory found in Chapter 5. We are not suggesting that one label is correct, and one is incorrect, only that it is important for researchers to pay attention to differences in the scale of the y-axis before summarizing trajectory research. We were guilty of this in our prior work (e.g., McCuish et al., 2014). The seductions of exciting methods made it difficult to see the forest through the trees. As another example of this, the statistical approach of accounting accounts for exposure time (e.g., Nagin, 2005) does not mean that the practice of doing so fully resolves all issues (McCuish, 2020).

We also found that several characteristics in childhood/adolescence (e.g., substance use, family dysfunction, school behavior problems) were associated with CPO trajectories. Moreover, for different CPO trajectories, different risk/needs factors mattered. There is a balance to be struck between denying the importance of risk factors in childhood/adolescence based on the assumption that random life events and human agency will alter an individual's trajectory (Laub & Sampson, 2003) and using such characteristics to make claims about the need for deterrence, punishment, and selective incapacitation (DeLisi, 2016). Specified services aimed at improving the health, education, and social outcomes of marginalized youth may, as a positive collateral consequence, also influence reductions in offending.

Chapter 6 used data on boys and girls from Cohort II to address developmental criminology questions about antisocial behavior onset and qualitatively distinct patterns of versatility versus propensity theory questions about antisocial behaviors as part of a general antisocial tendency. We looked at different types of antisocial behavior (e.g., substance use, aggression, delinquency) and antisocial behaviors in different contexts (e.g., at school, at home). Three themes were addressed: (1) the prevalence of antisocial behavior across different dimensions and correlations across dimensions, (2) qualitative patterns of antisocial behavior, and (3) the relationship between self-reported antisocial behavior and official offending.

Most participants engaged in criminal behavior prior to age 12, which is the age of criminal responsibility in Canada. For a smaller percentage of participants, their antisocial behavior before age 12 was persistent across different domains (e.g., at school, at home, aggressive behavior, substance use, criminal behavior). Their antisocial behavior at an early age, therefore, was well known to family members, teachers, principals, and perhaps even the child welfare system. A series of LCAs indicated that for some individuals, their antisocial behavior was frequent and versatile. For others, there was a tendency towards either authority conflict, covert, or overt behavior. These observations resembled developmental criminology perspectives about different behavioral pathways (e.g., Loeber & Hay, 1994). Boys generally showed a higher-risk pattern of behavior compared to girls. However, girls were twice as likely as boys to be associated with the most serious substance use profile, which was defined by high probabilities of the use of heroin, crack cocaine, and crystal methamphetamine. Differences in antisocial behavior profiles and associated risk/needs factors across gender (Chapter 3) reiterated that reasons for offending and treatment needs varied across boys and girls. Especially for girls in the sample, traumatic experiences and transient circumstances (e.g., homelessness) appeared to precipitate substance use as a possible self-medicating mechanism.

Antisocial behavior for the sample manifested early, in multiple settings, in multiple contexts, and in various ways. Although developmental criminology has identified risk factors for the course of antisocial and criminal behavior, it is still lacking a clear theory of rehabilitation and intervening factors that promote cognitive, emotional, and behavioral change and the maintenance of such change. Forensic psychology has recently taken up this challenge by using risk assessment tools, not just to understand risk factors and problem behavior, but how to most appropriately intervene with youth characterized by such factors and behaviors (Viljoen et al., 2019).

Chapter 7 detailed how, especially due to past mistakes from the psychiatrization of offending paradigm relating to inattention to construct validity, the ALC paradigm gave little to no consideration to psychopathology. Forensic psychology on the other hand showed that psychopathy is among the most important individual-level predictors of recidivism (Hart, 1998). Inattention to this construct may have influenced Sampson and Laub's (2003) assertion that there is no evidence that risk factors in childhood/adolescence are informative of offending in adulthood. We used this chapter to examine the relationship between features of psychopathy in adolescence and static (i.e., chronic offending) and dynamic (i.e., CPO trajectories) measures of offending. There are two different criminological perspectives on the relationship between psychopathy and offending. The first suggests that both psychopathy and chronic offending are static, meaning that strong features of psychopathy and chronic offending are both constant over time (DeLisi, 2016). Developmental criminology recognizes that both psychopathy and offending are changeable, but this does not discount the important relationship between the two. While we were unable to examine the changeable aspect of psychopathy (but see McCuish & Lussier, 2018), we did examine the changeable aspect of offending via the modeling of trajectories. PCL:YV scores were informative of both chronic offending and CPO trajectories. This included the prediction of convictions approximately 20 years after the assessment of features of psychopathy. Measuring longer-term and more dynamic indicators of offending, rather than single-item indicators of recidivism after short follow-up periods, helped illuminate the importance of interpersonal features of psychopathy such as manipulativeness, dominance, and pathological lying that are counterintuitive to classic turning points that require positive relationships with others (i.e., the antithesis to interpersonal features of psychopathy).

At the group-level, youth with strong features of psychopathy are more likely to show a long-term pattern of high rate offending compared to youth without such features. However, using such findings to make predictions about what any one individual might experience results in much more uncertainty. Chapter 7 looked closer at false positive cases in the sample (i.e., participants with a score of 30+ on the PCL:YV but a low rate of offending), which indicated that features of psychopathy in adolescence can change, or at least are difficult to accurately measure. Assessing psychopathy relies on a retrospective examination of a person's life history. Adults have decades of history to look back upon; therefore, it is easier to identify stability of personality features consistent with psychopathy. For youth, their past is much shorter and therefore less reliable. Our findings should not be used to suggest that high PCL:YV scores justify long-term, punitive sentences. Part of the challenge is getting individuals with strong features of psychopathy to successfully complete treatment; when they do, it is associated with a reduced likelihood of sexual and violent recidivism (Sewall & Olver, 2019). Cognitive behavioral therapy appears effective in reducing youth features of psychopathy and associated negative outcomes (Hecht et al., 2018).

Chapter 8 addressed the lack of information regarding the adult social outcomes of ISVYOS participants. Practitioners rated ISVYOS participants on a range of different sources of informal social control that were in turn used to examine questions about desistance. Sampson and Laub's (1993) age-graded theory of informal social control described desistance as the result of turning points like employment, marriage, and parenthood. From their perspective, human agency and the randomness of life events made prediction of informal social control difficult. Social structure mechanisms funnel individuals into adult roles. This perspective influenced Laub and Sampson's (2003) assertion that desistance occurs by default. Contrary to this perspective, in mature adulthood, most ISVYOS participants were involved in the justice system and in emerging adulthood rarely did they experience positive sources of informal social control.

Selection effects were present in that the highest-risk youth (e.g., greater number of risk factors, more time spent incarcerated in adolescence) were less likely to experience quality sources of informal social control. Despite these selection effects, when positive social controls in emerging adulthood were present, they were associated with a lower rate of future convictions. However, moderation analyses showed that informal social controls only influenced desistance if state dependent effects (e.g., lengthy incarceration in adolescence) and cumulative disadvantage (e.g., high individual-level risk, high family-level risk in adolescence) were absent. This contrasted with Laub and Sampson's (2003) description of "desistance by default" (p. 278-9) and the acquisition of positive sources of informal social control as a normative aspect of adulthood.

Using repeated measures of informal social control, within-individual improvement in total level of informal social control was associated with within-individual decreases in convictions during the same window of measurement (i.e., same year of age). However, this relationship disappeared when looking at the lagged effect of within-individual change in informal social control on within-individual change in convictions one year later. Baseline indicators of individual-level risk in adolescence were associated with within-individual increases in convictions during the adulthood follow-up period. Future research is needed to better understand the potentially reciprocal relationship between informal social control and offending by focusing on cognitive, emotional, behavioral, and social change and the factors promoting such change (McCuish et al., 2020b). This includes considering the role of different aspects of maturation as important, not only to desistance, but to a person's ability to perform in their adult roles in positive ways that can subsequently promote desistance.

Section III: Reflections on the ISVYOS

Participants were recruited between 1998–2011. About halfway through this period, Canada's youth justice legislation shifted from the YOA (Cohort I) to the YCJA (Cohort II). The shift resulted in an even greater emphasis on diverting youth from the formal justice system and reserving custody sentences for the most serious and violent youth. Under the YOA, the goal of incarceration was often deterrence or to protect the young person from a negative social environment (Doob & Sprott, 2001). The goal of incarceration under the YCJA was rehabilitation (Bala et al., 2009). We examined Cohort I and Cohort II differences in offending outcomes in adolescence, risk/needs factors in adolescence, and adult offending outcomes. As anticipated based on the more punitive nature of the YOA, Cohort I had more severe patterns of official offending in adolescence. Also as expected given the anticipation of a more serious risk factor profile among Cohort II, Cohort II self-reported a significantly greater number of different types of self-reported offenses. This likely reflected the YCJA's tendency to use diversionary measures in response to the initial offending of Cohort II, which means that this Cohort's offending detected by the justice system would not actually be officially recorded. As well, in adolescence, risk/needs factors were more prevalent and more severe for Cohort II compared to Cohort I.

When it came to justice system involvement in adulthood, Cohort II averaged significantly more convictions between ages 18 and 29. The relationship between youth justice system involvement and adult justice system involvement was stronger for Cohort I compared to Cohort II. For example, for Cohort I, onset of justice system involvement was negatively associated with their number of convictions in adulthood. The number of convictions in adulthood for Cohort II was not distinguished based on participants' age of onset of justice system invovlement. This may be evidence that the YCJA's use of diversion and emphasis on rehabilitation was more effective in disrupting the link between past and future offending. Finally, we examined whether the experience of changes in incarceration on changes in future convictions varied depending on the type of legislation that governed decisions about incarceration. Within-individual increases in time incarcerated were associated with within-individual decreases in frequency of convictions. The strength of this relationship was stronger for Cohort II participants. In effect, there was evidence that greater exposure to custody reduced the number of convictions incurred one year later, and this was especially true under the YCJA.

Chapter 10 reflected on the ISVYOS data collection process. Specific attention was given to strategies for conducting interviews with incarcerated youth who at times can be challenging due to difficulties with, for example, behavioral regulation. Other challenges related to the uniqueness of youth compared to adults. Youth can be more prone to embarrassment about answers that do not conform to what is typical for their peers. Using less confrontational follow-up questions (e.g., "how come?" rather than "why?") can facilitate more open responses from participants. It is also imperative that interviews designed for adults (e.g., the assessment of psychopathy) are adapted to the adolescence developmental stage (e.g., questions about high school cliques rather than political ideologies when assessing intolerant attitudes).

Participant boredom, antagonism, dishonesty, and low levels of motivation can threaten the reliability of interview information. We described different strategies for managing these threats. However, developing rapport is a more proactive strategy that helps ensure that threats to an interview's reliability do not need to be managed in the first place. Building rapport starts by showing respect for residents' living unit as if you were walking into their home. Once in their "home", understand that incarcerated youth have experienced particularly traumatic histories that may include having been lied to or manipulated by persons responsible for their care. Be genuine and do not try to force a close bond. Showing up, remaining calm, and being consistent help establish trust. Trust and rapport evolve over the course of the interview and so placing intrusive questions towards the end of the interview is important. That said, we recommend that RAs not end interviews on sensitive topics to avoid participant destabilization, which can lead to experiences of victimization when returning to their unit and being among their peers.

Farrington's widely accepted conclusions about the development of offending

Chapter 1 presented Farrington's (2003) widely accepted conclusions about the development of offending. These were largely based on longitudinal studies of community-based samples. The chapters in this book helped address whether Farrington's conclusions were true for youth who experienced incarceration (see Table 11.1 for a summary).

Farrington's first conclusion was that offending peaked in late adolescence. Chapter 4 showed that for the full sample, convictions peaked in late adolescence. However, Chapter 5 showed that for individuals associated with CPO trajectories, their average rate of offending while free in the community peaked in adulthood. Chapter 6 indicated that the prevalence of various antisocial and criminal behaviors was much higher in adolescence (from age 12 onwards) than in childhood (before age 12).

Farrington's (2003) second conclusion was that ages 8–14 marked the typical onset of offending. ISVYOS participants' average onset of first conviction was towards the end of this interval. Actual onset is likely much earlier given that it is unlikely that all individuals were caught, adjudicated, and convicted for their first crime. Indeed, Chapter 6 showed that participants' average age of onset for self-reported offending was 11.19 (SD = 2.95) years old. Just 10% of participants self-reported an onset of offending at age 15 or older. Boys had a significantly earlier self-reported age of onset (M = 11.06; SD = 2.98) compared to girls (M = 11.90; SD = 2.70). Farrington's second conclusion also asserted that termination from offending was most common in the 20s. In contrast, as shown in Chapter 4, nearly half the sample incurred at least one new conviction between ages 30–35. Interventions that are age-appropriate beyond a person's 20s are therefore important. As well, relying on convictions overestimated the prevalence of termination from offending because some individuals received lengthy sentences that preempted opportunities to incur new convictions.

Farrington's third conclusion was that onset of offending was negatively correlated with offending continuity and frequency. In Chapter 4, the

Table 11.1 Farrington's widely accepted conclusions about the development of offending

Conclusion	*Description of the conclusion*	*ISVYOS findings & interpretation*
#1	Offending peaks in late adolescence.	Prevalence of offending peaked in adolescence (Chapter 4). However, part of the reason convictions peaked in adolescence is because of recidivism sentencing premiums in adulthood that reduced the opportunity to maintain a high rate of offending. When accounting for exposure time, convictions peaked later in adulthood for some CPO trajectories (Chapter 5). Self-reported antisocial behavior was more prevalent from age 12 onward than before age 12. This was true for virtually all types of antisocial behavior from a wide range of domains (e.g., home, school, substance use; Chapter 6).
#2	Onset of offending is most common between ages 8 and 14 and termination from offending is most common during the 20s.	Conviction onset occurred towards the end of the age 8–14 interval, but age of onset was likely overestimated due to reliance on official data. Termination was rare in the 20s; most participants continued offending into their 30s (Chapter 4). Trajectories through mature adulthood revealed that most individuals were involved in at least one crime in their 30s (Chapter 5). Seventy-five percent of the sample self-reported at least one type of offense that occurred between ages 8–14. Although antisocial behavior was more prevalent in adolescence, antisocial behavior typically emerged *before* age 12 (Chapter 6).
#3	Onset of offending and continuity/frequency of offending are negatively correlated.	Onset of convictions was negatively related to the frequency of offending, but only with a longer follow-up period. Because all sample members were involved in crime in adolescence, a longer follow-up period was needed to make distinctions in conviction frequency based on onset (Chapter 4). Similar observations were made with respect to conviction trajectories shown in Chapter 5. Self-reporting an early onset of offending behavior is

(*Continued*)

Table 11.1 (Continued)

Conclusion	*Description of the conclusion*	*ISVYOS findings & interpretation*
		associated with involvement in more serious and versatile antisocial behavior (Chapter 6).
#4	There is some continuity between antisocial behavior across different developmental stages.	Stability of offending was more common through emerging adulthood; stability of non-offending was more common through mature adulthood. Robins' (1978) paradox was especially evident (Chapter 4). The trajectories defined by the highest rate of offending showed the most continuity. Continuity can be underestimated among individuals involved in especially serious crimes because they can be incarcerated for lengthy periods of time (Chapter 5). There was an association between higher levels of childhood/adolescence antisocial behavior and CPO trajectories through emerging adulthood (Chapter 6).
#5	Most of all crime is perpetrated by a minority of all persons.	As the sample aged, the proportion of the sample needed to account for 50% of all convictions declined from 23.5% in adolescence to 9.3% in mature adulthood (Chapter 4). When looking at CPO trajectories, by mature adulthood, a smaller proportion of the sample was associated with trajectories accounting for most of all crime (Chapter 5). Regardless of the type of antisocial behavior domain examined, the most versatile participants represented only about 20% of the sample (Chapter 6).
#6	Persistent offending is characterized by involvement in a wide range of crimes as opposed to specializing in a particular crime type.	Especially in adulthood, frequency and versatility of offending were nearly perfectly correlated (Chapter 4). The trajectories characterized by the most frequent and persistent offending were also characterized by the greatest levels of versatility (Chapter 5). Individuals associated with a CPO trajectory were significantly more likely to also be associated with more versatile patterns

(Continued)

Table 11.1 (Continued)

Conclusion	*Description of the conclusion*	*ISVYOS findings & interpretation*
		of self-reported antisocial behavior (Chapter 6).
#7	Specific types of crimes tend to be a manifestation of a general antisocial tendency as opposed to a proclivity for engaging in a certain crime type.	Individuals who were versatile in their antisocial behavior were more likely to endorse every type of antisocial behavior that was measured. There was a lack of evidence of individuals who "specialized" in one type of antisocial behavior, especially when looking at those involved in the most frequent forms of antisocial behavior (Chapter 6).
#8	Co-offending is more likely during adolescence than adulthood.	N/A.
#9	Motivations for crime in adolescence tend to be both reactive and instrumental, whereas crimes in adulthood tend to be driven by the latter motive only.	When it came to aggression, reactive motivations were more prevalent than instrumental motivations. For offending more broadly, the reactive and instrumental motivation types were similarly common. Individuals with a more versatile pattern of antisocial behavior were more likely to endorse instrumental motivations (Chapter 6).
#10	Different types of crime tend to be first committed at different ages.	Violations of court orders were more common in adolescence and drug and weapons-based offenses were more common in adulthood (see Lussier et al., 2017). Crimes that might require more skill or criminal social capital were more likely to manifest later in adolescence (Chapter 6).

expected negative relationship between onset and frequency of offending did not emerge until individuals were followed further into adulthood. That is, this relationship took time to develop, possibly because of the homogeneity of the sample (e.g., all experienced the rare event of being incarcerated in adolescence). Similar results emerged in Chapter 5 when modeling conviction trajectories across different age-ranges. These findings differed from life-course criminology assertions that the link between past and future offending will dissipate with a longer follow-up period (Sampson & Laub, 2005b). Chapter 6 examined the overlap between latent classes of antisocial behavior and self-reported age of onset of offending. Individuals with a more versatile/serious pattern of school behavioral problems, substance use, aggression, delinquency, and offending were associated with an earlier self-reported age of onset of first arrest.

Farrington's fourth conclusion was that there was continuity in offending over the life-course. Chapter 4 provided evidence of both stability and change in offending. Using retrospective analyses, virtually all individuals associated with chronic offending in mature adulthood (ages 30–35) were also associated with chronic offending in adolescence. However, only a minority of participants with a pattern of chronic offending in adolescence showed a pattern of chronic offending during mature adulthood. The latter analysis provided evidence against static notions of chronic offending; chronic offending at an earlier age period did not guarantee continued chronic offending. In Chapter 5, nearly all participants assigned to the EOSD or HRP trajectories were involved with the justice system in each age-stage examined (adolescence, emerging adulthood, full adulthood, and mature adulthood). Similarly, Chapter 6 found stability in self-reported delinquency and self-reported offending when measured before age 12 and from age 12 through age 17.

Farrington's fifth conclusion was that a minority of persons were responsible for the majority of all offending. Chapter 4 showed that this was true when looking at convictions for the ISVYOS sample. In adolescence, 23.5% of the sample accounted for 50% of all convictions. Just 9.3% of the sample were needed to account for 50% of all convictions during mature adulthood. In Chapter 5, modeling trajectories from ages 12–35 showed that the EOSD and HRP trajectories, representing less than a third of the sample, were responsible for the majority of all convictions. Where these findings differed from prior research was with respect to the volume of offending associated with chronicity. In Wolfgang et al.'s (1972) study, the minimum number of arrests needed to meet the chronic offending threshold in adolescence was five. For the ISVYOS sample, the minimum number of convictions needed to meet the threshold for chronic offending in adolescence was 17.

Farrington's sixth conclusion was that offending persistence and versatility were positively correlated. In Chapter 4, conviction versatility and conviction frequency were almost perfectly correlated in the full adulthood and mature adulthood age-stages. This finding contrasted with policies in the United States that presume that individuals are repeatedly involved in one specific crime type (e.g., sexual offending; see Lussier et al., 2020a). Chapter 6 showed that higher levels of self-reported offending versatility in adolescence were associated with CPO trajectories through emerging adulthood.

Farrington's seventh conclusion was that criminal behavior was a manifestation of a general antisocial tendency. In Chapter 4, the strong correlation between frequent and versatile offending supported Farrington's seventh conclusion. In Chapter 6, when looking at self-report data, there was mixed support for Farrington's conclusion. There were some participants who showed a tendency towards, for example, overt behavior only or covert behavior only. There were other individuals who were versatile in their antisocial behavior and had the highest probability of endorsing any given behavioral problem.

Farrington's eighth conclusion was that co-offending was more likely in adolescence than adulthood. This was not addressed in the book, but the ISVYOS recently received another four years of funding to use data from CORNET to code co-offending and other relationships as part of each participant's criminogenic network. We are examining these data through the lens of social network analysis to learn about who an individual is connected to, how many co-offenders they have, whether these criminogenic connections were forged while incarcerated, and whether these relationships in custody continue in the community.

Farrington's ninth conclusion was that offending was reactively and instrumentally motivated in adolescence but only instrumentally motivated in adulthood. While we were unable to examine motivations for offending in adulthood, Chapter 6 showed that for aggressive behavior, reactive motivations were more prevalent than instrumental motivations. Those least associated with aggressive behavior were only reactively motivated. More versatility in the types of aggressive acts perpetrated was associated with a greater variety of motivations for aggression. Similarly, more versatility in self-reported offending was associated with a greater variety of reactive and instrumental motivations. Instrumental motivation was more useful than reactive motivation for distinguishing between self-reported offending latent classes because reactive motivations were common for the entire sample.

Farrington's tenth conclusion was that different types of crime tended to be committed at different ages. Chapter 6 showed that certain crimes were more prevalent than others in childhood than in adolescence and vice-versa. Bullying was more typical in childhood than in adolescence. Crimes that required skills (e.g., motor vehicle theft, breaking and entering), overpowering others (e.g., robbery), or especially serious crimes like homicide were rarer in childhood than adolescence. Although not examined in this book, other publications using ISVYOS data showed that violations of court orders comprised a larger proportion of the crime-mix in adolescence compared to adulthood, whereas drug and weapons offenses comprised a larger proportion of the crime-mix in adulthood compared to adolescence (Lussier et al., 2017).

In sum, the main way in which findings from the ISVYOS departed from Farrington's conclusions related to the degree of continuity of offending, lack of conformity to the age-crime curve, and a later age at offending termination. This highlights a divide between what DLC criminology has reported about the nature of sequences of offending and what practitioners see in their own experiences working with individuals with a history of incarceration in adolescence. It highlights the need for criminology to do more to look at the problem of offending from the perspective of those responsible for helping to respond to this problem. This does not mean taking the side of agents of the justice system or agreeing with their approach. It means that more attention is needed to conducting research that can directly help these agents do their jobs in ways that bring about positive results (e.g., the promotion of desistance, prevention of victimization, and improvements in maturation, social outcomes, and quality of life).

Concluding thoughts

It could be easy to be pessimistic about the helpfulness of the youth justice system given that adult justice system involvement was regularly experienced by participants (see Chapter 4) and positive life outcomes in adulthood were rare (see Chapter 8). However, it is important to place these findings in the context of macro-level trends over the last several decades. Youth crime rates are down (Payne & Piquero, 2020). The transition from the YOA (Cohort I) to the more rehabilitation-oriented principles of the YCJA (Cohort II) was associated with less of a connection between past youth justice system involvement and future adult justice system involvement (see Chapter 9). A tentative conclusion is that the YCJA's emphasis on treatment, intervention, and community release planning helped break the typical connection between past and future crime. Fear-inducing notions of the highly-prevalent youth super predator (DiIulio, 1995) appear nothing more than poorly-conceived theories. We think it is important to find a balance between (1) the observation that crime rates for serious and violent offending appear to be on the decline and (2) for those involved in serious and violent offending, instead of making assumptions about desistance by default, it is more accurate to assume that there is much work to do to facilitate the path to desistance. ISVYOS participants were regularly raised in environments that were difficult to cope with. Relationships between mothers and fathers were often non-existent or characterized by shared substance use issues and intimate partner violence. Half the sample were placed in foster care. Half the sample used crack cocaine, heroin, or crystal methamphetamine. Only half the sample were attending school prior to their incarceration. Most participants who did attend school regularly skipped class. Participants were characterized by serious mental health issues, including features of psychopathy. They also experienced major physical health issues (e.g., tuberculosis, anemia, pneumonia).

These difficult circumstances continued in adulthood. Participants' parents died young and of non-natural causes (e.g., suicide, overdose, homicide). Their relationships were characterized by substance use, violence perpetration, and violence victimization. They experienced homelessness, difficulty finding and maintaining employment, car accidents, hospitalizations, and repeated experiences of victimization in prison and in the community. At the time of this book, 109 of the 1,620 members of the ISVYOS for whom we had data on experienced early mortality (6.7% of the sample). It was rare for young persons to escape negative social situations in adolescence and find new, more positive experiences in adulthood.

The negative criminal, health, and social outcomes of this sample were not a result of a passive justice system. Over the years, we met with policymakers from MCFD and directors from youth and adult custody centers. It was clear that practitioners wanted to know more about the high-risk persons housed within their facilities and how to improve their chances of rehabilitation. These practitioners did not endorse notions of "desistance by default" (Laub & Sampson, 2003, 278–9). Nor do we, at least when it comes to this sample. Participants received ratings from practitioners about whether various sources of informal social control were deemed to be, not just "not causing interference", but "strength" factors. Family relationships, living arrangements, intimate partner relationships, academic/vocational skills, and employment were rarely a positive source of strength for the sample. We found that participants whose adolescence was characterized by negative family situations, numerous individual-level risk factors, and lengthy periods of time incarcerated were especially unlikely to experience positive sources of informal social control. Even when these positive sources of informal social control were present, they were not enough to influence desistance if they were held by a person characterized by high levels of risk in adolescence. To talk of desistance by default is to potentially deny that anything needs to be done to help these young persons.

We prefer more recent thinking about how to promote desistance through assistance (Dufour et al., 2018). This is more than just social hooks for change (Giordano et al., 2002). It requires development of evidence-based treatment and intervention strategies that help alter a person's temperament, identity, and ability to perform in new adult roles in a prosocial way (McCuish et al., 2020b). We do not deny that human agency is important, but what is also important is acknowledging that two individuals with equal levels of agency may need to allocate this agency differently based on their life circumstances. Some are free to use this agency to find a job and housing. Others, like the case of Tyler presented in Chapter 6, use their agency to help care for family members dealing with substance addiction, suicidal ideation, and malnourishment. Agency is not infinite, and some need to use their agency in response to severe structural constraints and forms of oppression, making desistance by default more difficult. The magnitude of disadvantage experienced by members of the ISVYOS calls for resources similar in magnitude. Dufour et al. (2018) described the importance of identifying formal (e.g., initiated by agents of the justice system) and informal (e.g., initiated by mentors) strategies that help improve, not just the chances of desistance, but also an individual's self-identity and quality of life. Are individuals not offending simply because they are worn down from mental and physical health problems, family conflict, and employment difficulties? If persons are not experiencing happiness, love, and pride when it comes to their identity, their children, their relationships, and their work, then it is perhaps not true desistance (Bersani et al., 2018).

Accordingly, DLC research should move towards studying desistance as a process of change in offending *and* change in the person.

This approach may call into question the role of probation and parole officers who are acting in the interests of public safety and therefore may not always be acting in the best interests of the person before the justice system. The assessment of risk factors for recidivism and the presentation of statistical probabilities of recidivism have become the norm over the past two decades (Lussier et al., 2020). While public safety will remain the main focus of the justice system, this is not necessarily inconsistent with a paradigm shift that recognizes, through theory and research, that focusing on desistance can help protect the public. A clear research agenda focusing on desistance will necessitate a *theory of change*, not a revised theory of social control as a normative process of the life-course for youth with histories of incarceration.

References

Abram, K., Teplin, L., Charles, D., Longworth, S., McClelland, G., & Dulcan, M. (2004). Posttraumatic stress disorder and trauma in youth in juvenile detention. *Archives of General Psychiatry*, *61*, 403–410.

Abram, K., Teplin, L., McClelland, G., & Dulcan, M. (2003). Comorbid psychiatric disorders in youth in juvenile detention. *Archives of General Psychiatry*, *60*, 1097–1108.

ACLU. (2020). America's addiction to juvenile incarceration: State by state. https://www.aclu.org/issues/juvenile-justice/youth-incarceration/americas-addiction-juvenile-incarceration-state-state

Agnew, R. (1992). Foundation for a general strain theory of crime and delinquency. *Criminology*, *30*, 47–88.

Agnew, R., Brezina, T., Wright, J., & Cullen, F. (2002). Strain, personality traits, and delinquency: Extending general strain theory. *Criminology*, *40*, 43–72.

Aichorn, A. (1935). *Wayward youth*. The Viking Press.

Akers, R. (1992). Linking sociology and its specialties: The case of criminology. *Social Forces*, *71*, 1–16.

Akers, R., Krohn, M., Lanza-Kaduce, L., & Radosevich, M. (1979). Social learning and deviant behavior: A specific test of a general theory. *American Sociological Review*, *1*, 636–655.

Allison, P. (2015). Don't put lagged dependent variables in mixed models. *Statistical Horizons*, *2*. https://statisticalhorizons.com/lagged-dependent-variables#:~:text=Nowadays%2C%20mixed%20modeling%20is%20probably,as%20dynamic%20panel%20data%20models.

Allison, P. D. (2009). *Fixed Effects Regression Models*. London: Sage.

Altikriti, S., Theocharidou, K., & Sullivan, C. (2020). Specific theories of crime? A longitudinal assessment of the competing effects of psychopathy and self-control. *Journal of Crime and Justice*, 1–21. http://doi.org/10.1080/0735648X.2020.1727765

Andershed, H., Kerr, M., Stattin, H., & Levander, S. (2002). Psychopathic traits in non-referred youth: Initial test of a new assessment tool. In E. Blaauw, J. Philippa, K. Ferenschild, & B. van Lodensteijn (Eds.), *Psychopaths: Current international perspectives* (pp. 131–158). Elsevier.

Andrews, D., Bonta, J., & Wormith, J. (2006). The recent past and near future of risk and/or need assessment. *Crime & Delinquency*, *52*, 7–27.

Andrews, D., Zinger, I., Hoge, R., Bonta, J., Gendreau, P., & Cullen, F. (1990). Does correctional treatment work? A clinically relevant and psychologically informed meta-analysis. *Criminology*, *28*, 369–404.

Arnett, J. (2000). Emerging adulthood: A theory of development from late teens through the twenties. *American Psychologist*, *55*, 469–480.

Bachman, J., & Schulenberg, J. (1993). How part-time work intensity relates to drug use, problem behavior, time use, and satisfaction among high school seniors: Are these consequences or merely correlates? *Developmental Psychology*, *29*, 220–235.

Bala, N. (2003). *Youth criminal justice law*. Irwin Law.

Bala, N., Carrington, P., & Roberts, J. (2009). Evaluating the Youth Criminal Justice Act after five years: A qualified success. *Canadian Journal of Criminology and Criminal Justice*, *51*, 131–167.

Bala, N., Finlay, J., De Filippis, R., & Hunter, K. (2015). Child welfare adolescents & the youth justice system: Failing to respond effectively to crossover youth. *Canadian Criminal Law Review*, *19*, 129–151.

Bandura, A. (2006). Toward a psychology of human agency. *Perspectives on Psychological Science*, *1*, 164–180.

Barnes, J., El Sayed, S., TenEyck, M., Nedelec, J., Connolly, E., Schwartz, J., & Anderson, N. (2017). Estimating relative stability in developmental research: A critique of modern approaches and a novel method. *Journal of Quantitative Criminology*, *33*, 319–346.

Barnhorst, R. (2004). The youth criminal justice act: New directions and implementation issues. *Canadian Journal of Criminology and Criminal Justice*, *46*, 231–250.

Baron, S. W., & Kennedy, L. W. (1998). Deterrence and homeless male street youth. *Canadian Journal of Criminology*, *40*, 27–60.

Barrett, D., Katsiyannis, A., & Zhang, D. (2006). Predictors of offense severity, prosecution, incarceration, and repeat violations for adolescent male and female offenders. *Journal of Child and Family Studies*, *15*, 708–718.

Baskin-Sommers, A. R., & Baskin, D. (2016). Psychopathic traits mediate the relationship between exposure to violence and violent juvenile offending. *Journal of Psychopathology and Behavioral Assessment*, *3*, 341–349.

Basto-Pereira, M., & Farrington, D. (2020). Lifelong conviction pathways and self-reported offending: Towards a deeper comprehension of criminal career development. *The British Journal of Criminology*, *60*, 285–302.

BC Representative of Children and Youth. (2009). Kids, crime and care – Health and well-being of children in care: Youth justice experiences and outcomes. Office of the Provincial Health Officer.

Bei Li, L. (2018). Data privacy in the cyber age: Recommendations for regulating doxing and swatting. *Federal Communications Law Journal*, *70*, 317–328.

Bell, S. (2014). *Young offenders and juvenile justice: A century after the fact*. Nelson.

Bennett, W., DiIulio, J., & Walters, J. (1996). *Body count: Moral poverty – and how to win America's war against crime and drugs*. Simon & Schuster.

Bernard, T. (1990). Angry aggression among the "truly disadvantaged". *Criminology*, *28*, 73–96.

Bernard, T., & Snipes, J. (1996). Theoretical integration in criminology. *Crime and Justice*, *20*, 301–348.

Bernburg, J., Krohn, M., & Rivera, C. (2006). Official labeling, criminal embeddedness, and subsequent delinquency: A longitudinal test of labeling theory. *Journal of Research in Crime and Delinquency*, *43*, 67–88.

Bersani, B. & Doherty, E. E. (2018). Desistance from offending in the twenty-first century. *Annual Review of Criminology*, *1*, 311–334.

Blokland, A., Nagin, D., & Nieuwbeerta, P. (2005). Life span offending trajectories of a Dutch conviction cohort. *Criminology*, *43*, 919–954.

Blokland, A., & Nieuwbeerta, P. (2005). The effects of life circumstances on longitudinal trajectories of offending. *Criminology*, *43*, 1203–1240.

Blumstein, A., & Beck, A. (1999). Population growth in US prisons, 1980–1996. *Crime and Justice*, *26*, 17–61.

Blumstein, A., & Cohen, J. (1979). Estimation of individual crime rates from arrest records. *Journal of Criminal Law & Criminology*, *70*, 561–585.

Blumstein, A., Cohen, J., & Farrington, D. (1988a). Criminal career research: Its value for criminology. *Criminology*, *26*, 1–35.

Blumstein, A., Cohen, J., & Farrington, D. (1988b). Longitudinal and criminal career research: Further clarifications. *Criminology*, *26*, 57–74.

Blumstein, A., Cohen, J., & Hsieh, P. (1982). *The duration of adult criminal careers*. National Institute of Justice.

Blumstein A., Cohen, J., Roth J., & Visher C. (1986). Criminal careers and "career criminals." *Report of the National Academy of Sciences Panel on Research on Criminal Careers; Washington*. National Academy Press.

Blumstein, A., Farrington, D., & Moitra, S. (1985). Delinquency careers: Innocents, desisters, and persisters. *Crime and Justice*, *6*, 187–219.

Blumstein, A., & Moitra, S. (1980). The identification of "career criminals" from "chronic offenders" in a cohort. *Law & Policy*, *2*, 321–334.

Blumstein, A., Wallman, J., & Farrington, D. (Eds.). (2006). *The crime drop in America*. Cambridge University Press.

Bohmert, M., Duwe, G., & Hipple, N. (2018). Evaluating restorative justice circles of support and accountability: Can social support overcome structural barriers? *International Journal of Offender Therapy and Comparative Criminology*, *62*, 739–758.

Bolan, K. (2018). Metro's deadly gang war: Going after a familiar cast plus new players. *Vancouver Sun*. https://vancouversun.com/news/local-news/metros-deadly-gang-war-going-after-a-familiar-cast-plus-new-players.

Boman IV, J., & Mowen, T. (2018). The role of turning points in establishing baseline differences between people in developmental and life-course criminology. *Criminology*, *56*, 191–224.

Bonta, J., & Andrews, D. A. (2007). Risk-need-responsivity model for offender assessment and rehabilitation. *Rehabilitation*, *6*, 1–22.

Book, A., Holden, R., Starzyk, K., Wasylkiw, L., & Edwards, M. (2006). Psychopathic traits and experimental induced deception in self report assessment. *Personality and Individual Differences*, *41*, 601–608.

Borum R., Bartel P., & Forth A. (2002). *SAVRY: Manual for the structured assessment of violence risk in youth Tampa*. FL: Florida Mental Health Institute, University of South Florida.

Boykin, C. M., Brown, N. D., Carter, J. T., Dukes, K., Green, D. J., Harrison, T., ... & Williams, A. D. (2020). Anti-racist actions and accountability: Not more empty promises. *Equality, Diversity and Inclusion: An International Journal*, 1–12.

Brantingham, P. (1985). Sentencing disparity: An analysis of judicial consistency. *Journal of Quantitative Criminology*, *1*, 281–305.

Burt, C. (1925). *The young delinquent*. University of London Press.

Bushway, S. (2013). Life-course-persistent offenders. In F. Cullen & P. Wilcox (Eds.), *The Oxford handbook of criminological theory* (pp. 189–204). Guilford University Press.

Bushway, S., & Piehl, A. (2001). Judging judicial discretion: Legal factors and racial discrimination in sentencing. *Law & Society Review*, *35*, 733–764.

Bushway, S.D., & Paternoster, R. (2013). Desistance from crime: A review and ideas for moving forward. In C. Gibson & M. Krohn (Eds.), *Handbook of life-course criminology* (pp. 213–231). Springer.

Capaldi, D., & Patterson, G. (1996). Can violent offenders be distinguished from frequent offenders: Prediction from childhood to adolescence. *Journal of Research in Crime and Delinquency*, *33*, 206–231.

Caputo, T. (1987). The Young Offenders Act: Children's rights, children's wrongs. *Canadian Public Policy/Analyse de Politiques, 13*(2), 125–143.

Carrington, P., & Moyer, S. (1995). Factors affecting custodial dispositions under the *Young Offenders Act*. *Canadian Journal of Criminology*, *37*, 127–162.

Carrington, P., Matarazzo, A., & DeSouza, P. (2005). *Court careers of a Canadian birth cohort*. Canadian Centre for Justice Statistics.

Caspi, A., Moffitt, T., Silva, P., Stouthamer-Loeber, M., Krueger, R., & Schmutte, P. (1994). Are some people crime-prone? Replications of the personality-crime relationship across countries, genders, races, and methods. *Criminology*, *32*, 163–196.

Cauffman, E., Kimonis, E. R., Dmitrieva, J., & Monahan, K. C. (2009). A multi-method assessment of juvenile psychopathy: Comparing the predictive utility of the PCL: YV, YPI, and NEO PRI. *Psychological Assessment*, *21*, 528–542.

Cauffman, E., & Steinberg, L. (2012). Emerging findings from research on adolescent development and juvenile justice. *Victims & Offenders*, *7*, 428–449.

CBC News. (December, 2007). Man says he didn't laugh at sentence for axe attack. CBC News. https://www.cbc.ca/news/canada/british-columbia/man-says-he-didn-t-laugh-at-sentence-for-axe-attack-1.686601

Cernkovich, S., & Giordano, P. (2001). Stability and change in antisocial behavior: The transition from adolescence to early adulthood. *Criminology*, *39*, 371–410.

Cernkovich, S., Giordano, P., & Pugh, M. (1985). Chronic offenders: The missing cases in self-report delinquency research. *The Journal of Criminal Law and Criminology*, *76*, 705–732.

Cesaroni, C., & Bala, N. (2008). Deterrence as a principle of youth sentencing: No effect on youth, but a significant on judges. *Queen's Law Journal*, *34*, 447–482.

Chaiken, J., & Chaiken, M. (1982). *Varieties of criminal behavior*. Rand.

Chambliss, W. (1972). *Box man: A professional thief's journey*. Harper and Row.

Cicchetti, D., & Sparrow, S. (1981). Developing criteria for establishing interrater reliability of specific items: applications to assessment of adaptive behavior. *American Journal of Mental Deficiency*, *86*, 127–137.

Clancy, K., Bartolomeo, J., Richardson, D., & Wellford, C. (1981). Sentence decisionmaking: The logic of sentence decisions and the extent and sources of sentence disparity. *The Journal of Criminal Law and Criminology*, *72*, 524–554.

Cleckley, H. (1941). *The mask of sanity*. Mosby

Cleckley, H. (1976). *The mask of sanity* (5th Ed.). Mosby.

Coffee, J. (1975). The future of sentencing reform: Emerging legal issues in the individualization of justice. *Michigan Law Review*, *73*, 1361–1462.

Cohen, J. (1988). *Statistical power analysis for the behavioral sciences* (2nd Ed.). Earlbaum.

Cohn, E., & Farrington, D. (2008). Scholarly influence in criminology and criminal justice journals in 1990–2000. *Journal of Criminal Justice*, *36*, 11–21.

Colins, O., Andershed, H., & Pardini, D. (2015). Psychopathic traits as predictors of future criminality, intimate partner aggression, and substance use in young adult men. *Law and Human Behavior*, *39*, 547–558.

Collins, L., & Lanza, S. (2010). *Latent class and latent transition analysis: With applications in the social, behavioral, and health sciences*. Wiley.

Cooke, D., Hart, S., Logan, C., & Michie, C. (2004). *Comprehensive assessment of psychopathic personality – Institutional rating scale (CAPP-IRS)*. Department of Psychology, Glasgow Caledonian University

Cooke, D., Hart, S., Logan, C., & Michie, C. (2012). Explicating the construct of psychopathy: Development and validation of a conceptual model, the comprehensive assessment of psychopathic personality (CAPP). *International Journal of Forensic Mental Health*, *11*, 242–252.

Cooke, D., & Logan, C. (2018). Capturing psychopathic personality: Penetrating the mask of sanity through clinical interview. In. C. Patrick (Ed.), *Handbook of psychopathy*. Guilford Press.

Cooke, D., & Michie, C. (1997). An item response theory analysis of the Hare Psychopathy Checklist-Revised. *Psychological Assessment*, *9*, 3–14.

Cooke, D., & Michie, C. (1999). Psychopathy across cultures: North America and Scotland compared. *Journal of Abnormal Psychology*, *108*, 58–68.

Cooper, L., Longmore, M., Manning, W., & Giordano, P. (2020). The influence of demographic, relational, and risk asymmetries on the frequency of intimate partner violence in young adulthood. *Journal of Family Issues* (online first).

Copas, J., & Tarling, R. (1986). Some methodological issues in making predictions. In J. Weis (Ed.), *Criminal Careers and Career Criminals,* 2, 291–313.

Cornell, D., Warren, J., Hawk, G., Stafford, E., Oram, G., & Pine, D. (1996). Psychopathy in instrumental and reactive violent offenders. *Journal of Consulting and Clinical Psychology*, *64*, 783–790.

Corrado, R., DeLisi, M., Hart, S., & McCuish, E. (2015). Can the causal mechanisms underlying chronic, serious, and violent offending trajectories be elucidated using the psychopathy construct? *Journal of Criminal Justice*, *43*, 251–261.

Corrado, R., & Markwart, A. (1994). The need to reform the YOA in response to violent young offenders: Confusion, reality or myth. *Canadian Journal of Criminology*, *36*, 343–378.

Corrado, R., Gronsdahl, K., MacAlister, D., & Cohen, I. (2006). Should deterrence be a sentencing principle under the Youth Criminal Justice Act. *Canadian Bar Review*, *85*, 539–565.

Corrado, R., Gronsdahl, K., MacAlister, D., & Cohen, I. (2010). Youth justice in Canada: Theoretical perspectives of youth probation officers. *Canadian Journal of Criminology and Criminal Justice*, *52*, 397–426.

Corrado, R., Lussier, P., & Leschied, A. (Eds.). (2015). *Serious and violent young offenders and youth criminal justice: A Canadian perspective*. Simon Fraser University Publications.

Corrado, R., Odgers, C., & Cohen, I. (2000). Incarceration of female young offenders: Protection for whom? *Canadian Journal of Criminology*, *42*, 189–208.

Cortina, J. (1993). What is coefficient alpha? An examination of theory and applications. *Journal of Applied Psychology*, *78*, 98–104.

Côté, J. (2000). *Arrested adulthood: The changing nature of maturity and identity*. University Press.

Cotter, R., Burke, J., Stouthamer-Loeber, M., & Loeber, R. (2005). Contacting participants for follow-up: How much effort is required to retain participants in longitudinal studies? *Evaluation and Program Planning*, *28*, 15–21.

Crawford, T. (2016). Youth inmates riot at overcrowded, gang-ridden Burnaby 'super-jail. *Vancouver Sun*. https://vancouversun.com/news/local-news/riot-and-fire-at-burnaby-youth-detention-centre

Crewe, B. (2011). Soft power in prison: Implications for staff–prisoner relationships, liberty and legitimacy. *European Journal of Criminology*, *8*, 455–468.

Cronbach, L. J., & Meehl, P. E. (1955). Construct validity in psychological tests. *Psychological Bulletin*, *52*, 281–302.

Cullen, F. (2011). Beyond adolescence-limited criminology: Choosing our future—the American Society of Criminology 2010 Sutherland address. *Criminology*, *49*, 287–330.

Cusson, M., & Pinsonneault, P. (1986). The decision to give up crime. Cornish, D. & R. Clarke (Eds.) *The reasoning criminal: Rational choice perspectives on offending* (pp. 72–82). Springer.

da Silva, D., Rijo, D., & Salekin, R. (2020). Psychopathic traits in children and youth: The state-of-the-art after 30 years of research. *Aggression and Violent Behavior* (online first), 1–16.

Daftary-Kapur, T., & Zottoli, T. (2014). A first look at the plea deal experiences of juveniles tried in adult court. *International Journal of Forensic Mental Health, 13*, 323–336.

Davies, G. & Dawson, S. (2015). The 2011 Stanley Cup Riot: Police perspectives and lessons learned. *Policing: An International Journal of Police Strategies & Management*, *38*, 132–152.

Dawson, S., McCuish, E., Hart, S., & Corrado, R. (2012). Critical issues in the assessment of adolescent psychopathy: An illustration using two case studies. *International Journal of Forensic Mental Health*, *11*, 63–79.

Day, D., Nielsen, J., Ward, A., Sun, Y., Rosenthal, J., Duchesne, T., & Rossman, L. (2012). Long-term follow-up of criminal activity with adjudicated youth in Ontario: Identifying offence trajectories and predictors/correlates of trajectory group membership. *Canadian Journal of Criminology and Criminal Justice, 54*, 377–413.

DeLisi, M. (2001). Extreme career criminals. *American Journal of Criminal Justice*, *25*, 239–252.

DeLisi, M. (2016). *Psychopathy as unified theory of crime*. Palgrave Macmillan.

DeLisi, M., & Piquero, A. (2011). New frontiers in criminal careers research, 2000–2011: A state-of-the-art review. *Journal of Criminal Justice*, *39*, 289–301.

DeMatteo, D., Hart, S. D., Heilbrun, K., Boccaccini, M. T., Cunningham, M. D., Douglas, K. S. ... Reidy, T. J. (2020). Statement of concerned experts on the use of the Hare Psychopathy Checklist – Revised in capital sentencing to assess risk for institutional violence. *Psychology, Public Policy, and Law*. https://doi.org/10.1037/law0000223.

Department of Justice. (2007). *Pre-trial detention under the Youth Criminal Justice Act: A consultation paper*. Department of Justice Canada.

Department of Justice. (2019). *What we heard – Transforming Canada's criminal justice system*. Department of Justice Canada.

Deslauriers-Varin, N., & Beauregard, E. (2014). Unravelling crime series patterns amongst serial sex offenders: Duration, frequency, and environmental consistency. *Journal of Investigative Psychology and Offender Profiling*, *11*, 253–275.

DiIulio, J. (1995, December). Moral poverty: The coming of the Superpredators should scare us into wanting to get to the root causes of crime a lot faster. *Chicago Tribune*, Section 1, p. 31.

Doherty, E. E., & Ensminger, M. (2013). Marriage and offending among a cohort of disadvantaged African Americans. *Journal of Research in Crime and Delinquency*, *50*, 104–131.

Dombek, C., & Chitra, M. (1980). The pre-sentence report: An update. *Criminal Law Quarterly*, *23*, 216–238.

Doob, A. (1992). Trends in the use of custodial dispositions for young offenders. *Canadian Journal of Criminology*, *34*, 75–84.

Doob, A. (2001). Youth court judges' views of the youth justice system: The results of a survey. Centre of Criminology, University of Toronto.

Doob, A., & Sprott, J. (2004). Youth justice in Canada. *Crime and Justice*, *31*, 185–242.

Doob, A., & Sprott, J. (2007). The sentencing of Aboriginal and non-Aboriginal youth: Understanding local variation. *Canadian Journal of Criminology and Criminal Justice*, *49*, 109–123.

Dufour, I. F., Villeneuve, M-P. & Perron, C. (2018). Les interventions informelles de désistement assisté: une étude de la portée. *Canadian Journal of Criminology & Criminal Justice*, 60, 206–240.

D'Unger, A., Land, K., & McCall, P. (2002). Sex differences in age patterns of delinquent/criminal careers: Results from Poisson latent class analyses of the Philadelphia cohort study. *Journal of Quantitative Criminology*, *18*, 349–375.

Dyck, H. L., Campbell, M. A., Schmidt, F., & Wershler, J. L. (2013). Youth psychopathic traits and their impact on long-term criminal offending trajectories. *Youth Violence and Juvenile Justice*, *11*, 230–248.

Edens, J., Campbell, J., & Weir, J. (2007). Youth psychopathy and criminal recidivism: A meta-analysis of the psychopathy checklist measures. *Law and Human Behavior*, *31*, 53–75.

Edens, J., Marcus, D., Lilienfeld, S., & Poythress Jr, N. G. (2006). Psychopathic, not psychopath: Taxometric evidence for the dimensional structure of psychopathy. *Journal of Abnormal Psychology*, *115*, 131–144.

Eggleston, E., Laub, J., & Sampson, R. (2004). Methodological sensitivities to latent class analysis of long-term criminal trajectories. *Journal of Quantitative Criminology*, *20*, 1–25.

Elder, G. (1994). Time, human agency, and social change: Perspectives on the life course. *Social Psychology Quarterly*, *57*, 4–15.

Elder, G. (1998). The life course as developmental theory. *Child Development*, *69*, 1–12.

Ellis, H. (1890). *The criminal*. Walter Scott.

Endres, K. (2004). The Youth Criminal Justice Act: The new face of Canada's youth criminal justice system. *Family Court Review*, *42*, 526–539.

Erikson, E. (1968). *Identity: Youth and crisis*. Norton.

Eurostat. (2012). School-to-work Transition Statistics. http://ec.europa.eu/eurostat/statistics-explained/index.php/Main_Page

Eysenck, H. (1964). *Crime and personality*. Houghton Mifflin.

Fahmy, C., Clark, K., Mitchell, M., Decker, S., & Pyrooz, D. (2019). Method to the madness: tracking and interviewing respondents in a longitudinal study of prisoner reentry. *Sociological Methods & Research*. https://doi.org/10.1177/0049124119875962

Farrall, S., & Bowling, B. (1999). Structuration, human development and desistance from crime. *British Journal of Criminology*, *39*, 253–268.

Farrington, D. (1989). Early predictors of adolescent aggression and adult violence. *Violence and Victims*, *4*, 79–100.

Farrington, D. (1992). Explaining the beginning, progress, and ending of antisocial behavior from birth to adulthood. *Facts, Frameworks, and Forecasts*, *3*, 253–286.

Farrington, D. (2003). Developmental and life-course criminology: Key theoretical and empirical issues-the 2002 Sutherland Award address. *Criminology*, *41*, 221–225.

Farrington, D. (2005). The importance of child and adolescent psychopathy. *Journal of Abnormal Child Psychology*, *33*, 489–497.

Farrington, D. (2019). The integrated cognitive antisocial potential (ICAP) Theory: Past, present, and future. *Journal of Developmental and Life-Course Criminology*, *6*, 172–187.

Farrington, D. (2020) Donald J. West (June 9, 1924 - January 31, 2020). *The DLC Criminologist*, *8*, 22–24.

Farrington, D., & Welsh, B. (2008). *Saving children from a life of crime: Early risk factors and effective interventions*. Oxford University Press.

Farrington, D., Gaffney, H., Lösel, F., & Ttofi, M. (2017). Systematic reviews of the effectiveness of developmental prevention programs in reducing delinquency, aggression, and bullying. *Aggression and Violent Behavior*, *33*, 91–106.

Farrington, D., & Hawkins, J. (1991). Predicting participation, early onset and later persistence in officially recorded offending. *Criminal Behaviour and Mental Health*, *1*, 1–33.

Farrington, D., Jolliffe, D., Hawkins, J., Catalano, R., Hill, K., & Kosterman, R. (2003). Comparing delinquency careers in court records and self-reports. *Criminology*, *41*, 933–958.

Farrington, D., Kazemian, L., & Piquero, A. (2019). *The Oxford handbook of developmental and life-course criminology*. Oxford University Press.

Farrington, D., Ttofi, M., Crago, R., & Coid, J. (2014). Prevalence, frequency, onset, desistance and criminal career duration in self-reports compared with official records. *Criminal Behaviour and Mental Health*, *24*, 241–253.

Feld, B. (1993). Criminalizing the American juvenile court. *Crime and Justice*, *17*, 197–280.

Fenchel, F., & Winterdyk, J. (2019). Denis Szabo (1929–2018): Founder of Canadian Criminology in Québec. *Canadian Journal of Criminology and Criminal Justice*, *61*, 1–7.

Fergusson, D., & Horwood, L. (2002). Male and female offending trajectories. *Development and Psychopathology*, *14*, 159–177.

Fergusson, D.M., Horwood, L. J., & Nagin, D. S. (2000). Offending trajectories in a New Zealand birth cohort. *Criminology*, *38*, 525–551.

Fink, A. (1938). *Causes of crime: Biological theories in the United States 1800–1915*. A.S. Barnes.

Fontaine, N., Lacourse, E., Vitaro, F., & Tremblay, R. (2014). Links between trajectories of self-reported violent and nonviolent offending and official offending during adolescence and adulthood. *Criminal Behaviour and Mental Health*, *24*, 277–290.

Forth, A. (1995). *Psychopathy and young offenders: Prevalence, family background, and violence*. Unpublished manuscript. Carelton Univesity, Ottawa, Canada.

Forth, A., Kosson, D., & Hare, R. (2003). *The Hare Psychopathy Checklist: Youth Version*. Multi-Health Systems.

Fox, B., Jennings, W., & Farrington, D. (2015). Bringing psychopathy into developmental and life-course criminology theories and research. *Journal of Criminal Justice*, *43*, 274–289.

Fox, K., Zambrana, K., & Lane, J. (2011). Getting in (and staying in) when everyone else wants to get out: 10 lessons learned from conducting research with inmates. *Journal of Criminal Justice Education*, *22*, 304–327.

Fréchette, M., & Le Blanc, M. (1987). *Délinquances et délinquants*. Gaétan Morin.

Friedlander, K. (1945). Formation of the antisocial character. *The Psychoanalytic Study of the Child*, *1*, 189–203.

Gadermann, A., Guhn, M., & Zumbo, B. (2012). Estimating ordinal reliability for Likert-type and ordinal item response data: A conceptual, empirical, and practical guide. *Practical Assessment, Research & Evaluation*, *17*, 1–13.

Gao, Y., & Raine, A. (2010). Successful and unsuccessful psychopaths: A neurobiological model. *Behavioral Sciences & the Law*, *28*, 194–210.

Gendreau, P. (1996). Offender rehabilitation: What we know and what needs to be done. *Criminal Justice and Behavior*, *23*, 144–161.

Gendreau, P., & Ross, R. (1987). Revivification of rehabilitation: Evidence from the 1980s. *Justice Quarterly*, *4*, 349–407.

Gilman, A., Hill, K., Kim, B., Nevell, A., Hawkins, J., & Farrington, D. (2014). Understanding the relationship between self-reported offending and official criminal charges across early adulthood. *Criminal Behaviour and Mental Health*, *24*, 229–240.

Giordano, P., Cernkovich, S., & Rudolph, J. (2002). Gender, crime, and desistance: Toward a theory of cognitive transformation. *American Journal of Sociology*, *107*, 990–1064.

Glueck, S. (1958). Predictive devices and the individualization of justice. *Law and Contemporary Problems*, *23*, 461–476.

Goff, C., & Geis, G. (2008). The Michael-Adler report (1933): Criminology under the microscope. *Journal of the History of the Behavioral Sciences*, *44*, 350–363.

Gottfredson, M., & Hirschi, T. (1986). The true value of lambda would appear to be zero: An essay on career criminals, criminal careers, selective incapacitation, cohort studies, and related topics. *Criminology*, *24*, 213–234.

Glueck, S. & Glueck, E. (1937). *Later criminal careers*. The Commonwealth Fund.

Glueck, S., & Glueck, E. (1950). *Unraveling juvenile delinquency*. Commonwealth Fund.

Gonzales, R. (2011). Learning to be illegal: Undocumented youth and shifting legal contexts in the transition to adulthood. *American Sociological Review*, *76*, 602–619.

Goring, C. (1913). *The English convict: A statistical study*. Darling.

Gottfredson, M., & Hirschi, T. (1987). The methodological adequacy of longitudinal research on crime. *Criminology*, *25*, 581–614.

Gottfredson, M., & Hirschi, T. (1988). Science, public policy, and the career paradigm. *Criminology*, *26*, 37–55.

Gottfredson, M. & Hirschi, T. (1990). *A general theory of crime*. Stanford University Press.

Greenwood, P. & Abrahamse, A. (1982). *Selective incapacitation*. Rand.

Gunasekara, F., Richardson, K., Carter, K., & Blakely, T. (2014). Fixed effects analysis of repeated measures data. *International Journal of Epidemiology*, *43*, 264–269.

Hannah-Moffat, K. & Maurutto, P. (2003). *Youth risk/need assessment: An overview of issues and practices*. Department of Justice Canada.

Hare, R. (1980). A research scale for the assessment of psychopathy in criminal populations. *Personality and Individual Differences*, *1*, 111–117.

Hare, R. (1991). *The Hare Psychopathy Checklist-Revised: Manual*. Multi-Health Systems.

Hare, R. (2003). *The Hare PCL-R* (2nd Ed.). Multi Health Systems.

Hare, R. & Cox, D. (1978) Clinical and empirical conceptions of psychopathy, and the selection of subjects for research. In R. Hare & D. Schalling (Eds.), *Psychopathic behavior: Approaches to research* (pp. 1–21). Wiley.

Hart, S. (1998). The role of psychopathy in assessing risk for violence: Conceptual and methodological issues. *Legal and Criminological Psychology*, *3*, 121–137.

Hart, S. (2016). Culture and violence risk assessment: The case of Ewert v. Canada. *Journal of Threat Assessment and Management*, *3*, 76–96.

Hart, S., & Cook, A. (2012). Current issues in the assessment and diagnosis of psychopathy (psychopathic personality disorder). *Neuropsychiatry*, *2*, 497–508.

Hart, S., & Cooke, D. (2013). Another look at the (Im-) precision of individual risk estimates made using actuarial risk assessment instruments. *Behavioral Sciences & the Law*, *31*, 81–102.

Hart, S., Douglas, K., & Guy, L. (2016). The Structured Professional Judgement Approach to violence risk assessment: Origins, nature, and advances. In L. Craig & M. Rettenberger & (Eds.), *The Wiley handbook on the theories, assessment and treatment of sexual offending* (pp. 643–666). Wiley.

Hart, S., Michie, C., & Cooke, D. (2007). Precision of actuarial risk assessment instruments: Evaluating the "margins of error" of group v. individual predictions of violence. *The British Journal of Psychiatry*, *190*, s60–s65.

Harter, S. (1990). Self and identity development. In S. Feldman & G. Elliott (Eds.), *At the threshold: The developing adolescent* (pp. 352–387). Harvard University Press.

Hay, C., & Forrest, W. (2006). The development of self-control: Examining self-control theory's stability thesis. *Criminology*, *44*, 739–774.

Healy, D. (2010). Betwixt and between: The role of psychosocial factors in the early stages of desistance. *Journal of Research in Crime and Delinquency*, *47*, 419–438.

Hecht, L., Latzman, R., & Lilienfeld, S. (2018). The psychological treatment of psychopathy: Theory and research. In D. David, S. Lynn, & G. Montgomery (Eds.), *Evidence-based psychotherapy: The state of the science and practice* (pp. 271–298). Wiley-Blackwell.

Hill, J., & Holmbeck, G. (1986). Attachment and autonomy during adolescence. In G. Whitehurst (Ed.), *Annals of child development* (Vol. 3, pp. 145–189). JAI Press.

Hill, J., van der Geest, V., & Blokland, A. (2017). Leaving the bank of mum and dad: Financial independence and delinquency desistance in emerging adulthood. *Journal of Developmental and Life-Course Criminology*, *3*, 419–439.

Hirschi, T. (1969). *Causes of delinquency*. University of California Press.

Hirschi, T. (1979). Separate but unequal is better. *Journal of Research in Crime and Delinquency*, *16*, 34–38.

Hirschi, T., & Gottfredson, M. (1983). Age and the explanation of crime. *American Journal of Sociology*, *89*, 552–584.

Hirschi, T., & Hindelang, M. (1977). Intelligence and delinquency: A revisionist review. *American Sociological Review*, *42*, 571–587.

Hogarth, J. (1967). Towards the improvement of sentencing in Canada. *Canadian Journal of Corrections*, 9, 122–136.

Hogarth, J. (1971). *Sentencing as a human process*. University of Toronto Press.

Hogeveen, B. (2005). Toward "safer" and "better" communities?: Canada's Youth Criminal Justice Act, Aboriginal youth and the processes of exclusion. *Critical Criminology*, *13*, 287–305.

Hooton, E. (1939). *Crime and the man*. Harvard University Press.

Horley, J. (2014). The emergence and development of psychopathy. *History of the Human Sciences*, *27*, 91–110.

Horney, J., Osgood, D., & Marshall, I. (1995). Criminal careers in the short-term: Intra-individual variability in crime and its relation to local life circumstances. *American Sociological Review*, *60*, 655–673.

Howell, J. (2009). *Preventing and reducing juvenile delinquency: A comprehensive framework*. SAGE.

Howell, J., Krisberg, B., Hawkins, J., & Wilson, J. (Eds.). (1995). *Sourcebook: Serious, violent, and chronic juvenile offenders*. SAGE

Howell, J., & Lipsey, M. (2004). A practical approach to evaluating and improving juvenile justice programs. *Juvenile and Family Court Journal*, *55*, 35–48.

Hu, L., & Bentler, P. (1999). Cutoff criteria for fit indexes in covariance structure analysis: Conventional criteria versus new alternatives. *Structural Equation Modeling*, *6*, 1–55.

Isaacs, J. B., Sawhill, I. V., & Haskins, R. (2008). Getting ahead or losing ground:

Economic mobility in America. *Brookings Institution*. https://www.pewtrusts.org/~/media/legacy/uploadedfiles/pcs_assets/2008/PEWEMPGETTINGAHEADFULL2pdf.pdf.

Jennings, W., & Reingle, J. (2012). On the number and shape of developmental/life-course violence, aggression, and delinquency trajectories: A state-of-the-art review. *Journal of Criminal Justice*, *40*, 472–489.

Jesness, C. (1988). The Jesness inventory classification system. *Criminal Justice and Behavior*, *15*, 78–91.

Jolliffe, D., Farrington, D., Hawkins, J., Catalano, R, Hill, K., & Kosterman, R. (2003). Predictive, concurrent, prospective and retrospective validity of self-reported delinquency. *Criminal Behaviour and Mental Health*, *13*, 179–197.

Jolliffe, D., Farrington, D., Piquero, A., MacLeod, J., & Van de Weijer, S. (2017). Prevalence of life-course-persistent, adolescence-limited, and late-onset offenders: A systematic review of prospective longitudinal studies. *Aggression and Violent Behavior*, *33*, 4–14.

Jones, B. (2009). Meaningful consequences? Sentencing and the Youth Criminal Justice Act. *Criminal Reports (Articles)*, *62*, 1–13.

Jones, B., & Nagin, D. (2013). A note on a Stata plugin for estimating group-based trajectory models. *Sociological Methods & Research*, *42*, 608–613.

Karpman, B. (1951). The sexual psychopath. *Journal of Criminal Law, Criminology & Police Science*, *42*, 184–198.

Kazemian, L. (2007). Desistance from crime theoretical, empirical, methodological, and policy considerations. *Journal of Contemporary Criminal Justice*, *23*, 5–27.

Kazemian, L., & Farrington, D. (2006). Exploring residual career length and residual number of offenses for two generations of repeat offenders. *Journal of Research in Crime and Delinquency*, *43*, 89–113.

Kecmanović, D. (1983). Psychiatrization: A general view. *International Journal of Social Psychiatry*, 29, 308–310.

Kelley, S., Edens, J., Mowle, E., Penson, B, & Rulseh, A. (2019). Dangerous, depraved, and death-worthy: A meta-analysis of the correlates of perceived psychopathy in jury simulation studies. *Journal of Clinical Psychology*, *75*, 627–643.

Kempf, K. (1990). Career criminals in the 1958 Philadelphia birth cohort: A follow-up of the early adult years. *Criminal Justice Review*, *15*, 151–172.

Kempf-Leonard, K., Tracy, P., & Howell, J. (2001). Serious, violent, and chronic juvenile offenders: The relationship of delinquency career types to adult criminality. *Justice Quarterly*, *18*, 449–478.

Kennealy, P., Skeem, J., Walters, G., & Camp, J. (2010). Do core interpersonal and affective traits of PCL-R psychopathy interact with antisocial behavior and disinhibition to predict violence? *Psychological Assessment*, *22*, 569–580.

Kirk, D. (2009). A natural experiment on residential change and recidivism: Lessons from Hurricane Katrina. *American Sociological Review*, *74*, 484–505.

Koegl, C., & Day, D. (2019). The monetary costs of crime for a sample of offenders in Ontario. *Canadian Journal of Criminology and Criminal Justice*, *61*, 21–44.

Kornhauser, R. (1978). *Social Sources of Delinquency*. University of Chicago Press.

Koss, M., Gidycz, C., & Wisniewski, N. (1987). The scope of rape: Incidence and prevalence of sexual aggression and victimization in a national sample of higher education students. *Journal of Consulting and Clinical Psychology*, *55*, 162–170.

Kosson, D., Gacono, C., Klipfel, K., & Bodholdt, R. (2016). Understanding and assessing psychopathy. In C. Gacono (Ed.), *The clinical and forensic assessment of psychopathy: A practitioner's guide* (2nd Ed.), (pp. 252–275). Routledge.

Kreis, M., Cooke, D., Michie, C., Hoff, H., & Logan, C. (2012). The Comprehensive Assessment of Psychopathic Personality (CAPP): Content validation using prototypical analysis. *Journal of Personality Disorders*, *26*, 402–413.

Kropp, P., Hart, S., Webster, C., & Eaves, D. (1994). *Manual for the Spousal Assault Risk Assessment Guide*. British Columbia Institute on Family Violence.

Lahey, B., & Waldman, I. (2003). A developmental propensity model of the origins of conduct problems during childhood and adolescence. In B. Lahey, T. Moffitt, & A. Caspi. (Eds.), *Causes of Conduct Disorder and Juvenile Delinquency*. Guildford Press.

Lahey, B., & Waldman, I. (2005). A developmental model of the propensity to offend during childhood and adolescence. In D. Farrington (Ed.), *Advances in criminological theory Vol. 13* (pp. 15–50). Transaction Publishers.

Lalumière, M., Harris, G., Quinsey, V., & Rice, M. (2005). *The causes of rape: Understanding individual differences in male propensity for sexual aggression*. American Psychological Association.

Landsheer, J. & Dijkum, C. (2005). Male and female delinquency trajectories from pre through middle adolescence and their continuation in late adolescence. *Adolescence*, *40*, 729–748.

Lanza, S., Collins, L., Lemmon, D., & Schafer, J. (2007). PROC LCA: A SAS procedure for latent class analysis. *Structural Equation Modeling*, *14*, 671–694.

Laub, J. (2006). Edwin H. Sutherland and the Michael-Adler Report: Searching for the soul of criminology seventy years later. *Criminology*, *44*, 235–258.

Laub, J., Nagin, D., & Sampson, R. (1998). Trajectories of change in criminal offending: Good marriages and the desistance process. *American Sociological Review*, *63*, 225–238.

Laub, J., Rowan, Z., & Sampson, R. (2018). The status of the age-graded theory of informal social control. In D. Farrington, L. Kazemian, & A. Piquero (Eds.), *Oxford handbook of developmental and life-course criminology*. Oxford University Press.

Laub, J., & Sampson, R. (1988). Unraveling families and delinquency: A reanalysis of the Gluecks' data. *Criminology*, *26*, 355–380.

Laub, J., & Sampson, R. (1991). The Sutherland-Glueck debate: On the sociology of criminological knowledge. *American Journal of Sociology*, *96*, 1402–1440.

Laub, J., & Sampson, R. (1993). Turning points in the life course: Why change matters to the study of crime. *Criminology*, *31*, 301–325.

Laub, J., & Sampson, R. (2001). Understanding desistance from crime. *Crime and Justice*, *28*, 1–69.

Laub, J., & Sampson, R. (2003). *Shared beginnings, divergent lives: Delinquent boys to age 70*. Harvard University Press.

Le Blanc, M. (2005). An integrative personal control theory of deviant behavior: Answers to contemporary empirical and theoretical developmental criminological issues. In D. Farrington (Ed.), *Integrated developmental and life-course theories of offending* (pp. 125–163). Transaction.

Le Blanc, M. (2012). Twenty-five years of developmental criminology: What we know, what we need to know. In R. Loeber & B. Welsh (Eds.), *The future of criminology* (pp. 124–133). Oxford University Press.

Le Blanc, M., & Bouthillier, C. (2003). A developmental test of the general deviance syndrome with adjudicated girls and boys using hierarchical confirmatory factor analysis. *Criminal Behaviour and Mental Health*, *13*, 81–105.

Le Blanc, M., & Fréchette, M. (1989). *Male criminal activity from childhood through youth: Multilevel and developmental perspective.* Springer-Verlag.

Le Blanc, M., & Kaspy, N. (1998). Trajectories of delinquency and problem behavior: Comparison of social and personal control characteristics of adjudicated boys on synchronous and nonsynchronous paths. *Journal of Quantitative Criminology*, *14*, 181–214.

Le Blanc, M., & Loeber, R. (1998). Developmental criminology updated. *Crime and Justice*, *23*, 115–198.

Le Blanc, M., McDuff, P., & Montreal University. (1996). *Mesures de l'adaptation sociale et personnelle pour les adolescents québécois: manuel et guide d'utilisation [Social and personal adjustment measures for Quebec adolescents: User guide and manual]* (3rd ed.). Groupe de recherche sur les adolescents en difficulté, École de psychoéducation, Université de Montréal.

Leistico, A. M. R., Salekin, R., DeCoster, J., & Rogers, R. (2008). A large-scale meta-analysis relating the Hare measures of psychopathy to antisocial conduct. *Law and Human Behavior*, *32*, 28–45.

Leschied, A. & Gendreau, P. (1986). The declining role of rehabilitation in Canadian juvenile justice: Implications of underlying theory in the Young Offenders Act. *Canadian Journal of Criminology*, *28*, 315–322.

Lesieur, H. R., & Lehman, P. M. (1975). Remeasuring delinquency: A replication and critique. *The British Journal of Criminology*, *15*, 69–80.

Levy, D. J., Heissel, J. A., Richeson, J. A., & Adam, E. K. (2016). Psychological and biological responses to race-based social stress as pathways to disparities in educational outcomes. *American Psychologist*, *71*, 455–473.

Lieb, R., Quinsey, V., & Berliner, L. (1998). Sexual predators and social policy. *Crime and Justice*, *23*, 43–114.

Lilienfeld, S. (2018). The multidimensional nature of psychopathy: Five recommendations for research. *Journal of Psychopathology and Behavioral Assessment*, *40*, 79–85.

Lilienfeld, S., & Fowler, K. (2006). The self-report assessment of psychopathy: Problems, pitfalls, and promises. In C. Patrick (Ed.), *Handbook of psychopathy* (pp. 107–132). Guilford Press.

Loeber, R., & Farrington, D. (1998). Serious and violent juvenile offenders. In R. Loeber & D. Farrington (Eds.), *Serious and violent juvenile offenders: Risk factors and successful interventions* (pp. 13–29). SAGE.

Loeber, R., & Farrington, D. (2000). Young children who commit crime: Epidemiology, developmental origins, risk factors, early interventions, and policy implications. *Development and Psychopathology*, *12*, 737–762.

Loeber, R., & Farrington, D. (2001). *Child delinquents.* SAGE.

Loeber, R., Farrington, D., Stouthamer-Loeber, M., Moffitt, T., Caspi, A., & Lynam, D. (2001). Male mental health problems, psychopathy, and personality traits: Key findings from the first 14 years of the Pittsburgh Youth Study. *Clinical Child and Family Psychology Review*, *4*, 273–297.

Loeber, R., Farrington, D., Stouthamer-Loeber, M., & White, H. (2008). Introduction and key questions. In R. Loeber, D. Farrington, M. Stouthamer-Loeber, & H. White (Eds.), *Violence and serious theft: Development and prediction from childhood to adulthood* (pp. 3–24). Routledge.

Loeber, R., & Hay, D. (1994). Developmental approaches to aggression and conduct problems. In M. Rutter & D. Hay (Eds.), *Development through life: A handbook for clinicians* (pp. 448–516). Blackwell Scientific Publications.

Loeber, R., & Le Blanc, M. (1990). Toward a developmental criminology. In M. Tonry & N. Morris (Eds.), *Crime and justice* (pp. 375–473). University of Chicago Press.

Logan, C. (2013). Risk assessment: Specialist interviewing skills for forensic practitioners. In C. Logan & L. Johnstone (Eds.), *Managing clinical risk: A guide to effective practice*. Routledge.

Lussier, P., & Blokland, A. (2014). The adolescence-adulthood transition and Robins's continuity paradox: Criminal career patterns of juvenile and adult sex offenders in a prospective longitudinal birth cohort study. *Journal of Criminal Justice*, *42*, 153–163.

Lussier, P., & Davies, G. (2011). A person-oriented perspective on sexual offenders, offending trajectories, and risk of recidivism: A new challenge for policymakers, risk assessors, and actuarial prediction? *Psychology, Public Policy, and Law*, *17*, 530–561.

Lussier, P., & McCuish, E. (2016). Desistance from crime without reintegration: A longitudinal study of the social context and life course path to desistance in a sample of adults convicted of a sex crime. *International Journal of Offender Therapy and Comparative Criminology*, *60*, 1791–1812.

Lussier, P., & McCuish, E. (2020). A developmental life-course view of sexual offending: Taking stock of research on the life-course development of antisocial and criminal behavior. In J. Proulx, F. Cortoni, L. A. Craig, & Elizabeth J. Letourneau (Eds.), *The Wiley handbook of what works with sexual offenders: Contemporary perspectives in theory, assessment, treatment, and prevention*, 39–70.

Lussier, P., McCuish, E., & Cale, J. (2020a). *Understanding sexual offending: An evidence-based response to myths and misconceptions*. Springer.

Lussier, P., McCuish, E., & Corrado, R. (2020b). Psychopathy and the prospective prediction of adult offending through age 29: Revisiting unfulfilled promises of developmental criminology. *Journal of Criminal Justice*. https://doi.org/10.1016/j.jcrimjus.2020.101770

Lussier, P., McCuish, E., & Corrado, R. (2015). The adolescence-adulthood transition and desistance from crime: Examining the underlying structure of desistance. *Journal of Developmental and Life Course Criminology*, *1*, 87–117.

Lussier, P., McCuish, E., Deslauriers-Varin, N., & Corrado, R. (2017). Crime specialization as a dynamic process?: Criminal careers, crime mix, and crime specialization in chronic, serious, and violent offenders. In Arjan Blokland & Victor van der Geest (Eds.), *The Routledge international handbook of life-course criminology* (pp. 112–139). Routledge.

Lussier, P., McCuish, E., & James, J. (2020c). The developmental pathways of sexual deviance: More than 100 years of research in context. In J. Proulx, F. Cortoni, L. Craig, & E. Letourneau (Eds.), *The Wiley handbook of what works with sexual offenders*. Wiley.

Lynam, D. (1996). Early identification of chronic offenders: Who is the fledgling psychopath? *Psychological Bulletin*, *120*, 209–234.

Lynam, D., Miller, D., Vachon, D., Loeber, R., & Stouthamer-Loeber, M. (2009). Psychopathy in adolescence predicts official reports of offending in adulthood. *Youth Violence and Juvenile Justice*, *7*, 189–207.

MacLennan, R. (1988). Correlation, base-rates, and the predictability of behavior. *Personality & Individual Differences*, *9*, 675–684.

Magnusson, D., & Bergman, L. (1988). Individual and variable-based approaches to longitudinal research in early risk factors. In M. Rutter (Ed.), *Studies of psychosocial risk: The power of longitudinal data* (pp. 45–61). Cambridge University Press.

Malakieh, J. (2017). Youth correctional statistics in Canada, 2015/2016. *Statistics Canada*. https://www150.statcan.gc.ca/n1/pub/85-002-x/2017001/article/14702-eng.htm

Malakieh, J. (2019). Adult and youth correctional statistics from Canada, 2017/2018. *Statistics Canada*. https://www150.statcan.gc.ca/n1/pub/85-002-x/2019001/article/00010-eng.htm.

Martinson, R. (1974). What works? Questions and answers about prison reform. *The Public Interest*, *35*, 22–54

Masis, J. (2009). Good, bad of reform school recalled. *Boston.com*. http://archive.boston.com/news/local/articles/2009/07/19/boys_reform_school_in_shirley_brings_both_good_bad_memories/?page=3.

Mathesius, J., Lussier, P., & Corrado, R. (2017). Child and adolescent disposition model: an examination of the temperament factor structure within early childhood. *International Journal of Offender Therapy and Comparative Criminology*, *61*, 1500–1526.

Matsueda, R. (1988). The current state of differential association theory. *Crime & Delinquency*, *34*, 277–306.

Matsueda, R. L. (1997). Cultural deviance theory: The remarkable persistence of a flawed term. *Theoretical Criminology*, *1*, 429–452.

Maurer, D. (1940). *The big con: The story of the confidence man*. Anchor.

Maurutto, P., & Hannah-Moffat, K. (2007). Understanding risk in the context of the Youth Criminal Justice Act. *Canadian Journal of Criminology and Criminal Justice*, *49*, 465–491.

McAdams, D. (1993). *The stories we live by: Personal myths and the making of the self*. Guilford Press.

McCarthy, B., Hagan, J., & Martin, M. (2002). In and out of harm's way: Violent victimization and the social capital of fictive street families. *Criminology*, *40*, 831–866.

McCuish, E. (2016). *Bringing psychopathy into research on offending trajectories: Understanding the construct's role as a barrier to desistance* (Unpublished doctoral dissertation). Simon Fraser University.

McCuish, E. (2017). Substance use profiles among juvenile offenders: A lifestyles theoretical perspective. *Journal of Drug Issues*, *47*, 448–466.

McCuish, E. (2020). Seductions of exposure time: The mismeasurement of desistance among chronic and serious offenders. *Canadian Journal of Criminology and Criminal Justice, 62*, e20200003.

McCuish, E., Bouchard, M., & Beauregard, E. (2020a). A network-based examination of the longitudinal association between psychopathy and offending versatility. *Journal of Quantitative Criminology*. https://doi.org/10.1007/s10940-020-09462-w.

McCuish, E., Bouchard, M., Beauregard, E., & Corrado, R. (2019b). A network approach to understanding the structure of core symptoms of psychopathic personality disturbance in adolescent offenders. *Journal of Abnormal Child Psychology*, *47*, 1467–1482.

McCuish, E., & Corrado, R. (2018). Do risk and protective factors for chronic offending vary across Indigenous and White youth followed prospectively through full adulthood? *Crime & Delinquency*, *64*, 1247–1270.

McCuish, E. C., Corrado, R. R., & Yang, J. (2018). Narrowing the scope of psychopathy in explanations of offending: Towards an understanding of persistent violence. In J. Ireland, P. Birch, & C. Ireland (Eds.), *The Routledge international handbook of human aggression* (pp. 342–352). Routledge.

McCuish, E., Corrado, R., Hart, S., & DeLisi, M. (2015b). The role of symptoms of psychopathy in persistent violence over the criminal career into full adulthood. *Journal of Criminal Justice*, *43*, 345–356.

McCuish, E., Corrado, R., Lussier, P., & Hart, S. (2014). Psychopathic traits and offending trajectories from early adolescence to adulthood. *Journal of Criminal Justice*, *42*, 66–76.

McCuish, E., Hanniball, K., & Corrado, R. (2019a). The assessment of psychopathic personality disturbance among adolescent male offenders: Interview strategies and recommendations. *International Journal of Forensic Mental Health*, *18*, 35–49.

McCuish, E. C., & Lussier, P. (2018). A developmental perspective on the stability and change of psychopathic personality traits across the adolescence–adulthood transition. *Criminal Justice and Behavior*, *45*, 666–692.

McCuish, E., Lussier, P., & Corrado, R. (2018b). Incarceration as a turning point? The impact of custody experiences and identity change on community reentry. *Journal of Developmental and Life-Course Criminology*, 4(4), 427–448.

McCuish, E., Lussier, P., & Corrado, R. (2015a). Examining antisocial behavioral antecedents of juvenile sexual offenders and juvenile non-sexual offenders. *Sexual Abuse*, *27*, 414–438.

McCuish, E., Lussier, P., & Rocque, M. (2020b). Maturation beyond age: Interrelationships among psychosocial, adult role, and identity maturation and their implications for desistance from crime. *Journal of Youth and Adolescence*, *49*, 479–493.

McCuish, E., Mathesius, J., Lussier, P., & Corrado, R. (2018c). The cross-cultural generalizability of the Psychopathy Checklist: Youth Version for adjudicated indigenous youth. *Psychological Assessment*, *30*, 192–203.

McGee, T., Hayatbakhsh, M., Bor, W., Aird, R., Dean, A., & Najman, J. (2015). The impact of snares on the continuity of adolescent-onset antisocial behaviour: A test of Moffitt's developmental taxonomy. *Australian & New Zealand Journal of Criminology*, *48*, 345–366.

McGee, T., Whitten, T., Williams, C., Jolliffe, D., & Farrington, D. (2020). Classification of patterns of offending in developmental and life-course criminology, with special reference to persistence. *Aggression and Violent Behavior*. https://doi.org/10.1016/j.avb.2020.101460.

Megargee, E. (1976). Prediction of dangerous behavior. *Criminal Justice and Behavior*, *3*, 3–22.

Meldrum, R., Barnes, J., & Hay, C. (2015). Sleep deprivation, low self-control, and delinquency: A test of the strength model of self-control. *Journal of Youth and Adolescence*, *44*, 465–477.

Messner, S., & Rosenfeld, R. (2012). *Crime and the American Dream*. Wadsworth.

Michael, J., & Adler, M. (1933). *Crime, law and social science*. Harcourt, Brace.

Millon, T., & Davis, R. (1993). The Millon Adolescent Personality Inventory and the Millon Adolescent Clinical Inventory. *Journal of Counseling and Development*, *71*, 570–574.

Mitchell, M., McCullough, K., Wu, J., Pyrooz, D., & Decker, S. (2018). Survey research with gang and non-gang members in prison: Operational lessons from the LoneStar Project. *Trends in Organized Crime*, 1–29. https://doi.org/10.1007/s12117-018-9331-1.

Mitchell, O. (2005). A meta-analysis of race and sentencing research: Explaining the inconsistencies. *Journal of Quantitative Criminology*, *21*, 439–466.

Moffitt, T. (1993). "Life-course-persistent" and "adolescent-limited" antisocial behavior: A developmental taxonomy. *Psychological Review*, *100*, 674–701.

Moffitt, T., Caspi, A., Harrington, H., & Milne, B. (2002). Males on the life-course-persistent and adolescence-limited antisocial pathways: Follow-up at age 26 years. *Development and Psychopathology*, *14*, 179–207.

Monahan, K., Steinberg, L., Cauffman, E., & Mulvey, E. (2013). Psychosocial (im)maturity from adolescence to early adulthood: Distinguishing between adolescence-limited and persisting antisocial behavior. *Development and Psychopathology*, *25*, 1093–1105.

Monahan, K., Steinberg, L., & Piquero, A. R. (2015). Juvenile justice policy and practice: A developmental perspective. *Crime and Justice*, *44*, 577–619.

Morissette, R., Hou, F., & Schellenberg, G. (2015, November). Full-time employment, 1976 to 2014. *Statistics Canada*. https://www150.statcan.gc.ca/n1/pub/11-626-x/11-626-x2015049-eng.htm

Morizot, J., & Kazemian, L. (2014). *The development of criminal and antisocial behavior*. Springer.

Morselli, C., Tremblay, P., & McCarthy, B. (2006). Mentors and criminal achievement. *Criminology*, *44*, 17–43.

Mosher, C., Miethe, T., & Hart, T. (2010). *The mismeasure of crime*. SAGE.

Moyer, S. (2005). *A comparison of case processing under the Young Offenders Act and the first six months of the Youth Criminal Justice Act*. Department of Justice Canada.

Mulvey, E., Steinberg, L., Fagan, J., Cauffman, E., Piquero, A., Chassin, L., & Losoya, S. (2004). Theory and research on desistance from antisocial activity among serious adolescent offenders. *Youth Violence and Juvenile Justice*, *2*, 213–236.

Murrie, D., Cornell, D., Kaplan, S., McConville, D., & Levy-Elkon, A. (2004). Psychopathy scores and violence among juvenile offenders: A multi-measure study. *Behavioral Sciences & the Law*, *22*, 49–67.

Murrie, D., Marcus, D., Douglas, K., Lee, Z., Salekin, R., & Vincent, G. (2007). Youth with psychopathy features are not a discrete class: A taxometric analysis. *Journal of Child Psychology and Psychiatry*, *48*, 714–723.

Mustaine, E., Tewksbury, R., & Stengel, K. (2006). Social disorganization and residential locations of registered sex offenders: Is this a collateral consequence? *Deviant Behavior*, *27*, 329–350.

Na, C. (2016). The consequences of fatherhood transition among disadvantaged male offenders: Does timing matter? *Journal of Developmental and Life-Course Criminology*, *2*, 182–208.

Na, C., & Paternoster, R. (2012). Can self-control change substantially over time? Rethinking the relationship between self-and social control. *Criminology*, *50*, 427–462.

Nagin, D. (2005). *Group-based modeling of development*. Harvard University Press.

Nagin, D., Farrington, D., & Moffitt, T. (1995). Life-course trajectories of different types of offenders. *Criminology*, *33*, 111–139.

Nagin, D., & Land, K. (1993). Age, criminal careers and population heterogeneity: Specification and estimation of nonparametric mixed poisson model. *Criminology*, *31*, 327–354.

Nagin, D. & Paternoster, R. (1991). On the relationship of past to future participation in delinquency. *Criminology*, *29*, 163–189.

Nagin, D. & Paternoster, R. (1993). Enduring individual differences and rational choice theories of crime. *Law and Society Review*, *27*, 467–496.

Nagin, D. & Paternoster, R. (2000). Population heterogeneity and state dependence: State of the evidence and directions for future research. *Journal of Quantitative Criminology*, *16*, 117–144.

Nagin, D., & Snodgrass, G. (2013). The effect of incarceration on re-offending: Evidence from a natural experiment in Pennsylvania. *Journal of Quantitative Criminology*, *29*, 601–642.

Nagin, D., & Tremblay, R. (2005). Developmental trajectory groups: Fact or a useful statistical fiction? *Criminology*, *43*, 873–904.

Nguyen, H. & Loughran, T. (2018). On the measurement and identification of turning points in criminology. *Annual Review of Criminology*, *1*, 335–358.

OJJDP. (2019). *Easy access to the Census of Juveniles in Residential Placement: 1997–2017*. https://www.ojjdp.gov/ojstatbb/ezacjrp/asp/State_Race.asp?state=&topic=State_Race&year=2001&percent=rate.

Olver, M., Lewis, K., & Wong, S. (2013). Risk reduction treatment of high-risk psychopathic offenders: The relationship of psychopathy and treatment change to violent recidivism. *Personality Disorders: Theory, Research, and Treatment*, *4*, 160–167.

Oudekerk, B., Erbacher, M., & Reppucci, D. (2012). A comparison of diversity, frequency, and severity self-reported offending scores among female offending youth. *Psychological Assessment*, *24*, 738–750.

Ouimet, M. (2002). Explaining the American and Canadian Crime "Drop" in the 1990s. *Canadian Journal of Criminology*, *44*, 33–50.

Ouimet, M., & Le Blanc, M. (1996). The role of life experiences in the continuation of the adult criminal career. *Criminal Behaviour and Mental Health*, *6*, 73–97.

Parsons, T. (1958). Social structure and the development of personality: Freud's contribution to the integration of psychology and sociology. *Psychiatry*, *21*, 321–340.

Paternoster, R., & Brame, R. (1997). Multiple routes to delinquency? A test of developmental and general theories of crime. *Criminology*, *35*, 49–84.

Paternoster, R., & Brame, R. (2000). On the association among self-control, crime, and analogous behaviors. *Criminology*, *38*, 971–982.

Patterson, G. (1993). Orderly change in a stable world: The antisocial trait as a chimera. *Journal of Consulting and Clinical Psychology*, *61*, 911–919.

Paternoster, R., & Bushway, S. (2009). Desistance and the "feared self": Toward an identity theory of criminal desistance. *The Journal of Criminal Law and Criminology*, 1103–1156.

Patterson, G., & Yoerger, K. (1993). Developmental models for delinquent behavior. In S. Hodgins (Ed.), *Crime and mental disorder* (pp. 140–172). SAGE.

Payne, J., & Piquero, A. (2020). *Developmental criminology and the crime decline: A comparative analysis of the criminal careers of two New South Wales birth cohorts.* Cambridge Elements.

Penner, E., Roesch, R., & Viljoen, J. (2011). Young offenders in custody: An international comparison of mental health services. *International Journal of Forensic Mental Health, 10*, 215–232.

Peters, D. (2018, November). What it is like to be an unusually young university student. *The Globe and Mail.* https://www.theglobeandmail.com/canada/education/canadian-university-report/article-what-it-is-like-to-be-an-unusually-young-university-student/

Petkovsek, M., Boutwell, B., Barnes, J., & Beaver, K. (2016). Moffitt's developmental taxonomy and gang membership: An alternative test of the snares hypothesis. *Youth Violence and Juvenile Justice, 14*, 335–349.

Petrunik, M. (1994). *Models of dangerousness: A cross jurisdictional review of dangerousness legislation and practice.* Solicitor General Canada, Ministry Secretariat.

Pinel, P. (1806). A *Treatise on Insanity.* Todd.

Piquero, A. (2008). Taking stock of developmental trajectories of criminal activity over the life course. In A. Liberman (Ed.), *The long view of crime: a synthesis of longitudinal research* (pp. 23–53). Springer.

Piquero, A. (2013). Somewhere between persistence and desistance: The intermittency of criminal careers. In S. Maruna (Ed.), *After crime and punishment: Pathways to offender reintegration* (pp. 120–144). Willan.

Piquero, A., Blumstein, A., Brame, R., Haapanen, R., Mulvey, E., & Nagin, D. (2001). Assessing the impact of exposure time and incapacitation on longitudinal trajectories of criminal offending. *Journal of Adolescent Research, 16*, 54–74.

Piquero, A., Brame, R., & Lynam, D. (2004). Studying criminal career length through early adulthood among serious offenders. *Crime & Delinquency, 50*, 412–435.

Piquero, A., Farrington, D., & Blumstein, A. (2003). The criminal career paradigm. In M. Tonry (Ed.), *Crime and justice: A review of research* (Vol. 30) (pp. 359–506). University of Chicago Press.

Piquero, A., Farrington, D., & Blumstein, A. (2007). *Key issues in criminal career research: New analyses of the Cambridge Study in Delinquent Development.* Cambridge University Press.

Piquero, A., Farrington, D., Fontaine, N., Vincent, G., Coid, J., & Ullrich, S. (2012). Childhood risk, offending trajectories, and psychopathy at age 48 years in the Cambridge Study in Delinquent Development. *Psychology, Public Policy, and Law, 18*, 577–598.

Piquero, A, Farrington, D., Nagin, D., & Moffitt, T. (2010). Trajectories of offending and their relation to life failure in late middle age: Findings from the

Cambridge Study in Delinquent Development. *Journal of Research in Crime and Delinquency*, *47*, 151–173.

Piquero, A., Jennings, W., Diamond, B., Farrington, D., Tremblay, R., Welsh, B., & Gonzalez, J. (2016). A meta-analysis update on the effects of early family/parent training programs on antisocial behavior and delinquency. *Journal of Experimental Criminology*, *12*, 229–248.

Piquero, A., Oster, R., Mazerolle, P., Brame, R., & Dean, C. (1999). Onset age and offense specialization. *Journal of Research in Crime and Delinquency*, *36*, 275–299.

Polaschek, D. & Skeem, J. (2018). Treatment of adults and juveniles with psychopathy. In C. Patrick (Ed.), *Handbook of psychopathy* (pp. 710–731). Guilford Press.

Posick, C., & Rocque, M. (2018). *Great debates in criminology*. Routledge.

Potegal, M., & Davidson, R. (2003). Temper tantrums in young children: Behavioral composition. *Journal of Developmental & Behavioral Pediatrics*, *24*, 140–147.

Pratt, T., & Cullen, F. (2000). The empirical status of Gottfredson and Hirschi's general theory of crime: A meta-analysis. *Criminology*, *38*, 931–964.

Preszler, J., Marcus, D., Edens, J., & McDermott, B. (2018). Network analysis of psychopathy in forensic patients. *Journal of Abnormal Psychology*, *127*, 171–182.

Pridemore, W., Makel, M., & Plucker, J. (2018). Replication in criminology and the social sciences. *Annual Review of Criminology*, *1*, 19–38.

Pulis, J., & Sprott, J. (2005). Probation sentences and proportionality under the Young Offenders Act and the Youth Criminal Justice Act. *Canadian Journal of Criminology and Criminal Justice*, *47*, 709–724.

Quay, H. (1964). Personality dimensions in delinquent males as inferred from the factor analysis of behavior ratings. *Journal of Research in Crime and Delinquency*, *1*, 33–37.

Quinn, M., Rutherford, R., Leone, P., Osher, D., & Poirier, J. (2005). Youth with disabilities in juvenile corrections: A national survey. *Exceptional Children*, *71*, 339–345.

Rafter, N. (1997). Psychopathy and the evolution of criminological knowledge. *Theoretical Criminology*, *1*, 235–259.

Remschmidt, H., & Walter, R. (2010). What becomes of delinquent children? Results of the Marburg child delinquency study. *Deutsches Arzteblatt International*, *107*, 477–483.

Richardson, G., Gudjonsson, G., & Kelly, T. (1995). Interrogative suggestibility in an adolescent forensic population. *Journal of Adolescence*, *18*, 211–216.

Roach, K. (1998). Four models of the criminal process. *Journal of Criminal Law & Criminology*, *89*, 671–716.

Roberts, J. (2003). Sentencing juvenile offenders in Canada: An analysis of recent reform legislation. *Journal of Contemporary Criminal Justice*, *19*, 413–434.

Roberts, J. (2004). Harmonizing the sentencing of young and adult offenders: A comparison of the Youth Criminal Justice Act and Part XXIII of the Criminal Code. *Canadian Journal of Criminology and Criminal Justice*, *46*, 301–326.

Roberts, J. (2008). *Punishing persistent offenders: Exploring community and offender perspectives*. Oxford University Press.

Roberts, J. (2010). First offender sentencing discounts: Exploring the justifications. In J. Roberts & A. von Hirschi (Eds.), *Previous Convictions at Sentencing: Theoretical and Applied Perspectives* (pp. 17–35). Hart Publishing.

Roberts, J., & Bala, N. (2003). Understanding sentencing under the Youth Criminal Justice Act. *Alberta Law Review*, *41*, 395–423.

Robins, L. (1978). Sturdy childhood predictors of adult antisocial behavior: Replications from longitudinal studies. *Psychological Medicine*, *8*, 611–622.

Robins, L. (1991). Conduct disorder. *Journal of Child Psychology and Psychiatry*, *32*, 193–212.

Robins, L. (2005). Explaining when arrests end for serious juvenile offenders: comments on the Sampson and Laub study. *The Annals of the American Academy of Political and Social Science*, *602*, 57–72.

Salekin, R. (2016). Psychopathy in childhood: Toward better informing the DSM–5 and ICD-11 conduct disorder specifiers. *Personality Disorders: Theory, Research, and Treatment*, *7*, 180–191.

Salekin, R., & Lynam, D. (2010). Child and adolescent psychopathy: An introduction. In. R. Salekin & D. Lynam (Eds.), *Handbook of child and adolescent psychopathy* (pp. 1–14). Guilford Press.

Sampson, R., & Laub, J. (1993). *Crime in the making: Pathways and turning points through life*. Harvard University Press.

Sampson, R., & Laub, J. (1997). A life-course theory of cumulative disadvantage and the stability of delinquency. In T. Thornberry (Ed.), *Development theories of crime and delinquency* (pp. 133–161). Transaction Publishers.

Sampson, R., & Laub, J. (2003). Life-course desisters? Trajectories of crime among delinquent boys followed to age 70. *Criminology*, *41*, 555–592.

Sampson, R., & Laub, J. (2005a). A life-course view of the development of crime. *The Annals of the American Academy of Political and Social Science*, *602*, 12–45.

Sampson, R., & Laub, J. (2005b). When prediction fails: From crime-prone boys to heterogeneity in adulthood. *The Annals of the American Academy of Political and Social Science*, *602*, 73–79.

Sampson, R., & Laub, J. (2005c). Seductions of method: Rejoinder to Nagin and Tremblay's "Developmental trajectory groups: Fact or fiction?". *Criminology*, *43*, 905–913.

Sampson, R., & Laub, J. (2016). Turning points and the future of life-course criminology: Reflections on the 1986 Criminal Careers Report. *Journal of Research in Crime and Delinquency*, *53*, 321–335.

Sampson, R., Laub, J., & Wimer, C. (2006). Does marriage reduce crime? A counterfactual approach to within-individual causal effects. *Criminology*, *44*, 465–508.

Sawyer, W. (2019). Youth confinement: The whole pie 2019. *Prison Policy Initiative.* https://www.prisonpolicy.org/reports/youth2019.html#:~:text=4%2C535%20confined%20youth%20%E2%80%94%20nearly%201,services%20are%20available%20to%20them.

Schroeder, R., Giordano, P., & Cernkovich, S. (2007). Drug use and desistance processes. *Criminology*, *45*, 191–222.

Schubert, C., Mulvey, E., Steinberg, L., Cauffman, E., Losoya, S., Hecker, T., ... & Knight, G. (2004). Operational lessons from the pathways to desistance project. *Youth Violence and Juvenile Justice*, *2*, 237–255.

Schuessler, K. & Cressey, D. (1950). Personality characteristics of criminals. *American Journal of Sociology*, *55*, 476–484.

Scott, E. & Steinberg, L. (2009). *Rethinking juvenile justice*. Harvard University Press.

Seagrave, D., & Grisso, T. (2002). Adolescent development and the measurement of juvenile psychopathy. *Law and Human Behavior*, *26*, 219–239.

Sebba, L. (1980). Is mens rea a component of perceived offense seriousness. *The Journal of Criminal Law and Criminology*, *71*, 124–135.

Sebba, L. (1984). Crime seriousness and criminal intent. *Criminology*, *30*, 227–244.

Sellin, T., Wolfgang, M. (1964). *The measurement of delinquency*. Wiley.

Selman, R. (1980). *The growth of interpersonal understanding: Developmental and clinical analyses*. New York: Academic.

Sewall, L. A., & Olver, M. (2019). Psychopathy and treatment outcome: Results from a sexual violence reduction program. *Personality Disorders: Theory, Research, and Treatment*, *10*, 59–69.

Sharkey, P., & Sampson, R. (2010). Destination effects: Residential mobility and trajectories of adolescent violence in a stratified metropolis. *Criminology*, *48*, 639–682.

Shaw, C. (1930). *The jack-roller: A delinquent boy's own story*. University of Chicago Press.

Shepherd, E. (2007). *Investigative interviewing: The conversation management approach*. Oxford University Press.

Shepherd, E., & Griffiths, A. (2013). *Investigative interviewing*. Oxford University Press.

Short, J. (1960). Differential association as a hypothesis: Problems of empirical testing. *Social Problems*, *8*, 14–25.

Shover, N. (1996). *Great Pretenders: Pursuits and Careers of Persistent Thieves*. Boulder: Westview Press.

Silva, K., Chein, J., & Steinberg, L. (2020). The influence of romantic partners on male risk-taking. *Journal of Social and Personal Relationships*, *37*, 1405–1415.

Skardhamar, T. (2010). Distinguishing facts and artifacts in group-based modeling. *Criminology*, *48*, 295–320.

Skardhamar, T., & Savolainen, J. (2014). Changes in criminal offending around the time of job entry: A study of employment and desistance. *Criminology*, *52*, 263–291.

Skardhamar, T., Savolainen, J., Aase, K., & Lyngstad, T. (2015). Does marriage reduce crime? *Crime and Justice*, *44*, 385–446.

Skeem, J., & Cooke, D. (2010). Is criminal behavior a central component of psychopathy? Conceptual directions for resolving the debate. *Psychological Assessment*, *22*, 433–445.

Skeem, J., & Mulvey, E. (2001). Psychopathy and community violence among civil psychiatric patients: Results from the MacArthur Violence Risk Assessment Study. *Journal of Consulting and Clinical Psychology*, *69*, 358–374.

Skeem, J., Johansson, P., Andershed, H., Kerr, M., & Louden, J. (2007). Two subtypes of psychopathic violent offenders that parallel primary and secondary variants. *Journal of Abnormal Psychology*, *116*, 395–409.

Smith, B. (1998). Children in custody: 20-year trends in juvenile detention, correctional, and shelter facilities. *Crime and Delinquency*, *44*, 526–543

Snyder, H. (1999). Serious, violent, and chronic juvenile offenders: An assessment of the extent of and trends in officially recognized serious criminal behavior in a delinquent population. In R. Loeber & D. Farrington (Eds.), *Serious & violent juvenile offenders: Risk factors and successful interventions* (pp. 428–444). SAGE.

Sprott, J., & Myers, N. (2011). Set up to fail: The unintended consequences of multiple bail conditions. *Canadian Journal of Criminology and Criminal Justice*, *53*, 404–423.

Statistics Canada. (2013). *British Columbia (Code 59) (table). National Household Survey (NHS) Aboriginal Population Profile. 2011 National Household Survey. Statistics Canada Catalogue no. 99-011-X2011007. Ottawa.* http://www12.statcan.gc.ca/nhs-enm/2011/dp-pd/aprof/index.cfm?Lang=E.

Statistics Canada. (2015a). *Guilty cases completed in youth court, by type of offence and select sentence, Canada, 2013/2014.* https://www150.statcan.gc.ca/n1/pub/85-002-x/2015001/article/14224/tbl/tbl06-eng.htm

Statistics Canada. (2015b). *Marital status: Overview, 2011.* https://www150.statcan.gc.ca/n1/pub/91-209-x/2013001/article/11788-eng.htm

Statistics Canada. (2017, June). *Father's Day... by the numbers.* https://www150.statcan.gc.ca/n1/daily-quotidien/190501/dq190501b-eng.htm

Statistics Canada. (2018a, May). *Canadian youth and full-time work: A slower transition.* https://www150.statcan.gc.ca/n1/pub/11-630-x/11-630-x2017004-eng.htm

Statistics Canada. (2018b, May). *Fertility: Fewer children, older moms.* https://www150.statcan.gc.ca/n1/pub/11-630-x/11-630-x2014002-eng.htm

Statistics Canada. (2018c, July). *Living arrangements of young adults aged 20 to 29.* https://www12.statcan.gc.ca/census-recensement/2011/as-sa/98-312-x/98-312-x2011003_3-eng.cfm

Statistics Canada. (2019a, May). *Family matters: Being common law, married, separated or divorced in Canada.* https://www150.statcan.gc.ca/n1/daily-quotidien/190501/dq190501b-eng.htm

Statistics Canada. (2019b, May). *Proportion of workers in full-time and part-time jobs by sex, annual.* Statistics Canada.

Statistics Canada. (2020a). *Average counts of young persons in provincial and territorial correctional services (Table: 35-10-0003-01 (formerly CANSIM 251-0008)).* https://www150.statcan.gc.ca/t1/tbl1/en/tv.action?pid=3510000301.

Statistics Canada. (2020b, March). *Data.* https://www150.statcan.gc.ca/n1/en/type/data

Statistics Canada. (2020c, March). *Household characteristics, by tenure including first-time homebuyer status.* https://www150.statcan.gc.ca/t1/tbl1/en/cv.action?pid=4610004501

Statistics Canada. (2020d, March). *Total income and characteristics of single-property owners by home buyers' amount (HBA) claimant status.* https://www150.statcan.gc.ca/t1/tbl1/en/tv.action?pid=4610004801

Steffensmeier, D., & Demuth, S. (2000). Ethnicity and sentencing outcomes in U.S. Federal Courts: Who is punished more harshly? *American Sociological Review*, *65*, 705–729.

Steinberg, L. (2009). Adolescent development and juvenile justice. *Annual Review of Clinical Psychology*, *5*, 459–485.

Steinberg, L. (2017). Adolescent brain science and juvenile justice policymaking. *Psychology, Public Policy, and Law*, *23*, 410–420.

Stouthamer-Loeber, M., Loeber, R., Stallings, R., & Lacourse, E. (2008). Desistance from and persistence in offending. In *Violence and serious theft: Development and prediction from childhood to adulthood* (pp. 269–308). Routledge.

Sullivan, C. J. (2019). *Taking Juvenile Justice Seriously: Developmental Insights and System Challenges*. Temple University Press.

Sutherland, E. (1937). *The professional thief, By a professional thief*. University of Chicago Press.

Sutherland, E. (1947). *Criminology* (4th ed.). Philadelphia: Lippincott.

Sutherland, E. (1949). The sexual psychopath laws. *Journal of Criminal Law & Criminology*, *40*, 543–554.

Sweeten, G., Piquero, A., & Steinberg, L. (2013). Age and the explanation of crime, revisited. *Journal of Youth and Adolescence*, *42*, 921–938.

Sykes, G. M. (1958). *The Society of Captives: A Study of a Maximum Security Prison*. Princeton: Princeton University Press.

Sykes, G., & Matza, D. (1957). Techniques of neutralization: A theory of delinquency. *American Sociological Review*, *22*, 664–670.

Tamminga, M. (October, 2012). Dona Cadman to speak alongside mother of her son's killer. *Surrey Now-Leader*. https://www.surreynowleader.com/news/dona-cadman-to-speak-alongside-mother-of-her-sons-killer/.

Tappan, P.W. (1955). Some myths about the sex offender. *Federal Probation*, *19*, 7–11.

Tennenbaum, D. (1977). Personality and criminality a summary and implications of the literature. *Journal of Criminal Justice*, *5*, 225–235.

Teplin, L., Abram, K., McClelland, G., Dulcan, M., & Mericle, A. (2002). Psychiatric disorders in youth in juvenile detention. *Archives of General Psychiatry*, *59*, 1133–1143.

Thomas, C. W., & Foster, S. C. (1972). Prisonization in the inmate contraculture. *Social Problems*, 20, 229–239.

Thornberry, T. (2004). Introduction: Some advantages of developmental and life-course perspectives for the study of crime and delinquency. In T. Thornberry (Ed.), *Developmental theories of crime and delinquency* (v.7), 1–10. Transaction Publishers.

Tibbetts, J. (2009). Reforming young offender laws won't enhance public safety: Academics. National Post. http://www.nationalpost.com/news/Reforming+young+offender+laws+enhance+public+safety+academics/1166092/story.html

Tolan, P. H., & Gorman-Smith, D. (1998). Development of serious and violent offending careers. In R. Loeber & D. Farrington (Eds.), *Serious and violent juvenile offenders: Risk factors and successful interventions* (pp. 68–85). SAGE.

Tonry, M. (1999). Why are US incarceration rates so high? *Crime & Delinquency*, *45*, 419–437.

Toumbourou, J., Rowland, B., Williams, J., Smith, R., & Patton, G. (2019). Community intervention to prevent adolescent health behavior problems: Evaluation of communities that care in Australia. *Health Psychology*, *38*, 536–544.

Tracy, P. & Kempf-Leonard, K. (1996). *Continuity and discontinuity in criminal careers*. Plenum.

Tracy, P., Wolfgang, M., & Figlio, R. (1990). *Delinquency careers in two birth cohorts*. Plenum Press.

Trépanier, J. (1999a). Juvenile courts after 100 years: Past and present orientations. *European Journal of Criminal Policy and Research*, *7*, 303–327.

Trépanier, J. (2004). What did Quebec not want? Opposition to the adoption of the Youth Criminal Justice Act in Quebec. *Canadian Journal of Criminology and Criminal Justice*, *46*, 273–300.

Trull, T., & Durrett, C. (2005). Categorical and dimensional models of personality disorder. *Annual Review of Clinical Psychology*, *1*, 355–380.

Trulson, C., Marquart, J., & Mullings, J. (2004). Breaking in: Gaining entry to prisons and other hard-to-access criminal justice organizations. *Journal of Criminal Justice Education*, *15*, 451–478.

Tsang, S., Schmidt, K., Vincent, G., Salekin, R., Moretti, M., & Odgers, C. (2015). Assessing psychopathy among justice involved adolescents with the PCL: YV: An item response theory examination across gender. *Personality Disorders: Theory, Research, and Treatment*, *6*, 22–31.

Uggen, C. (2000). Work as a turning point in the life course of criminals: A duration model of age, employment, and recidivism. *American Sociological Review, 54*, 529–546.

UN. (2019). *Patterns and trends in household size and composition: Evidence from a United Nations dataset*. Retrieved from https://www.un.org/en/development/desa/population/publications/pdf/ageing/household_size_and_composition_technical_report.pdf July 30 2020.

van der Geest, V., Bijleveld, C., & Blokland, A. (2011). The effects of employment on longitudinal trajectories of offending: A follow-up of high-risk youth from 18 to 32 years of age. *Criminology*, *49*, 1195–1234.

van der Geest, V., Blokland, A., & Bijleveld, C. (2009). Delinquent development in a sample of high-risk youth: Shape, content, and predictors of delinquent trajectories from age 12 to 32. *Journal of Research in Crime and Delinquency*, *46*, 111–143.

van Domburgh, L., Vermeiren, R. R., Blokland, A., & Doreleijers, T. (2009). Delinquent development in Dutch childhood arrestees: Developmental trajectories, risk factors and co-morbidity with adverse outcomes during adolescence. *Journal of Abnormal Child Psychology*, *37*, 93–105.

van Koppen, V., Rodermond, E., & Blokland, A. (2020). Waxing and waning: Periods of intermittency in criminal careers. *Journal of Developmental and Life-Course Criminology*, 6, 1–24.

Vaughn, M., & DeLisi, M. (2008). Were Wolfgang's chronic offenders psychopaths? On the convergent validity between psychopathy and career criminality. *Journal of Criminal Justice*, *36*, 33–42.

Vaughn, M., Howard, M., & DeLisi, M. (2008). Psychopathic personality traits and delinquent careers: An empirical examination. *International Journal of Law and Psychiatry*, *31*, 407–416.

Verschuere, B., van Ghesel Grothe, S., Waldorp, L., Watts, A., Lilienfeld, S., Edens, J., & Noordhof, A. (2018). What features of psychopathy might be central? A network analysis of the Psychopathy Checklist-Revised (PCL-R) in three large samples. *Journal of Abnormal Psychology*, *127*, 51–65.

Viljoen, J., Cochrane, D., Shaffer, C., Muir, N., Brodersen, E., Rogers, B. & Vincent, G. (2019). Bridging risk assessments to case planning: Development and evaluation of an intervention-planning tool for adolescents on probation. *Criminal Justice and Behavior*, *46*, 1587–1610.

Viljoen, J., McLachlan, K., & Vincent, G. (2010). Assessing violence risk and psychopathy in juvenile and adult offenders: A survey of clinical practices. *Assessment*, *17*, 377–395.

Vincent, G. (2002). *Investigating the legitimacy of adolescent psychopathy assessments: Contributions of item response theory. Unpublished doctoral dissertation.* Burnaby, BC: Simon Fraser University.

Vincent, G., Odgers, C., McCormick, A., & Corrado, R. (2008). The PCL: YV and recidivism in male and female juveniles: A follow-up into young adulthood. *International Journal of Law and Psychiatry*, *31*, 287–296.

Vrij, A., Akehurst, L., Brown, L., & Mann, S. (2006). Detecting lies in young children, adolescents and adults. *Applied Cognitive Psychology*, *20*, 1225–1237.

Waldo, G., & Dinitz, S. (1967). Personality attributes of the criminal: An analysis of research studies, 1950-65. *Journal of Research in Crime and Delinquency*, *4*, 185–202.

Walters, G. (2012). Psychopathy and crime: Testing the incremental validity of PCL-R-measured psychopathy as a predictor of general and violent recidivism. *Law and Human Behavior*, *36*, 404–412.

Ward, A., Day, D., Bevc, I., Sun, Y., Rosenthal, J., & Duchesne, T. (2010). Criminal trajectories and risk factors in a Canadian sample of offenders. *Criminal Justice and Behavior*, *37*, 1278–1300.

Warr, M. (1989). What is the perceived seriousness of crimes? *Criminology*, *27*, 795–821.

Warr, M. (1998). Life-course transitions and desistance from crime. *Criminology*, *36*, 183–216.

West, D., & Farrington, D. (1973). *Who becomes delinquent? Second report of the Cambridge study in delinquent development* (Vol. 34). Heinemann Educational.

Whitten, T., McGee, T., Homel, R., Farrington, D., & Ttofi, M. (2017). Disentangling operationalizations of persistent offending. *Journal of Criminal Justice*, *52*, 22–33.

Wikström, P.-O.H. (2006). Individuals, settings, and acts of crime: Situational mechanisms and the explanation of crime. In P. O. H. Wikström & R. Sampson (Eds.), *The explanation of crime: Context, mechanism, and development* (pp. 61–107). Cambridge University Press.

Wikström, P.-O.H., & Treiber, K. (2009). Violence as situational action. *International Journal of Conflict and Violence*, *3*, 75–96.

Williams, R., Allison, P., & Moral-Benito, E. (2018). Linear dynamic panel-data estimation using maximum likelihood and structural equation modeling. *Stata Journal*, 18, 293–326.

Wilson, J. Q. & Hernstein, W. (1985). *Crim and human nature*. Simon & Schuster.

Wolfgang, M. E. (1983). Delinquency in two birth cohorts. In K. Teilmann Van Duesen & S. Mednick (Eds.), *Prospective studies of crime and delinquency* (pp. 7–16). Kluwer-Nijhoff.

Wolfgang, M., Figlio, R., & Sellin, T. (1972). *Delinquency in a birth cohort*. University of Chicago Press.

Yang, J. & McCuish, E. (in progress). *The revolving door of youth justice: Exploring the role of familial trauma among chronic offenders.*

Yang, J., McCuish, E., & Corrado, R. (2017). Foster care beyond placement: Offending outcomes in emerging adulthood. *Journal of Criminal Justice*, *53*, 46–54.

Yang, J., McCuish, E., & Corrado, R. (2020). Is the foster care-crime relationship a consequence of exposure? Examining potential moderating factors. *Youth Violence and Juvenile Justice*, *19*, 94–112.

Yip, T., Cheon, Y., Wang, Y., Cham, H., Tryon, W., & El-Sheikh, M. (2020). Racial disparities in sleep: Associations with discrimination among ethnic/racial minority adolescents. *Child Development*, *91*, 914–931.

Yochelson, S., & Samenow, S. (1976). *The criminal personality: Vol I. A profile for change*. Aronson.

Zingraff, M. T. (1975). Prisonization as an inhibitor of effective resocialization. *Criminology*, *13*, 366–388.

Zulawski, D., & Wicklander, D. (1993). *Practical aspects of interview and interrogation*. Elsevier.

Zytaruk, T. (November, 2018). Domestic silence: Parents of Surrey gangsters won't speak up. *The Abbotsford News*. https://www.abbynews.com/news/domestic-silence-parents-of-surrey-gangsters-wont-speak-up/

Criminal Code, RSC 1985, c C-46 s 718.

R. *v*. D.B., [2008] 2 S.C.R. 3, 2008 SCC 25

R. *v*. B.W.P.; R. *v*. B.V.N., [2006] 1 S.C.R. 941, 2006 SCC 27

Youth Criminal Justice Act, S.C. 2002. c. 1.

Index

www.ingramcontent.com/pod-product-compliance
Lightning Source LLC
LaVergne TN
LVHW021118300926
849160LV00010B/769
9781032060811